HEALTH-CARE CAREERS

for the 21st Century

Dr. Saul Wischnitzer
& Edith Wischnitzer

jist

Publishing

HEALTH-CARE CAREERS
FOR THE 21ST CENTURY

Dr. Saul Wischnitzer & Edith Wischnitzer

© 2000 by Dr. Saul and Edith Wischnitzer

Published by JIST Works, Inc., an imprint of JIST Publishing, Inc.
8902 Otis Avenue
Indianapolis, IN 46216-1033
Phone: 1-800-648-JIST   Fax: 1-800-JIST-FAX   E-mail: info@jist.com

Visit our Web site at **www.jist.com** for information on JIST, free job search information, and ordering information on our many products!

Quantity discounts are available for JIST books. Please call our Sales Department at 1-800-648-5478 for a free catalog and more information.

Cover design by: Katy Bodenmiller
Editing and interior design by: Blue Moon Editorial & Design

Library of Congress Cataloging-in-Publication Data

Wischnitzer, Saul.
   Health-care careers for the 21st century / Saul Wischnitzer & Edith Wischnitzer.
   p. cm.
   Includes index.
   ISBN 1-56370-667-9
   1. Medicine—Vocational guidance—Forecasting. I. Title: Health-care careers for the
     twenty first century. II. Wischnitzer, Edith. III. Title.

R690 .W565 2000
610.69—dc21

                                              00-023970

Printed in the United States of America

05 04 03 02 01   9 8 7 6 5 4 3 2

ISBN 1-56370-667-9

CONTENTS

PART IV
ALLIED HEALTH CAREERS 91

12   Rehabilitation Careers 295

13   Affiliated Health-Care Careers 361

APPENDICES

A Health-Care Career Options; Alternative Listing

B Admissions Examinations

C Allied Health Professional Organizations

D Job Search Resources

E Web Sites for National Allied Health Organizations

LIST OF TABLES, FIGURES, & FORMS

PREFACE

The health-care professions represent one of the largest employment areas in the United States, annually absorbing thousands of newly trained workers. The field attracts people with a wide range of educational backgrounds, from high school through graduate school, because it offers such a variety of career options. The explosive growth of the health-care industry stems from a variety of forces:

- Our growing and aging population continually demands more health care. This translates into explosive growth in home health care and clinical out-patient services.

- Managed care and cost-control efforts generate a host of new positions, such as physician assistant and dental hygienist. These workers now do many of the routine tasks doctors and dentists used to perform—at a much lower cost to patients and insurance companies.

- Technological advances create entirely new jobs, such as sonographer and nuclear medical technologist.

- Our society's increased health consciousness has placed a strong emphasis on the role of health advocates and counselors—in fields as diverse as enhancing nutrition and improving mental health.

This book is a complete career guidance manual and directory. It will help you decide on a health-care career, find the education or training you'll need for that career, and walk you through the actual job-search process.

The book is divided into four sections:

In **Part I**, we'll help you determine whether you want to work in the health-care field and, if so, which career is best for you. *Chapter 1* presents an overview of the field, listing what kinds of positions are available and where. *Chapter 2* offers several checklists and exercises to help you assess where your skills and interests lie. We'll also outline the major categories of career options. In *Chapter 3*, we'll look at where and how you can get the education and training you need for your chosen career—from finding the best program to financing your schooling.

In **Part II**, we'll give you a feel for what it's like to work in health care. *Chapter 4* outlines the basic characteristics and skills a helping professional needs. *Chapter 5* presents the professional's role from the *patient's* point of view and discusses several patient-relations issues. *Chapter 6* details the relationship between health-care professionals and patients.

Part III covers the job-search process. In *Chapter 7*, we'll help you define your career goals, target prospective employers, learn to network, and market yourself effectively. *Chapter 8* will teach you to find job openings, create an effective resume, handle applications and examinations, and hone your interview skills.

Finally, **Part IV** gives detailed descriptions of the top 81 allied health-care careers, outlining the basic characteristics of each. Each career outline also lists schools that offer educational and training programs in the field. The career descriptions are organized into five categories:

1. Diagnosing and treating practitioners

2. Associated health-care workers

3. Technologists, technicians, and assistants

4. Therapists and therapist assistants

5. Affiliated health-care workers

This book stems from the senior author's extensive background as a college prehealth professions advisor and private health careers consultant. The authors can be reached by email at wischman@juno.com.

DEDICATION & ACKNOWLEDGMENTS

This book is dedicated to the memory of our parents,
Solomon and Ray Wischnitzer
and
Miksa and Gali Lefkovits
who, through their devotion and
by example, provided us
with the ethical and spiritual
values that have served as
our guiding lights throughout life.

We are especially grateful to our son Judah Wischnitzer, who applied his computer skills to prepare all of the bar graphs and data capsules in the book, and who was always ready to help with the many technical problems that arose in the course of preparing this manuscript.

RESUME & COVER LETTER CONTRIBUTORS

The following persons contributed resumes and cover letters to this book. They are all professional resume writers. I appreciation their voluntary submissions.

California

Susan Britton Whitcomb, CPRW
Alpha Omega Services
440 East Princeton
Fresno, CA 93704
Phone: (209) 222-7474
Fax: (209) 222-9538
Cover letter on page 82.

Florida

Diane McGoldrick
Business Services of Tampa Bay
2803 West Busch Blvd., #103
Tampa, FL 33618
Phone: (813) 935-2700
Fax: (813) 935-4777
E-mail: mcgoldrk@ix.netcom.com
Resume on page 79.

Michigan

Janet L. Beckstrom
Word Crafter
1717 Montclair Avenue
Flint, MI 48503
Phone/Fax: (800) 351-9818
Phone/Fax: (810) 232-9257
E-mail: wordcrafter@voyager.net
Resume on page 78.

New Jersey

Rhoda Kopy
A HIRE IMAGE®
26 Main Street, Suite E
Toms River, NJ 08753
Phone: (908) 505-9515
E-mail: ahi@infi.net
Cover letter on page 81.

Melanie A. Noonan, CPS
Peripheral Pro
560 Lackawanna Avenue
West Paterson, NJ 07424
Phone: (201) 785-3011
Fax: (201) 785-3071/(201) 256-6285
Resume on page 77.

New York

Kristin Mroz Coleman
Custom Career Services
44 Hillcrest Drive
Poughkeepsie, NY 12603
Phone: (914) 452-8274
Fax: (914) 452-7789
E-mail: kcoleman@idsi.net
Cover letter on page 84.

South Carolina

Gwen P. Noffz
Your Girl Friday of Greenwood, Inc.
P.O. Box 1212
Greenwood, SC 29648
Phone: (864) 223-3030
Fax: (864) 229-6377
Resume on page 76.

West Virginia

Barbie Dallman, CPRW
Happy Fingers Word Processing & Resume Service
1205 Wilkie Drive
Charleston, WV 25314
Phone: (304) 345-4495
Fax: (304) 342-7120
Cover letter on page 83.

Choosing a Health-Care Career

In recent years, we've witnessed an extensive debate on how best to assure our society of quality health care delivered both efficiently and cost-effectively. This issue is especially complex because we have an expanding and aging population which needs, expects, and deserves adequate and competent health care. As a consequence, more and different types of health-care providers will be needed in the 21st century to cope with both population increases and technological advances. The majority of positions being created in the health-care industry are in the allied health fields.

Professionals in many allied health-care fields have direct patient contact in offices, clinics, and hospitals. These professionals educate and advise patients on illness prevention, proper nutrition, and therapeutic management of health-related problems.

In the past, allied health-care workers were not in great demand; nor did they receive the recognition they deserved. Today their impact on treatment outcomes is more fully appreciated—and rewarded.

According to the U.S. Department of Labor, some professions will see greater growth than others. This is reflected in the list below, projecting the percentage of anticipated increase in employment by occupation from 1996 to 2006.

Health Area	% Increase
Home health aides	130
Physical therapy assistants and aides	95
Physical therapists	90
Medical assistants	70
Radiologic technologists and technicians	65
Medical record technicians	63
Occupational therapists	60
Speech–language pathologists and audiologists	50
Respiratory therapists	45

Many people expect a major restructuring of the health-care industry over the next decade; as a result, it is difficult to project personnel needs with absolute certainty. In addition, rapid changes in technology affect this issue. However, it is certain that our growing and aging population will require enormous resources in the area of health care.

The Health-Care Field

 ## An Overview

Until the turn of the 20th century, there were only three kinds of health-care practitioners in the United States: doctors, dentists, and nurses. Although many cities boasted hospitals, most doctors made house calls, treating patients in their homes. Today, health care is offered in offices, clinics, hospitals, and several other kinds of facilities. Nurses and health support personnel are much more involved in diagnosing and treating patients. As a direct consequence of the revolutionary advances made in both prevention and treatment of illnesses, the life span of the average American has expanded about 25 years in the 20th century—from 47 to 72 years.

Evidence of the growth in health-care services is all around you. Simply taking a walk through nearly any business district reveals the number and variety of health-care facilities at hand. You might be surprised by the number of people engaged in health-care services in your own community. Of course these include the skilled personnel working in the offices of doctors, dentists, podiatrists, optometrists, and chiropractors. But they also include allied health-care professionals employed at local hospitals, storefront clinics, nursing homes, rehab centers, and even small animal care establishments. In addition to doctors and nurses, your neighborhood health-care offices and facilities employ technologists, technicians, therapists, assistants, administrative and office workers, and other support personnel.

The technological advances of the past century have also created many new types of health-care careers, resulting in a huge industry that employs many millions of people. In fact, the health-care field is one of the largest employers in this country. Its broad spectrum of careers offers satisfying and rewarding jobs to people of all educational levels and abilities. These careers differ widely in complexity, variety of activities, and level of responsibility.

Well over 5 million people work in health-care industries. These include physicians, dentists, nurses, pharmacists, therapists, technologists, technicians, assistants, and many others. At least an additional 1 million are employed as health support personnel, holding clerical and maintenance staff positions in health facilities. Their skills and knowledge are vital to the routine operations of the workplace. Many thousands more work in facilities that manufacture drugs and other health supplies.

At least one of these many challenging careers in the health-care industry might be just the right one for you!

EMPLOYMENT SITES

Where you work is an important issue. Health service workers generally are employed in one of two kinds of facilities: inpatient and outpatient. Inpatient facilities include hospitals, senior residences, and other residential homes. Outpatient facilities vary widely in function and style.

Inpatient Facilities

Hospitals

The greatest number of health-care workers are employed at hospitals. But not all hospitals are alike. They are categorized by their nature of ownership and by the type of service they provide.

Hospital ownership is categorized in one of three ways: government, voluntary, or proprietary.

Government hospitals are operated by federal, state, and local government agencies. The federal government operates the nationwide Veterans' Administration hospitals; states maintain psychiatric hospitals; and cities are responsible for municipal hospitals.

Voluntary hospitals are local, private, not-for-profit institutions. Many are owned by religious organizations.

Proprietary hospitals are operated for profit and are owned either by private individuals or by companies.

Based on the type of service they provide, hospitals are further categorized as either acute-care or long-term care facilities:

Acute-care facilities treat patients with sudden-onset illnesses and conditions (e.g., heart attacks or fractures). Patients typically stay in such facilities no more than a few days or weeks.

Long-term hospitals treat patients with chronic and psychiatric illnesses. They also provide rehabilitative services, often extending over many months or even years.

Finally, some cities in the United States have *specialty hospitals*, which are devoted to caring for a specific population, such as children or patients suffering from one disease (e.g., pulmonary, orthopedics, or cancer).

Senior Residences

The aging of the U.S. population and our increased mobility have led to a rapid increase in the number of senior residences (including nursing homes) that provide long-term care for the elderly. Today, more than 25,000 such facilities nationwide employ about 1 million people.

Some of these facilities provide short-term care for people of all ages who are convalescing from illness or injury. But most are geared toward the elderly, providing residents with services ranging from simple personal assistance to skilled nursing care.

Special Residential Facilities

In addition to senior residences, more than 7,000 inpatient facilities serve the special needs of those who require ongoing assistance but do not need to be hospitalized. These include residential homes for mentally retarded, emotionally disturbed, and physically handicapped people, as well as those who are impaired due to alcohol or substance abuse. Such facilities not only provide living accommodations but also arrange for the medical care of their clients, usually at outpatient sites.

Outpatient Facilities and Services

More than half a million people work in a wide variety of facilities that provide direct health-care services, such as those listed below:

Ambulance services transport patients to hospitals and other health-care facilities. These services are operated by both municipal and private agencies.

Blood banks—located within hospitals or operated independently—draw, type, process, and store blood for medical use.

Clinical laboratories usually are located in hospitals, but they can be operated privately. Workers in these labs draw blood and secure other body specimens for use in diagnosing illnesses.

Community mental health centers offer 24-hour emergency assistance, inpatient or outpatient help, and counseling for mental health problems.

Dental laboratories employ people to prepare crowns, bridges, and other dental appliances based on specifications submitted to them by dentists. Most are privately owned and operated.

Family planning centers employ trained professionals who provide counseling on birth control, sterility, and questions concerning abortion.

Genetic counseling centers usually are located in hospitals. Trained professionals counsel couples who are concerned about the possibility of birth defects—either because of hereditary problems or because the mother is especially at risk. These centers also arrange for fetal testing during pregnancy.

Governmental health agencies—operated by all levels of government—promote and maintain public health. They employ scientists to determine if standards are being observed in food preparation, water supply, and waste disposal facilities. They may also evaluate if industrial health and safety standards are being met. In addition, they promote health education and offer inoculations and other health-care services to low-income people.

Health maintenance organizations (HMOs) are prepaid insurance programs that provide medical coverage for office and hospital care at their own or affiliated institutions. They employ physicians, physician assistants, nurses, clinical laboratory workers, and others.

Health practitioner offices are local sites in neighborhoods, city centers, or even private hospitals where physicians, dentists, and other practitioners render their services. These professionals may be engaged in solo or group practices and employ a variety of personnel.

Home health-care agencies are public and private organizations that provide help (e.g., nursing or homemaker care) for those who are ill or disabled but don't need to be confined to a hospital or nursing home.

Industrial organizations are involved in the research, development, and marketing of both prescription and over-the-counter drugs. They also produce medical devices, such as cardiac pacemakers and hearing aids, and sophisticated diagnostic and treatment equipment. They employ a variety of chemists, engineers, and marketing professionals.

Migrant health centers provide essential health services to migrant and seasonal farm workers. Since migrant workers often don't have access to medical care because of their nonpermanent resident status, such centers employ many kinds of allied health workers.

Neighborhood health centers provide residents in their areas with medical, dental, pharmaceutical, and counseling services. They provide both acute and preventive care.

Optical centers usually are store-front businesses that are individually owned or belong to a chain. They provide eyeglasses or contact lenses, prepared according to an ophthalmologist's or optometrist's prescription. They employ a variety of workers who do vision testing, write prescriptions, and prepare and fit glasses and lenses.

Poison control centers are state- or city-supported agencies that provide both general and specific information on the hazards of and treatments for poisons.

Professional health associations are organized on national, state, and local levels. They represent the members of specific health professions or types of health facilities. They work to improve standards of practice or operations, enhance the professional education of their members, and perform research. They employ members of their profession to help meet their commitments; for example, the American Physical Therapy Association employs physical therapists as administrative personnel.

Rehabilitation centers may be hospital-affiliated or independently operated. They serve patients who have been disabled because of accidents, injuries, strokes, or birth defects. They employ a variety of therapists who help patients recover as much of their functional abilities as possible.

Voluntary health promotion agencies function on all three government levels to address specific health problems or services. They provide health education, make health services more available, and support research (usually through grants). The American Cancer Society is an example of this type of agency.

 # EMPLOYMENT OPPORTUNITIES

The Bureau of Labor Statistics—a division of the U.S. Department of Labor—makes 10-year employment projections for most job categories, including those in the health field (see Figure 1.1). Their data show that many of the fastest growing occupations are found in health services, which are expected to increase more than twice as fast as the economy as a whole.

The validity of the data, however, depends on the state of the economy, government support, geographic location, technological advances, and changes in existing facilities to meet altering population needs.

Government Funding

The government, at all levels, is a major source of funds for health-care services. The extent of such support is worked out between the current administration and Congress. This has been the subject of intense debate in recent years, with strong pressures brought to hold down expenditures. Thus, the availability of future funding is uncertain.

Geographic Location

Health services employers are unevenly distributed in this country. As a result, there are job opportunities in some areas and scarcities in others. Thus, there is a shortage of health-care professionals in both rural and inner-city areas—even though the former areas are underpopulated and the latter are overpopulated.

Population shifts due to changes in economic opportunities also greatly affect the number of job opportunities. For example, when people began flocking to the West Coast and Sun Belt states, there were thousands of new job openings for health-care workers, as well.

Expanding Careers

The time of diagnosing and treating practitioners is both valuable and costly. Thus, there has been a drive to reassign certain routine tasks to suitably trained and qualified allied health workers. As a result, workers such as physician assistants and dental hygienists are in high demand. With the restructuring of the medical profession under managed care, the use of physician assistants in a wide variety of settings is increasing significantly.

Technological Advances

Modern technology has created many career opportunities for health-care personnel. Early in the 20th century, for example, the use of x-rays for diagnostic purposes virtually created the field of radiology and the need for qualified technologists and technicians. In the latter part of this century, the development of CAT scans, MRIs, and ultrasound equipment has resulted in even more new career opportunities.

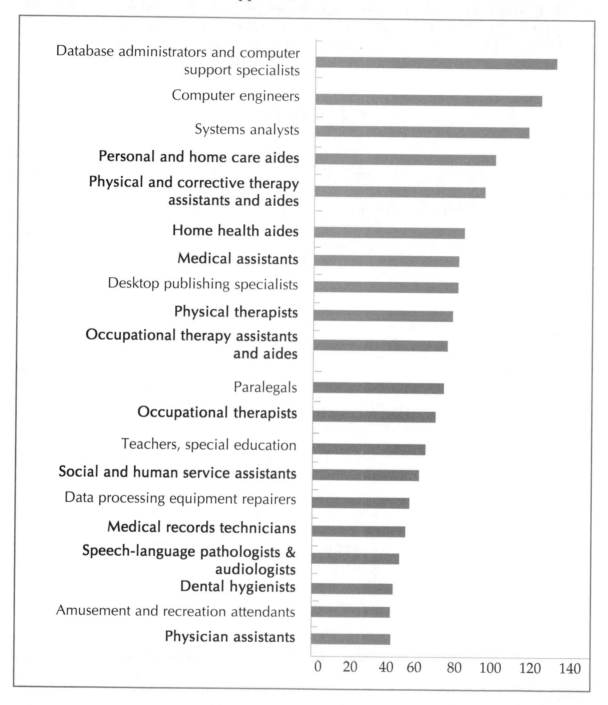

Figure 1.1. The fastest-growing occupations reflect growth in computer technology and health-care services, 1996–2006. Health-care careers are shown in bold. The numbers at the bottom represent the percentage increase anticipated.

Facility and Service Expansion

Health care is undergoing a major restructuring because of the expansion of Health Maintenance Organizations. HMOs put an increased emphasis on primary care and preventive medicine. As a consequence, the family practice specialty has grown, creating the need for support personnel. On the other hand, cost-cutting efforts on the part of the federal government and HMOs will act to hold down job opportunities in other fields. However, increased pressure for services by the growing population of elderly has generated a strong demand for home-care services in various categories. The lower cost of providing health care at home rather than at inpatient facilities has driven the need for personnel qualified to provide such services. The overall outlook for future funding in this field, however, is uncertain.

Women and Minorities

There has been a significant increase in the number of women and minorities in the health services field in recent years. Hospitals, medical schools, and other institutions have made concerted efforts to increase participation by these groups as health professionals, with some significant, positive results. For example, more than 40 percent of students entering freshman medical school classes today are women; and more than 10 percent are minorities.

Other health professions where these groups traditionally have been under-represented—such as dentistry, optometry, podiatry, veterinary medicine, and health services administration—have also seen increases. These sustained advances should serve as encouragement to women and minority students who are contemplating careers in the health professions.

Your Career

 ## THE IMPORTANCE OF YOUR CAREER

One of the most important decisions you will make in life is what career you will pursue. Why, you may ask, is it such a big deal? Well, assuming that your professional life lasts from age 25 to age 65, you'll spend 40 years on the job. If you average 40 hours a week at work, you'll devote around 80,000 hours of your life to your career. Add to that the time and money you spend getting the right education and training, and you've got a large chunk of your life—and your resources—invested in your career choice.

Additionally, your career choice determines, to a large degree, the number of hours you'll work, the kinds of people you'll meet, and the lifestyle you'll be able to maintain. All of this points out why it's so important to spend some time and effort choosing a career that suits your personal needs, abilities, and goals—rather than simply "falling into" a job or letting someone else decide for you. This chapter will help you make your decision for yourself.

 ## CHOOSING YOUR CAREER

Choosing a health-care career that's right for you involves a three-step process:

Step 1   You must prove *to your own satisfaction* (not just to your parents, your friends, and your teachers) that you *want* to focus your attention on possible employment in the allied health professions.

Step 2   You must determine which of five health occupational groups is most interesting to you.

Step 3   You must decide which of the career options in that occupational group you want to investigate further.

STEP 1. CHOOSING A CAREER IN HEALTH CARE

Your first step is deciding if you are well-suited to a career in health care. To do this, it's helpful to match the characteristics of your "ideal job" to those commonly found in health-care careers. In the list below, mark with an *X* each of the characteristics that *must* be a component of your future career.

_____ *Using instruments.* You enjoy using your manual dexterity or skills and working with your hands.

_____ *Teaching others.* You like instructing or showing people how to do or understand things.

_____ *Being precise.* You expect to meet high standards of accuracy in your work.

_____ *Complex tasks.* You enjoy jobs with many specific details and steps.

_____ *Frequent public contact.* You enjoy working with people—for example, clients seeking services.

_____ *Evident results.* You want to see your progress or tangible results of your work.

_____ *Team effort.* You like working as part of a group.

_____ *Ample employment.* You want to work in a field with lots of job opportunities.

_____ *Problem-solving capacity.* You enjoy pinpointing problems and determining how to solve them.

_____ *Routine.* You want a job with repetitive activities that does not present many challenges.

_____ *Working outdoors.* You would like to work primarily outside.

_____ *Fixed location.* You want to stay in one site for most of the workday.

_____ *Creativity.* You like taking the initiative; devising original or novel concepts, products, or programs; and acting upon them.

_____ *Independence.* You want the flexibility to work on your own without a high degree of supervision.

_____ *Competition.* You want a high-achievement position in which your success is based on reaching tough goals.

Reviewing a wide variety of jobs shows that the first nine characteristics are associated with many health-care positions. If you checked five or more of these characteristics, we encourage you to explore health-care careers in greater depth by proceeding to Steps 2 and 3.

Naturally, the list is only a simplified self-assessment profile, designed primarily to encourage further career investigation.[1] Your initial assessment will either be reinforced or weakened as you explore. As you focus on choosing an occupation cluster and then on specific health-care careers, your interests may or may not be validated.

Next, compare your own assessment of desirable job characteristics with those that are associated with health-care positions in general (see Table 2.1).

Now you can proceed in your career determining process by choosing the appropriate health occupation group. The group you select will, in turn, point you toward a number of specific professions to consider.

STEP 2. CHOOSING A HEALTH OCCUPATION GROUP

Step 2 in your career assessment process involves deciding which of five health occupation clusters best fits your interests. Each of these groups consists of a number of specific professions that have a variety of similar characteristics, which are defined below.

In Part IV of this book, we'll outline 81 different allied health-care careers. These careers have been grouped into five different occupational clusters:

- Diagnosing and treating practitioners (4 careers)

- Associate health careers related to medicine and dentistry (11 careers)

- Adjunctive health careers: technologists, technicians, and assistants (33 careers)

- Rehabilitation careers: therapists and therapy assistants (15 careers)

- Affiliated health careers: medical scientists, educators, and information workers (18 careers)

The first four clusters are organized primarily by education and training requirements, the nature of job responsibilities, and the type of work. The first of these characteristics—career preparation time—is especially important, since it affects the total cost of your education. Because this is such a decisive issue, let's look at career preparation time in more detail.

High School Preparation

A key part of preparing for a successful career is completing high school. Your work here provides the foundation upon which you'll build your advanced education and training.

---

1. If you'd like to try more sophisticated, thorough self-assessment, ask your school guidance counselor. Many guidance offices carry the *JIST Career Exploration Inventory* and the *Strong Interest Inventory*, either of which will give you a much more detailed assessment.

TABLE 2.1 Desirable Personal Characteristics for Various Health Careers

	Problem-solving ability	Uses instruments	Instructs others	Repetitious work	Hazardous	Outdoors	Physical stamina	Generally confined	Precision	Works with detail	Frequent public contact	Part-time	Can see results	Creativity	Influences others	Competition on the job	Is part of a team	Jobs widely scattered	Initiative
Diagnosing and Treating Practitioners																			
Chiropractors	•	•	•				•		•	•	•	•	•		•		•	•	•
Optometrists	•	•	•				•		•	•	•	•	•		•		•	•	•
Podiatrists	•	•	•				•		•	•	•		•		•		•	•	•
Veterinarians	•	•	•		•		•		•	•	•		•		•		•	•	•
Associated Health Careers																			
Dental hygienists		•	•	•			•			•	•	•					•	•	
Registered nurses	•	•	•		•		•		•	•	•	•	•		•		•	•	•
Licensed practical nurses		•	•		•		•		•	•	•	•	•		•		•	•	
Pharmacists	•		•					•	•	•	•						•	•	•
Technologist, Technician, and Assistant Careers																			
Dental assistants		•	•	•						•	•	•					•	•	
Dental laboratory technicians	•	•		•				•	•				•				•	•	
Electrocardiograph technicians		•	•	•					•	•	•	•					•	•	
EEG technologists & technicians		•	•	•					•	•	•						•	•	
Emergency medical technicians	•	•	•		•	•	•		•	•	•						•	•	
Medical laboratory workers		•		•	•			•	•	•							•	•	
Nursing aides, orderlies, and attendants		•	•	•	•		•				•	•	•				•	•	
Operating room technicians		•	•	•					•	•	•						•	•	
Optometric assistants		•	•						•	•	•						•	•	
Radiologic (X-ray) technologists		•	•	•					•	•	•	•						•	
Respiratory therapy workers		•	•						•	•	•						•	•	
Rehabilitation Careers																			
Occupational therapists	•	•	•							•	•		•	•			•	•	•
Occupational therapy assistants		•	•				•			•	•	•	•				•	•	
Physical therapists	•	•	•				•			•	•		•	•			•	•	•
Physical therapist assistants and aides		•	•								•		•				•	•	
Speech pathologists and audiologists	•	•	•						•	•	•		•	•			•	•	•
Other Health Careers																			
Health services administrators	•									•					•		•	•	•
Medical records administrators	•								•	•							•	•	•
Medical record technicians and clerks				•				•	•	•							•	•	

While you are in high school, you should work at learning good oral and written communication skills and get a solid grounding in the sciences (including mathematics). Your high school diploma is an essential prerequisite for advanced training programs, technical institutes, apprenticeships, and college. A good high school record is one of the keys that unlocks the door to a bright career in health care.

Post-High School Preparation

Once you have your high school diploma securely in hand, it's time to consider your next move: First you must decide how much time you want to invest in your education and training. Careers in the allied health professions vary widely in their educational requirements. Some require as little as nine months of post-high school training; others require as much as nine years of schooling. These varying educational requirements are reflected in Figure 2.1 (pp. 16–18), which lists all of the health-care careers discussed in this book and the time needed to train for each. The length of time you invest in your education will determine the cost of your education: The more education a job requires, the greater the cost.

Depending on the career you choose, you can prepare for work in one of the following ways:

- Secure on-the-job training.

- Join an apprenticeship program and secure classroom and/or on-the-job training.

- Enroll in a vocational-technical school.

- Complete a training program at a hospital, medical center, or blood bank.

- Attend an accredited college and, if necessary, graduate school.

Confirming Your Group Choice

Choosing a suitable occupational group is a key element in determining the specific health-care career you want. Now that you've decided on an occupational group, it's a good idea to confirm your choice. To do this, you'll use an approach called *categorization*. This involves seeing in which of four groupings your personal attributes best fit.

Categorization

People's occupational interests vary widely—all the way from actor to zoologist. Generally, career interests can be subdivided into four categories. Associated with each of these categories are four sets of attributes related to personal interests, personality, behavior patterns, and preferred social environment. The characteristics of the four categories are described on pages 18–20.

FIGURE 2.1 Preparation Time for Health-Care Careers

	On-the-job training	1 year of college	Associate degree (2 years)	3 years of college	Bachelor's degree (4 years)	Postgraduate	
PRACTITIONERS CAREERS							
Chiropractor							
Optometrist							
Podiatrist							
Veterinarian							
ASSOCIATED HEALTH CAREERS							
Dental hygienist							
Dietitian							
Nurse anesthetist							
Nurse–licensed practical							
Nurse–midwife							
Nurse–practitioner							
Nurse–registered							
Pharmacist							
Physician assistant							
Surgeon assistant							
ADJUNCTIVE HEALTH CAREERS							
Anesthesiologist assistant							
Blood bank personnel							
Cardiovascular technology personnel							
Clinical laboratory technician							
Clinical laboratory technologist							
Cytotechnologist							
Dental assistant							
Dental laboratory technician							
Diagnostic medical sonographer							
Dietetic technician							
Electroencephalograph technician							
Electroencephalograph technologist							
Emergency medical technician							
Food technologist							
Histology technician							

Note: Darker bar extensions represent additional time needed for advanced training.

FIGURE 2.1 *Continued*

	On-the-job training	1 year of college	Associate degree (2 years)	3 years of college	Bachelor's degree (4 years)	Postgraduate	
Medical assistant	▓	▓	▓				
Mental health assistant	▓	▓	▓				
Nuclear medicine technologist	▓	▓	▓				
Nurse's aide/psychiatric aide	▓						
Ophthalmic assistant	▓	▓					
Ophthalmic technician	▓	▓	▓				
Ophthalmic technologist	▓	▓	▓				
Optician	▓	▓	▓				
Optometric assistant	▓	▓					
Optometric technician	▓	▓					
Orthoptist	▓	▓	▓				
Perfusionist	▓	▓	▓				
Pulmonary function technologist	▓	▓	▓	▓	▓		
Radiation therapy technologist	▓	▓	▓				
Radiological technologist	▓	▓	▓				
Surgical technologist	▓	▓	▓				
Veterinary assistant	▓	▓	▓				
REHABILITATION CAREERS							
Art therapist	▓	▓	▓	▓	▓	▓	
Dance/movement therapist	▓	▓	▓	▓	▓	▓	
Home health aide	▓						
Horticultural therapist	▓	▓	▓	▓	▓		
Music therapist	▓	▓	▓	▓	▓		
Occupational therapist	▓	▓	▓	▓	▓		
Occupational therapy assistant	▓	▓	▓				
Orthotic-prosthetic technician	▓	▓	▓	▓	▓		
Patient representative	▓	▓	▓	▓	▓	▓	
Physical therapist	▓	▓	▓	▓	▓		
Physical therapy assistant	▓	▓	▓				
Recreational therapist	▓	▓	▓	▓	▓		
Respiratory therapist	▓	▓	▓	▓	▓		
Respiratory therapy assistant	▓	▓	▓				

continues

FIGURE 2.1   *Continued*

	On-the-job training	1 year of college	Associate degree (2 years)	3 years of college	Bachelor's degree (4 years)	Postgraduate
Speech–language pathologist	▓	▓	▓	▓	▓	▓
AFFILIATED HEALTH CAREERS						
Biomedical engineer	▓	▓	▓	▓	▓	▓
Biomedical equipment technician	▓	▓	▓			
Biomedical photographer	▓	▓	▓			
Biomedical writer	▓	▓	▓	▓	▓	
Certified athletic trainer	▓	▓	▓	▓	▓	
Child life specialist	▓	▓	▓	▓	▓	
Dietary manager	▓	▓				
Environmental health scientist	▓	▓	▓	▓	▓	
Health educator	▓	▓	▓	▓	▓	
Health information technician	▓	▓	▓			
Health sciences librarian	▓	▓	▓	▓	▓	
Health services administrator	▓	▓	▓	▓	▓	
Health sociologist	▓	▓	▓	▓	▓	
Instructor for the blind	▓	▓	▓	▓	▓	
Medical illustrator	▓	▓	▓	▓	▓	
Medical/psychiatric social worker	▓	▓	▓	▓	▓	▓
Mental health worker	▓	▓	▓	▓	▓	▓

Category A: Practitioners

Interests	Behavior	Personality	Environment
Organizing	Objective	Authoritative	Hierarchical
Creating	Forceful	Resourceful	Self-structured
Solving practical problems	Competitive	Logical	Pressured
Seeing completed product	Practical	Practical	Achievement-oriented
Working with people	Cooperative	Personable	Competitive

Sample careers in this category are:

Chiropractor   Physician assistant
Veterinarian   Anesthesiologist assistant
Surgeon assistant   Pharmacist
Nurse-midwife   Emergency medical technician
Optometrist   Nurse-practitioner
Podiatrist   Engineer
Technicians and technologists

Category B: Therapists and Counselors

Interests	Behavior	Personality	Environment
Influencing	Personable	Spontaneous	Innovative
Motivating	Independent	Enthusiastic	Team-oriented
Persuading	Determined	Outgoing	Informal
Consensus building	Outspoken	Talkative	Competitive
Delegating authority	Welcomes challenge	Risk assuming	Tolerant

Sample careers in this category are:

Dietitian   Genetic counselor
Therapist   Medical and psychiatric social worker

Category C: Inventors, Teachers, Writers

Interests	Behavior	Personality	Environment
Abstract thinking	Reflective	Reflective	Informal
Planning	Conscientious	Imaginative	Self-motivated
Innovating	Creative	Thoughtful	Low-key
Conceptualizing	Perceptive	Sensitive	Long-term goal-oriented
Implementing ideas	Cautious	Emotional	Challenging

Sample careers in this category are:

Biomedical writer   Certified athletic trainer
Health educator   Instructor of the blind
Nurse   Medical photographer
Environmental health scientist

Category D: Engineers, Researchers, Office Managers			
Interests	*Behavior*	*Personality*	*Environment*
Ordering	Orderly	Methodical	Controlled
Doing detailed work	Cooperative	Organized	Established
Working with systems	Consistent	Solitary	Orderly
Employing numbers	Careful	Systematic	Measurable
Keeping tight control	Sociable	Self-reliant	Predictable

Sample careers in this category are:

Health-care administrator   Medical librarian
Biomedical engineer   Environmental health scientist

STEP 3. IDENTIFYING YOUR SPECIFIC CAREER

Step 3 in the career assessment process consists of identifying within an occupational cluster the specific careers that merit detailed exploration. The number of careers encompassed by a group varies (see Table 2.2). (For an alternative presentation of career options, see Appendix A.)

In Table 2.2 (on pages 21–22), check all of the careers that are appealing in the categories you chose in Step 2. Then read the detailed descriptions for those careers in Part 4 and select those few that are of special interest to you. Finally, list these in Form 2.1 (on page 23). The listing should be in order of your interest. If none of the careers checked-off are especially appealing to you, read up on some others in the same category and then identify those of special interest to you here.With several specific career options available, you should now explore your first and second chances more thoroughly in order to affirm the suitability of your selections. If you lose interest in your initial choices, proceed to the other careers that are further down on your interest list.

There are at least four ways to explore a career: reading in-depth, visiting facilities, gaining volunteer experience, and securing work experience. These options are not mutually exclusive; rather, they reinforce each other. In the sections that follow, we'll discuss each of these approaches.

In-Depth Reading

Once you've read the preliminary overview of your prospective career in Part 4 of this book, write to the professional organizations listed at the end of the description or to one of the training programs in your area, or check out their Web sites on the Internet for more information. In addition, your local library has a wide selection of career books, where you can find more detailed information. Appendix D also suggests reference sources.

TABLE 2.2   The Five Groups of Career Options

Group 1. Practitioner Careers

___ Chiropractor   ___ Optometrist

___ Podiatrist   ___ Veterinarian

Group 2. Associated Health Careers

___ Dental hygienist   ___ Dietitian

___ Genetic counselor   ___ Nurse anesthetist

___ Nurse–licensed practical   ___ Nurse–midwife

___ Nurse–practitioner   ___ Nurse–registered

___ Pharmacist   ___ Physician assistant

___ Surgeon assistant

Group 3. Adjunctive Health Careers: Technologists and Technicians

___ Anesthesiologist assistant   ___ Blood bank technologist and specialist

___ Cardiovascular technology personnel   ___ Clinical laboratory technician

___ Clinical laboratory technologist ___ Cytotechnologist

___ Dental assistant   ___ Dental laboratory technician

___ Diagnostic medical sonographer   ___ Dietetic technician

___ Electroencephalograph technician ___ Electroencephalograph technologist

___ Emergency medical technician   ___ Food technologist

___ Histology technician   ___ Medical assistant

___ Mental health assistant   ___ Nuclear medicine technologist

___ Nurse's aide/psychiatric aide   ___ Ophthalmic assistant

___ Ophthalmic technician   ___ Ophthalmic technologist

___ Optician   ___ Optometric assistant

___ Optometric technician   ___ Orthopist

___ Orthotic–prosthetic technician   ___ Perfusionist

___ Pulmonary technologist   ___ Radiation therapy technologist

___ Radiological technologist   ___ Surgical technologist

___ Veterinary assistant

Group 4. Rehabilitation Careers: Therapists and Therapist Assistants

___ Art therapist   ___ Dance/movement therapist

___ Home health aide   ___ Horticultural therapist

___ Music therapist   ___ Occupational therapist

___ Occupational therapy assistant   ___ Patient representative

___ Physical therapist   ___ Physical therapy assistant

___ Recreational therapist   ___ Respiratory therapist

___ Respiratory therapy technician   ___ Speech–language pathologist and audiologist

TABLE 2.2 *Continued*

Group 5. Affiliated Health Careers

___ Biomedical engineer   ___ Biomedical equipment technician

___ Biomedical photographer   ___ Biomedical writer

___ Certified athletic trainer   ___ Child life specialist

___ Dietary manager   ___ Environmental health scientist

___ Health educator   ___ Health information technician

___ Health services administrator   ___ Health sociologist

___ Instructor for the blind   ___ Medical Illustrator

___ Medical librarian   ___ Medical and psychiatric social worker

___ Mental health worker

Visit Facilities

Getting a close-up look at a health-care institution or professional office can be very helpful in making your decision. Most facilities give tours to prospective students. Obviously, you should call for an appointment before visiting. Contact the administrative center, public relations department, or the manager to arrange such a visit. The value of your visit will be enhanced if you come prepared with a list of questions you would like answered and knowing specifically what you want to see. If, at a later date, you focus your career plans on one specific choice, you may want to make a return visit to clarify or elaborate on the information you received.

If your visit reinforces your career choice, your next step is to visit a school that trains students for that profession. Training facilities welcome prospective students, and their admissions officers usually will be happy to arrange for a site visit. To get the most from such a visit, plan to speak with both teachers and students. You should ask about admissions requirements, tuition, quality of instruction, adequacy of the facilities and equipment, and the school's job placement policy. Also ask about job prospects in your community.

Volunteer Experience

You can benefit greatly—both personally and professionally— by volunteering at a facility that employs people in the career you are contemplating. For example, if the career involves working in a hospital, then volunteering at a hospital can give you great experience, even if you are not assigned to the department or duty in which you are interested. While you are there, you may find an opportunity to get at least some exposure (e.g., during free time) in your specific area of interest. Thus, when asking for a position with the volunteer office of a facility, inform them of your special interests, but be prepared to accept something other than your first choice.

Work Experience

In some special situations, you may be able to secure part-time or summer work in the field of your choice. Obviously with limited knowledge and experience, getting a paid job

FORM 2.1   Career Interest List

Career Selection	Training	Education Level	Income	Future Prospects
1.				
2.				
3.				
4.				
5.				

can be quite difficult and, to a large extent, is dependent on the general employment situation in the field and in your area. In addition, the type of jobs for which you can apply will obviously be restricted if you don't yet have your training. Yet, being employed in any capacity in a health-care facility can help you get a realistic view of your eventual career activities.

Using several of these exploratory approaches—and, when necessary, applying them to more than one career option—you should be able to arrive at a sound tentative decision about one or more health-care careers.

 # CONFIRMING YOUR CAREER CHOICE

To find personal satisfaction as an allied health-care professional, you must objectively determine your own unique abilities, interests, and temperament. Once you have done this and focused on an appropriate career goal, your next step is to get the right education or training for your field. We'll cover that in Chapter 3.

Self-Evaluation

Having tentatively identified one or two possible health careers, you must now evaluate how reasonable your choices are. You can do this by matching your personal attributes with those essential for the careers in question. To gain insight into your personal attributes, you must engage in some serious self-evaluation. This is helpful in confirming your career choices; it also encourages you to proceed further in pursuing your goal.

Self-evaluation can also be useful for enhancing your future job employment prospects (as we will discuss in Chapter 7). Knowing and understanding your own blend of interests, capabilities, and potential allows you to better market yourself to prospective employers. This knowledge also can help you compensate for any deficiencies you may have, so you can put your best foot forward in interviews. Being aware of your ultimate goal allows you to focus precisely on the right education and training for your career. If you do your homework, ultimately you will find the right match between your personality and your career.

The Self-Evaluation Process
The key to meaningful self-evaluation is being fully honest with yourself. The actual procedure is straightforward; you simply consider several aspects of your personality and experience as realistically and honestly as you possibly can. Using Form 2.2 (on pages 25–26), outline your responses in all of the categories defined.

FORM 2.2 Self-Evaluation Protocol

1. **Strengths.** Describe your personal attributes that an employer would find attractive: for example, determination, organization, ambition, intelligence, effective leadership, and dependability.

   _____

   _____

   _____

2. **Weaknesses.** Describe your personal attributes that an employer might find unattractive: for example, overly aggressive, abrasive, impatient, lazy, confrontational, or sloppy.

   _____

   _____

   _____

3. **Skills.** List all the things you can do well, even if you don't consider them marketable: for example, computer literacy, foreign language skill, good handwriting, speed reading, and retentive memory.

   _____

   _____

   _____

4. **Hobbies.** Identify the things you enjoy and at which you especially excel: for example, building model ships, playing a musical instrument, reading, and traveling.

   _____

   _____

   _____

5. **Education courses.** List courses you have taken that are either marketable or enjoyable.

   _____

   _____

   _____

6. **Experience.** List any work positions you have held on a full- or part-time basis.

_____

_____

_____

7. **Personal preferences.** Provide information in areas not covered above. This may include your choice for working indoors or outside, in large or small cities, at a fast- or slow- paced activity, for small or large companies, and being lightly or heavily supervised.

_____

_____

_____

8. **Personal dislikes.** Provide information on types of places, activities, and people you would find unacceptable.

_____

_____

_____

9. **Education/training commitment.** List how much time you are willing to invest in education and training activities. Check below the time commitment you are prepared to make.

    ____ 2 years   ____ 4 years

    ____ 6 years   ____ more than 6 years

Your next step in self-evaluation is completing Form 2.3 (on page 27), which identifies 25 characteristics that may be relevant to you. Completing this form will help you discover the match (or maybe the mismatch) between your career choice and your personal characteristics. You also might want to review Form 2.3 with your parents, spouse, or a friend to get an objective opinion of your responses and perhaps additional information.

Matching Your Career Choices and Personal Attributes

You have already identified the specific careers that especially interest you (Form 2.1); and (presumably) you followed this up by investigating them further. The result should be that you narrowed down your choice to one or two careers. In Form 2.3, you will match the attributes for the career(s) you set your sights on with your own personal attributes.

FORM 2.3   Personal Self-Assessment

Attribute	High	Average	Low	Unknown
Responsible				
Efficient				
Resourceful				
Flexible				
Cooperative				
Objective				
Neat				
Self-confident				
Sincere				
Compassionate				
Outgoing				
Persevering				
Realistic				
Mature				
Ethical				
Self-centered				
Hard working				
Quick thinking				
Competitive				
Emotional				
Self-reliant				
Thorough				
Calm under stress				
Communicate well				
Analytical				

Your personal attributes. These are the qualities you checked in Form 2.3. Now list the five that are most important to you in column 3 of Form 2.4 (on page 25). Then check these attributes against the features listed for the occupational group you've chosen.

Profession characteristics. In Part IV of this book, you'll find profession characteristics for each of the 81 fields listed. These are located in the *Prerequisites* section of each career description. List the five most important ones in column 1 (and 2, if you've chosen more than one career) of Form 2.4.

FORM 2.4   Defining Your Career Choices

Profession's Characteristics		Personal Characteristics
Career 1	**Career 2**	**You**

When matching columns 1 and 2 with column 3, you can achieve three goals:

1. Determine if you are on the right track in your career choice. You can see if you have selected career choices from the most appropriate grouping out of the five.

2. Determine which of the two careers outlined above are best suited for you, as reflected by how they match up with your personal attributes.

3. Determine how close your favored career choice is to your attributes.

Once you have attained a close match between your personal attributes and a prospective career, you should gather as much information about it as possible.

- Write to the professional organization associated with the career. Addresses are listed at the end of each career description.

- Secure additional information from sources listed in Appendix D.

- Get more details about the education and training required for the career by visiting schools that offer relevant programs.

- Research the number of prospective job openings in your area. You can do this by visiting a medical library at a hospital or medical school and scanning the want-ad section of journals published by professional organizations. Be sure to look through several recent issues.

Planning Your Career

After you have decided which health-care career is right for you, your next decision is vitally important. You must choose the most appropriate educational institution—one that provides the training you need for your professional responsibilities.

YOUR EDUCATION

Where you get your professional training has a strong impact on your future success. Training programs for health-care careers are offered at a variety of trade schools, private vocational schools, technical institutes, colleges (both two- and four-year), universities, professional schools, and hospitals, as well as in the armed forces. In most cases, your career choice will determine the kind of institution you choose.

You'll find very few health-care jobs that require only on-the-job training or an apprenticeship. Almost all positions require college-level work. Some of these programs are offered by vocational-technical schools and community and junior colleges; others are offered only at universities and professional schools.

Vo-Tech Schools

Vocational-technical schools offer a variety of health-care programs, including dental assistant and medical technology. If you opt for a vo-tech school, you will receive classroom instruction and realistic training. When you complete such a program, you are awarded a certificate of achievement. At this point you are qualified to begin work, provided no license is required for your chosen career. Your first employer may ask that you receive some on-the-job training when you begin.

Before enrolling in a vocational-technical school, you should make sure it is accredited. Two organizations offer accreditation: the National Association of Trade and Technical Schools (NATTS) and the Association of Independent Colleges and Schools (AICS). You might also get the names of some alumni from different schools. Call these people and ask them about the schools: For example, how well were they were prepared for their jobs? How interested were prospective employers in hiring them? The more you know about each program, the easier it will be to decide on one.

Hospital Programs

Many hospitals, medical centers, and blood banks also offer health-care programs in a variety of technologist and technician fields. They provide both classroom and on-the-job training and award a certificate upon completion. Often, it is easier to get a job with a certain facility if you are a graduate of its educational program.

Community Colleges

Many community colleges offer health-care programs. Most of these programs can be completed in two years, at the end of which you receive an associate degree. Most programs have a limited number of required general courses. The bulk of your coursework is specialized in the area for which you are training.

An associate degree can serve as an intermediate step toward a bachelor's degree. So, for example, if you have completed two years of training as a licensed practical nurse, your training can be credited toward a four-year degree in a registered nurse program.

Four-Year Colleges and Universities

The more advanced and complex health careers (e.g., dietitian and physician assistant) require a bachelor's degree. Many people seeking such jobs enroll directly in a four-year program at a college or university. These schools require you to complete a variety of basic courses—including English composition, history, math, and others—as well as advanced courses in your major field of study. The courses in your major are designed to prepare you for your future work activities.

Post-Graduate Training

A number of health-care careers, such as podiatry and optometry, require education and training beyond a bachelor's degree. To enter these professions, you must earn a doctorate degree. These degrees are awarded to students who complete three to four years of highly specialized study. An internship usually follows, and licensure is required in order to practice.

 # Choosing a Program

General Information

One of the best ways to choose a program is to speak to people who are already working in the field you have chosen. Ask them which schools they recommend. This will give you some initial leads to investigate.

Once you have gotten the names of several appropriate schools, write to their admissions offices and ask for catalogs, applications, and financial aid forms. The catalogs should provide you with much of the basic information you need to become familiar with the school. Finally, arrange to tour the school, sit in on classes, and get the feel of the campus.

Accreditation

Make sure the school you're considering is accredited. A statement to this effect usually appears near the front of a school's catalog. *Accreditation* means that an independent agency has sent a team of professionals to the school to evaluate its program. These teams focus on a variety of issues, including the quality of the faculty, the nature of the curriculum, and the adequacy of the classrooms, laboratories, and library. They then submit a report to the accreditation agency, which decides whether to accredit the school or not.

The issue of accreditation is vital. In order to take the qualifying exams for your certification or license, you must provide proof that you have graduated from an accredited school. If you are unable to do so, your career will be seriously impaired. Additionally, many facilities will not hire graduates of unaccredited institutions.

Prerequisites

The prerequisites for admission into a program should be listed in the school's catalog. Read through these to make sure that the classes you are taking in high school will help you meet the requirements.

Find out if the school requires you to take a special admissions test, such as the Allied Health Professions Admissions Test. If it does, you'll need to find out which test you must take and arrange to take it. (For more information on admissions tests, see Appendix B.)

Specific Information

School Characteristics

The school catalog should give detailed information about tuition, fees, curriculum, and the course of study in your major. It probably will also list the names of the faculty and their educational background, and the overall requirements for graduation. You should become familiar with these so you don't run into difficulties as you near graduation.

The catalog might also give specific information on the layout of the campus, student organizations, and school services (including health, counseling, and tutoring), as well as extracurricular options.

Site Visit

If possible, you should make a personal visit to the schools you are seriously considering. That way you can see for yourself if the facilities measure up to those described in the institutions' literature. While you're on campus, try to accomplish several objectives:

- Meet with several students and ask about the quality of teaching and the dedication of the instructors.

- Visit the library and take note of the computer resources it offers. Also check to see that its books and journals are up-to-date.

- Chat with the dean and other faculty members to get an idea of how demanding the school's program really is. See if the "official view" matches the impressions you get from the students, which are of special importance.

- Meet with admissions personnel and guidance counselors. Ask for information on class makeup; faculty-student ratios for lectures, laboratories, and clinical classes; and the school's job placement record.

- Try to sit in on a lecture or see a laboratory class in operation.

At the end of your visit you should have a sense if the school is right for you. Above all, you should come away with the firm impression that the school will adequately prepare you for your chosen professional career. If you don't get that impression, you should look for another school.

Don't hesitate to investigate two or more institutions and compare them. Obviously, each school has its strengths and weaknesses, and some of your considerations in choosing a school will be highly subjective. Thus, some students prefer a large campus that offers several disciplines, while others prefer the unique atmosphere of a small school.

There is some value in attending an institution that offers multiple career tracks. Consider the case of a student who discovers halfway through a program that the field he has chosen is not appropriate for him. At a large institution, he might transfer to another discipline without losing all the credits he has earned. Obviously, you shouldn't choose a school solely on this basis, but it does merit consideration when evaluating your options.

Your education involves a huge investment of time, effort, and financial resources. So it is worthwhile to do all you can to make sure the program you choose is the right one for you. Copy Form 3.1 to record information about each school you investigate. Then, when it's time to make a choice, you can simply compare the facts.

After you've completed your school evaluations and arrived at your decision, it's time to submit an application. In the next section, we'll describe the admissions process.

 # GETTING IN

Competition for school programs varies by discipline and by school. Some are more competitive than others. So how many schools should you apply to? That depends on how strong a candidate you are and how many applications your chosen schools receive in an average year. Obviously, the more institutions you approach, the better your chances of getting accepted. But remember, you will have to pay a fee with each application, which means the process can become costly, especially if you have to visit out-of-town schools.

If you did not receive an application for admission when you requested a school catalog, you should call and ask for one. Find out the deadline for submission. Remember, *this usually is a firm date*; missing it makes you ineligible until the next admission cycle—often a full year away. Read the application carefully and see what supplementary materials you must submit; these might include transcripts; letters of recommendation; and SAT, ACT, or other test scores. Copy Form 3.2 (on page 34) and keep a log for each school to which you are applying, so that you have a permanent record of all the information and dates associated with each.

It is widely recognized by admissions officers that academic standards vary widely between schools. Thus, the level of achievement shown on student transcripts may not accurately reflect actual ability. Students with modest grades from more demanding schools may well have the same potential as those with impressive grades from less demanding ones. Moreover, a grade point average alone does not reflect special circumstances a student may face, such as the need to hold a part-time job while going to school, the absence of a positive study environment, or other personal problems.

In light of grade inflation, admissions officers handle the issue of fair evaluations in two ways: First, they usually are well aware of the academic standards of most of the schools from which their applicants come. They can thus more fully appreciate the real meaning of a student's academic performance and realistically estimate her potential for college. Second, they ask students to take an aptitude or admission test (see the section that follows).

FORM 3.1   School Information

School: _____ Application deadline: _____

Accredited by: _____

Cost of tuition: _____

Cost of room & board (if you will live on campus): _____

Cost of books & supplies: _____

Transportation costs: _____

Financial aid available?   yes   no   Application deadline: _____

Length of program: _____

Prerequisites: _____

Dropout rate: _____

Placement rate for graduates: _____

Job placement assistance?   yes   no

Other comments: _____

Finally, most college applications provide space for an essay or personal statement. This allows you to explain any mitigating circumstances that have affected your academic performance. It also allows you to present evidence to support your request for admission; in other words, it lets you sell yourself as an attractive prospective student.

 # ADMISSION/APTITUDE TESTS

Their Purpose

Aptitude tests are widely used to provide a nationally standardized measure of academic ability and achievement. With such tests there are no established passing or failing grades; scores are rated by means of a scale, with the percentile or ranking in each subtest given. This kind of scoring allows comparison of applicants independent of academic background

FORM 3.2 Application Tracking Record

Name of school: _____

Address: _____

City:_____ State:_____ Zip: _____

Phone:_____   Application deadline:_____

Admissions office contact person: _____

Check when completed

___ Catalog received   ___ Application received

___ Financial aid information received

___ Facility visited   Date: _____

___ Application filed   Date: _____

___ Transcript sent   Date: _____

___ Aptitude test scores sent   Date: _____

___ Recommendations sent   Date: _____

Name:_____   Date: _____

Name:_____   Date: _____

Name:_____   Date: _____

___ Financial aid application filed   Date: _____

or school record. The extent to which these test results are used in deciding whether an applicant is admitted to a program varies from one school to another. In general, admissions officers consider test results along with other information—such as school performance records, references, and an interview—in arriving at a decision.

The Various Tests

Five aptitude tests are relevant to students in allied health programs. Four of these are used in the admissions processes for specific professions:

1. *Medical College Admission Test* (MCAT) for admission to medical and podiatry schools

2. *Optometry Admission Test* (OAT) for admission to optometry schools

3. *Veterinary College Admission Test* (VCAT) for admission to veterinary schools

4. *Pharmacy College Admission Test* (PCAT) for admission to pharmacy schools.

The fifth test—the *Allied Health Professions Admission Test* (AHPAT)—is used by many schools to screen applicants for a wide variety of health-care programs.

These tests will be covered in more detail in Appendix B. In the meantime, Table 3.1 (on pages 36–37) summarizes the characteristics of each.

Preparing for the Tests

It is vital that you allow yourself adequate time to study for an aptitude test. The following general guidelines should help you in your preparation.

- Familiarize yourself with the major topics for each of the subtests. This will provide you with an overview of areas you should study.

- Start your studies with the subject you are most knowledgeable about or comfortable with. This helps to boost your confidence as you prepare for more challenging segments of the exam.

- Do a preliminary review of the material before starting intensive study. Then, if you spot areas of weakness, you can start working on them right away. This will lessen your anxiety.

- When you're learning new facts, try to put them into a logical framework rather than simply memorizing them. Understanding how a fact relates to the whole actually will help you to remember it better.

- Decide which study techniques work best for you, and stick with those. For example, try repeated reading of material, outlining the subject, writing a summary of the text, or reciting the information out loud.

- Before memorizing information, be sure you fully understand it. Remember, it's harder to unlearn erroneous material than to learn it right in the first place.

TABLE 3.1 Summary of Data Relevant to Exams for Health Science Schools

Exam	# times offered per year	Length of exam in hours	Sunday exam offered	Exam fee	Extra Sunday exam fee	Add'l score report fee/extra
MCAT	2	6	yes	55	5	n/a
OAT	2	$4^{1/4}$	yes	30	none	5
VCAT	4	$4^{1/4}$	n/a	20	n/a	3
PCAT	3	$4^{1/4}$	yes	25	10	5
AHPAT		4	yes	30	10	5

n/a = Information not available

- Study when you are alert, and only for as long as you stay alert. If you get tired, take a break or stop. You won't retain information if you're exhausted.

- Repetition is a key to learning retention. Frequent short, intense review periods will help you incorporate the information into your memory base.

- Get a good night's sleep after your study session—especially the night before the test!

 # FINANCIAL AID

Getting your post-secondary education can be quite expensive. Tuition and related costs have been rising faster than inflation for a long time. Yet this problem has not deterred students from entering the allied health-care professions. This is because students have been receiving financial aid from a variety of different sources, including federal and state governments, large corporations, philanthropic foundations, and colleges and universities themselves. In recent years, an average of $35 billion has been distributed annually to U.S. students, mostly in the form of grants, scholarships, and low-interest loans.

You've probably heard a number of myths about financial aid. Many students think aid is available only to the poor; that applying for aid is a difficult, complex process; that eligibility requirements are hard to meet; and that there is a social stigma in accepting financial aid. In reality, although some federal programs are designed for students from low-income families, many others are not. Many students from middle- and even upper-income families also receive financial aid. In fact, the vast majority of students attending college in this country receive some kind of financial aid.

Applying for financial aid is a time-consuming but straightforward process. Before you begin, you'll have to gather data on your family's financial status. The application form will show you how to add up your own and your family's assets, then use the total to

TABLE 3.1 *Continued*

Add'l test center fee/extra	Resched. fee	Change of center fee	Refund	# schools getting report	Special test handi-capped
5	0	0	35	6	n/a
50	15	10	0	3	no fee
10	10	5	0	n/a	n/a
50	n/a	n/a	10	3	no fee
50	15	10	0	3	no fee

calculate how much you can afford to pay for your education. You then deduct that amount from the total cost of attending a specific school. (You can get that number from the school's catalog.) The amount left over typically is what you qualify for in financial aid.

The amount you actually receive, however, is determined by a variety of factors, especially your grade point average and your test scores.

Government regulations impose strict guidelines on financial aid distribution, but colleges have much greater flexibility with their own institutional aid, such as tuition discounts. Such assistance amounts to about 25 percent of what the government dispenses. While some schools use the government formula in granting aid, others use financial aid to entice good students to enroll in their programs. So, if you are at the top of your class and your test scores are good, you may have some leverage in how much aid you receive.

Forms of Financial Aid

Financial aid grants vary from a few hundred to several thousand dollars a year. This money may be applied to tuition, fees, or personal expenses, although the terms of its use are usually clearly stipulated. Financial aid is offered in various forms, including scholarships, grants, loans, and stipends. Frequently more than one form is offered to make up a "financial aid package."

Scholarships

Scholarships are awarded for *prior achievement* in areas such as academic performance, leadership activities, athletic ability, and community service. You don't have to repay this money, and the amount usually is fixed by the terms of the scholarship fund. But, in some cases, need can be the determining factor.

Grants

Grants also do not have to be repaid. These are awarded for *potential ability*, as reflected by previous accomplishments. They are usually based on a student's financial need.

Loans

Student loans must be repaid. However, they usually carry low interest rates, and you don't have to repay them until your education is completed. Moreover, some loans offer deferment or cancellation of the debt in return for special services—such as working at a nonprofit facility in a low-income area.

Stipends

Stipends typically are *fixed amounts of money paid to students for their services*; a good example is a work-study program. Occasionally a school will offer free room and board in lieu of or in addition to a stipend.

Work

Taking a part-time job can also help you fund your education. Some schools have placement offices that will help you find a part-time job. Many colleges offer work-study programs, as well. However, before you take a job, be sure it will not seriously interfere with your course of studies. Remember, your first priority is your education.

Sources of Financial Aid

Your first step in learning more about financial aid sources is to visit the financial aid officer at your chosen school. He or she can give you the forms you need, help you determine your eligibility, tell you about the school's aid packages, and direct you to other potential aid sources.

Your high school guidance counselor and your school or public librarian can also direct you to information about government and private sources of financial aid.

Below is a list of the major sources of financial aid in this country:

Schools. Many schools offer financial aid in various forms. Look through your chosen school's catalog for information about the packages it provides.

Government. Federal and state governments are major sources of financial aid. Some of the biggest federal programs and sources for state aid are listed in Tables 3.2 and 3.3 (on pages 40–43).

Private Organizations. A variety of local and national businesses (especially health-related facilities), as well as fraternal, civic, and service organizations offer financial assistance to young people. Your local librarian (and the reference sources listed below) can provide further information. In addition, many professional health organizations have financial aid programs in their areas of interest. You should contact them directly for more information.

Foundations. Many foundations and charitable organizations offer aid for educational purposes. Some labor unions also provide assistance to members and their families.

Banks. Most banks and other lending institutions loan money to students; but this assistance can be costly, since their interest rates are often high. So check out your other options before approaching the bank.

Applying for Aid

As soon as possible after you've chosen a school, call the financial aid office and ask for a financial aid form, the school's catalog, and information about any other aid programs the school offers.

- Read the application carefully and be sure you understand what it asks for.

- Use the catalog to determine how much the program will cost *in total*. Include tuition, room and board, book and supply fees, and any other costs listed in the catalog.

- Gather all the financial data you'll need to complete the application. Remember to include all of your own assets as well as your family's.

- Carefully and neatly complete the entire application and securely attach any necessary documents.

- Review the application to make sure you have answered all the questions accurately and completely; then obtain all the needed signatures.

- Make a photocopy of the completed application for your files.

- Send off the application well before the deadline (by certified mail, if possible) to ensure its arrival on time.

- Set up a folder to keep accurate records about the applications and all relevant correspondence.

Are You Eligible?

Eligibility for financial aid depends on three factors: (1) the type of aid you're seeking; (2) the individual program requirements; and (3) your financial status.

Most schools use the government's standardized formula to determine how much financial aid you can receive and how much you will be expected to pay yourself. The financial aid office probably will give you one of two forms to record your family's financial information. These forms are then sent to the appropriate service—either the College Scholarship Service (CSS) or American College Testing (ACT)—for need analysis. Schools use this analysis to determine if you qualify for aid, and how much they will offer.

The responses you receive will vary from school to school. You may be offered different aid packages for different schools. You should not base your decision regarding which school to attend solely on the aid package you are offered, although this is a significant consideration. You should also take into account each school's location, its quality of instruction and facilities, its reputation, and its job placement record.

You must submit a new financial aid application each year. You can also reapply next year if you are rejected this year.

Remember, if you don't qualify for financial aid, you can always ask about merit scholarships, student stipends, work-study programs, and low-interest student loans. If you are really determined, you can almost always find a way to finance your education.

TABLE 3.2   Financial Aid Programs—General Education

Program	Financial Aid Available	Eligibility Requirements	More Information & Applications
Basic Education Opportunity Grants (BEOG)	Grants up to $1,600 per academic year.	Financial need. Under-graduate student enrolled in an approved post-secondary institution on at least a half-time basis, which is at least six months in length.	Contact your high school guidance office, financial aid office of post-secondary insti-tution, or write to the BEOG at P.O. Box 84, Washington, DC 20044.
College Work Study	Provides financial aid in the form of part-time employ-ment. Jobs limited to 40 hours per week. Hourly wage varies.	Financial need. A student must be enrolled at least half-time as an under-graduate, vocational, or graduate student in an approved educational institution.	Contact school financial aid office of student employment.
Guaranteed Student Loans	Undergraduate: Loans to $2,500 per year to total $7,500 maximum; graduate: up to $5,000 per year to total $15,000 maximum. Loan carries 7% interest; loan subsi-dation and deferment available.	Enrolled in or accepted as at least a half-time student in eligible college, university, school of nursing, vocational, technical, trade, business, or home study school.	Contact school financial aid office or your state office of education.
Social Security Administration Program	Amount varies.	Available to students of deceased, disabled, or retired parents (and, in some cases, grandparents) who qualify under the Social Security Act. Student must be enrolled full-time in an accredited educational institution.	Contact the Social Security Office in your community.
Supplemental Education Opportunity Grant	$200–$1,500 per year; Total $4,000 maximum for 4 years, or $5,000 for 5 years.	Exceptional financial need. Must be enrolled at least half-time as an undergraduate or vocational student in a participating educational institution.	Contact the school financial aid office.

TABLE 3.2 *Continued*

Program	Financial Aid Available	Eligibility Requirements	More Information & Applications
United Student Aid Fund	Undergraduate: Loans up to $2,500 per year to the maximum; Graduate: up to $5,000 maximum. 7% interest rate; loan subsidization available.	Must be enrolled in a participating educational institution	Contact school financial aid office or write: United Student Aid Funds, P.O. Box 50827, Indianapolis, IN 46250.
Veterans' Administration Program	Loans and grants. Amount varies.	Benefits for veterans and children of veterans who meet specific requirements. Eligibility requirements vary with different programs available.	Contact Veterans' Administration.
National Direct Student Loan (NDSL)	Undergraduate: Loans $2,500 maximum if enrolled in vocational program or have completed less than 2 years college toward bachelor's degree; $5,000 maximum if student *has completed* 2 years of study toward bachelor's degree. Graduate: Loans to $10,000 maximum *including* any amount borrowed under NDSL for undergraduate study. 3% interest rate; 10 years to repay loan. Loan deferment and cancellation provisions available.	Financial need. Must be enrolled at least half-time in participating education institution.	Contact school's financial aid office.

NOTE: This financial aid chart should be used only as a general guideline. Financial aid programs, the dollars available, and eligibility requirements change annually. Readers are urged to contact the programs directly for the most current information available.

TABLE 3.3 Financial Aid Programs—Health Careers

Program	Financial Aid Available	Eligibility Requirements	More Information/Applications
Armed Forces Health Professions Scholarships	All educational expenses exclusive of room and board, plus a $400-per-month living stipend.	Graduate students in professional schools of medicine, osteopathy, dentistry, optometry, podiatry, veterinary medicine, clinical psychology at Ph.D. level after graduation must serve minimum of 2 years active duty.	Contact local recruiter or write: Armed Forces, Scholarships, Box A, University City, TX 78148.
Federal Insurance Student Loans for Health Professions	Loans up to $10,000 per year to total $50,000 maximum (up to $7,000 per year to $37,500 for pharmacy students). Loan deferment available.	Graduate students in medicine, osteopathy, dentistry, veterinary medicine, optometry, pharmacy, podiatry, and public health.	Contact school financial aid office or write: U.S. Office of Education, Bureau of Financial Assistance, 400 Maryland Ave. S.W., Washington, DC 20202.
Health Profession Student Loans	Loans up to cost of tuition plus $2,500 per year for other education expenses. 7% interest rate; loan deferment and federal loan repayment available.	Graduate students in medicine, osteopathy, optometry, podiatry, and pharmacy.	Contact school financial aid office or write: U.S. Public Health Service, Bureau of Health Manpower, Student Assistance Branch, Center Bldg., Room 5–41, 3700 East-West Hwy., Hyattsville, MD 20782.

NOTE: This financial aid chart should be used only as a general guideline. Financial aid programs, the dollars available, and eligibility requirements change annually. Readers are urged to contact the programs directly for the most current information available.

TABLE 3.3   Continued

Program	Financial Aid Available	Eligibility Requirements	More Information/Applications
National Health Service Corps Scholarships (NHSC)	All tuition fees plus $400-per-month stipend.	Full-time students enrolled in professional study of medicine, osteopathy, dentistry, baccalaureate nursing, nurse practitioner, nurse midwife, public health nursing, and public health nutrition.	Contact school financial aid office or write: NHSC Scholarship Program, Center Bldg., Room 5–44, 3700 East-West Hwy,, Hyattsville, MD 20782.
Nursing Scholarship Program	$2,000 per year maximum for school expenses.	Exceptional financial need. Half-time or full-time beginning registered students.	Contact school financial aid office or write: U.S. Public Health Service Bureau of Health Manpower, Center Bldg., Room 5–41, 3700 East-West Hwy., Hyattsville, MD 20782.
Nursing Student Loans	Loans up to $2,500 per year maximum; deferment and loan cancellation available.	Half-time or full-time beginning registered students.	Same as above.
Loan Repayment Provision for Nursing Students	Partial (up to 85%) federal cancellation of loan repayment of all loans for registered nursing education	Student must serve a minimum 2 years in health manpower shortage area.	Same as above.

HEALTH PROFESSIONALISM

Working as a health-care professional means living between two worlds: that of the healthy and that of the infirm. The atmosphere, attitude, and attributes of these two worlds are essentially opposite to each other. The world of the healthy is one of activity, broadly focused, and of future planning. The world of the ill is usually sedentary, narrowly focused on recovery or adjustment, and thinking primarily in the short term.

Potential workers in the field of health care thus must be aware of the impact of the profession on their own lives, to understand the role they play and what it means to be a patient. The following three chapters will explore these areas.

The Health-Care Professional

 ## YOUR EDUCATION

Becoming a health-care professional is a formidable challenge. It involves much more than merely accumulating the required number of course credits to graduate from a program. Rather, it is an experience in intellectual and personal growth and maturation. Thus, the educational phase of this endeavor should involve mastering basic theoretical knowledge, acquiring specific professional skills, and developing a positive attitude toward working in the healing arts.

Theoretical Knowledge

The foundation for providing health-care service rests on solid science skills. These include the basic sciences—biology, chemistry, and physics—and the behavioral sciences of psychology and sociology. These courses provide a framework for understanding the human body's form and function and how people behave. Supplementing this background, it is helpful to learn about legal concepts, economics, statistics, and computers. Knowledge of the liberal arts also can broaden your perspective. Finally, understanding the theoretical basis of techniques facilitates their proper application.

Professional Skills

Prior to undertaking a program of professional training, your formal education takes place mostly in the classroom and laboratory. This continues in professional school, but a new learning site is introduced: namely, the clinic. This is the essential learning environment for gaining professional practice experience. During your training, you will acquire skills in four areas, which are listed below.

Technical Skills

Technical skills include the ability to properly apply given techniques to evaluate, diagnose, and treat illnesses. These skills may include reading lab results, giving inoculations, or using sophisticated lab equipment.

Communication Skills

Health professionals must interact with a wide variety of people. So they must have a good understanding of the unique relationship that exists in health-care establishments: the authority-dependency component. This means being able to accept responsibility and criticism from your supervisor while being constructively critical of those you are supervising. In essence, you must develop the interpersonal and communication skills that allow you to function in a responsible, challenging, and stress-filled environment.

Instruction and Management Skills

Health-care professions frequently are called upon to instruct patients or their families. They also may have to be innovative and design practical solutions to health-care problems. Workers with administrative skills and obligations may be asked to develop short- or long-term goals for their facilities and to supervise the allocation of equipment and supplies.

Research Skills

As part of your health-care activities, you may be called upon to design an investigative project, which includes formulating a hypothesis and collecting data to test it. The results may be valuable in your own facility or somewhere else.

Mastering these clinical skills is time-consuming and requires practice and patience. The steps involved to achieve success are listed below:

- Secure detailed knowledge about the skill.

- When possible, have the skill applied to yourself.

- Observe a professional using the skills

- When possible, assist the professional in using the skill.

- Initially, use the new skill only under close supervision.

- When possible, employ the skill in a variety of situations without direct supervision.

- Take a test to demonstrate your capability with the skill.

Your Attitude

If you hope to succeed in the health-care (or any other) field, you must develop a positive attitude. This is especially true for three major issues:

1. *Learning* is *always* a positive experience. Learning skills are not merely devices to pass courses or graduate. Rather, you should look upon learning as a challenge to your intellect and pursue it throughout your professional life.

2. *Inquisitiveness* implies a sense of adventure, because it involves venturing into the unknown as you move forward toward developing professional expertise.

3. *Commitment* implies a willingness to put forth your best effort to obtain results—whether you are mastering a subject, providing therapy to a patient, or carrying out a procedure.

The Clinical Component

Your clinical education is an introduction to the core of your future work. The key element in this critical educational phase is *refinement*. You expand your basic knowledge and skills by broadening your exposure. The ultimate goal is developing professional competence. Clinical work may include several components:

- working with several patients who have varied medical problems,

- observing different manifestations of a single pathological condition,

- working under time limitations, and

- having multiple responsibilities.

Starting off properly in a clinical context helps ensure you will have a meaningful learning experience. There are several steps you can take to get off on the right foot:

1. Introduce yourself to those with whom you will be associated.

2. Keep your eyes open to get an idea of how things are done in the work setting.

3. Ask your questions politely and try to determine what is expected of you.

4. Don't be offended by questions others ask because of your student status.

5. Assume that those around you will work to enhance your clinical abilities.

6. Try to act as if you are a member of the team by contributing to the group's activities in a meaningful way.

Remember that the beginning awkwardness will dissipate soon, as your responsibilities, independence, and self-confidence increase.

Anticipation and Anxiety

Sometime during your clinical training, you may be struck by the reality that *you* can have a positive impact on the lives of others. This should be a strong motivator during this challenging time.

If you find yourself having trouble on tests or with mastering skills, you may experience some self-doubt and anxiety. Learning and mastering new skills will help alleviate the inherent difficulties your new situation presents. You'll find that the positive impact that comes from improving your knowledge base and clinical skills is a significant counterbalance to the anxiety.

Other points to remember when you experience anxiety are listed below:

- The admissions people at your educational program based your admission on their confidence that you *are* capable of achieving your goals.

- Most people have periodic episodes of anxiety, especially when facing new situations.

- Mild anxiety usually is temporary. It *will* pass.

- Anxiety can be a positive force if you take it as wake-up call. It can stimulate your emotional reserves so you can better face the challenges of school.

- Finally, keep in mind the rewards of attaining your goal.

If you find yourself facing long-term anxiety, try to find the underlying issues generating the anxiety and then seek to remedy the situation. Maybe you can do this by improving your study habits. If you can't get on top of the situation, don't be afraid to seek the help of a school advisor or faculty member.

THE PROFESSIONAL AS A HELPER

Traditionally health professionals have been viewed as providing direct patient assistance (e.g., nurses and therapists). While this is true for many professionals, others provide services that help patients only indirectly (e.g., biomedical engineers and hospital administrators). Nevertheless, professionals in the latter category also work for the well being of patients, and their services are vital to the proper functioning of health-care institutions.

The Helping Relationship

Almost every adult has had the opportunity to serve as a helper for others at some time in life. This may involve teaching an activity or rendering a service. Consequently, you may have experienced the satisfaction that comes from being a helper.

There are two types of helping relationships: social and therapeutic. A *social* relationship is defined as

- providing a personal act of service,

- when a wide variety of resources are used,

- when the service is not goal-oriented,

- when the service may foster dependence, and/or

- when the relationship may not prove constructive.

A therapeutic relationship is defined as

- providing a professional act of service,

- using established professional skill,

- providing service that is goal-oriented,

- providing service that does not foster dependence,

- when the relationship should prove constructive.

From this brief comparison, you can see that therapeutic help providers are characterized by the professional nature of the services they render, which are aimed at both the short- and long-term benefit of the patient.

Professional help may be provided by means of two other approaches: The first involves the use of assistants, and the second involves referrals. *Professional assistant* programs (see Chapters 11 and 12) were introduced to help provide lower-cost health care without diminishing quality, to create employment possibilities for those unable to take extensive programs, and to reduce a shortage of personnel. These positions involve the appropriate division of responsibilities and skills between the professional and assistant. This may involve the professional delegating some responsibilities and assuming a supervisory role.

Referral to another professional helper may be mandated under certain conditions:

- if the professional lacks the experience or equipment to provide the appropriate service;

- if helper-patient personality conflicts hinder progress; and/or

- if dependence becomes excessive between the parties.

Teamwork

Many people believe that overall health care is best provided using a team approach. A team approach requires that each member skillfully applies his or her professional abilities, bearing in mind the supplementary and complementary activities of other team members. This approach allows patients to be viewed from a *multiple perspective*.

To be effective, a health-care team must be able to accommodate the personal and professional differences of its members. A team may function based on a hierarchical arrangement, with both power and responsibility resting heavily on top to maximize efficiency. An alternative approach is a community structure, in which power is far less centralized, and mutual support is paramount. Team health care can enhance professional development and capabilities.

 # THE PROFESSIONAL'S PERSONAL LIFE

In fairness to yourself and your patients or clients, you must stay healthy, be job-satisfied, and keep an optimistic view of life.

Caring for Yourself

When you maintain your good health, you feel, look, and function better. Good health refers to your physical *and* your psychological well-being—both of which need to be maintained to function optimally.

The Illusion of Invincibility

It seems obvious that health professionals should maintain sound lifestyles. Unfortunately, this is not always the case. This may be due to the fact that professional helpers sometimes subconsciously develop a sense of invincibility to illness, and thus do not practice preventive health care. You can overcome the tendency to feel invulnerable in two ways:

Establish periods of "aloneness." The principal function of a health-care professional is being a helper. This means that one-sided demands are constantly being placed on you, which automatically generates stress. You'll find a strong need at times for a respite that is more than a mere coffee-break. When this happens, you should seek time to be alone with yourself. A short period of self-imposed solitude can have a rejuvenating effect on your mental and physical faculties.

Develop good work habits. This means seeking an approach that values efficient decision making and competence while being open to innovation and experimentation. The optimal balance between these opposing goals serves to avoid burnout, on one hand, and ineffectiveness, on the other.

Networking for Support

Self-preservation is not enough as a work ethic. Career satisfaction involves sharing with your coworkers the joys and frustrations of your job. You'll find a commonality of interest with your colleagues about the progress of individual patients, events in your department or institution, or trends in your profession. There is a bond of language between health-care professionals that allows for a unique dialogue. Expressions of appreciation from coworkers also contribute to your sense of belonging within the professional network. These factors can enhance your working environment and foster opportunities for securing support during difficult periods. You should also consider your personal friends and family when you are seeking support sources.

Accountability

It is obviously important to maintain high standards of practice for health-care professionals. This is achieved by peer review. This term refers to the formal procedure for evaluating a colleague's work. A written evaluation is a means of constructive criticism that enhances self-awareness. It also is a basis for judging competency, thus providing protection to patients.

If you detect incompetent or unethical behavior outside of the realm of peer review, *you need to act*, even if it is personally difficult to do so. Follow your institution's policies for reporting the situation to the proper authorities.

The Patient

 ## MAINTAINING HEALTH

Did you know that, to a substantial extent, a person can control his or her own well-being by maintaining a healthy lifestyle? This involves eating a balanced diet, getting adequate exercise and sleep, and getting periodic, thorough medical checkups. Despite these steps, however, illness may result from a genetic predisposition, accidents, or the aging process. Similarly, some viral and bacterial infections (e.g., influenza) are unavoidable. Thus, even under the best of circumstances, people become ill, and some cases are serious enough to require hospitalization.

 ## THE IMPACT OF HOSPITALIZATION

An individual's hospitalization may be voluntary—for example, resulting from a decision to have elective surgery such as knee replacement—or it may be mandated by an acute illness such as appendicitis. In either case, hospitalization often has a powerful impact, because it significantly disrupts an individual's personal life. It also can negatively affect family, coworkers, and even friends. The effect varies, depending on each person's circumstances. When the patient is the family breadwinner or a single parent and the illness is prolonged, its impact obviously can be severe and seriously dislocate the stability of the family.

Admission to a hospital obviously implies that an illness requires more sophisticated treatment than is available at home or at a local clinic. This naturally raises a patient's level of anxiety; after all, placing one's well-being largely in the hands of strangers is an unnerving prospect. This anxiety is enhanced after a patient is assigned to a room with one or more strangers and gives up his or her regular clothing for a hospital gown.

Patients suddenly are exposed to multiple losses—including a loss of the ability to live at home and a sense of privacy. In addition, they experience a loss of independence. In the hospital, their activities are determined by staff routine and their own specific medical problems. Even their diets are not fully under their control and may be altered dramatically at a physician's request. The necessary hospital procedure of monitoring vital signs both day and night can prove most disturbing of all. This loss of independence compounds an already difficult situation, which for the acutely ill may cause temporary frustration. In the chronically ill, it can cause more severe responses, including depression.

Another consideration associated with hospitalization is the patient's loss of self-image. We all carry in our minds a psychosocial concept of ourselves, which serves as a built-in frame of reference. A change in how we think we look (as opposed to how we actually look), because of the impact of an illness or injury, can have a strong influence on our psyches. If a change in appearance or function looks like it may be prolonged, it can induce a stage of denial that can even inhibit recovery. This may be due to our tendency to generate an exaggerated view of the change in our physical appearance.

On top of it all, all of these losses and changes occur at the same time that patients feel most vulnerable and inadequate because of their illnesses. This can generate considerable inner emotional turmoil—turmoil to which the health-care professional must respond in a reassuring and thoughtful manner.

This is why health-care professionals must know how to reassure patients questioning their loss of self-image. These professionals must determine if they are justified in advising patients that they will be able to "reclaim" their former images once recovery occurs. Otherwise, they must help patients to discover realistic and satisfactory new body images as acceptable alternatives.

PATIENT STATUS

Our society places a high value on youth and independence. Serious illness can stigmatize a person as markedly different from healthy members of society. This is more severe when the illness is compounded by a disability. A patient facing disability may feel that he or she has been diminished as a person by having lost an essential element of humanity.

When a physical loss is permanent, or when it is evident (e.g., in the case of amputation), the potential impact is much greater. Thus the visual response of others is an important consideration and must be carefully and tactfully managed by health-care professionals. Those working with disabled patients do well to advise their patients to seek help from support groups. Simply seeing how others with similar conditions have succeeded in spite of their problems is helpful. Encouraging families to be supportive also contributes to a patient's sense of well-being.

PATIENT PRIVILEGES

Those who are sick enough to be hospitalized are granted certain amenities to make them more comfortable and encourage their recovery. Among these prerogatives is a release from obligations to work or to care for themselves to the extent that is medically justified.

Increasingly today, people are becoming more conscious of their health and more involved in managing their own treatment. Naturally, this depends on the state of a patient's illness. When treatment options exist, patients deserve to be consulted; most patients and their families appreciate this courtesy. In fact, consulting with patients actually enhances their momentum toward recovery.

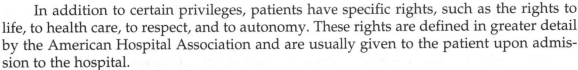

In addition to certain privileges, patients have specific rights, such as the rights to life, to health care, to respect, and to autonomy. These rights are defined in greater detail by the American Hospital Association and are usually given to the patient upon admission to the hospital.

Privileges, however, are not rights; rather, they are amenities that should be given only when they are warranted.

For example, some patients may find it advantageous to remain "sick," for this status protects them from the outside world. It may also provide financial and social gain. If you suspect such a situation, you should document it before drawing any conclusions. If established as valid, you should cooperate with the institution's mental health personnel to resolve the issue with a minimum of embarrassment to the patient.

 # POST-HOSPITALIZATION ANXIETY

Upon a patient's discharge from the hospital, he or she may face uncertainties about the future. This is especially the case for patients who must adjust to a disability or chronic condition. But even for those who have made a full recovery, concerns about future health may arise. They may have experienced some disappointment with how their treatment was handled, with the manner in which they were treated by the hospital personnel, or in the length of time it took to recover. Of special concern to such individuals is the possibility of a reoccurrence of their illness, or some other illness, that may necessitate another hospitalization.

This all points to the vital need for health-care professionals to be sensitive to the long-term impact they have on patients. Indeed, this is exactly why you must always be tactful and sensitive in what you say and do when you are in earshot of patients. Being discreet and tactful goes a long way toward assuring that patients have a positive association with your institution. Being sensitive means reassuring patients of your genuine interest in their welfare and your intent to do what you can to be helpful. Above all, avoid giving false information or raising false hopes. If a patient asks questions that lie beyond your competence to answer, suggest that they be referred to the attending physician.

Patient Adjustment

Hospitalized patients who respond to medical care and are fully recovered can proceed with their lives upon discharge. But those whose illnesses leave them vulnerable to future illness (e.g., heart attack victims) and disabled individuals (e.g., stroke or accident victims) are in a far different situation. These people may face a reevaluation of basic values to cope with their new circumstances. This adaptation may prove essential for both their physical and their emotional readjustment.

Health-care professionals who deal with such patients—both those who are hospitalized and those receiving post-discharge therapy—must be sensitive in helping them acquire these new values, a process that can take weeks and even months. The success of this process is critical to patients' optimal rehabilitation; it is achieved when patients come to the realization that, although their former potentials are no longer attainable, they can set new, more realistic goals.

When they receive medical treatment or therapy, patients are forced into new modes of interpersonal contact. While interacting with health-care professionals, they may even develop an unhealthy dependency. In this case, it is critical that the health-care provider directs the relationship so that it is constructive rather than detrimental. Thus, as a patient proceeds from the acute stage to the recovery process, he or she should be encouraged to become more independent.

The transition from hospitalized to outpatient status can be emotionally troubling, since it may involve a realization that recovery is incomplete. Also, the camaraderie of hospital patients cannot be found in the home.

THE OUTPATIENT

To reduce costs, many HMOs and other facilities make strenuous efforts to treat patients on an outpatient basis. This applies even to some types of surgical operations.

While not stigmatized as "sick," outpatients may nevertheless suffer from a loss of self-image. This is because they view themselves in comparison with a society of healthy individuals and so feel deficient. Inpatients, who live in an environment of sick people, may feel this loss of self-image less intensely. On the other hand, outpatients do not feel the various losses associated with hospitalization.

Finally, remember that the outpatient typically is on the road to recovery, as opposed to the permanently disabled individual, who is only on the road to adjustment.

The Professional–Patient Relationship

 ## COMMUNICATING EFFECTIVELY

Health professionals interact daily with people from all walks of life. Their basic needs may be similar, but their lifestyles probably vary widely. So, the health professional must be able to communicate effectively with a wide variety of people in both verbal and non-verbal ways.

Verbal Skills

Verbal communication obviously is essential in order to secure information on a patient's medical history, current condition, and therapeutic progress; to establish rapport with the patient; to provide instructions to the patient; and to relay information to other health-care team members.

Success with verbal communication depends on several factors:

Vocabulary. Sometimes choosing the wrong words can result in a patient's misunderstanding her condition and her treatment. For this reason, you should avoid using technical jargon when talking to patients. Make a genuine effort to understand what your patients are saying to you, and to ensure that they've understood you properly. To ensure good communication, you might try the *echoing technique*: Repeat back what a patient says to be sure you've got it right. And ask him to explain to you in his own words what you've said to him.

Organized presentation. When a complex explanation is needed (for example, if you must explain a procedure), be direct, clear, and to the point. Again, avoid using technical jargon. Instead, try using a logical, step-by-step approach, and avoid overwhelming the patient with details.

Attitude. To a large degree, your manner of delivery determines the effectiveness of your message. Convey genuine concern in your tone of voice and in the words you choose. When appropriate and if suitable, you might inject some humor into the conversation to lighten the atmosphere.

Effective listening. It is not enough to ensure that patients hear what you say to them; you must also be sure that you are hearing what they say to you. Be sensitive to your patients' nuances of expression and avoid prejudging what you think they will say. Try not to distort situations so that they fit into your preconceived notion of a patient's attitude.

Nonverbal Skills

Your nonverbal communication skills can be as important as your verbal skills. These are manifested in several ways:

- When you are dealing with patients who don't speak English and those with perceptual deficiencies, you might use the *demonstration approach*, in which hand gestures and posturing serve as substitutes for the spoken word.

- A second nonverbal approach involves *gestures, facial expressions, touch, and other signs* comparable with pantomime. Eye contact is a major element of facial expression and reflects the potential for positive communication.

  Your nonverbal communication can either put your patients at ease or make them uncomfortable. Remember, you can convey disapproval simply by raising an eyebrow or pointing at a person. Watch your body language!

- Another way we communicate nonverbally is through our *personal appearance.* This is best reflected by the practice of wearing of a uniform. Some health-care professionals feel uniforms are important because they quickly establish one's credentials and position of authority.

- Finally, remember that *touch* is a very powerful way of communicating. Studies have shown that touch can be tremendously comforting and even therapeutic.

CULTURAL INFLUENCES

Cultural variations and personal biases obviously affect the way people interpret both verbal and nonverbal messages. For example, different cultural groups have different definitions of *comfortable personal space*. In mainstream U.S. society, we define four interacting-distance zones: namely, intimate, personal, social, and public. Health professionals often must function within the first two zones. Outside the examining room, however, you should adhere to each patient's preference for acceptable distance. This helps patients feel more secure in the health-care facility.

A second culturally dependent variable is *time*. Some groups are highly conscious of punctuality, while others are very lax about such things. Being aware of such differences can help you improve the effectiveness of your interactions with patients. While maintaining a schedule is important, you should try to accommodate your patients' needs. Be conscious of the difference between a formal visit and a social-professional visit. In other words, take a few minutes to talk to your patients and answer their questions. Striking a proper balance is a valuable tool for professional success.

Be aware of your own biases—and remember that patients have biases, too. Above all, avoid manifesting prejudice in any manner during the course of your professional activities.

 # THE NATURE OF THE RELATIONSHIP

While it is important to maintain good relationships with your patients, remember that these relationships are not friendships. In order to get optimal results for your patients, you must understand the nature of the patient–professional relationship, which encompasses three distinct stages:

- First, there is an initial acquaintanceship phase.

- Second, you enter the task implementation phase.

- Finally, you go through a disengagement phase.

These three phases are experienced no matter how long or how short the relationship.

Both you and your patient will enter the relationship with your own needs, expectations, and perceptions. These background factors determine the nature of your relationship with each patient.

The element of *trust* is central to the patient–professional relationship. Since the interaction between you and your patients occurs in a public context, trust becomes the vehicle that converts casualness to caring. You build trust when you express genuine concern, respect, and feelings of responsibility.

 # MAINTAINING PROFESSIONALISM

Remember, professionalism does not mean being competent, efficient, and aloof. On the other hand, to move from a totally impersonal to a highly personal relationship is equally inappropriate and not in the patient's (or your own) best interests. You must find a proper balance between the two, and then fine-tune that balance for each individual case. A key factor in attaining this goal is establishing good social relationships in your personal life and being flexible in meeting the challenges of daily life. Then you will have the tools to be more effective in your therapeutic relationships.

Use the guidelines below to help you strike the right balance between acting in a cold, distant manner and being excessively casual.

- Determine your own feelings about wearing a uniform. Wearing a white coat will not necessarily generate a sense of aloofness; nor will casual dress imply greater caring. But how you dress does affect how you feel, so you should give some consideration to your attitude toward uniforms.

- When dealing with a new patient, exercise good judgment in deciding whether to call him by his first name. As a general rule, address people older than you by their surnames, until they ask you to do otherwise.

- Try to communicate a sense of caring in your relationship with patients. Avoid establishing rigid limits in your interactions, but do try to keep to a schedule as well.

Your goal should be to combine a friendly approach with professional competence. This means demonstrating respect for each patient's values, beliefs, and needs in the context of proper professional care.

 # CARING FOR THE YOUNG

Infants

Some infants have medical problems from birth. These babies require continued, demanding, and dedicated care. They cannot express their wants and needs clearly, other than by crying. The needs of the infant fall into two categories: material and psychosocial.

The infant's primary *material consideration* is the need to eliminate physical discomfort, which may be due to hunger, thirst, irritation from a soiled diaper, or pain. Environmental discomforts may be due to noise, bright lights, or an unpleasant smell.

Because infants cannot talk, you must be perceptive to their typical behavior patterns, so you will recognize any unusual behavior when providing care.

You also must address the infant patient's *psychosocial needs*. Above all, this means you must generate trust—for example, by acting in a consistent, gentle manner with your tiny patients.

If you work with infant patients, you should take advantage of the bridge parents can provide between you and their babies. Parents can be invaluable in providing feedback on an infant's behavior so the impact of treatment can be fully evaluated and the real needs of the infant can be met.

Children

Children deserve the same respect you would give to any other patients. While they spend most of childhood learning to be independent, when they become ill children tend to regress toward infancy and give up the independence they have worked so hard to acquire. You must recognize this situation and provide needed and tactful support, thus reinforcing their sense of security.

When interacting with children, it is essential to enhance their self-esteem, which may need strengthening due to illness. Approaching the child-patient respectfully, as an individual, will maximize your chance of a successful outcome. Here, too, the family can facilitate a positive response. Remember, the sick child is not your only client—you must support the parents, as well. Doing so enables them to support the child, which helps in the recovery process.

You must also be attentive to the sick child's siblings, especially when their relationship is close. A sudden separation between two (or more) such siblings, plus the special attention given to the sick child, can generate a hostile response from those who are well.

You should make an effort, where feasible, to minimize the impact of illness on the relationships between siblings. In the long run, doing so will help in the therapeutic process.

Adolescents

It is hard to generalize about adolescents, because their development happens at such variable rates. During the adolescent stage, the individual must establish her own identity, value system, and philosophy of life.

You face special challenges when dealing with adolescents, since they may seek to assert their autonomy in decision making and yet are not legally able to do so. The most prominent viewpoint in this area is the *Mature Minors Doctrine*, which allows for parents or the state to speak on behalf of a minor's interest only as long as the minor is unable to represent him- or herself. Consequently, an adolescent's maturity level is the essential decisive factor.

Because of this, you should try to assess the maturity of your adolescent patients and respect their autonomy as far as is possible. At the same time, you cannot exclude the parents from the decision-making process.

It is important to realize that an adolescent's feelings may fluctuate between the desire for autonomy and a retreat to the submissive state of childhood. An assessment of family relationships will help you decide how to deal with the decision-making process.

CARING FOR ACTIVE ADULTS

Most health professionals have generally positive relationships with patients in their middle years, but beyond this point, interfacing may prove more difficult. This is because physical ailments during the prime of life are secondary to psychosocial issues, such as work, parenting, and relationships—all of which generate stress. The individual's lifestyle also influences his physical and mental well-being.

Most people in their middle years consider themselves invulnerable to the aches and pains of the elderly. So, if a middle-aged patient experiences these ailments, she may respond with anger or confusion at the disruption in her life. Thus, when a catastrophic illness or injury occurs at this life stage, you may have to help the patient contend with denial, depression, and hostility.

In treating active adults, therefore, you must consider their psychosocial as well as their physical needs. If a patient is unable to meet his established responsibilities and life goals, he may feel a sense of estrangement, vulnerability, and frustration coupled with a devastating loss of self-image. All of this engenders stress, which can have profound physical manifestations. As a professional, you must distinguish these manifestations from the genuine physical pain the patient may be experiencing.

You can help diminish your adult patients' anxiety by listening carefully to their concerns and adjusting your treatment approach accordingly.

CARING FOR THE ELDERLY

As a society, we must recognize that health-care delivery to the elderly is deficient because of a negative bias in this country known as *ageism*. This is reflected in many aspects of their treatment and typically results in elderly people receiving lower quality care. Becoming cognizant of the problem is the first step toward combating this prejudice.

In general, treating the elderly is comparable to working with other age groups. However, there are some specific issues of direct relevance to elderly patients. To begin with, many older people experience diminished sensory capacity (e.g., poor eyesight or bad hearing). Being aware of these limitations will help you interact with your elderly patients effectively and respectfully.

In addition, many older people need routine and schedule to help orient themselves to the time of day. In other words, a stable and predictable lifestyle helps them maintain emotional stability. If you can avoid altering their treatment routines, you can help provide the security and stability they need to recover their health.

Finally, you should remember that elderly patients face a continuing series of devastating losses as they age: They lose friends and family members to death; they lose their work identities to retirement; and many lose their independence to illness and the ravages of age. Being sincere in your care, listening carefully to their concerns, and sometimes just sitting quietly with them can help your older patients more than we know.

III

The Job Search

Once you have elected to enter the health-care field, chosen your prospective career, and completed your education and training, you are ready to enter the last phase of your endeavor to become a health-care professional: Finding a job.

Securing employment as a health-care professional requires the same approach as for any other position. This means you must prepare a resume and cover letter to send to prospective employers. You must also hone your skills for the critical interview that follows if your resume is of interest to a prospective employer. You will find advice on all these aspects of the job search in this section.

Preparing for the Job Search

Your job search should be directed at finding both the right job and the right employer. You should begin planning your search long before you start sending out resumes to prospective employers. Because your first job can have a big impact on your future success, your preparation is crucial. This chapter will help you avoid some common pitfalls and make good decisions as you proceed in the search process. To do this, we outline a series of sequential steps that are essential to your career success.

The preliminary steps of the search process were laid out in Chapter 2. If you haven't yet done so, complete the self-evaluation exercises there. If you completed them earlier, review your responses now. With this information in hand, you will be in a better position to assess your suitability for openings that come your way. You will be better focused on your specific needs and the kind of jobs that will meet your intellectual and personal requirements.

 ## DEFINING YOUR GOALS

Before you begin contacting prospective employers, you should develop your own unique job profile. In Table 7.1 on page 66, list the preferable, acceptable, and unacceptable conditions of any position you would consider.

Now you have a profile of your "ideal" hypothetical position. You can use this to judge potential jobs in your field. As you learn more about positions available in your area, you may want to revise your answers.

 ## IDENTIFYING PROSPECTIVE EMPLOYERS

Your next step in the job search process is to target the potential employers that best meet your needs. Your first stop should be your school's job placement office. The staff there can help you put together an effective resume or portfolio. Often, they maintain lists of

TABLE 7.1   Characteristics of Your Ideal Position

1. Do you want to work in the United States?

    ___ Yes   ___ No   ___ Preferable, but not mandatory

2. Are you willing to relocate to secure your first job?

    ___ Yes   ___ No

3. Are you willing to relocate periodically if you employer asks you to?

    ___ Yes   ___ No

4. Are you willing to travel as part of your job?

    ___ Yes   ___ No

5. Which part of the country do you prefer? (Number your preferences—1 being most desirable.)

    ___ Northeast   ___ Southeast   ___ Southwest

    ___ Upper Midwest   ___ Lower Midwest   ___ Northwest

6. What kind of location do you prefer? (Number your preferences.)

    ___ Large city   ___ Mid-sized city

    ___ Small town   ___ Rural/outdoors

7. What size of employer do you prefer? (Number your preferences.)

    ___ Large corporation   ___ Mid-sized company   ___ Small company

8. What kind of facility do you prefer? (Number your preferences.)

    ___ Hospital   ___ Residential facility   ___ Outpatient facility

9. If you find a position that meets your preferred working conditions, would you decline it solely because of:

    (a) Salary?

    ___ Yes   ___ No

    (b) Fringe benefits (e.g., health insurance, travel allowance, vacation days, tuition reimbursement, retirement benefits)?

    ___ Yes   ___ No

    (c) The absence of a formal training program?

    ___ Yes   ___ No

employers in your area and field. They may also direct you to other graduates who are working in the field. These contacts can be invaluable in your job search.

One of the best and most overlooked sources of job leads is your local *Yellow Pages*. Look through the listings of facilities in your field, check the ones that most interest you, then call or visit them directly. Ask if you can tour the facility and meet the human resources staff. Even if they have no openings available, they can give you valuable information about the field. They may even direct you to other organizations that do have openings.

Other sources of information on potential job openings are want ads, professional organizations and journals, employment agencies, database services, and the Internet.

Want Ads

Most newspapers carry employment ads in the Sunday classified ads section. You should recognize at the outset, however, that while these ads are sometimes helpful, they are more often frustrating. Because they generate so many responses, the competition for jobs listed in the want ads is intense. You may find yourself sending in resume after resume, with no response. Some people do find jobs through the wants ads, so you probably will want to spend some time and effort following up on them. But you clearly should not exclude the other approaches that may be more productive.

Read each want ad carefully and see how well it matches with your background and interests. If the match fits well, you should write a cover letter to match the particular position. Wait a week or so before sending this letter and your resume; this ensures that the initial wave of applicants has passed and your letter will receive closer attention.

Professional Organizations and Journals

Professional organizations are great sources of possible job leads. You'll find complete listings of these organizations by field in Appendix C and by state in Appendix D of this book.

You should also spend some time in a medical school or hospital library reviewing the classified ads in the professional journal for your field. Some sample journals are listed by field below. For a more complete list of professional journals, handbooks, and directories, see Appendix D.

Biomedical technology:

Biomedical Instrumentation and Technology
Association for the Advancement of
Medical Instrumentation
3330 Washington Blvd.
Arlington, VA 22201

Cytogenetics:

Applied Cytogenetics
Association of Cytogenetics Technologists
616 South Orchard Drive
Burbank, CA 91506

Cardiovascular technology:

CP NEWS
National Society for Cardiovascular/
Pulmonary Technology
1101 14th Street, NW
Washington, DC 20003

Nuclear medical technology:

Journal of Nuclear Medicine Technology
Society of Nuclear Medicine
136 Madison Avenue
New York, NY 10016

Laboratory medicine:

Archives of Pathology & Laboratory Medicine
American Medical Association
515 North State Street
Chicago, IL 60610

Medical laboratory technology:

Endocrinology
Endocrinology Society
9650 Rockville Pike
Bethesda, MD 20814

Medical records service:

Journal of the AMRA
American Medical Record Association
919 North Michigan Avenue
Chicago, IL 60611

Radiological technology:

Radiological Technology
American Society of Radiotechnologists
15000 Central Avenue SE
Albuquerque, NM 87123

Surgical assistant:

The Surgical Technologist
Association of Surgical Technologists
8307 Shaffer
Littleton, CO 80127

Ultrasound technology:

Journal of Ultrasound in Medicine
11200 Rockville Pike, Suite C-205
Rockville, MD 20852

A valuable source of information on health-care trade magazines is the *Magazine Industry Marketplace*. This reference book is available at your local library and is revised annually.

Finally, you'll find lists of openings with the federal government in two biweeklies:

Federal Career Opportunities
Federal Research Services Inc.
243 Church Street, NW
Vienna, VA 22183

Federal Jobs Digest
325 Pennsylvania, SE
Washington, DC 20003

Employment Agencies and Executive Recruiters

To effectively use this resource, you must first identify those agencies in your area that actively recruit health-care personnel. It is even more valuable if you can locate those that specialize in securing positions for people *in your field*. When you are checking out an agency, ask how many people it has placed in your field in the last two years. Contact local health-care agencies and ask if they have hired employees from that agency. Finally, be sure to find out if the agency is paid by the employer who hires you, or if you must pay for services yourself. Doing your homework first can save you from wasting time and money on the wrong agency.

Your next step is to meet with a counselor from your chosen agency. Try to work with only one counselor; send all correspondence and queries to that person. That way, the counselor is more likely to remember you and to recommend you to potential employers. Treat each meeting with your counselor as you would a job interview. Dress neatly, have all of your materials at hand, and focus on making good impression. Remember, this is the person who will be recommending you (or *not* recommending you) for a job! After each meeting, send a thank-you note to your counselor for his or her time and help.

Every other week or so, call your employment counselor to check in and remind him or her of your continued availability.

Because some agencies are paid by the employers they recruit for, and some charge the job-seeker for their placement services, you can expect different services from each.

- If you pay for an agency's services, that agency is working for *you*. The counselor's job is to find you a job, and therefore may be more willing to spend time helping you with your resume and cover letter. While this help is obviously valuable, it is not cheap. Many agencies charge as much as 10 percent of your first year's salary for placing you in a job.

- If an agency is paid by the employer to recruit workers, that agency is working for the *company*. You will not be charged for their services, but their efforts on your behalf may be limited. The same is true for executive recruiters, who are paid by employers to find high-paid workers such as veterinarians, biomedical engineers, and therapists.

Database Services

A growing number of database services today offer useful information for those seeking employment. Such services are available at many local libraries. Two examples are listed below. Ask your librarian for more information about these and other database services.

The Ultimate Job Finder. This lists about 5,000 trade and specialty journals.

Standard & Poor. This listing provides information on many public and private companies.

The Internet

Most new college graduates today do at least part of their job searching on the Internet. All of the major online commercial services provide networking opportunities as well as job search capabilities in health care. Make use of bulletin boards to focus on your particular employment needs. You should introduce yourself, clearly indicate what kind of position you are seeking, and mention any help you can offer to others. You then have to patiently wait for replies.

A more direct approach is to look for a job directly on the Internet. Many organizations today maintain Web sites listing their current employment opportunities. You can check out your target facility's Web site, learn more about the organization and its openings, and even apply directly online.

Another option is to locate Web sites that list job opportunities for allied health professionals or jobs in your specific area of interest. Some of these let you post your resume online for employers to see. Others simply list the openings. You then submit your resume and cover letter by regular mail.

Some of the most popular job-search Web sites include these:

www.monster.com   www.jobsleuth.com

www.job-listings.com   www.joblocator.com

www.execsearches.com

Some sites devoted to health-care careers include:

www.embbs.com

www.medimorphus.com

www.HealthCareSource.com

www.hirehealth.com

www.healthcareers-online.com

www.healthcareerweb.com

NETWORKING: YOUR BEST SOURCE OF JOB LEADS

Securing a job, especially the right one, requires a strong proactive approach. You need to take the initiative and establish your own web of family, friends, and acquaintances who can pass relevant job information along to you. This kind of activity is known as *networking,* and it is the single most effective way to find job leads. Networking involves contacting everyone you know and asking them if they know of any job openings in your field, or if they can refer you to someone else who might know of any openings. Chances are, if you keep at it persistently, networking will lead you to a job interview— or at least to an informational interview.

Informational Interviews

Use your network of contacts to get names of people who are working in positions similar to the one you want. Then call these people and ask if they will meet with you to talk about their jobs. These are not job interviews per se; you are simply gathering information at this stage.

During an informational interview, ask the person about the field you're interested in, the company he or she works for, and the responsibilities of the position. Specifically, you should ask about three issues at this interview:

Training. Ask if the company has a training program and how long it lasts. Also ask if the company provides training for updating or upgrading your skills. Some companies provide their employees with financial help to complete educational course work in their specialties.

Salary. Ask about the industry standard of compensation for entry-level positions in your field. (Figure 7.1 can provide guidance in this area.)

Benefits. Ask what benefits the company offers. For example, does it provide health and disability insurance? What about vacation days, stock options, and retirement plans? These are an important part of any compensation package.

This can give you a realistic picture of what to expect and what you might ask for when you go to an actual job interview. Keep a record of the information you get during your informational interviews. You'll find it invaluable in preparing for job interviews.

FIGURE 7.1   Average Salaries for Health-Care Careers

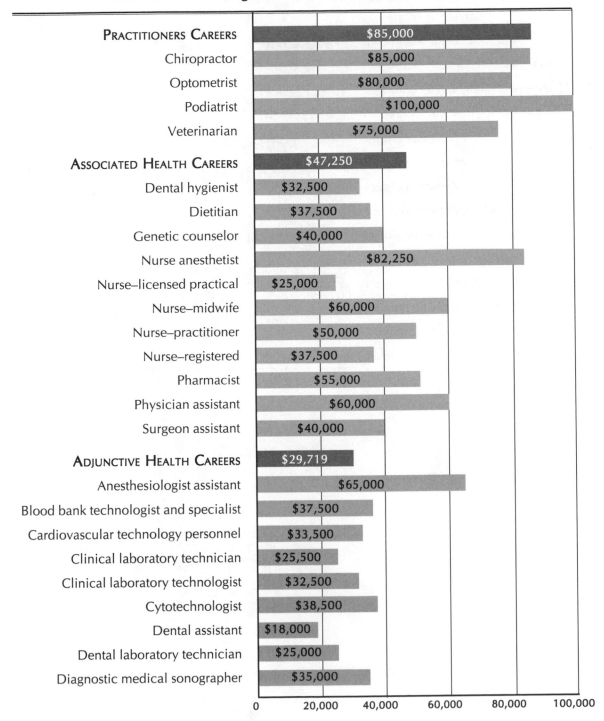

FIGURE 7.1 *Continued*

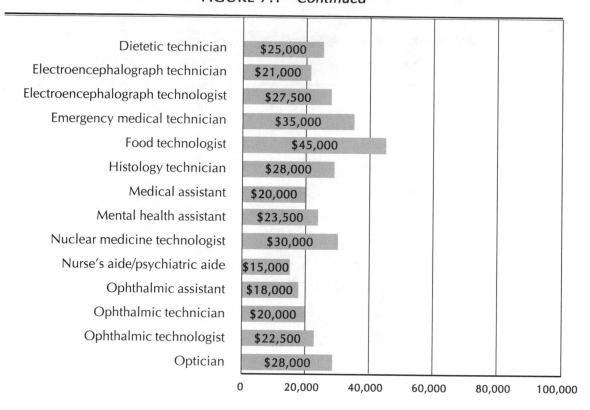

Securing a Position

The second major phase of the job search process involves actually securing a position. Your challenge now is to sell yourself. In this chapter you'll find suggestions for creating your marketing tools—your resume and cover letter—for handling applications and exams, and for being effective in interviews.

YOUR RESUME

Your resume is, in reality, your letter of introduction. To prepare it properly you have to be fully acquainted with the details of your career and of the job you seek. An attractive resume is aimed at securing an invitation to come for an interview. This is the next step in the job search process.

Your resume should contain the following information:

Your location. You should provide your full home address, phone number, and e-mail address.

Your career goal. Carefully and precisely summarize the kind of job you are seeking.

Your education. Beginning with the most recent educational institution you've attended, list all of your completed degrees, diplomas, and certificates going back to high school. List the name and address of each institution, the years you attended, the degree or diploma your received, and (where appropriate) your major.

Honors, awards, and recognition. List any recognition of special abilities or service you received during your school years. These may include specific awards, membership in honor societies, or being elected to school office.

Work experience. List all the places you've worked, starting with the most recent. Include summer, part-time, and volunteer positions. Identify the length of time you were employed, your job title, and your major accomplishments on the job.

Qualifications. As specifically as possible, list the skills you have to do the job you want. Include the names and types of software and equipment you can use.

Special abilities. This section gives you an opportunity to promote yourself by identifying your special skills or unique achievements. If you set up a successful mini-business during school, list it here. If you held a job, ran track, belonged to a service club, and still managed good grades in school, that's something to list! Try to demonstrate your creativity, organizational skills, team spirit, and social/cultural activities. Indicate your special musical skills, community service activities, foreign language ability, and hobbies.

Position Information

Knowing the facts about the position you want allows you to demonstrate your suitability for the position. After reviewing the job openings you've located, identify the educational requirements and qualifications for each one. Make note of any prior experience required and the job's responsibilities. Then match these requirements and responsibilities with your personal assets. Now you can customize your resume to meet the prospective employer's needs.

Keep in mind that most employers receive many resumes for each job opening. Frequently personnel managers expedite their review by simply scanning cover letters and resumes. That's why these marketing tools should be as attractive as possible. Your resume should be eye-catching and focus the reviewer's attention on your candidacy and your credentials.

There are a number of issues to focused on in preparing your resume:

Brevity. Don't assume that a longer resume is a better resume. Your resume should be no more than two pages. This means you must write in a brief, concise fashion. When presenting a project you successfully completed, list only the major elements of your activities rather than describing the protocol in detail. Try to get the basics across and leave the details for an interview.

Word choice. Use action words that reflect accomplishment, such as *organized, designed,* and *implemented.* These imply intense personal involvement; they show you have potential. Other words that leave a positive impression are *analyzed, created, developed, planned,* and *increased.* Whenever possible use numbers or figures to document your achievements.

Presentation. Make your resume as attractive as possible, without resorting to gimmicks. The layout should be simple and clean. Proper spacing and use of margins, headings, and italics can make your information clear and more interesting. Your resume is like a personal commercial; the better it looks, the more likely your chances for success. Use a laser printer or have it reproduced by a professional printer. In either case, use a high-quality paper in white, off-white, or pale gray with a contrasting ink.

Clarity. Be sure the information you provide is accurate and as complete as possible for the reader to evaluate your abilities and potential. Don't exaggerate to enhance your appeal, and avoid being vague if you are trying to "cover up" information. It may be a red flag that arouses the reader's attention. Have someone review your resume to ensure there are no grammatical errors, and use the computer spell-check for accuracy. Set the draft copy aside for a short while and then proofread it carefully before printing the final draft.

On pages 76–79, you will find some sample resumes for various positions in the health-care field. The resumes were written by professional resume writers and originally appeared in either *Gallery of Best Resumes for People Without a Four-Year Degree*, by David F. Noble (published by JIST Works) or *The Quick Resume & Cover Letter Book*, by J. Michael Farr (published by JIST Works).

ELIZABETH M. BARKLEY
104 Maple St.
Montgomery, AL 00000
(000) 000-0000

PROFILE: *Licensed Practical Nurse desirous of securing a nursing position in fulfillment of a lifelong dream. Stable and promotable with over seventeen years with the same organization.*

EDUCATION:	Tri-County Technical College, Montgomery, AL *Practical Nursing*	1995
	Tri-County Technical College, Montgomery, AL *A.S. Business Education*	1989

Honors:
Distinguished Practical Nurse Graduate
Magnolia Leadership Graduate
Board of Visitors – Tri-County Tec
Montgomery County Highest Academic Achievement Award
USSA Academic Collegiate All-American
Phi Theta Kappa Honor Society
Collegiate National Deans' List
President's List
Dean's List

WORK EXPERIENCE:

Synthetic Technologies, Montgomery, AL *Materials Manager*	1988 – Present

Supervised materials management department including purchasing, traffic, materials control, production, planning, and distribution. Developed objectives, policies, and programs covering the administration and operation of materials management.

Davidson Cable Corp., Montgomery, Al *Distribution Center Manager* (1986 – 1988)	1970 – 1988

Directed all aspects of distribution center for manufacturing facility with $95 million sales. Supervised 8 managers and 40 hourly associates.

Manager of Materials and Sales (1982 – 1986)

Managed purchasing, customer services, shipping/receiving, primary warehouse and plant services departments. Supervised 5 management employees and 8 hourly employees.

Warehouse Manager (1979 – 1982)

Assumed responsibility for shipping finished goods and maintaining $2.5 million in inventory.

Purchasing Agent (1974 – 1979)

Negotiated competitive prices and delivery of raw materials, supplies, small tools, office and janitorial supplies. Performed physical inventories and periodic cycle counts.

Buyer (1970 – 1974)

Procured raw materials by means of bills of materials. Expedited delivery of raw materials, manufacturing, janitorial, and maintenance supplies.

This resume was created by *Gwen P. Noffz, Greenwood, South Carolina.* The Profile explains a career change after many years in management. Re-created with permission from D. Noble, *Gallery of Best Resumes for People Without a Four-Year Degree* (JIST Works).

Maria Eléna Navarro, CRTT

127 Pine Street, Unit D
Morris Plains, NJ 55555

(000) 000-000

OBJECTIVE

Respiratory therapist *in a hospital where previous experience in clinical settings such as ICU, CCU, and NICU would be put to use and valued.*

EDUCATION

County College of Morris, Randolph, NJ
Completed AMA approved certificate program in Repiratory Therapy, 1992

William Paterson College, Wayne, NJ
Associates in Applied Science, Allied Health, 1988

TECHNICAL SKILLS

Equipment: *MA-1, Puritan-Bennett 7200, and Bear series ventilator initiation and management, including transport, set up and maintenance.*

Treatment Modalities: *Under the direction of a physician, perform gas, aerosol and humidity therapies; intermittant positive pressure breathing (IPPB); chest physiotherapy; cardiopulminary rehabilitation.*

Techniques: *Endotrachael intubation/extubation; administration of medical gases, drugs, treatments and tests as prescribed by an authorized physician; drawing and interpretation of arterial blood gases; airway management; bedside spirometry for checking pulmonary functioning and recording patient progress; quality control checks for optimal equipment performance of respiratory equipment.*

Patient Interaction: *Implementation of patient care plans and follow-up treatment on patients of all ages, newborn through geriatric; instruction of patients on use of liquid oxygen, concentrators, c-paps, bipaps and apnea monitors as well as use, care and troubleshooting of their ventilators; direct responsibility for the management of respiratory compromised patients; assistance to crisis team in the administration of basic life support in code situations.*

WORK EXPERIENCE

3/95 to Present **Respiratory Technician**
HomeCare Agency, Rockaway, NJ

2/93 to 3/95 and currently **Respiratory Therapist**
on per diem basis *Memorial Hospital, Morristown, NJ*

1/92 to 2/93 **Respiratory Technician**
Wayne General Hospital, Wayne, NJ

10/90 to 12/91 **Telemetry Technician**
Cardiologics, Inc., Glenridge, NJ

8/87 to 10/90 **Telemetry Technician/Nurses Assistant**
Beth Israel Hospital, Passaic, NJ

LANGUAGES

Bilingual Fluency in English and Spanish

This resume was created by **Melanie Noonan, CPS, West Paterson, New Jersey.** The separation of the headings in the left column adds an interesting visual element. Re-created with permission from D. Noble, *Gallery of Best Resumes for People Without a Four-Year Degree* (JIST Works).

Margaret P. Jameson

1843 McMillan Drive
Jackson, MI 49444

517-555-7454

Radiologic Technologist

Summary of Clinical Skills and Experience
- Produce diagnostic radiographs
- Assist radiologist in fluoroscopic exams
- Operate mobile radiographic equipment
- Perform laboratory tests
- Received introduction to CT, MRI and mammography
- Completed rotation in surgical unit

Education
GENESEE COMMUNITY COLLEGE • Genesee, MI
Associate in Applied Science with Honors xxxx
Consistently named to Dean's List

Certification
A.R.R.T. Candidate
Will sit for exam in July xxxx

Clinical Experience

URGENT CARE CENTER • Dixon, MI	xxxx-Present
HEALTH RESOURCES • St. Johns, MI	xxxx-xxxx
SPARROW MEDICAL CENTER* • Lansing, MI	xxxx-xxxx
PERRYVILLE HOSPITAL* • Perryville, MI	xxxx-xxxx

Denotes clinical experience as student

Other Experience

JOHNSON BROTHERS & ASSOC. • Flint, MI xxxx-Present
Clerical Assistant [part-time]

JACKSON AUTO PLAZA • Jackson, MI xxxx-xxxx
Cashier/Receptionist

This resume was created by *Janet L. Beckstrom, Flint, Michigan*. The candidate is a new graduate without much experience. The writer has listed her credentials in an eye-catching format. Re-created with permission from J. Michael Farr, *The Quick Resume & Cover Letter Book* (JIST Works).

Danielle Lewis

28044 Tea Rose Court • Tampa, Florida 33500 • (000) 000-0000

— Career Focus: Medical Assistant —

Profile

- Self-starter with solid employment history throughout high school and technical school; financed 100% of education.
- Trained in handling medical front/back office duties, assisting patients, and early childhood development.
- Strong organizational skills; exhibit ability to handle multiple tasks efficiently and accurately.
- "People" person, able to establish working rapport with patients, co-workers, and professional levels.

Education & Certifications

Concord Institute - Tampa, FL (Graduated October 19XX)
Medical Assistant Certification

Formal Training:
Clinical: Anatomy, Phlebotomy, Injections, EKG, X-ray, Clinical Equipment Use, Elements of Patient Care
Office: Standard Front & Back Office Procedures, Typing, Computer Training (Medical Manager Software, Windows, WordPerfect), Peg Boarding, Basic Insurance Coding

Chamberlain High School - Tampa, FL (Graduated 19XX)
Diploma (Emphasis on Early Childhood Development)

CPR and First-Aid Certified

20-hour Day Care Teaching Certificate

Relevant Experience

Family Medical Center - Lutz, FL (Externship Program)   4/XX - 8/XX
Medical Assistant

- Assisted Doctor in patient care; obtained medical history, took vital signs, blood draws, administered injections, handled wound care and dressings, obtained specimens, and followed up on lab work.
- Performed EKGs, ear washes, removal of stitches, patient prep procedures, and set up patient rooms.
- Worked with Office Manager to provide assistance with front office clerical duties.

Other Experience

Youth Academy - Tampa, FL (part-time while attending Concord Institute   9/XX - 3/XX
Child Care Technician (Infant Room)

Home Day Care - Tampa, FL   4/XX - 9/XX
Nanny (two children — 6 months and 3-year old)

Bay Area Learning Center - Tampa, FL   6/XX - 4/XX
Day Care Teacher (Lesson planning and supervision — infants through two-year olds)

Highland Pre-school - Tampa, FL (Work Study Program - Chamberlain High School)   4/XX - 6/XX
Teacher Assistant (3 and 4 year olds)

This resume was created by *Diane McGoldrick, Tampa, Florida*. The candidate's background is in child care. The writer leaves open other possibilities. Re-created with permission from J. Michael Farr, *The Quick Resume & Cover Letter Book* (JIST Works).

YOUR COVER LETTER

Your resume should be accompanied by a *cover letter*. This is the initial exposure a potential employer will have with you. It should entice the reader to look carefully at your resume. The resume outlines your skills and experience; the cover letter ties these features to a future employer's specific needs. Thus, while the resumes you send out will be fairly standardized, each cover letter should be modified to meet a potential employer's requirements.

A good cover letter accomplishes several things:

- It generates interest in your resume.

- It markets you as an attractive prospective employee.

- It provides a favorable indication of your communication skills.

- It gives attractive, concrete facts about you and your background.

The cover letter usually consists of four elements: the salutation, the opening, the body, and the closing.

Salutation. If at all possible, address your letter to a specific individual. This may be someone in the personnel department, a department head, or a prospective supervisor. *Be sure you spell the person's name correctly.*

Opening. Your focus should be to secure the reader's interest. If a mutual acquaintance suggested you write to this person, mention that acquaintance by name. If you are responding to an ad, note that in the letter.

Body. Emphasize your special interest in the company by noting some of its favorable aspects (e.g., awards it has received, research breakthroughs, or a close match with your background and interest). You can secure this information from the business press or local newspapers.

Closing. To close the letter, clearly emphasize your genuine interest in the position and ask to meet with the reader at his or her earliest convenience. Beneath the closing paragraph, type "Sincerely," and then leave three blank lines for your signature. Type your name beneath your signature. Make sure your phone number is listed on both your cover letter and your resume.

Type your letter on high-quality paper to match your resume. Be sure to keep a copy of each letter you send for your files.

On pages 81–84, you'll find some sample cover letters for positions in the health-care field. These letters were written by professional resume writers and originally appeared in either *Gallery of Best Cover Letters* or *Gallery of Best Resumes for People Without a Four-Year Degree*, both by David F. Noble and published by JIST Works.

Rhonda Nilson, R.N.

10 Langford Avenue, Elliott, NJ 00000 • (555) 555-5555 • Willing to Relocate

July 16, 20XX

Wecare Behavioral Health Center
35 Edge Way
Elliot, NJ 00000

Attention: Nurse Recruiter

Dear Nurse Recruiter:

I am interested in pursuing the nursing position recently advertised in the *Elliot Tribune*. I am confident that my strong critical and human relations skills, conscientiousness, and ability to work effectively under pressure will make me a valuable addition to your nursing staff.

I recently graduated summa cum laude from Elliot Community College, and received an award for academic excellence and outstanding achievement in nursing practice. My classmates frequently relied on me to assist them with their studies, and I often led tutoring sessions.

My life experiences prior to nursing school will strengthen my abilities as a nurse. After earning my B.A. degree from Midland State College, I pursued an acting career in Manhattan. In trying to launch this career, I held numerous positions requiring strong interpersonal, communication, and presentation skills, and the ability to think and respond quickly. These experiences have also helped me to relate easily and comfortably with all types of people and to appreciate each person's uniqueness.

If your facility is in need of a competent, energetic registered nurse with a mature attitude, please contact me at (555) 555-5555. My schedule is extremely flexible, and I am available to work whatever hours or days you require.

Sincerely,

Rhonda Nilson, R.N.

Enclosure

Written by *Rhoda Kopy, Toms River, New Jersey*. A strong, convincing letter that displays interest, confidence, academic excellence, and a willingness to work any hours or days. Re-created with permission from D. Noble, *Gallery of Best Resumes for People Without a Four-Year Degree* (JIST Works).

ROBIN BRIMM, MHSL
0000 North West Avenue
Anywhere, USA
(000) 000-0000

December 15, 2000

John Shirley, Ph.D.
Associate Vice President for Academic Administration
THE UNIVERSITY OF FLORIDA MEDICAL BRANCH
000 Miami Boulevard
Miama, Florida 00000-0000

Dear Dr. Shirley:

John Daggle, Administrator–Pediatrics with Children's Hospital, suggested I contact you regarding the position of Program Development Manager, Department of Radiology, with The University of Florida Medical Branch. The enclosed resume outlines my management experience in health care, as well as pertinent industry involvement and graduate preparation in health systems leadership. With respect to your requirements, my qualifications include:

Administration: Presently hold full administrative authority for the nation's largest freestanding radiology center ... accountable for strategic planning, management of operating and capital equipment budgets, contract negotiations, business development, marketing ... positioned center to control major market share despite nationwide decline in imaging center services.

Development of Service Lines: Identified and developed comprehensive service line, augmenting facility with women's services, 3D imaging, and MRI mammography. Successfully introduced new lines through strategic marketing and communications campaign.

Human Relations: Strength in establishing and fostering cohesive relationships, particularly with physicians ... equally effective with administrators, employees, the medical community, and the community at large ... extensive experience in addressing sensitive physician-related matters.

Dr. Shirley, based on my brief conversation with John, I am very interested in this position. Given my background, I believe I have much to contribute toward your center's evolution and expansion, as well as the administrative expertise to support new business growth.

I will be in touch and look forward to learning more about this opportunity.

Sincerely,

Robin Brimm, MHSL
Enclosure

Written by *Susan Britton Whitcomb, CPRW, Fresno, California*. Mentioning the name of a mutual acquaintance is a good way to get your letter noticed. Re-created with permission from D. Noble, *Gallery of Best Resumes for People Without a Four-Year Degree* (JIST Works).

Melanie Stone, CRNA

1555 Main Street • Charleston, WV 25302 • (304) 555-5555

November 4, 20XX

Roger Cummings, MD
Pleasants Hospital
411 Pleasants Drive
Boston, MA 55555

Dear Dr. Cummings:

For the last several years, whenever I've thought about New England—Boston in particular—I've found myself musing about its opportunities for professional growth and continuing education. Boston is the heart of medicine in America. Its reputation for significant research and professional excellence is world-renowned. More than anything, I want to make myself a valuable member of Boston's medical community.

As a CRNA with four years' experience at a busy teaching hospital, I am proud of my reputation for outstanding clinical performance. I can offer top-notch skills as well as clinical instructor experience and a balanced background that includes both nursing and fine arts. Because I love my career, you'll find me eager to be an involved employee, serving on committees and assisting in any area where I can be effective. Locally, I have played an active role in maintaining CRNA professional standards and expanding our scope of practice.

My resume is enclosed for your consideration. I would appreciate the chance to talk with you personally regarding opportunities within your facility. I'll follow up next week to see if there's an interest. In the meantime, please feel free to call me at the number listed above.

Respectfully,

Melanie Stone

Enclosure

Written by *Barbie Dallman, CPRW, Charleston, West Virginia.* An interesting letter because the first two paragraphs are fresh, without any cliché commonly found in cover letters. Re-created with permission from D. Noble, *Gallery of Best Resumes for People Without a Four-Year Degree* (JIST Works).

BRYAN ENEA

Home: 811 66th Avenue N. • Herkimer, NY 00000 • (555) 555-5555
School: 123 Sunny Avenue • Boston, MA 00000 • (555) 555-5555

August 19, xxxx

Ms. Jane Smith
123 Street
Poughkeepsie, NY 12603

Dear Ms. Smith:

I am a pediatric physical therapy major at Northeastern University who would like to explore employment opportunities within your practice. Northeastern's program is based on a cooperative educational approach which requires students to pursue paid employment opportunities within their field of study. Therefore, I would accept any position where my skills and abilities would benefit your practice while enabling me to gain an insight into the office environment as well as a realistic understanding of the role of a physical therapist.

If given the opportunity, I will work hard to make positive contributions to your practice. As a sophomore, I realize that I cannot offer you an abundance of experience. However, I would bring with me an exceptional work ethic, an eagerness to learn, and a commitment to my chosen profession. I would also bring general clerical skills—data entry, word processing, and the Internet—and personal qualities which include organized and disciplined work habits, an ability to relate well with people, a high energy level, and problem-solving aptitude.

Enclosed is my resume for your review. Should you have any questions regarding my abilities, please contact me at the above. number. Thank you for your time and attention in reviewing my qualifications. I look forward to hearing from you.

Sincerely,

Bryan Enea

Enclosure

Written by *Kristin Mroz Coleman, Poughkeepsie, New York.* This person is upfront about having little experience but offers energy and commitment. Recreated with permission from D. Noble, *Gallery of Best Cover Letters* (JIST Works).

JOB APPLICATIONS

Some large firms, government agencies, and hospitals use their own application forms rather than resumes (or in addition to them) to evaluate prospective candidates. The application's uniform structure helps the evaluator find the information he or she needs and allows for easy comparisons between candidates. Because applications don't let you present your qualifications the way you typically would, you should plan ahead of time how to present them under the categories most applications contain.

When completing an application, keep in mind the following tips:

Ask for two copies of the application. That way, you can use one copy to prepare a first draft. And, if you make a mistake, you can use the second form. Whenever possible, make a copy for your own files.

Read it before you complete it. Familiarize yourself with the form so you can relate it with sections in your resume. Then you can use your resume as a reference source.

When possible, complete the application at home and photocopy it.

Use a typewriter or print neatly in dark blue or black ink.

Processing Guidelines

When you are applying for several positions in the same company, you can leave the specific job title blank. Do not leave any other blanks on the application. If a question is not relevant to you, write N/A (not applicable) in the space provided.

Sometimes you must fill out an application at the employment site, so be sure to take a copy of your resume with you. You might also find it useful to take a list of standard answers to commonly asked questions. Be sure to take a dark-blue or black ink pen and your complete list of references, along with their addresses and phone numbers.

As with your resume, the answers you provide on an application form should be direct, accurate, and honest.

JOB EXAMINATIONS

The most common job exams are those for civil service appointments. For these and similar tests you can and should prepare adequately. Government agencies usually will provide samples of exams, and copies may be available at your local library. You can also find standardized test preparation books in a wide variety of fields at your local bookstore.

By practicing beforehand, you will improve your performance level, you'll be less nervous the day of the test, and you'll be familiar with the kinds of questions you'll have to answer.

Listed below are some general study guidelines for preparing for tests:

- Familiarize yourself with the major topics you must master.

- Begin your study sessions with your strongest area.

- Do a quick review of the material before beginning your intensive study.

- Determine the sequence of the information you must learn. Try to master it in a logical grouping rather than as isolated facts.

- Use your most successful study techniques to prepare for the exam.

- Before memorizing information, make sure you understand it.

- Keep your study sessions to a reasonable time limit, bearing in mind your physical and mental well-being.

- Remember that you will remember facts better if you can associate them with something you already know.

- Frequent, short, intense review periods are more useful than long study sessions.

- Getting a good night's sleep after intense evening study consolidates the material in your memory and thus enhances retention.

For the test day itself, make the following preparations:

- Prepare what you will need the night before (e.g., #2 pencils, a calculator, any reference materials you are allowed to bring).

- Get a good night's sleep the night before the exam. Avoid last-minute cramming.

- Arrive at the test center 5 to 30 minutes prior to the starting time.

- Use the restroom before the test begins.

- Before answering any questions, read through the instructions carefully and make sure you understand them.

- Do not spend too much time on any one question. Since you have only a limited amount of time, speed counts; a significant delay can prove costly if you don't have time to answer the questions you do know.

 # THE INTERVIEW

The interview is probably the most critical element in securing any job. The entire goal of your cover letter and resume is to secure this opportunity to sell yourself and to see what the position is all about.

Your interview goals are twofold:

1. *You want to show the employer you have the qualifications and the personality characteristics necessary for the job.* The interviewer will be looking for signs that you can do the work, and that you will fit into the organization's

social structure. He or she may also have unanswered questions about your records.

2. **You want to gather information** about working conditions, job responsibilities, and your compatibility with your potential supervisor.

Preparing

To a large extent, your success in an interview depends on the amount of preparation you do *before* the interview. This is one instance when doing your homework pays off in a big way!

Know your background. Your resume is a "cold" outline of your professional life. During the interview, you can add the details that will enhance your chances. You might say, for example, "I had to work occasionally until late at night to meet emergency needs of the position." Or, "I recommended, ordered, and set up this piece of equipment that enhanced the efficiency of my workplace." Or, "I am especially proud of the following accomplishment ..."

Take stock of your assets. Make a list of your personal and professional abilities that will enhance your appeal to a prospective employer. On the personal side these might include punctuality, dependability, and good interpersonal relationship skills. Professionally you may want to emphasize a sense of commitment and dedication, loyalty, inquisitiveness, and a desire to take the initiative.

Be informed about the position. Get as much information about the job as you possibly can. Try to learn about its duties, responsibilities, and requirements. This will help you to match up your assets with the needs of the position, so you can present this match to your interviewer.

Do a mock interview. It is natural to be nervous when facing an interview. You can ease this nervousness by practicing the interview experience. Have a friend pretend to be the interviewer. Prepare a list of questions you think will be asked. Have your friend ask them, and practice giving your answers until they come to you naturally and fluently. You can use the questions below as the basis for your mock interview:

- Why did you apply for this position?

- Tell me about yourself.

- What are your career goals?

- What are your greatest assets and liabilities?

- What aspects of the position do you find most appealing?

- Where do you want to be five years from now?

- What from your education or work experience is most relevant to this job?

- Were you ever terminated from a position? If so, why?

- What challenges do you find to be most appealing?

- What are your salary requirements?

- How did you learn about this opening?

- Do you have any questions?

In addition to practicing for the interview, there are some simple things you can do to increase your chances of success:

Get a good night's sleep so that you are rested and alert.

Shower in the morning; it will help you relax.

Dress neatly and be properly groomed, so that you make a good first impression.

Arrive 15 minutes early for the interview so you can adjust to the surroundings.

Don't be upset if your interview session is delayed.

When the interviewer arrives, greet him or her with a firm handshake.

Stay as relaxed as possible. Try taking several deep breaths and exhaling slowly just before you enter the interviewer's office.

Carry a copy of your resume with you.

Make small talk in the beginning of the interview by commenting on the weather or something of interest in the person's office.

Be courteous and friendly. Remember to smile.

Maintain eye contact throughout the interview.

Answer the questions honestly. Don't try to anticipate what the interviewer might want to hear.

Be as straightforward and as accurate as possible in your answers.

If you respond poorly to a question, let it pass. Don't let it upset you for the rest of the interview.

Try to be as natural as possible.

Try to sell your favorable assets by fitting them into the interview. (This presupposes that you know your strengths thoroughly.)

Once the interviewer has asked all of his or her questions, it's your turn. The interviewer probably will ask if you have any questions. If not, seize the moment yourself by saying, "May I ask you some questions?" You will undoubtedly receive a positive response. Be sure to have some questions prepared ahead of time. Listed below are some good examples:

- How important is this position in the company?

- Would I be working alone, or will I be part of a group?

- To whom would I report? Would it be possible to meet that person?

- Would I supervise anyone? If yes, could I meet them?

- What challenges does the position present?

- How can I advance in the company?

- Is the company expanding?

- Who will evaluate my performance? How, and how often?

- How did this opening come about?

- What fringe benefits does the company offer its employees?

Don't bring up salary during a first interview. If the interviewer brings it up, be as general as possible. For example, if you are asked how much you expect to make, you might say, "That depends on the work and on what kinds of opportunities are available." Wait until you have a job offer before you begin negotiating salary.

At the end of the interview, thank the interviewer and ask about the next step in the hiring process. Ask if you can provide any additional information. Express your genuine interest in the position (if that is the case), and say you are looking forward to hearing from the interviewer.

Following Up

As soon as you arrive home from the interview, sit down and write a brief note, thanking the interviewer for his or her time. Mention how much you enjoyed meeting the person, recap any pertinent things you have in common, and again emphasize that you'd like to talk again. Send the note the same day, so that it arrives only a day or two after the interview.

Don't spend a lot of time and agony trying to judge your chances based on your interview performance. You may misjudge the impression you left. In any case you don't know how many other candidates are being interviewed. Try to relax, knowing you did your best.

ALLIED HEALTH CAREERS

This section contains detailed descriptions of 80 allied health careers. These are divided into five categories based on the nature of the professional activity:

- diagnosing and treating practitioners,

- associated health-care personnel,

- adjunctive health-care personnel,

- rehabilitative personnel, and

- affiliated personnel.

The form of presentation is the same for each of the careers:

Capsule. A seven-heading summary precedes each career description and provides an overview of the critical components of the career.

Scope. This section introduces the career in broad terms, outlining the significance of the work, the general duties and responsibilities, and the patients or clients served.

Activities. This section gives a detailed description of the actual work done by people in the field.

Work setting. Health-care professionals work in a variety of situations—public, private, home, office, and several different kinds of institutions. This section lists the options commonly available to personnel in the field.

Advancement. The section lists prospects moving up and assuming more significant responsibilities in the field.

Prerequisites. This lists the educational prerequisites for career studies in the field. In addition, it lists the personal attributes that are natural prerequisites for successfully carrying out the professional activities.

Education/training. This section outlines the educational route for the field, including the make-up of courses in the program leading to a certificate, diploma, or degree. It also lists training requirements that are specific to the career.

Certification/registration/licensure. This lists any professional certification or licenses needed to practice in the field.

Career potential. In this section, we discuss future prospects for employment in the field.

For more information. This section lists resources for those interested in learning more about the field, including the names and addresses of professional organizations. Also listed (when available) are agencies to contact regarding certification or registration.

Training programs. These are listed by state. When writing for an application or catalog, address your request to the department at the school on the list (e.g., Department of Physical Therapy). For some careers, there are hundreds of educational programs available. In these cases, listings are not given. There are also fields for which a listing is inappropriate, since no formal education is required. In a few cases information could not be secured and, for that reason, lists are not provided.

Diagnosing and Treating Practitioners

When a physical health problem arises, it manifests in various ways, such as pain, swelling, color change, or some other disfigurement. Physicians and dentists who are involved in active practice and are called upon to treat patients exhibiting symptoms of illness and distress need to first make a diagnosis about the causes of the problem. This is the *diagnostic phase*, which is carried out by means of a history, physical examination, and various tests (e.g., x-rays). Once a reliable diagnosis has been made, the next phase is to design a treatment plan. This is the standard approach used by physicians and dentists.

But there are other diagnosing and treating health practitioners who employ the same methods of handling illnesses within the scope of their practices:

Chiropractors are specialists in the structural adjustment of the body skeleton, especially the vertebral column.

Optometrists specialize in various aspects of eye care.

Podiatrists are specialists in the care of the feet.

Veterinarians specialize in the care of animals.

The education and training programs for these fields are quite rigorous, requiring between five and nine years of study and experience beyond high school. Students must secure a solid grounding in the natural sciences while in college, in the biomedical disciplines in professional school, and finally in intensive patient contact during a residency. Before setting up a practice in any of these fields, you must also pass various exams to obtain licensure.

CHIROPRACTORS

Principal activity: Practicing chiropractic medicine—a nonmedication, nonsurgical treatment approach to healing

Work commitment: Full-time

Preprofessional education: 2 years of college

Program length: 3 to 4 years

Work prerequisites: Doctor of Chiropractic degree (DC) and a license

Career opportunities: Favorable

Income range: $50,000 to $120,000

Scope

Chiropractors are health-care professionals who are trained to perform structural adjustments, especially to the vertebral column, as a means of treatment. The name *chiropractor* is derived from two Greek words: *cheir*, which means hand, and *praktokos*, meaning practical or operative. Taken together, the words mean "done by hand." This healing approach is based on the hypothesis that misalignment of the spine results in neurological dysfunction and consequently a disturbance in various parts of the body. By manual adjustment or use of other nonsurgical or nonmedicinal methods, chirophractors restore the body to a healthy state.

Activities

Chiropractors form a diagnosis about patients' problems by obtaining a medical history, performing a physical examination involving spinal postural analysis, taking and evaluating x-rays and measurements, and ordering laboratory tests. Patients treated by chiropractors may have either acute or chronic problems, including headaches, stiff neck, backaches, or fatigue. After arriving at a diagnosis, chiropractors seek to correct any structural problems found by reducing or immobilizing the abnormality. Many chiropractors supplement their standard manual adjustment methods by using traction, diathermy, galvanic currents, ultraviolet light, ultrasound, massage, paraffin baths, hot or cold compresses or baths, and sole or heel lifts. They may treat injuries of the limbs with first aid, strapping, or casting. They use supportive collars and braces to treat neck, lower back, elbow, knee, and ankle injuries. In addition to performing structural adjustments, chiropractors may make recommendations for dietary regimes and nutritional supplements in order to improve health. Some specialize in such areas as orthopedics, sports medicine, and nutrition. These fields require specialized postgraduate education programs.

Work Settings

The principal work sites are private chiropractic offices. Other locations include alternative health care centers, health spas, and chiropractic colleges.

Advancement

Chiropractors may advance by moving to a bigger or more prestigious facility, opening a private practice, or specializing.

Prerequisites

Two years of college education are required for this field, including courses in general biology, chemistry, and physics.

Desirable personal attributes for the field include empathy for the sick, manual dexterity, good interpersonal skills (especially in communication), a detail-oriented personality, above average intelligence, and superior observation skills.

Education/Training

The chiropractic educational program extends over eight semesters, which may be completed in three or four years, depending on the school's curriculum. The first half of the program emphasizes the basic sciences: anatomy, physiology, microbiology, biochemistry, pathology, and public health. This is followed by classes in physical, clinical, and laboratory diagnosis; gynecology and obstetrics; pediatrics; geriatrics; dermatology; otolaryngology; rontgeneology; dietetics; orthopedics; physical therapy; emergency procedures; spinal analysis; and principles and practices of chiropractic and adjustive techniques. Clinical experience is incorporated into the curriculum.

Certification/Registration/Licensure

A written and practical examination taken under a state board of examiners is the standard route to licensure.

Career Potential

The increasing acceptance of chiropractic medicine as a healing approach strongly suggests that more practitioners will be needed over the next decade. The expanding older population of the United States, with their increased likelihood of structural problems, will also increase demand for chiropractors.

For More Information

The professional organization is the American Chiropractic Association, 1701 Clarendon Blvd. Arlington, VA 22209. Additional information can be secured from the Council on Chiropractic Education, 4401 Westown Parkway, W Des Moines, IA 50265.

Colleges of Chiropractic Medicine

California

Cleveland Chiropractic College
590 North Vermont Avenue
Los Angeles, CA 90004
www.lagoon.com

Life Chiropractic College
2005 Via Barrett
P.O.Box 367
San Lorenzo, CA 94580
www.lifewest.com

Los Angeles College of Chiropractic
16200 East Amber Valley Drive
Box 1166
Whittier, CA 90609
ww.lacc.edu

Palmer College of Chiropractic-West
90 East Tasman Drive
San Jose, CA 95134
www.palmer.com

Pasadena College of Chiropractic
1505 North Marengo Avenue
Pasadena, CA 91101

Connecticut

University of Bridgeport
College of Chiropractic
75 Linden Ave.
Bridgeport, CT 06601
www.bridgeport.edu/ubpage/chiro/ubcc.html

Georgia

Life Chiropractic College
1269 Barcley Circle
Marietta, GA 30060
http://lifenet.life.edu

Illinois

National College of Chiropractic
200 East Roosevelt Road
Lombard, IL 60148
http://national.chiropractic.edu/

Iowa

Palmer College of Chiropractic
1000 Brady Street
Davenport, IA 52803
www.palmer.edu/

Minnesota

Northwestern College of Chiropractic
2501 West 84th Street
Bloomington, MN 55431
www.nw.chiro.edu/

Missouri

Logan College of Chiropractic
2501 Schoettler Road,
P O Box 1065
Chesterfield, MO 63106
www.logan.edu/

Cleveland Chiropractic College
6401 Rockhill Road
Kansas City, MO 64131
www.lagoon.com/

New York

New York Chiropractic College
P.O. Box 800
2360 State Route 89
Seneca Falls, NY 13148
www.nycc.edu/

Oregon

Western States Chiropractic College
2900 NE 132nd Avenue
Portland, OR 97230
www.wschiro.edu/

Sherman College of Straight Chiropractic
P.O. Box 1452
Spartanburg, SC 29304

Texas

Texas Chiropractic College
5912 Spencer Highway
Pasadena, TX 77505
www.txchiro.edu/

Parker College of Chiropractic
2500 Walnut Hill Lane
Dallas, TX 75229
www.parkercc.edu/

Canada

Canadian Memorial Chiropractic College
1900 Bayview Avenue
Toronto, Ontario
Canada M4G 3E6
www.netaccess.on.ca/~drwatson.educate.html

OPTOMETRISTS

Principal activity: Providing corrective lenses and eye care

Work commitment: Usually full-time

Preprofessional education: College degree

Program length: 4 years

Work prerequisites: Doctor of Optometry degree (OD) and license

Career opportunities: Average

Income range: $70,000 to $90,000

Scope

More than half of the people in the Unted States wear glasses or contact lenses to help their vision. These lenses are generally prescribed and secured by optometrists or doctors of optometry (ODs). These professionals examine patients' eyes to determine if they have any visual problems or eye diseases.

When necessary optometrists prescribe eye glasses and lenses and provide them for their clients.

Activities

Optometrists perform comprehensive examinations of the external and internal structures of the eye. They use both subjective and objective tests to evaluate a patient's vision. This evaluation includes determining visual acuity, depth and color perception, and the ability to focus and coordinate the eyes. The optometrist then forms a treatment plan based on an analysis of the eye examination and test results. Treatment may involve prescribing glasses or contact lenses or recommending vision therapy. In most states optometrists also treat certain eye diseases, such as conjunctivitis and corneal infections, and check eye pressure for signs of glaucoma. Optometrists may prescribe topical or oral drugs for certain eye problems. If they observe conditions that lie outside the scope of their practice (such as diabetese), they refer the patient to another eye care practitioner.

Work Settings

Most optometrists work in their own private offices in solo, partnership, or group practices. They also may be employed by chain vision care centers based in store-fronts or by hospitals, HMOs, ophthalmologists, or other optometrists.

Advancement

Optometrists may move up to managerial positions in larger establishments. Those who seek to specialize in family practice, pediatrics, geriatrics, or vision therapy for ocular diseases may enroll in one-year post-graduate residency programs. In addition, those interested in teaching or research may seek a master's or Ph.D. degree in visual science, physiological optics, or neurophysiology of the eye.

Prerequisites

Students who want to enter optometry should seek admission to a college or university that offers courses in the basic pre-optometry requirements, including one year each of biology, chemistry (inorganic and organic), physics, math, and English. Additional courses are required by individual schools and may include advanced biology (especially microbiology), psychology, speech, statistics, and business. Although prerequisites may be completed in two or three years, most applicants have a college degree at the time they enter optometry school. More than half of current optometry students are women.

Applicants seeking admission to an optometry school must take the Optometry Admission Test (OAT), which is administered by the Optometry Admission Testing Program, 211 East Chicago Avenue, Chicago, IL 60611. It is given three times a year (in February, April, and October) at established centers. The test measures general academic ability and science knowledge. The results—along with the student's undergraduate record, recommendations, and an interview—help determine admission to optometry school.

Optometry schools do not have a central application service. Applications must be secured from and returned to individual schools. Students must also make their own arrangements made to have their OAT scores sent to their chosen schools. Competition for admission is keen. You'll find more information about the OAT in Appendix B.

Desirable personal attributes for a career in optometry include self-discipline, business skills, a talent for dealing with patients tactfully, a strong interest in helping people, good communication skills, and superior vision.

Education/Training

The program of studies for the Doctor of Optometry degree extends over a four year period. During the first two years, students take courses in the basic medical sciences (such as anatomy, biochemistry, pharmacology, and pathology) as well as in optics, visual sciences, and clinical techniques. During the third and fourth years, the emphasis is on patient care, with training in both primary eye care and specialty services. Training covers such areas of contemporary practice as contact lenses, binocular and low-vision therapy, and eye disease diagnosis and treatment.

Certification/Registration/Licensure

All U.S. states require a license to practice optometry. Licensure requires graduation from an accredited college of optometry and successful completion of both written and clinical examinations.

Career Potential

Employment prospects over the next ten years are expected grow at an average rate, consistent with the growth and aging of the U.S. population. As a substantial segment of the population passes the age of 45, they will need increased vision care. Greater awareness of the importance of vision, rising personal incomes, and the growth in employee vision care plans will also enhance employment opportunities for optometrists.

For More Information

The professional organization for optometrists is the American Optometric Association, 243 North Lindbergh Boulevard, St. Louis, MO 63141.

You can get additional information from the Association of Schools and Colleges of Optometry, 6110 Executive Boulevard, Rockville, MD 20852.

Schools and Colleges of Optometry

Alabama

School of Optometry
University of Alabama at Birmingham
UAB Station
Birmingham, AL 35294
http://intopt.opt.uab.edu/care/

California

Southern California College of Optometry
2575 Yorba Linda Boulevard
Fullerton, CA 92631
www.scco.edu/

School of Optometry
University of California, Berkeley
Minor Hall
Berkeley, CA 94720
http://spectacle.berkeley.edu

Florida

College of Optometry
Nova Southeastern University
3200 South University Drive
Fort Lauderdale, FL 3328
www.nova.edu/

Illinois

Illinois College of Optometry
3241 South Michigan Avenue
Chicago, IL 60616
www.ico.edu/

Indiana

School of Optometry
Indiana University
800 East Atwater Avenue
Bloomington, IN 47401
www.opt.indiana.edu/graduate/main/html/

Massachusetts

New England College of Optometry
424 Beacon Street
Boston, MA 02115
www.ne~optometry.edu/

Michigan

Michigan College of Optometry at
Ferris State University
1310 Cramer Circle
Big Rapids, MI 49307
www.ferris.edu/

Missouri

School of Optometry
University of Missouri–St. Louis
8001 Natural Bridge Road
St. Louis, MO 63121
www.umsl.edu/

New York

State College of Optometry
State University of New York
100 East 24th Street
New York, NY 10010
http://trex.sunyopt.edu/

Ohio

College of Optometry
Ohio State University
338 West Tenth Avenue
Columbus, OH 43210
www.optometry.ohio-state.edu/

Oklahoma

College of Optometry
Northeastern State University
600 North Grand Avenue
Tahlequah, OK 74464
http://arapaho.nsuok.edu/~optometry/

Oregon

College of Optometry
Pacific University
2043 College Way
Forest Grove, OR 97116
www.opt.pacificu.edu/

Pennsylvania

Pennsylvania College of Optometry
1200 West Godfrey Avenue
Philadelphia, PA 19141
www.pco.edu/

Tennessee

Southern College of Optometry
1245 Madison Avenue
Memphis, TN 38104
www.sco.edu/

Texas

College of Optometry
University of Houston
4800 Calhoun Road
Houston, TX 77204
www.opt.uh.edu/

Canada

School of Optometry
University of Montreal
3744 Gean Brillant, Local 110
Montreal, Quebec
Canada, H3T 1P1
www.umontreal.ca/

School of Optometry
University of Waterloo
Faculty of Sciences
Waterloo, Ontario
Canada, N2L 3G1
www.optometry.uwaterloo.ca/

PODIATRISTS

Principal activity: Providing medical and surgical foot care for both the healthy and infirm

Work commitment: Usually full-time

Preprofessional education: Bachelor's degree

Program length: 4 years

Work prerequisites: Doctor of Podiatry Medicine degree (DPM) and license

Career opportunities: Favorable

Income range: $80,000 to $120,000

Scope

Doctors of podiatry specialize in the prevention, diagnosis, and treatment of diseases, injuries, and disorders of the foot and ankle. They use medical, surgical, mechanical, and physical treatment methods, and may prescribe corrective footwear and shoe insert devices. The profession traces its origins as far back as ancient Egypt. The first practitioner in the United States was Julius Davidson, who set up an office in Philadelphia in 1841.

Activities

The typical podiatry practice covers the full range of pediatric problems, including corns, calluses, warts, ingrown toenails, bunions, and the treatment of foot injuries. Podiatrists use computerized machines to determine the exact size, shape, and dimensions for corrective shoes and inserts. Some specialize in such areas as *pedopodiatrics* (the care of children's feet), *podogeriatrics* (foot care for the aged), podiatry sports medicine (diagnosis and treatment of sports-related problems), and podiatric surgery. A newer specialty is diabetic and disease-related foot care.

Work Settings

Traditionally, podiatrists have worked in solo practices, often establishing offices in their homes or in professional buildings, but today group practices have become more common. Podiatrists also serve on the staffs of clinics, hospitals, and nursing homes; in municipal health departments; at sports health facilities; and on the faculty of podiatry schools. Many also serve professionally as members of the U.S. armed forces.

Advancement

Podiatrists can advance by joining the staffs of prestigious facilities, by moving into a private practice, or by specialization.

Prerequisites

The initial goal of a pre-podiatry student is to secure a high school diploma or its equivalent with good grades in the sciences. The next step is to gain admission to an accredited college or university, where the basic science courses should be completed. These courses include one year of biology, chemistry, and physics as well as mathematics and English composition. Other courses may be recommended by individual schools. A minimum of three years of college (90 semester hours) is required for admission to podiatry schools, but most applicants have graduated by the time they begin their professional studies.

Applicants to podiatry schools must take the Medical College Admissions Test (MCAT) and arrange for official transcripts and letters of recommendation to be sent to their chosen schools. A single application can be used to apply to any or all of the six podiatry schools belonging to the application service AAPMAS (see below).

Desirable personal attributes of those planning to enter this field include good interpersonal and business skills, proficiency in science, and superior manual dexterity.

Education/Training

Podiatry involves four years of study followed by one to three years of residency training. There are some differences in curriculum content among schools; however, the general pattern involves two years of basic medical science courses and two years of clinical course work. The overall pattern of the curriculum is arranged so that students move from learning fundamental knowledge about the normal structure and function of the human body to a mix of basic and preliminary clinical science work in the second year. The third year is devoted primarily to clinical learning experience, with advanced seminars and electives. During this time students gain proficiency in the treatment of podiatric patients suffering from various problems.

Certification/Registration/Licensure

Podiatrists must be licensed by the state in which they will work. Licensing requirements differ from state to state, but they generally involve earning a D.P.M. degree; passing written and/or oral proficiency exams; and satisfactorily completing at least a year of residency training, which is arranged through a matching program. In some states, exams administered by the National Board of Podiatric Examiners substitute for written state examinations. The Board exams are taken in two parts. The first, at the end of a student's second year of podiatry school, covers the basic sciences. The second, taken in the spring of the fourth year, covers the clinical areas. Podiatrists also may be certified in one of three specialty areas: primary medicine, orthopedics, and surgery.

Career Potential

Podiatrists are compensated by both private and governmental insurance agencies. Their income potential has increased as a result of the rise in fitness, sports, and exercise programs, all of which may cause foot problems or injuries. An aging population also has resulted in a greater need for treatment by the elderly. Thus, employment prospects for podiatrists are favorable; and their level of income, which increases with experience, is quite high.

For More Information

The professional organization in this field is the American Podiatric Medical Association, 9312 Old Georgetown Road, Bethesda, MD 20814. You can get additional information from the American Association of Colleges of Podiatric Medicine, 1350 Piccard Drive, Rockville, MD 20850. The certifying organization is the American Board of Podiatric Surgery, 3330 Mission Street, San Francisco, CA 94110.

The seven accredited podiatry schools in United States are scattered widely. The deadline for fall admission is June 1. For more iformation about this service, contact the American Association of Colleges of Podiatric Medicine Application Service, 1350 Picard Drive, Rockville, MD 20850.

The tuition at podiatry schools varies from $15,000 to $20,000. Freshman class sizes range from 80 to 130 students. Applicants must take the Medical College Admission Test (MCAT), which is given twice a year, in April and August. Those applying for September admission must take the MCAT no later than April of the year of desired admission. For more information on the MCAT, contact the MCAT Program Office, P.O. Box 4056, Iowa City, IA 52243.

You must designate the school to which your MCAT scores should be sent. The test usually is given on Saturdays, but it can be taken on Sundays if religious convictions prevent you from taking it on Saturday. The MCAT can be retaken without special permission, but you should do so only if there is a significant discrepancy between your college grades and your MCAT scores.

Colleges of Podiatry

California

College of Podiatric Medicine
1210 Scott Street
San Francisco, CA 94115
www.phactor.com/ccpm/

Florida

Barry University
College of Podiatric Medicine
11300 NE Second Avenue
Miami Shores, FL 33161
www2.barry.edu/

Illinois

Dr. William M. Scholl
College of Podiatric Medicine
1001 North Dearborn Street
Chicago, IL 60610
http://scholl.edu/

Iowa

University of Osteopathic Medicine
College of Podiatric Medicine and Surgery
3200 Grand Avenue
Des Moines, IA 50312
www.uomhs.edu/cpms/

New York

New York College of Podiatric Medicine
53 East 124th Street
New York, NY 10035
www.nycpm.edu/

Ohio

Ohio College of Podiatric Medicine
10515 Carnage Avenue
Cleveland, OH 44106
www.ocpm.edu/

Pennsylvania

Pennsylvania College of Podiatric Medicine
Eight at Race Street
Philadelphia, PA 19107
www.pcpm.edu/

VETERINARIANS

Principal activity: Providing animal care to maintain and restore health

Work commitment: Usually full-time

Preprofessional education: Bachelor's degree

Program length: 4 years

Work prerequisites: Doctor of Veterinary Medicine degree (DVM) and license

Career opportunities: Good

Income range: $50,000 to 85,000

Scope

Veterinarians provide care for pets, livestock, sporting, and laboratory animals. They contribute to animal health as well as to the well-being of human beings. Some are engaged in research, food safety inspection, or teaching. The majority treat only small companion animals, such as dogs, cats, and birds. Others treat only large animals, such as cattle and horses. Still others (mostly in rural areas) deal with both small and large animals.

Activities

Veterinarians advise owners on both the care and breeding of animals. They have the skill and training to diagnose medical problems, dress wounds, set fractured bones, and perform surgery. They also are qualified to prescribe and administer medicines and to vaccinate animals against diseases. Some veterinarians work with physicians and scientists to prevent and treat disease in humans. Those involved in health safety work may serve as livestock inspectors, checking for diseased animals. Those engaged in meat inspection examine slaughtering and processing plants, checking both live animals and carcasses for disease to see if standards and sanitation are adequate.

Work Settings

Veterinarians are employed in private clinics and hospitals, and by federal, state, and local government agencies. Some work at teaching institutions, zoos, and aquariums. Horse racing farms need resident veterinarians. Research laboratories, pharmaceutical companies, and animal food manufacturers also employ them.

Advancement

Those employed by others can move on to solo or group practices. Those employed by government agencies can move up the civil service ladder. Specialized training in one of a variety of specialty areas enhances career status.

Prerequisites

If you want to be a veterinarian, you must first earn a high school diploma or its equivalent. The next phase is getting admitted to an accredited college or university where all of the pre-veterinary requirement can be met. These include one year of biology, chemistry (both inorganic and organic), and physics and other courses taken by pre-health profession students as well as the Veterinary College Admission Test (VCAT). Admission to veterinary colleges is highly competitive.

Desirable personal attributes include a love for animals, superior manual dexterity, a pleasant personality, good reasoning abilities, quick thinking, and the ability to soothe anxious animals.

Education/Training

A Doctor of Veterinary Medicine degree (DVM) requires four years of professional study. In a traditional curriculum, the first two years of school are devoted to basic sciences—including the study of anatomy and physiology of dogs, cats, horses, cows, and other representative forms—along with biochemistry. The second year is devoted to the pathology of animal diseases and pharmacology. The last two years are devoted to clinical veterinary medicine, including surgery, radiology, public health, and preventive medicine as well as principles of outpatient and farm practice. The veterinary clinical experience includes diagnosing and treating animal diseases and performing surgery and various laboratory tests. Some schools use a core elective curriculum, which reduces the number of required courses while increasing the number of electives; this allows students to design a more personalized program of studies.

Certification/Registration/Licensure

Before practicing veterinary medicine, students must earn a DVM degree and successfully complete the National Board Examination to secure a license. Some states have additional board examinations of their own.

Career Potential

Employment prospects for veterinarians in the next decade are favorable, especially for those with specialized training in laboratory animal medicine, toxicology, pathology, animal behavior, and farm animals. Employment in this field is expected to grow as the number of pet owners increases and current practitioners retire.

For More Information

The professional organization for veterinarians is the American Veterinary Medical Association, 1931 North Meachem Road, Schaumburg, Illinois 60173. Another good source of information about the field is the Association of American Veterinary Medical Colleges, 1101 Vermont Avenue NW, Washington, DC 20005.

Schools and Colleges of Veterinary Medicine

Alabama

College of Veterinary Medicine
Auburn University
104 Greene Hall
Auburn, Al 36849
www.vetmed.auburn.edu/

College of Veterinary Medicine, Nursing,
& Allied Health
Tuskegee University
Tuskegee, Al 36088
http://sumc107.tusk.edu/

California

School of Veterinary Medicine
University of California-Davis
Davis, CA 95616
www.ucd.edu/

Colorado

College of Veterinary Medicine & Biomedical
Sciences
Colorado State University
Fort Collins, CO 80523
www.cvmbs.colostate.edu/physio/

Florida

College of Veterinary Medicine
University of Florida
215 SW 16th Avenue
P.O. Box 100125
Gainesville, FL 32610
www.vetmed.ufl.edu/

Georgia

College of Veterinary Medicine
University of Georgia
Athens, GA 30602
www.vet.uga.edu/

Illinois

College of Veterinary Medicine
University of Illinois-Urbana
2001 South Lincoln Avenue
Urbana, IL 61801
www.cvm.uiuc.edu/

Indiana

School of Veterinary Medicine
Purdue University
1240 Lynn Hall
West Lafayette, IN 49707
www.vet.purdue.edu/

Iowa

College of Veterinary Medicine
Iowa State University
2508 Veterinary Administration
Ames, IO 50011
www.vetmed.iastate.edu/vetmed.html

Kansas

College of Veterinary Medicine
Kansas State University
Trotter Hall 101
Manhattan, KS 66506
www.vet.ksu.edu/

Louisiana

School of Veterinary Medicine
Louisiana State University
Baton Rouge, LA 70803
www.vetmed.lus.edu/ech/

Massachusetts

School of Veterinary Medicine
Tufts University
200 Westboro Road
North Grafton, MA 01536
www.vec.tufts.edu/vetschool.html

Michigan

College of Veterinary Medicine
Michigan State University
G-100 Veterinary Medical Center
East Lansing, MI 48824
www.cvm.msu.edu/

Minneapolis

College of Veterinary Medicine
University of Minnesota
1365 Gortner Avenue
St. Paul, MN 55108
www.cvm.umn.edu/

Mississippi

College of Veterinary Medicine
Mississippi State University
Box 9825
Mississippi State, MS 39762
www.cvm.msstate.edu

Missouri

College of Veterinary Medicine
University of Missouri
Columbia, MO 65211
www.cvm.missouri.edu/

New York

College of Veterinary Medicine
Cornell University
S2005 Schurman Hall
Ithaca, NY 14853
http://web.vet.cornell.edu/

North Carolina

College Of Veterinary Medicine
North Carolina State University
4700 Hillsborough Street
Raleigh, NC 27606
www.cvm.ncsu.edu/

Ohio

College of Veterinary Medicine
Ohio State University
101 Sisson Hall
1900 Coffey Road
Columbus, OH 43210
www.vet.ohio-state.edu/docs/

Oklahoma

College of Veterinary Medicine
Oklahoma State University
205 Veterinary Medicine
Stillwater, OK 74078
www.cvm.okstate.edu/

Oregon

College of Veterinary Medicine
Oregon State University
200 Magruder Hall
Corvallis, OR 97331
www.osu.orst.edu

Pennsylvania

School of Veterinary Medicine
University of Pennsylvania
3800 Spruce Street
Philadelphia, PA 19104
www.vet.upenn.edu/

Tennessee

College of Veterinary Medicine
University of Tennessee
PO Box 1071
Knoxville, TN 37901
www.vet.utk.edu/

Texas

College of Veterinary Medicine
Texas A&M University
College Station, TX 77843
www.cvm.tamu.edu/

Virginia

VA-MD Regional College of Veterinary Medicine
Duckpond Drive
Blacksburg, VA 24061
http://education.vetmed.vt/edu/

Washington

College of Veterinary Medicine
Washington State University
Pullman, WA 99164
www.wsulibs.wsu.edu/vet/vetsrvcs.htm

Wisconsin

School of Veterinary Medicine
University of Wisconsin-Madison
2015 Linden Drive W
Madison, WI 53706
www.vetmed.wisc.edu/

Canada

Ontario Veterinary College
University of Guelph
Guelph, Ontario
Canada N1G 2W1
www.uoguelph.ca/

Faculte de Medicine Veterinaire
Universite de Montreal-Quebec
St. Hycinthe, Montreal
Canada J2S 7C6
brise.ere.umontreal.ca/~jettip/Med_vet/

Atlantic Veterinary College
University of Prince Edward
550 University Avenue
Charlottetown, PE1
Canada C1A 4P3
www.upei.ca:80/~avc/

Western College of Veterinary Medicine
University of Saskatchewan
52 Campus Drive
Saskatoon SK
Canada S7N 5B4
www.usask.ca/wcvm/ultratalk/

Associated Health Careers

Physicians and dentists are highly educated and rigorously trained health-care professionals. Since their time is limited and costly, they often delegate some of their responsibilities to other health professionals. Although they have less training, these people are well qualified to efficiently perform certain tasks and procedures, which allows physicians and dentists to focus their attention exclusively on diagnosis and treatment.

This section outlines seven health-care careers, all involving direct patient contact and providing valuable services that enhance the public's health.

Dental hygienists carry out oral care procedures and educate patients in the daily care of their teeth.

Dietitians prescribe appropriate nutritional components of meals to restore and maintain good health.

Genetic counselors provide information and guidance about medical issues that have a hereditary basis.

Nurses of various types (registered, practical, practitioners, midwives, anesthetists) provide a wide variety of hands-on daily patient care and services.

Pharmacists compound and dispense medications prescribed by doctors.

Physician assistants perform many routine and sophisticated medical and diagnostic tasks and procedures.

Surgeon assistants help doctors and nurses in the surgical arena.

This field has grown rapidly as a result of major advances in medical care. While pharmacists may be self-employed, the other professionals in this field work in private offices or hospital settings. All seven careers require specialized education and some training, and all offer good long-term prospects for employment.

DENTAL HYGIENISTS

Principal activity: Providing teeth and gum care

Work commitment: Part- or full-time

Preprofessional education: 2 years of college

Program length: 2 years minimum

Work prerequisites: Degree and license

Career opportunities: Very favorable

Income range: $24,000 to $40,000

Scope

Dental hygienists are important members of the dental health-care team. Their knowledge and training enhance the quality of care dental patients receive. Their work requires superior technical and interpersonal skills. The hygienist represents an extension of the dentist and provides both clinical treatment and education. The first school to train dental hygienists was founded by a dentist in 1917 in Bridgeport, Connecticut, to help improve the oral health of school children.

Activities

Each state licenses its own dental hygienists. The extent of their permissible activities varies in different states. Their major activity involves cleaning teeth. This service usually is provided to patients on a regular basis and involves removing soft and hard deposits, which requires scraping and sometimes gumline curettage. Hygienists also apply fluorides and sealers to help retard the formation of cavities and the buildup of plaque. In addition to performing these duties (known as oral prophylaxis), hygienists teach patients good oral hygiene techniques to maintain the health of their teeth and gums by demonstrating the proper way to brush and floss. These measures enhance the chances of preventing oral disease. In the course of their work, hygienists note and report on abnormalities (e.g., loose teeth and missing fillings) they observe. They also may assist the dentist by taking and developing patient x-rays and helping identify problem or prospective problem sites.

Some states permit dental hygienists to perform preliminary examinations, identifying and charting missing teeth, cavities, and any abnormal growths. In certain states, hygienists may even remove sutures, apply dressings, and administer anesthesia during surgeries.

Laws governing dental hygienists are being changed in some states, and this will expand their duties significantly. Under these new laws, hygienists would be allowed to take impressions for making models of teeth, insert filings, and polish existing restorations. This frees the dentist to provide the many services that require their specialized expertise. Finally, in some practices, hygienists serve as office managers.

Work Settings

Most dental hygienists work for dentists on a part- or full-time basis. They may find employment in private or group practices or at hospitals or clinics. They may also find employment opportunities in schools, where they educate students about oral health. Dental hygienists can secure appointments in the armed forces as commissioned officers. There is a big need for hygienists to work in nursing homes, in extended care facilities, and at state health departments. Overseas service opportunities also exist in governmental or privately sponsored health-care projects.

Prerequisites

To enter a dental hygienist program, you must have a high school diploma or its equivalent. It is helpful to have an above-average record and a science background.

Those entering the field should enjoy working with people; they also should be meticulous and patient and have good manual dexterity.

Education/Training

To enter this field, you must complete an accredited dental hygiene program at a community college or university. The standard program involves courses in the liberal arts, basic sciences, and clinical sciences, as well as supervised patient care experiences. Training in oral health education techniques and community health education are also provided.

Three educational paths are offered in this field:

Certificate or associate degree. This is a two- or three-year program that prepares the student for dental office practice.

Bachelor's degree. This is a four-year program. At this level, once a graduate has gained work experience, he or she is eligible for teaching, administrative, or public health positions.

Master's degree. This two-year post-graduate program qualifies individuals for advanced positions in teaching, administration, and public health.

Certification/Registration/Licensure

Graduates with any of these degrees from an accredited program are eligible to take licensing examinations. Once they satisfactorily complete the exams, they can identify themselves as *registered dental hygienists.*

To secure a license, almost all states require candidates to earn a passing score on a comprehensive, written Dental Hygiene National Board Examination. In addition they must pass a state-approved licensure exam that tests both knowledge and clinical skills.

Career Potential

With the introduction of fluorides, a strong emphasis has been placed on preventive dentistry. As part of this program, regular dental checkups and cleanings are routinely prescribed. This and the increased lifespan of people in the United States has greatly increased the need for dental hygienists; job opportunities are quite favorable. Job openings are advertised in the classified or display sections of most newspapers. Salaries vary considerably, depending on the hygienist's training, experience, and responsibilities, and the position's geographical location. Wages are paid by the hour, day, week, or number of patients seen. Benefit packages are often provided.

For More Information

The American Dental Hygienist's Association is the professional organization in this field. It publishes a journal and has a student's counterpart. The association is located at 444 North Michigan Avenue, Chicago, IL 60611.

You may want to arrange a visit with your family dentist's hygienist to observe him or her at work. You may also arrange to speak with a counselor at a school that offers a dental hygiene program.

All of the schools listed below offer dental hygiene programs accredited by the American Dental Association.

Dental Hygienist Programs

Alabama

University of Alabama
1919 Seventh Avenue
Box 59
Birmingham, AL 35294
www.us.edu/

Alaska

University of Alaska
3211 Providence Drive
Anchorage, Alaska 99508
www.uaa.alaska.edu/

Arizona

Northern Arizona University
P.O. Box 15065
Flagstaff, AZ 86011
www.nau.edu/

Phoenix College
1202 West Thomas Road
Phoenix, AZ 85013
www.pc.maricopa.edu/

Pima County Community College
2202 West Anklam Road
Tucson, AZ 85709
www.pima.edu/

Arkansas

University of Arkansas-Medical Science
4301 West Markham Street
Little Rock, AR 72205
www.uams.edu/

California

Cabrillo College
6500 Soquel Drive
Aptos, CA 95003
www.cabrillo.cc.ca.us/

West Los Angeles College
4800 Freshman Drive
Culver City, CA 90230
www.wlac.cc.ca.us/

Cypress College
9200 Valley View
Cypress, CA 90630
www.cypress.cc.ca.us/

Chabot College
25555 Hesperian Boulevard
Hayward, CA 94545
www.clpccd.cc.ca.us/

Loma Linda University
School of Dentistry
Loma Linda, CA 92350
www.llu.edu/llu/dentistry/

Foothill College
12345 El Monte Road
Los Altos Hills, CA 94022
www.foothill.fhda.edu/

University of Southern California
University Park-MC0641
Los Angeles, CA 90089
www.usc.edu/

Cerritos College
11110 East Allondra Boulevard
Norwalk, CA 90650
www3.cerritos.edu/

Pasadena City College
1570 East Colorado Boulevard
Pasadena, CA 91106
www.paccd.cc.ca.us/

Diablo Valley College
321 Golf Club Road
Pleasant Hill, CA 94523
www.DVC.edu/

Sacramento City College
3835 Freeport Boulevard
Sacramento, CA 95822
http://wserver.scc.losrios.cc.ca.us/

University of California
School of Dentistry
P.O. Box 0754
San Francisco, CA 94143
http://itsa.ucs.edu/~dental/

Colorado

University of Colorado
Medical Center
4200 East Ninth Avenue
Denver, CO 80262
www.uchsc.edu/sd/sd/

Pueblo Community College
415 Harrison Avenue
Pueblo, CO 81004
http://cis.pcc.ccoes.edu/

Colorado Northwestern Community College
500 Kennedy Drive
Rangely, CO 81648
www.cncc.cc.co.us/

Connecticut

University of Bridgeport
30 Hazel Street
Bridgeport, CT 06601
www.bridgeport.edu/

Tunxis Community College
Routes 6 and 177
Farmington, CT 06032
http://tunxis.commnet.edu/

Delaware

Delaware Technical College
333 Shipley Street
Wilmington, DE 19801
www.dtcc.edu/

District of Columbia

Howard University
600 West Street NW
Washington, DC 20059
www.howard.edu/

Florida

Brevard Community College
1519 Clearlake Road
Cocoa, FL 32922
www.brevard.cc.fl.us/

Indian River Community College
3209 Virginia Avenue
Ft. Pierce, FL 33981
www.ircc.cc.fl.us/

Santa Fe Community College
3000 NW 83 Street
Gainesville, FL 32606
www.santefe.cc.fl.us/

Florida Community College
4501 Capper Road
Jacksonville, FL 32218
www.fccj.cc.fl.us/

Palm Beach Community College
4200 South Congress Avenue
Lake Worth, FL 33461
www.pbcc.cc.fl.us/

Miami-Dade Community College
950 NW 20th Street
Miami, FL 33127
www.mdcc.edu/

Valencia Community College
1800 South Kirkman Road
Orlando, FL 32811
www.valencia.cc.fl.us/

Pensacola Junior College
5555 Highway 98
Pensacola, FL 32507
www.pcci.edu/

St. Petersburg Junior College
P.O. Box 13489
St. Petersburg, FL 33733
www.spjc.cc.fl.us/

Tallahassee Community College
444 Appleyard Drive
Tallahassee, FL 32304
www.talahassee.cc.fl.us/

Georgia

Darton College
2400 Gillionville Road
Albany, GA 31707
www.dartnet.peachnet.edu/

Medical College of Georgia
1120 15th Street
Augusta, GA 30912
www.mcg.edu/

Columbus State University
4225 University Ave.
Columbus, GA 31907
www.colstate.edu/

DeKalb College/Georgia Perimeter College
2101 Womack Road
Dunwoody, GA 30338
www.dekalb.dc.peachnet.edu/

Macon College
100 College Station Drive
Macon, GA 31297
www.mc.peachnet.edu/

Clayton College and State University
5900 Lee Street North
Morrow, GA 30260
www.csc.peachnet.edu/

Armstrong Atlantic State University
11935 Abercorn
Savannah, GA 31406
www.armstrong.edu/

Hawaii

University of Hawaii
2528 the Mall
Honolulu, HI 96822
www.hawaii.edu/

Idaho

Idaho State University
741 South 8th Street
Pocatello, Idaho
www.isu.edu/

Illinois

Southern Illinois University
College for Technical Careers
Carbondale, IL. 62901
www.siu.edu/siuc/

Parkland College
2400 West Bradley
Champaign, IL 61821
www.parkland.cc.il.us/

Prairie State College
202 South Halstead Street
Chicago Heights, IL 60411

Lake Land College
South Route 45
Mattoon, IL 61938
www.lakeland.cc.il.us/

William Rainey Harper College
1200 West Algonquin Road
Palatine, IL 60067
www.harper.cc.il.us/

Indiana

University of Southern Indiana
8600 University Boulevard
Evansville, IN 47712
www.usi.edu/

Indiana University Medical Center
1121 West Michigan Street
Indianapolis, IN 46202
www.indiana.edu/

Indiana University/Purdue University
2101 Coliseum Boulevard East
Fort Wayne, IN 46805
www.purdue.edu/

Indiana University of South Bend
1700 Mishawaka Avenue
South Bend, IN 46634
www.indiana.edu/

Iowa

Des Moines Area Community College
2006 Ankeny Boulevard
Ankeny, IA 50021
www.dmacc.cc.ia.us/

University of Iowa
College of Dentistry
Iowa City, IA 52242
www.uiowa.edu/

Hawkeye Institute of Technology
1501 East Orange Road
P.O. Box 8015
Waterloo, IA 50704

Kansas

Johnson County Community College
12345 College Boulevard
Overland Park, KS 66210
www.johnco.cc.ks.us/

Wichita Area Vocational Technical School
324 North Emporia
Wichita, KS 67202
www.ed-oha.org/

Kentucky

Western Kentucky University
Academic Complex, Room 207
Bowling Green, KY 42101
www.wku.edu/

Northern Kentucky University
Mayville Community College
1401 Dixie Highway
Covington, KY 41011
www.nku.edu/

Hopkinsville Community College
P.O. Box 2100
Hopkinsville, KY 42240
www.hopntsvl.hopcc.uky.edu/

Lexington Community College
Cooper Drive-Oswald Boulevard
Lexington, KY 40506
www.uky.edu/lcc/

University of Louisville
School of Dentistry
Louisville, KY 40292
www.louiseville.edu/

Louisiana

Northeast Louisiana University
700 University Avenue
Monroe, LA 71209
www.nlu.edu/

Louisiana State University
1100 Florida Avenue
New Orleans, LA 70119
www.lsu.edu/

Maine

University of Maine
Lincoln Hall, 29 TX Avenue
Bangor, ME 04401
www.ume.edu/

Westbrook College
716 Stevens Avenue
Portland, ME 04103
www.une.edu/

Maryland

Allegany Community College
Willowbrook Road
Cumberland, MD 21502
www.ac.cc.md.us/

Baltimore City Community College
2901 Liberty Heights Avenue
Baltimore, MD 21215

University of Maryland
666 West Baltimore Street
Baltimore, MD 21201
www.ab.umd.edu/

Massachusetts

Middlesex Community College
Springs Road
Bedford, MA 01730
www.middlesex.cc.ma.us/

Forsyth School of Dental Hygienists
140 The Fenway
Boston, MA 02115
www.forsyth.org/

Bristol Community College
777 Elsbree Street
Fall River, MA 02720
http://bullwinkle.bristol.mass.edu/

Springfield Technical Community College
1 Armory Square
Springfield, MA 01105
www.stcc.mass.edu/

Cape Code Community College
Route 132
West Barnstable, MA 02668
(508) 362-2131

Quinisgamond Community College
670 West Boylston Street
Worcester, MA 01606
www.qcc.mass.edu/

Michigan

University of Michigan
1101 North University
Ann Arbor, MI 48109
www.umich.edu/

Ferris State University
901 South State Street
Big Rapids, MI 49307
www.ferris.edu/

Wayne County Community College
8551 Greenfield, Room 308-A
Detroit, MI 48228

University of Detroit-Mercy
2985 East Jefferson Avenue
Detroit, MI 48207
www.udmercy.edu/

C.S. Mott Community College
1401 East Court Street
Flint, MI 48901
www.mcc.edu/

Grand Rapids Community College
143 Bostwick, NE
Grand Rapids, MI 49009
www.grcc.cc.mi.us/

Kalamazoo Valley Community College
6767 West O Avenue
Kalamazoo, MI 49009
www.kzoo.edu/

Lansing Community College
P.O. Box 40010
Lansing, MI 48901
www.lansing.cc.mi.us/

Oakland Community College
7350 Cooley Lake Road
Union Lake, MI 48387
www.occ.cc.mi.us/

Delta College
University Center, MI 48710
www.delta.edu/

Minnesota

Normandale Community College
9700 France Avenue South
Bloomington, MN 55431
www.hr.cc.mn.us/

Duluth Technical College
2101 Trinity Road
Duluth, MN 55811
www.hibbing.tec.mn.us/

Mankato State University
Box 8400, P.O. Box 81
Mankato, MN 56002
www.mankato.msus.edu/

University of Minnesota
9-436 Moos Tower
Minneapolis, MN 55455
www.umn.edu/

Rochester Community College
1926 College View Road
Rochester, MN 55904
www.roch.edu/rctc/

Mississippi

Northeast Mississippi Community College
Booneville, MS 38829
www.nmcc.cc.ms.us/

Pearl River Community College
5448 US Highway 49 South
Hattiesburg, MS 39401
www.prcc.cc.ms.us/

University of Mississippi
2500 North State Street
Jackson, MS 339216
www.olemiss.edu/

Meridian Community College
5500 Highway 19 North
Meridian, MS 39307
www.mcc.cc.ms.us/

Missouri

Missouri Southern State College
Newman & Dunquesne Roads
Joplin, MO 64801
www.mssc.edu/

University of Missouri
650 East 25th Street
Kansas City, MO 64108
www.umkc.edu/

St. Louis Community College of Forest Park
5600 Oakland Avenue
St. Louis, MO 63110
www.stlcc.cc.mo.us/

Nebraska

Central Technical Community College
P.O. Box 1024
Hastings, NE 68902
www.cccneb.edu/

University of Nebraska Medical Center
40th & Holdrege Streets
Lincoln, NE 68583
www.unl.edu/

Nevada

Community College of Southern Nevada
6375 West Charleston Boulevard
Las Vegas, NV 89102
www.ccsn.nevada.edu/

New Hampshire

New Hampshire Technical Institute
11 Institute Drive
Concord, NH 03301
www.conc.tec.nh.us/

New Jersey

Camden County College
P.O. Box 200
Blackwood, NJ 08012
www.camdencc.edu/

Middlesex County College
153 Mill Road
Edison, NJ 08818
www.middlesex.cc.nj.us/

University of Medicine & Dentistry
65 Bergen Street
Newark, NJ 07107
www.umdnj.edu/

Bergen Community College
400 Paramus Road
Paramus, NJ 07652
www.bergen.cc.nj.us/

New Mexico

The University of New Mexico
Novitski Hall
Albuquerque, NM 87131
www.unm.edu/

New York

Broome Community College
P.O. Box 1017
Binghamton, NY 13902
www.sunybroome.edu/

New York City Technical College
300 Jay Street
Brooklyn, NY 11201
www.nyctc.cuny.edu/

Eugenio Maria de Hostos College
475 Grand Concourse
Bronx, NY 10451
www.hostos.cuny.edu/

Erie Community College
6205 Main Street
Buffalo, NY 14221
www.sunyerie.edu/

Orange County Community College
115 South Street
Middletown, NY 10940
http://orange.cc.ny.us/

New York University Dental Center
345 East 24th Street
New York, NY 10010
www.nyu.edu/

State University of New York
Melville Road
Farmingdale, NY 11735
www.farmingdale.edu/

Monroe Community College
1000 East Henrietta Road
Rochester, NY 14127
www.monroecc.edu/

Hudson Valley Community College
80 Vandenburgh Avenue
Troy, NY 12180
www.hrcc.edu/

Onondaga Community College
Route 173
Syracuse, NY 13215
www.sunyocc.edu/

North Carolina

Asheville-Buncombe Technical Institute
340 Victoria Road
Asheville, NC 28801
www.asheville.cc.nc.us/

University of North Carolina
367 Old Dental Bldg. CB#7450
Chapel Hill, NC 27599
www.unc.edu/

Central Piedmont Community College
1201 Elizabeth Avenue-Kings Drive
Charlotte, NC 28204
www.cpcc.cc.nc.us/

Fayetteville Technical Community College
2201 Hull Road, P.O. Box 35236
Fayetteville, NC 28303
www.faytech.cc.nc.us/

Wayne Community College
Caller Box 8002
Goldsboro, NC 27530
www.wyne.cc.nc.us/

Coastal Carolina Community College
444 Western Boulevard
Jacksonville, NC 28540
www.ccarolina.cc.nc.us

Guilford Technical Institute
P.O. Box 309
Jamestown, NC 27282
http://technet.gtcc.cc.nc.us/

North Dakota

North Dakota State
College of Science
800 N. Sixth St.
Wahpeton, ND 58076
www.ndscs.nodak.edu/

Ohio

University of Cincinnati/Raymond Walters
College
9555 Plainfield Road
Cincinnati, OH 45236
www.uc.edu/

Cuyahoga Community College
2900 Community College Avenue
Cleveland, OH 44115
www.tri-c.cc.oh.us/

Ohio State University
305 West 12th Avenue
Columbus, OH 43210
www.acs.ohio-state.edu/

Sinclair Community College
444 West Third Street
Dayton, OH 45402
www.sinclair.edu/

Lima Technical College
4240 Campus Drive
Lima, OH 45804
www.ltc.tec.oh.us/

Lakeland Community College
7700 Clocktower Drive
Mentor, OH 44060
www.lakeland.cc.oh.us/

Owens Technical College
P.O. Box 10000
Toledo, OH 43699
www.owens.cc.oh.us/

Shawnee State University
940 Second Street
Portsmouth, OH 45662
www.shawnee.edu/

Youngstown State University
410 Wick Avenue
Youngstown, OH 44555
www.yus.edu/

Oklahoma

Rose State College
6420 Southeast Fifteenth
Midwest City, OK 73110
www.rose.cc.ok.us/

University of Oklahoma
Health Science Center
P.O.Box 26901
Oklahoma City, OK 73190
http://web.ouhsc.edu/

Tulsa Junior College
909 S. Boston Avenue
Tulsa, OK 74119
www.tulsa.cc.ok.us/

Oregon

Lane Community College
4000 East 30th Avenue
Eugene, OR 97405
www.lanecc.edu/

Mt. Hood Community College
26000 SE Stark Street
Gresham, OR 97030
www.mhcc.cc.or.us/

Oregon Institute of Technology
3201 Campus Drive
Klamath Falls, OR 97601
www.oit.osshe.edu/

Portland Community College
P.O. Box 19000
Portland, OR 97219
www.pcc.edu/

Oregon University Health Sciences
611 SW Campus Drive
Portland, OR 97201
www.pcc.edu/

Pennsylvania

Northampton County Community College
3835 Green Pond Road
Bethlehem, PA 18017

Montgomery County Community College
340 DeKalb Pike
Blue Bell, PA 19422
www.mc3.edu/

Luzerne County Community College
13333 South Prospect Street
Nanticoke, PA 18634
www.luzerne.edu/

University of Pittsburgh
B-23 Salk Hall
Pittsburgh, PA 15261
www.upenn.edu/

Community College of Philadelphia
1700 Spring Garden Street
Philadelphia, PA 19130
www.ccp.cc.pa.us/

Thomas Jefferson University
130 South 9th Street, 22nd Floor
Philadelphia, PA 19107
www.tju.edu/

Westmoreland County Community College
Armbrust Road
Youngwood, PA 15697
www.westmoreland.cc.pa.us/

Pennsylvania Technical College
1 College Avenue
Williamsport, PA 17701
www.pct.edu/

Rhode Island

University of Rhode Island
8 Washburn Hall
Kingston, RI 02881
www.uri.edu/

Community College of Rhode Island
Louisquisset Pike
Lincoln, RI 02865
www.ccri.cc.ri.us/

South Carolina

Trident Technical College
P.O. Box 10367
Charleston, SC 29411
www.trident.tec.sc.us/

Midland Technical College
P.O. Box 2408
Columbia, SC 29202
www.mid.tec.sc.us/edu/

Florence Darlington Technical College
P.O. Box F-800
Florence, SC 29606
www.flo.tec.sc.us/

Greenville Technical College
P.O. Box 5616, Station B
Greenville, SC 29606
www.greenvilletech.com/

Tennessee

Chattanooga State Technical Community College
4501 Amnicola Highway
Chattanooga, TN 37406
www.cstcc.cc.tn.us/

East Tennessee State University
P.O. Box 70690
Johnson City, TN 37614
www.etsu-tn.edu/

University of Tennessee
822 Beale Street, Room 321E
Memphis, TN 38163
www.utm.edu/

Meharry Medical College
John A. Merritt Boulevard
Nashville, TN 37209
www.mcc.edu/

Roane State Community College
Oak Ridge, TN 37830
www.rscc.cc.tn.us/

Texas

Amarillo College
P.O. Box 477
Amarillo, TX 79178
www.actx.edu/

Lamar University
P.O. Box 10096
Beaumont, TX 77710
www.lamar.edu/

Bee County College
3800 Charco Road
Beeville, TX 78102
www.bcc.cc.tx.us/

Howard College
1001 Birdwell Lane
Big Spring, TX 79720
www.hc.cc.tx.us/

Del Mar College
Baldwin at Ayers Streets
Corpus Christi, TX 78404
www.delmar.edu/

Baylor College of Dentistry
3302 Gaston Avenue
Dallas, TX 75246
www.tambcd.edu/

Texas Woman's University
Box 22665-TWU Station
Denton, TX 76204
www.twu.edu/

El Paso Community College
P.O. Box 20500
El Paso, TX 79998
www.epcc.edu/

University of Texas Dental Branch
P.O. Box 20068
Houston, TX 75225
www.utexas.edu/

Tarrant County Junior College
828 Harwood Road
Hurst, TX 76054
www.tcjc.cc.tx.us/

University of Texas
Health Sciences Building
7703 Floyd Curl Drive
San Antonio, TX 78284
www.utexas.edu/

Tyler Junior College
P.O. Box 90020
Tyler, TX 75711
www.tyler.cc.tx.us/

Wharton County Junior College
911 Boling Highway
Wharton,TX 77488
http://198.64.57.10/tgcccc/wharton/
cjchome.htm

Midwestern State University
34–Taft
Wichita, TX 76308
www.mwsu.edu/

Utah

Weber University
3750 Harrison Boulevard
Ogden, Utah 84408
www.weber.edu/

Vermont

University of Vermont
Rowell Boulevard
Burlington, VT 05405
www.uvm.edu/

Virginia

Northern Virginia Community College
8333 Little River Turnpike
Annandale, VA 22003
www.nv.cc.va.us/

Old Dominion University
G.W. Hirschfeld School
Norfolk, VA 23529
www.odu.edu/

Virginia Commonwealth University
School of Dentistry
Box 566
Richmond, VA 23298
www.vcu.edu/

Virginia Western Community
3095 Colonial Avenue SW
Roanoke, VA 24038
www.vw.cc.va.us/

Wytheville Community College
1000 East Main Street
Wytheville, VA 24382
www.wc.cc.va.us/

Washington

Shoreline Community College
16101 Greenwood Avenue North
Seattle, WA 98133
http://oscar.ctc.edu/shoreline/

Pierce Community College
9401 Farwest Drive SW
Tacoma, WA 98498
www.pierce.ctc.edu/

Clark College
1800 East McLoughlin Boulevard
Vancouver, WA 98663
www.clark.edu/

Yakima Valley College
16th Avenue South & Nob Hill Boulevard
Yakima, WA 98907
www.rfttc.org/

West Virginia

West Virginia Institute of Technology
Montgomery, WV 25136
www.wvutech.edu/

West Virginia University
P.O. Box 9425
Morgantown, WV 26506
www.wvu.edu/

West Liberty State College
West Liberty, WV 26074
www.wlse.wvnet.edu/

Wisconsin

Northeast Wisconsin Technical Institute
2740 West Mason Street
P.O. Box 19042
Green Bay, WI 54307
www.nwtc.tec.wi.us/

Madison Area Technical College
3550 Anderson, Room 300F
Madison, WI 53704
www.madison.tec.wi.us/

Marquette University
604 North 16th Street
Milwaukee, WI 53223
www.mu.edu/

Milwaukee Area Technical College
700 West State Street
Milwaukee, WI 53233
www.milwaukee.tec.wi.us/

North Central Technical College
100 Campus Drive
Wausau, WI 54401
http://wausauchamber.com/members/NTC/index.htm

Wyoming

Laramie County Community College
1440 East College Drive
Cheyenne, WY 82007
www.lcc.whecn.edu/

Sheridan College
3059 Coffeen Avenue
Sheridan, WY 82801
http://siswww.uwyo.edu/sf/sch/book/nwcc.html

Canada

Algonquin College
1385 Woodruffe Avenue
Nepean, Ontario
Canada K2G 1V8
www.algonquin.on.ca/

Cegep Francois Xavier Garneau
1600 Boulevard De L'Entente
Sillery, Quebec
Canada G1T 2S3

Cegep St-Hyacinthe
300 Rue Boulle
St. Hyacinthe, Quebec
Canada J2S 1H9

College of de Maisonneuve
3800 Sherbrooke Street East
Montreal, Quebec
Canada HIX 2A2

Dalhousie University
1308 Robie Street
Halifax, Nova Scotia
Canada B3H 3J5
www.dentistry.dal.ca/

University of Alberta
3032 Dental Pharmacy Bldg.
Edmonton, Alberta
Canada T6G 2NB
www,debt,yakberta,ca.

University of Manitoba
780 Bannatyne Avenue
Winnipeg, Manitoba
Canada R3E OW3
www.umanitoba.ca/

Vancouver Community College
250 West Pender
Vancouver, BC
Canada V6B 159
www.vcc.bc.ca/

DIETITIANS

Principal activity: Planning appropriate nutritional diets and providing nutritional education to maintain health

Work commitment: Part- or full-time

Preprofessional education: High school diploma

Program length: 4 years

Work prerequisites: Bachelor's degree in dietetics or related field on nutrition

Career opportunities: Quite favorable

Income range: $30,000 to $45,000

Scope

Dietitians are professionals who provide advice on nutritional food selection and preparation. They both plan and supervise preparation and serving of foods suitable for specific dietary needs. Their activities promote proper eating habits to enhance health. After scientifically evaluating their clients' diets, dietitians offer suggestions for modifications and improvements. They are knowledgeable about the most appropriate diets to maintain health and prevent disease at different phases of life and about what dietary modifications will improve certain health conditions.

Activities

There are seven distinct areas of dietetic practice:

Clinical dietitians work in health-care institutions such as hospitals and nursing homes. They evaluate patients' nutritional needs, formulate and implement appropriate nutritional programs, and assess and report results. To coordinate medical and nutritional needs, dietitians confer with physicians and other health-care providers. They provide patients and their families with detailed instructions on maintaining a proper diet upon discharge from the hospital. Within this general area there are several subspecialties: For example, some dietitians deal only with overweight or critically ill patients. In small hospitals or clinics, dietitians may be responsible for managing all food services.

Community dietitians, also known as *nutritionists,* advise both individuals and groups about proper nutritional practices that enhance health and prevent diseases. Those who work in clinics, nursing homes, HMOs, hospitals, and home care agencies evaluate facilities, develop nutritional care plans, and teach clients and their families about nutrition. They also advise health-care agencies on food shopping and preparation for the elderly and the chronically ill. Because of current public interest in nutrition, these professionals are now finding employment with food manufacturers and in advertising and marketing agencies, where they analyze foods and prepare literature on nutritional content and other health-related issues.

Management dietitians supervise large-scale meal planning in long-term health-care facilities, restaurants, companies, hotels, schools, colleges, and prisons. Typically, they have a wide range of duties and responsibilities, including hiring and training food-preparation workers, purchasing food and equipment, enforcing safety and sanitary conditions, and developing budgets.

Dietetic educators are primarily involved in teaching dietetic principles at colleges, health-care facilities, and community centers.

Research dietitians typically hold advanced degrees (i.e., a master's degree or Ph.D.) that enable them to undertake research studies at medical centers, government agencies, and educational facilities. Their work may involve developing and evaluating new nutritional approaches to treating diseases.

Consulting dietitians provide a variety of services for health-care facilities. Typically, they work in private practice or under contract for others. They perform nutrition screening and offer advice on weight loss, cholesterol reduction, and diabetes management.

Business dietitians technically are not health-care providers, but they do work in dietary planning and so are worth mentioning here. They work in private industry, advising companies on purchasing, food development, marketing, advertising, and sales.

Work Settings

Dietitians can find employment in a broad range of places, especially in medical facilities such as hospitals, clinics, and nursing homes. In addition, federal, state, and local government agencies offer positions in health departments and other health-related sites. Other dietitians find work with social service agencies, residential care facilities, educational institutions, industrial food services, restaurants, catering services, and hotels. Some work for physicians with practices devoted to weight management.

Advancement

Advancement is possible in all dietetic areas and comes with experience and successful performance. Promotion typically involves assuming supervisory responsibilities. Earning a graduate degree facilitates advancement in this field.

Prerequisites

In the course of earning their high school diplomas, students who want to enter this field should take courses in biology, chemistry, mathematics, home economics, and business management.

Desirable personal attributes include strong interpersonal and communication skills. Those who want to be dietitians should have the ability to speak before a group, since occasional lectures in special settings and one-on-one teaching may be a big part of the job. Obviously, those entering the field should be interested in food preparation and its impact on the well-being of others.

Education/Training

The basic requirement for entering this field is a bachelor's degree from an accredited institution, with a major in dietetics, nutrition food science, food preparation, or food services management. Undergraduate course work should include general biology, inorganic and organic chemistry, biochemistry, anatomy, physiology, microbiology, diet therapy, advanced nutrition, food services systems, food services management, quality food production, accounting, data processing, business management, and statistics.

Certification/Registration/Licensure

Dietitians in most states must satisfy specific academic and experience requirements to meet the standards set by the Commission on Dietetic Registration. Most positions are open exclusively to *registered dietitians* (*RDs*). An RD degree reflects that a candidate has met a specified high standard of education and training.

Career Potential

The job outlook for dietitians for the foreseeable future is quite favorable. There is a continuous demand for more dietitians to meet the needs of an aging and more health-conscious population in the United States. The impact of health-care reforms on the field is unclear at present. Nevertheless, as the public becomes increasingly aware of the need for good dietary habits, the services of professionals in this field should be increasingly stimulated at various community levels.

For More Information

The professional organization in this field is the American Dietetic Association, 216 West Jackson Blvd., Chicago, IL 60606

Dietitian Programs

Alabama

Auburn University
Auburn, AL 36117
www.auburn.edu/

Oakwood College
Huntsville, AL 35896
www.oakwood.edu/

Jacksonville State University
Jacksonville, AL 36265
www.jsu.edu/

University of Alabama
Livingston, AL 35740
www.uab.edu/

University of Montevallo
UM Station 6720
Montevallo, AL 35115
www.montevaallo.edu/

Alabama A & M University
P.O. Box 908
Normal, AL 35762
http://aphal.aamu.edu/

Tuskegee University
Carnegie Hall
Tuskegee, AL 36088
www.tusk.edu/

University of Alabama
Tuskaloosa, AL 35487
www.ua.edu/

Arizona

Northern Arizona University
P.O. Box 4084
Flagstaff, AZ 86011
www.nau.edu/

Arkansas

Ouachita Baptist University
Arkadelphia, AR 71998
www.obu.edu/

University of Central Arkansas
Conway, AR 72035
www.uca.edu/

University of Arkansas at Pine Bluff
UAPB Box 17
1200 University Drive
Pine Bluff, AR 71601
www.uapp.edu/

California

Pacific Union College
Augurin, CA 94508
www.puc.edu/

University of California–Berkeley
Berkeley, CA 94720
www.berkeley.edu/

California State University–Chico
Chico, CA 95929
www.csuchico.edu/

University of California–Davis
Davis, CA 95616
www.ucdavis.edu/

California State University–Fresno
5241 North Maple Avenue
Fresno, CA 93740
www.csufresno.edu/

California State University–Long Beach
1250 Bellflower Blvd.
Long Beach, CA 90840
www.acs.sculb.edu/

California State University–Northridge
18111 Nordhoff Street
Northridge, CA 91330
www.csun.edu/

California State Polytechnic University
3801 West Temple Avenue
Pomona, CA 91768
www.csupomona.edu/

California State University–San Bernardino
5500 University Parkway
San Bernardino, CA 92407
www.wcsusb.edu/

Point Loma Nazarene College
San Diego, CA 92106
www.ptloma.edu/

San Francisco State University
1600 Holloway Avenue
San Francisco, CA 94132
www.sfsu.edu/

San Jose Sate University
1 Washington Square
San Jose, CA 95192
www.sjsu.edu/

Colorado

Colorado State University
Fort Collins, CO 80523
www.colostate.edu/

University of Northern Colorado
Greeley, CO 80639
www.univnorthco.edu/

Connecticut

University of Connecticut
2131 Hillside Road U-88
Storrs, CT 06269
www.uconn.edu/

St. Joseph College
West Hartford, CT 06117
www.sjc.edu/

University of New Haven
New Haven, CT 06516
www.newhaven.edu/

Delaware

University of Delaware
Newark, DE 19716
www.udel.edu/

District Of Columbia

Howard University
2400 6th Street NW
Washington, DC 20059
www.howard.edu/

Florida

Florida International University
University Park
Miami, FL 333199
www.fiu.edu/

Florida State University
Tallahassee, FL 32306
www.fsu.edu/

Georgia

Georgia State University
University Plaza
Atlanta, GA 30303
www.gsu.edu/

University of Georgia
Athens, GA 30602
www.uga.edu/

Idaho

Idaho State University
P.O. Box 8054
Pocatello, IA 50614
www.uni.edu

Iowa

University of Northern Iowa
Cedar Falls, IA 50614
www.wisu.edu

Illinois

Southern Illinois University at Carbondale
Carbondale, IL 62901
www.siu.edu/

University of Illinois at Urbana–Champaign
1206 South 4th Street
Champaign, IL 61820
www.uiuc.edu

Eastern Illinois University
600 Lincoln Avenue
Charleston, IL 61920
www.eiu.edu/

University of Illinois at Chicago
P.O. Box 5220
Chicago, IL 60680
www.uiuc.edu/

Northern Illinois University
De Kalb, IL 60115
www.niu.edu/

Olivete Nazarene University
Kankakee, IL 60901
www.olivet.edu/

Benedictine University
Lisle, IL 60532
www.ben.edu/

Western Illinois University
Macomb, IL 61455
www.wiu.edu/

Illinois State University
Normal, IL 61790
www.ilstu.edu/

Finch University of Health Sciences
Chicago Medical School
3333 Green Bay Road
North Chicago, IL 60064
www.finchsms.edu/

Bradley University
1501 West Bradley Avenue
Peoria, IL 61625
www.bradley.edu/

Dominican Univesity
River Forest, IL 60305
www.dom.edu/

Indiana

Indiana University
300 North Jordan Avenue
Bloomington, IN 47405
www.indiana.edu/

IUPUI
Cavanaugh Hall, Room 129
Indianapolis, IN 46202
www.IUPUI.edu/

Goshen College
Goshen, IN 46526
www.goshen.edu

Purdue University
173rd & Woodmar Avenue
Hammond, IN 46323
www.purdue.edu/

Ball State University
2000 University Avenue
Muncie, IN 47306
www.bsu.edu/

Indiana State University
Terre Haute, IN 47806
www.indstate.edu/

Purdue University
Schleman Hall
West Lafayette, IN 47906
www.purdue.edu/

Kentucky

Berea College
CPO 2344
Berea, KY 40404
www.berea.edu/

Western Kentucky University
Bowling Green, KY 42101
www.ku.edu/

Morehead State University
Morehead, KY 40351
www.morehead-st.edu/

Murray State University
Murray, KY 42071
www.mursuky.edu

Louisiana

Louisiana State University
A & M College
Baton Rouge, LA 70803
www.lsu.edu/

Grambling State University
Grambling, LA 71245
www.lus/edu/

University of Southern Louisiana
104 University Circle
Lafayette, LA 70504
www.usl.edu/

Louisiana Tech University
Ruston, LA 71272
www.latech.edu/

Nicholls State University
Thibodaux, LA 70301
www.lsu.edu/

Maryland

Hood College
401 Rosemont Avenue
Frederick, MD 21701
www.hood.edu/

Massachusetts

Framingham State College
Framingham, MA 01701
www.framingham.edu/

Michigan

Andrews University
Berrien Springs, MI 49104
www.andrews.edu/

Marygrove College
8425 West McNichols Road
Detroit, MI 48221

Wayne State University
Detroit, MI 48221
www.wayne.edu/

Michigan State University
East Lansing, MI 48824
wwwlmsu.edu/

Western Michigan University
West Michigan Avenue
Kalamazoo, MI 49008
www.wmich.edu/

Madonna University
36600 Schoolcraft Road
Livonia, MI 48150
www.umunet.edu/

Northern Michigan University
Marquette, MI 49855
www.nmu.edu/

Central Michigan University
Mount Pleasant, MI 48859
www.cmich.edu/

Eastern Michigan University
Ypsilanti, MI 48197
www.emich.edu/

Minnesota

College of St. Scholastica
Duluth, MN 55811
www.css.edu/

Mankato State University
Mankato, MN 56002
www.mankato.msus.edu/

Concordia College
901 8th Street South
Moorehead, MN 56562
www.cord.edu/

Mississippi

University of Southern Mississippi
Hattiesburg, MS 39906
http://eos.gp.usm.edu/

Missouri

Southeast Missouri State University
One University Plaza
Cape Girardeau, MO 63701
www.semo.edu/

University of Missouri–Columbia
Columbia, MO 65211
www.umc.edu/

Fontbonne College
6800 Wydown Blvd.
St. Louis, MO 63105
www.fontbonne.edu/

Southwest Missouri State University
901 S. National Ave.
Springfield, MO 65804
www.smsu.edu/

Central Missouri State University
Warrensburg, MO 64093
http://cmsuvmb.cmsu.edu/

New Hampshire

University of New Hampshire
Grant House
Durham, NH 03824
www.uhn.edu/

New Jersey

Rutgers State University of New Jersey
Cook College
New Brunswick, NJ 08903
www.rutgers.edu/

Montclair State University
1 Normal Avenue
Upper Montclair, NJ 07043
www.montclair.edu/

New Mexico

New Mexico State University
Box 30001, Dept. 3-A
Las Cruces, NM 88003
www.nmsu.edu/

New York

Lehmann College of the City of New York
250 Bedford Park
Bronx, NY 10468
www.lehman.cuny.edu/

D'Youville College
320 Porter Avenue
Buffalo, NY 14201
www.dyc.edu/

Queens College of the City of New York
65-30 Kissena Blvd.
Flushing, NY 11367
www.cqu.edu.edu/

Cornell University
410 Thurston Avenue
Ithaca, NY 14850
www.cornell.edu/

New York University
22 Washington Square
New York, NY 10012
www.nyu.edu/

Syracuse University
201 Tolley Administration Boulevard
Syracuse, NY 13244
www.syr.edu/

Marymount College
100 Marymount Avenue
Tarrytown, NY 10591
www.marymt.edu/

North Carolina

Western Carolina University
Cullowhee, NC 18723
www.wcu.edu/

Bennett College
900 E Washington Street
Greensboro, NC 27401
www.bennett.edu/

North Carolina Ag. & Tech. State University
107 Benbow Hall
Greensboro, NC 27411
www.ncat.edu/

University of North Carolina at Greensboro
1000 Spring Garden Street
Greensboro, NC 27412
www.uncg.edu/

East Carolina University
East 5th Street
Greenville, NC 27858
www.edu.edu/

North Dakota

North Dakota State University
University Station
Fargo, ND 58105
www.ndsu.nodak.edu/

University of North Dakota
Box 8382
Grand Forks, ND 58202
www.und.nodak.edu/

Ohio

University of Akron
381 Buchtel Common
Akron, OH 44325
www.uakron.edu/

Ohio University
416 Tower
Athens, OH 45701
www.ohiou.edu/

Bluffton College
Bluffton, OH 45817
www.bluffton.edu/

Bowling Green State University
Bowling Green, OH 43403
www.bgsu.deu/

Case Western Reserve University
10900 Euclid Avenue
Cleveland, OH 44106
www.cwru.edu/

Ohio State University
3rd Floor, Lincoln Tower
Columbus, OH 43210
www.acs.ohio-state.edu/

Kent State University
161 Michael Schwartz Center
Kent, OH 44240
www.kent.edu/

Miami University
Oxford, OH 45056
www.muohio.edu

Youngstown State University
410 Wick Avenue
Youngstown, OH 44555
www.ysu.edu/

Oklahoma

Langston University
P.O. Box 728
Langston, OK 73050
www.lunet.edu/

University of Oklahoma
P.O. Box 26901
Oklahoma City, OK 73190
www.ou.edu/

Oklahoma State University
Stillwater, OK 74078
www.pio.okstate.edu/

Oregon

Oregon State University
Corvallis, OR 97331
www.orst.edu/

Pennsylvania

Cheyney University of PA
Cheyney, PA 19319
www.cheney.edu/

Edinboro University of PA
Edinboro, PA 16444
www.edinboro.edu/

Gannon University
University Square
Erie, PA 16541
www.gannon.edu/

Mercyhurst College
501 E. 38th St.
Erie, PA 16546
www.mercy.edu

Messiah College
Grantham, PA 17027
www.messiah.edu/

Immaculata College
Immaculata, PA 19345
www.immaculata.edu/

Indiana University of Pennsylvania
216 Pratthall
Indiana, PA 15705
www.iup.edu

Saint Vincent College
300 Fraser Purchase Road
Latrobe, PA 15650
www.stvincent.edu/

Mansfield University of Pennsylvania
Beecher House
Mansfield, PA 16933
www.mnsfld.edu/

University of Pittsburgh
Bruce Hall, 2nd Floor
Pittsburgh, PA 15260
www.pitt.edu/

Marywood College
2300 Adams. Ave.
Scranton, PA 18509
www.marywood.edu/

Rhode Island

University of Rhode Island
Kingston, RI 02881
www.uri.edu/

South Dakota

South Dakota State University
P.O. Box 72025
Brooking, SD 57007
www.sdstate.edu/

Tennessee

Carson-Newman College
P.O. Box 72025
Jefferson City, TN 37760
www.cn.edu/

University of Tennessee
Knoxville, TN 37996
www.utk.edu/

University of Tennessee at Martin
Martin, TN 38238
www.utm.edu/

Middle Tennessee State University
301 E. Main Street
Murfreesboro, TN 37132
www.mtsu.edu/

David Lipscomb University
3901 Granny White Pike
Nashville, TN 37204
www.dlu.edu/

Texas

Abilene Christian University
ACU Box 8483
Abilene, TX 79699
www.acu.edu/

University of Texas at Austin
Austin, TX 78712
www.utexas.edu/

Lamar University–Beaumont
4400 Martin Luther King Place
Beaumont, TX 77710
www.lamar.edu/

University of Texas
Southwestern Medical Center of Dallas
5323 Harry Hines Boulevard
Dallas, TX 75235
www.swmed.edu/

Texas Woman's University
P.O. Box 425648
Denton, TX 76204
www.two.edu/

University of Texas–Pan America
Edinburg, TX 78539
www.panam.edu/

Texas Christian University
2800 University Drive
Fort Worth, TX 76129
www.tcu.edu/

Texas Southern University
3100 Cleburne
Houston, TX 77004
www.tsu.edu/

University of Texas–Houston
Health Science Center
P.O. Box 20036
Houston, TX 77225
www.uthouston.edu/

University of Houston
4800 Calhoun
Houston, TX 77204
www.dt.uh.edu/

Utah

Brigham Young University
Provo, UT 84602
www.byu.edu/

Vermont

University of Vermont
Burlington, VT 05401
www.uvm.edu/

Virginia

Virginia Polytechnic Institute & State University
104 Burruss Hall
Blacksburg, VA 24061
www.vt.edu/

James Madison University
800 S. Main Street
Harrisonburg, VA 22807
www.jmu.edu/

Radford University
P.O. Box 6903
Radford, VA 24142
www.runet.edu/

Washington

Central Washington University
Mitchell Hall
Ellensburg, WA 98926
www.cwu.edu/

Washington State University
342 French Administration Bldg.
Pullman, WA 99164
www.wsu.edu/

West Virginia

West Virginia Wesleyan College
Buckhannon, WV 26201
www.wvwc.edu/

Marshall University
400 Hall Greer Blvd.
Huntington, WV 25755
www.marshall.ecu/

Wisconsin

University of Wisconsin–Green Bay
Green Bay, WI 54311
www.uwgb.edu/

Viterbo College
815 South 4th Street
La Crosse, WI 54601
www.viterbo.edu/

University of Wisconsin–Madison
B 117/109 Education Bldg.
1000 Bascom Mall
Madison, WI 53706
www.wisc.edu/

University of Wisconsin–Stout
Menomonic, WI 54751
www.uwstout.edu/

Mount Mary College
Milwaukee, WI 53222
www.mtmary.edu/

University of Wisconsin–Stevens Point
131 Quandt
Stevens Point, WI 54481
www.uwsp.edu/

 # Genetic Counselors

Principal activity: Providing information and advice on hereditary disorders and risks

Work commitment: Usually full-time

Preprofessional education: Bachelor's degree with a biology major

Program length: Two years

Work prerequisites: Master's degree

Career opportunities: Very favorable

Income range: $30,000 to $50,000

Scope

Genetic counselors are trained health-care professionals who help people seeking information about hereditary disorders. They have learned communication skills that help them to serve concerned patients in a variety of ways, including helping them to place their concerns in a proper perspective.

Activities

Genetics is the study of gene transmission from parents to their children. A genetic profile of a fetus can be medically useful in predicting potential health problems. Over the past few decades, medical technology has made remarkable progress in this area. Today, a multitude of genetically transmitted conditions and diseases can be identified in fetuses, including Down syndrome, muscular dystrophy, cystic fibrosis, Tay-Sachs disease, sickle cell anemia, and some forms of mental retardation. Diagnosing such diseases involves microscopic analysis of the number and appearance of chromosomes. Chromosome samples are obtained from fetal cells extracted from the amniotic fluid bathing the developing fetus. Other techniques also are available for studying fetal chromosomes and proteins.

Complementing this cellular approach is *ultrasound imaging*, which can uncover anatomical malformations in the heart, lungs, and spine. In some situations, physicians can perform surgery on the developing fetus *in utero* (in the womb); in others, physicians can correct abnormalities after birth.

Genetic counselors get the information from medical geneticists and other sources about individual patients. They help potential and prospective parents by providing them with information about prenatal screening tests, the meaning of the results of such tests, and medical options. They deal with couples who have serious concerns about the well-being of future children on general medical grounds—for example, those of late child-bearing age (in their upper 30s and 40s)—those belonging to specific races or nationalities—for example, Tay-Sachs disease is most prevalent in those of Eastern European Jewish origin—and those with a known family history of disease. Genetic counselors help such patients become better informed and provide assistance in coping with the psychological issues generated by the stresses of genetic disorders.

Work Settings

The majority of genetic counselors are employed by major medical centers. That's where both genetic screening and prenatal diagnosis take place. Genetic counselors may be affiliated with pediatric and obstetric/gynecology departments at such medical centers. Some genetic counselors are employed by federal and state health-care agencies. Some professionals are in private practice.

Advancement

In centers that employ several counselors, one may move up to a supervisory position.

Prerequisites

In order to enter this field, you must earn a bachelor's degree with a major in biology. Required courses include general biology, developmental biology (vertebrate embryology), genetics, molecular genetics, general chemistry, psychology, and statistics. Recommended courses include organic chemistry, advanced psychology, and Spanish.

Desirable attributes for those planning a career in this field include a sense of empathy and superior communication and counseling skills.

Education/Training

Courses taken as part of a master's degree program include human anatomy and physiology, biochemistry, human genetics, clinical medicine, animal genetics, medical genetics, client counseling, and delivery of genetic services. As part of their field work, students are placed in clinical settings (for several hundred hours) and are exposed to cytogenetics and laboratory work.

Certification/Registration/Licensure

Graduates of genetics counseling master's degree programs can take a certification examination offered by the American Board of Genetic Counseling.

Career Potential

Genetic counseling is a relatively new profession. But there is a definite demand for genetic counselors, as reflected by the fact that all those who have graduated from the educational programs in this field have secured employment in the field.

For More Information

The professional organization for this field is the National Society of Genetic Counselors Inc., 283 Canterbury Drive, Wallingford, PA 19086.

Genetic Counselor Programs

Alabama

University South Alabama Medical School
Mobile, AL 36698
www.ua.edu/

Alaska

Alaska Genetics Clinic
1231 Gambell Street
Anchorage, AK 99501
(907) 269-3430

Arizona

Phoenix Children's Hospital
1300 North 12th Street, #404
Phoenix, AZ 85006
www.phxchildrens.com/

Arkansas

University of Arkansas Medical School
4301 West Markham
Little Rock, AR 72205
www.uark.edu/

California

University of California, Berkeley
570 University Hall
Berkeley, CA 94720
www.berkeley.edu/

Valley Children's Hospital
3291 North Hilliard
Fresno, CA 93726
www.valleychildrens.org/

University of California-Los Angeles
300 UCLA Medical Plaza
Los Angeles, CA 90024
www.ucla/edu/

Kaiser Permanente
2025 Morse Avenue
Sacramento, CA 95825
www.ca.kaiserpermanente.org/

Colorado

Repro Genetics Center
455 S. Hudson, Level 3
Denver, CO 80246
(303) 399-5393

Children's Hospital
1056 East 19th Avenue
Denver, CO 80219
www.tchden.org/

Connecticut

Yale University School of Medicine
Box 208063
New Haven, CT 06520
www.yale.edu/

Delaware

Alfred I. duPont Institute
P O Box 269
Wilmington, DE 19899
http://aidi.udel.edu/

District of Columbia

George Washington University
2300 Eye Street NW
Washington, DC 20037
www.gwu.edu/

Howard University
520 West Street, NW, Box 75
Washington, DC 20059
www.howard.edu/

Florida

Arnold Palmer Hospital
92 West Miller Street
Orlando, FL 32806
www.orhs.org/

Georgia

Scottish Rite Children's
Medical Center
1001 Johnson Ferry Road
Atlanta, GA 30342
www.scottishritechildrens.org/

Memorial Medical Center
4750 Waters Avenue #202
Savannah, GA 31404
www.memorialcares.com/

Hawaii

Kapiolani Medical Center
1319 Punahou Street
Honolulu, HI 96826
www.aloha.net/~peters/kmcnucs.html

Idaho

St. Luke's Regional Medical Center
190 East Bannock Street
Boise, ID 83712
(208) 381-3088

Illinois

Northwestern University Medical School
333 East Superior
Chicago, IL 60611
www.nwu.edu/

Lutheran General Prenatal Center
1875 Dempster Street
Park Ridge, IL 60068
www.advocatehealth.com/sites/luthgen.html

Indiana

Indiana University School of Medicine
550 North University Boulevard
Indianapolis, IN 46202
www.indiana.edu/

Iowa

University Iowa Hospitals
Department of Pediatrics, 2601 JCP
Iowa City, IA 52240
www.uiowa.edu/uhs.accp.html

Kansas

University of Kansas Medical Center
Rainbow at 39th
Kansas City, KS 66013
www.ukans.edu/

Kentucky

University of Kentucky Medical Center
Kentucky Clinic
Lexington, KY 40536
www.uky.edu/

University of Louisville
Child Evaluation Center
571 South Floyd Street
Louisville, KY 40202
www.louisville.edu/

Louisiana

Tulane University School of Medicine
1430 Tulane Avenue
New Orleans, LA 70112
www.tulane.edu/

Maine

Foundation for Blood Research
Box 109
Scarborough, ME 04070
www.fbr.org/

Maryland

John Hopkins Hospital
Center for Medical Genetics
Blalock 1008
Baltimore, MD 21287
www.jhu.edu/

Massachusetts

Beth Israel Hospital
330 Brookline Avenue
Boston, MA 02215
http://smi.bih.harvard.edu/

Michigan

Michigan State University
B240 Life Sciences B
East Lansing, MI 48824
www.msu.edu/

Sinai-Grace Hospital
6767 Outer Drive
Detroit, MI 48235
(313) 966-3300

Minnesota

University of Minnesota Hospital & Clinics
420 Delaware Street, SE
Minneapolis, MN 55455
www.umn.edu/

Mississippi

University Mississippi Medical Center
2500 North State Street
Jackson, MS 39216
www.olemiss.edu/

Missouri

University of Missouri Hospital & Clinics
#1 Hospital Drive
Columbia, MO 65212
www.missouri.edu/

Montana

Shodair Hospital, Medical Genetics
Box 5539
Helena, MT 59604
(406) 444-7530

Nebraska

University of Nebraska Medical Center
600 South 42nd Street
Omaha, NE 68198
www.unomahu.edu/

Nevada

University of Nevada School of Medicine
2040 West Charleston Boulevard
Las Vegas, NV 89102
www.unlv.edu/

New Jersey

Cooper Hospital
University Medical Center
636-638 Benson Street
Camden, NJ 08103
www.cooperhealth.org/

Hackensack University Medical Center
Pediatric Center
30 Prospect Avenue
Hackensack, NJ 07601
www.humed.com/

New Hampshire

Dartmouth-Hitchock Medical Center
Lebanon, NH 03756
www.Hitchcock.org/

New Mexico

University of New Mexico
2350 Alamo SE
Albuquerque, NM 87106
www.unm.edu/

New York

New York State Department Health
WCLR Empire State Plaza
Albany, NY 12201
www.health.state.ny.us/

Binghamton University Genetic Counseling
Program
124 Front St.
Binghamton, NY 13905
www.binghamton.edu/

New York University School of Medicine
550 First Avenue
New York, NY 10016
www.nyu.edu/

North Carolina

Carolinas Medical Center
Box 32861
Charlotte, NC 28232
www.warolinas.org/

Ohio

Children's Hospital Medical Center
One Perkins Square
Akron, OH 44308
www.medcenter.uc.edu/

Children's Hospital
3333 Burnet Street
Cincinnati, OH 45229
www.cincinnatichildrens.org/

Oklahoma

Oklahoma State Department of Health
MCH-Genetics,
1000 NE 10th Street
Oklahoma City, OK 73117
www.health.state.ok.us/

Oregon

Oregon Health Science University
P.O. Box 574
Portland, OR 97207
www.ohsu.edu/

Pennsylvania

Thomas Jefferson University Hospital
11th & Walnut
Philadelphia, PA 19107
www.jeffersonhealth.org/tjuh

University of Pittsburgh
130 DeSoto St.
Pittsburgh, PA 15261
www.pitt.edu/

Hershey Medical Center
Department of Pediatrics
Box 850
Hershey, PA 17033
www.psu.edu/

Rhode Island

Women's and Infant's Hospital
79 Plain Street
Providence, RI 02902
www.brown.edu/

South Carolina

University of South Carolina
School of Medicine
2 Medical Park
Columbia, SC 29203
www.sc.edu/

South Dakota

University of South Dakota
School of Medicine
3625 Fifth Street
Rapid City, SD 57701
www.usd.edu/

Tennessee

Vanderbilt University
Genetics Department
Box DD2205
2200 West End Ave.
Nashville, TN 37240
www.vanderbilt.edu/

Texas

Central Texas Genetics Center
4201 Marathon B
Austin, TX 78756
(512) 451-5173

Baylor College of Medicine
T538 One Baylor Plaza
Houston, TX 77030
www.baylor.edu/

Utah

University of Utah Medical Center
Department of Pediatrics
Salt Lake City, UT 84112
www.utah.edu/

Vermont

Vermont Regional Genetics Center
1 Mill Street
Burlington, VT 05401
www.vtmednet.org/vhgi/vrgc/vrgc.htm

Virginia

University of Virginia
Department of Pediatric Genetics
Box 386
Charlottesville, VA 22908
www.virginia.edu/

Washington

University of Washington Medical Center
Box 357720
Seattle, WA 98195
www.washington.edu/

West Virginia

West Virginia University
Health Sciences Center
Morgantown, WV 26506
www.wvu.edu/

Wisconsin

University of Wisconsin
1500 Highland Avenue
Madison, WI 53705
www.wisc.edu/

St. Vincent Hospital
P.O. Box 13508
Green Bay, WI 54307
(940) 433-0111

LaCrosse Regional Genetic Service
P.O. Box 1326
LaCrosse, WI 54602
www.uwlax.edu/

Wyoming

State Health Department
Hathaway Building
Cheyenne, WY 82001
www.health.state.wy.us.

Canada

Montreal Children's Hospital
2300 Tupper Street
Montreal, Quebec
Canada H3H 1P3
www.mcgill.ca/

Hospital for Sick Children
555 University Avenue
Toronto, Ontario
Canada M5G 1X8
www.genet.sickkids.on.ca/rommens/

Nurse Anesthetists

Principal activity: Administering anesthesia to surgical and obstetric patients

Work commitment: Usually full-time

Preprofessional education: Licensed registered nurse

Program length: 2 years

Work prerequisites: Certified, registered RN status

Career opportunities: Favorable

Income range: $70,000 to $95,000

Scope

A nurse anesthetist is a registered nurse who is certified to administer anesthesia to patients. It is estimated that more than half of all anesthesia procedures are performed by nurse anesthetists. This is especially true in rural areas. Nurse anesthetists differ from anesthesiology assistants, who can work only under the direct supervision of an anesthesiologist. Nurse anesthetists also are capable of independently performing their responsibilities, being only under the general oversight of an anesthesiologist, who usually supervises the entire department.

Activities

The nurse anesthetist selects the proper anesthetic and the appropriate dosage for the specific procedure to be performed. They may assist with surgical, obstetrical, or dental procedures. During their activities they monitor patients' vital signs, note their conditions, and follow their postoperative course in the recovery room.

Work Settings

Nurse anesthetists work in hospital operating rooms, in ambulatory surgery sites, and in dentists' offices.

Advancement

In a facility that relies primarily on nurse anesthetists, gaining experience and having managerial skills may result in a worker gaining supervisory responsibilities.

Prerequisites

A BS degree in nursing along with a license is required for admission to most nurse-anesthetist programs.

Education/Training

Programs for nurse anesthetists last from 18 to 20 months. Course work involves anatomy, physiology, pharmacology, and anesthetic procedures. Practical experience in administering anesthesia also is provided.

Certification/Registration/Licensure

All states require nurse anesthetists to be licensed. To secure certification, candidates must pass an examination administered by the American Association of Nurse Anesthetists. Successfully passing this exam means the candidate may be designated a CRNA, a certified registered nurse anesthetist. To retain this status, nurses must undergoe a biannual recertification process. This involves completing continuing education courses.

Career Potential

Nurse anesthetists are in high demand and have many opportunities for general or specialty practice throughout the United States. This is one of the best paid nursing specialties and has been ranked in the top 20 percent of income-earning professions.

For More Information

The professional organization for this field is the American Association of Nurse Anesthetists, 222 South Prospect Avenue, Park Ridge, IL 60068.

Nurse Anesthesia Programs

Alabama

University of Alabama at Birmingham
1714 Ninth Avenue South
Birmingham, AL 35294
www.uab.edu/

California

University of Southern California
1540 Alcazar Street
Los Angeles, CA 90033
www.usc.edu/

Samuel Merritt College
370 Hawthorne Avenue
Oakland, CA 94609
www.summitmed.com/school.shtm/

University of California, San Francisco
N611Y-Box 0610
San Francisco, CA 94143
www.ucsf.edu/

Connecticut

Bridgeport Hospital and Southern
State Connecticut State University
267 Grant Street
Bridgeport, CT 06610
www.ctstateu.edu/

New Britain School of Nurse Anesthesia
100 Grand Street
New Britain, CT 06050
www.ccsu.ctstate.edu/

New Haven-Hospital of Saint Raphael
1423 Chapel Street
New Haven, CT 06511
www.srhs.org/

District of Columbia

Georgetown University
3700 Reservoir Road NW
Washington, DC 20007
www.georgetown.edu/

Florida

Barry University/Mount Sinai Medical Center
11300 NE Second Avenue
Miami Shore, FL 33161
www.barry.edu/

Bay Medical Center
615 North Bonita Avenue
Panama City, FL 32401
www.baymedical.org/

Georgia

Medical College of Georgia
1120 15th Street
Augusta, GA 30912
www.mcg.edu/

Illinois

Ravenswood Hospital Medical Center
4550 North Winchester Avenue
Chicago, IL 60640
www.advocatehealth.com/sites/hospitals/ravn/

Rush University, College of Nursing
1653 Congress Parkway
Chicago, IL 60612
www.rush.edu/univ/

Decatur Memorial Hospital
Bradley University
2300 North Edward Street
Decatur, IL 62526
www.bradley.edu/

Southern Illinois University at Edwardsville
School of Nursing
Campus Box 1066
Edwardsville, IL 62026
www.siue.edu/

Iowa

Department of Veteran's Affairs
Drake University
2507 University
Des Moines, IO 50311
www.drake.edu/

University of Iowa
College of Nursing
Iowa City, IO 52242
www.uiowa.edu/

Kansas

University of Kansas Medical Center
3901 Rainbow Boulevard
Kansas City, KS 66160
www.ukans.edu/

Kentucky

Trover Clinic Foundation/
Murray State University
435 North Kentucky Avenue
Madisonville, KY 42431
www.mursuky.edu/

Louisiana

Charity Hospital/Xavier University
1532 Tulane Avenue
New Orleans, LA 70112
www.xula.edu/

Maine

Eastern Maine Medical Center
489 State Street
P.O. Box 404
Bangor, ME 04402
www.emh.org/

University of New England
11 Hills Beach Road
Biddeford, ME 04405
www.une.edu/

Maryland

Naval School of Health Sciences
Navy Nurse Corpse Anesthesia Program
8901 Wisconsin Avenue, Bldg. 141
Bethesda, MD 20889
http://nshs.med.navy.mil/

Uniformed Services University of the Health
Sciences
11426 Rockville Pike
Rockville, MD 20852
www.usuhs.mil/

Massachusetts

Northeastern University
New England Medical Center
360 Huntington Avenue
Boston, MA 02115
www.northeastern.edu/

Berkshire Medical Center
725 North Street
Pittsfield, MA 01201
(413) 447-2000

Michigan

Henry Ford Hospital/University of Detroit
Mercy
2799 West Grand Boulevard
Detroit, MI 48202
www.udmercy.edu/

Wayne State University College of Pharmacy
and Allied Health Professions
4201 St. Antoine
Detroit, MI 48201
www.wayne.edu/

University of Michigan–Flint/Hurley Medical
Center
One Hurley Plaza
Flint, MI 48503
www.flint.umich.edu/

University of Detroit Mercy
900 Woodward Avenue, Box 600
Pontiac, MI 48341
www.udmercy.edu/

Oakland University–Beaumont
3601 West 13 Mile Road
Royal Oak, MI 48073
www.acs.oakland.edu/

Minnesota

Abbott Northwestern Hospital
800 East 28th Street
Minneapolis, MN 55407
www.abbottnorthwestern.com/

Minneapolis VA School of Anesthesia
One Veterans Drive/112A
Minneapolis, MN 55417
www.mnana.org/

Mayo School of Health-Related Sciences
200 1st Street SW
Rochester, MN 55905
www.mayo.edu/

Minneapolis School of Anesthesia
6715 Minnetonka Blvd.
St. Louis Park, MN 55426
www.smumn.edu/

Missouri

Truman Medical Center
2301 Holmes Street
Kansas City, MO 64108
www.med.umkc.edu/crna/

Springfield Southwest Missouri School of
Anesthesia
1900 South National Avenue,
Springfield, MO 65804
www.smsu.edu/

Nebraska

Bryan Memorial Hospital
University of Kansas
1600 South 48th Street
Lincoln, NE 68506
www.bryan.org/

New Jersey

Our Lady of Lourdes Medical Center
1600 Haddon Avenue
Camden, NJ 08103
www.lourdesnet.org/

New York

Albany Medical College
A-131-43 New Scotland Avenue
Albany, NY 12208
www.albanyanesth.com/

Kings County Hospital Center
450 Clarkson Avenue, Box 22
Brooklyn, NY 11203
www.uhfnyc.org/

State University at Buffalo
3435 Main Street
Buffalo, NY 14214
www.smbs.buffalo.edu/

Columbia University School of Nursing
630 West 168th Street
New York, NY 10032
www.columbia.edu/

Harlem Hospital Center
506 Lenox Avenue
New York, NY 10037
www.uhfnyc.org/

North Carolina

Carolinas Health Care System
P.O. Box 32861
Charlotte, NC 28232
www.carolinas.org/

University of North Carolina at Greensboro
2500 Blue Ridge Road
Raleigh, NC 27607
www.uncg.edu/nur/

North Carolina Baptist Hospital/
Bowman Gray School of Medicine
University of North Carolina at Greensboro
Medical Center Boulevard
Winston-Salem, NC 27157
http://isnet.is.wfu.edu/medcenter.html

North Dakota

University North Dakota
P.O. Box 9025
Grand Forks, NC 58202
www.und.nodak.edu/

Ohio

United States Air Force
74th Medical Group/SGOSA
4881 Sugar Maple Drive
Wright-Patterson AFB 45433
www.wpafb.af.mil/

University of Akron
209 Carroll Street
Akron, OH 44325
www.uakron.edu/

University of Cincinnati
College of Nursing and Health
P.O. Box 210038
Cincinnati, OH 45221
www.nursing.uc.edu/

Cleveland Clinic Foundation
Frances Payne Bolton School of Nursing
Case Western Reserve University
9500 Euclid Avenue, E-31
Cleveland, OH 44195
http://misd.wcb1.ccf.org/ed/allied/
ahconted.htm

Mt. Sinai Medical Center
Frances Payne Bolton School of Nursing
Case Western Reserve University
2121 Abington Road
Cleveland, OH 44106
www.mtsinai.org/

St. Elizabeth Health Center
1044 Belmont Avenue
Youngstown, OH 44501
www.hmhs.org/StElizabeth/physician/

Pennsylvania

Altoona Hospital
620 Howard Avenue
Altoona, PA 16601
www.altoonahosp.org/

Geisinger Medical Center
100 North Academy Avenue
Danville, PA 17822
www.pcom.edu/

Hamot Medical Center
201 State Street
Erie, PA 16550
www.hamot.org/

Westmoreland-Latrobe Hospitals
La Roche College
532 West Pittsburgh Street
Greensburg, PA 15601
www.westmoreland.org/

Allegheny Valley Hospital/La Roche College
1301 Carlisle Street
Natrona Heights, PA 15065
www.laroche.edu/

Montgomery Hospital
1301 Powell Street
P.O.Box 992
Norristown, PA 19401
(610) 270-2770

Allegheny University of the Health Sciences
Broad & Vine Streets, Mailstop 501
Philadelphia, PA 19102
http://nursing.auhs.edu/

Nazareth Hospital
2601 Holme Avenue
Philadelphia, PA 19152
http://chc.hcwp.org/na-nh.htm

Pennsylvania Hospital
800 Spruce Street
Philadelphia, PA 19107
www.pahosp.com/

St. Francis Medical Center
La Roche College
400-45th Street
Pittsburgh, PA 15201
www.sfhs.edu/

University of Pittsburgh
School of Nursing
3500 Victoria Street
314 Victoria Building
Pittsburgh, PA 15261
www.pitt.edu/

Washington Hospital
155 Wilson Avenue
Washington, PA 15301
www.wpho.com/

Wyoming Valley Health Care System/
Wilkes University
575 North River Street
Wilkes-Barre, PA 18764
http://wilkes1.wilkes.edu

Lankenau Hospital
100 Lancaster Avenue
Wynnewood, PA 19096
www.jeffersonhealth.org/lh.index.html/

Rhode Island

St. Joseph Health Services
200 High Service Avenue
North Providence, RI 02904
www.staintjosephri.com/

Memorial Hospital of Rhode Island
111 Brewster Street
Pawtucket, RI 02860
www.mjri.org/

South Carolina

Medical University of South Carolina
171 Ashley Avenue
Charleston, SC 29425
www.musc.edu/nursing/

University of South Carolina
Five Richland Medical Park
Columbia, SC 29203
www.sc.edu/

South Dakota

Mount-Marty College
3109 South Kiwanis Avenue
Sioux Falls, SD 57105
www.mtmc.edu/

Tennessee

University of Tennessee at Chattanooga/
Erlanger Medical Center
615 McCallie Avenue
Chattanooga, TN 37403
www.utc.edu/

University of Tennessee
Medical Center at Knoxville
1924 Alcoa Highway, Drawer U109
Knoxville, TN 37920
www.utk.edu/

Middle-Tennessee School of Anesthesia
P.O. Box 6414
Madison, TN 37116
www.mtsu.edu/

Texas

Army Medical Department Center
2250 Stanley Road
Fort Sam Houston, TX 78234
www.acs.amedd.army.mil

Texas Wesleyan University
1201 Wesleyan Street
Ft-Worth, TX 76105
www.txwesleyan.edu/

Baylor College of Medicine
6550 Fannin, Suite #1003
Houston, TX 77030
www.bcm.tmc.edu/

University of Texas–
Houston Health Science Center
1100 Holcombe Boulevard
Houston, TX 77030
www.uthouston.edu/

Virginia

DePaul Medical Center
150 Kingsley Lane
Norfolk, VA 23505
www.depaul.com/

Old Dominion University
School of Nursing
Norfolk, VA 23529
www.odu.edu/

Medical College of Virginia
P.O. Box 980226, MCV Campus
Richmond, VA 23298
www.vcu.edu/

Washington

Sacred Heart Medical Center/
Gonzaga University
101 West 8th Avenue
Spokane, WA 99220
www.gonzaga.edu/

West Virginia

Charleston Area Medical Center
3110 MacCorkle Avenue SE
Charleston, WV 25304
(304) 388-9981

United Hospital Center
La Roche College
P.O. Box 1680
Clarksburg, WV 26302
www.uhcwv.org/

Wisconsin

Franciscan Skemp Healthcare
700 West Avenue
La Crosse, WI 54601
www.myo.edu/fsh/

LICENSED PRACTICAL NURSES

Principal activity: Providing nursing care for the infirm and injured

Work commitment: Full-time

Preprofessional education: High school diploma

Program length: 1 to 1½ years

Work prerequisites: Certificate/diploma/license

Career opportunities: Probably favorable

Income range: $16,000 to $35,000

Scope

Licensed practical nurses (LPNs) provide bedside care to a wide variety of patients, including the injured, ill, convalescent, and disabled. They work under the supervision of a registered nurse (RN). Having lesser responsibilities, the LPN's education and training is more limited than that of an RN. In a few states, they are known as Licensed Vocational Nurses (LVNs).

Activities

A major job for LPNs is securing and recording, at prescribed intervals during the day, vital signs of patients, including blood pressure, temperature, and pulse rate. They also assist in caring for patients by feeding, bathing, and dressing them. They may dress wounds and prepare patients for exams. They also assist in medical examinations by physicians. They need to note any significant changes in their patients' conditions and record these; when appropriate, they report changes immediately to their supervisor.

In non-hospital settings such as doctor offices, LPNs prepare patients for exams, change dressings, advise patients about home health care, and carry out a variety of administrative chores. Aside from serving on general hospital wards, LPNs may work in specialty areas such as obstetrics, pediatrics, or surgery.

Work Settings

The major work sites for LPNs are medical centers and hospitals. The second largest employment field is nursing homes. Openings are also available in HMOs, clinics, physicians' and dentists' offices, rehabilitation centers, prison medical offices, sanitariums, industrial health clinics, long-term facilities, and even private homes.

Advancement

Advancement may come by getting a supervisory position with responsibilities over nursing assistants and nurse's aides. By completing additional course work, an LPN can become a registered nurse. Some LPNs receive salary advancements by seeking employment in larger or more prestigious health-care facilities.

Prerequisites

A high school diploma or its equivalent is usually required to become a licensed practical nurse.

Desirable personal attributes for work in this field include a genuine sense of compassion, personal strength, good communication skills, the ability to follow instructions, concern for detail, and a desire to help the infirm and disabled.

Education/Training

State-approved practical nursing programs are offered by many institutions, including technical, vocational, and trade schools; hospitals; and community and junior colleges. The basic curriculum includes courses in anatomy and physiology, and in medical, surgical, psychiatric, pediatric, and obstetrical nursing. In addition, prospective LPNs are taught about nutrition and diet, first aid, administering medications, community development, and community health. They also learn various nursing concepts and basic nursing skills and techniques. Part of the training includes supervised clinical experience in a hospital. After candidates successfully complete the educational and training program, they are awarded a certificate or diploma.

Certification/Registration/Licensure

Earning a certificate or diploma from a state-approved practical nursing program qualifies a candidate to take the written state-board licensing examination. Once the candidate passes the exam, he or she is awarded a license to practice.

Career Potential

The employment outlook for LPNs appears, on the whole, to be favorable. However, recent history has seen marked cyclical fluctuations between surpluses and shortages of nurses. The surpluses were generated by the limitations placed on the length of hospital stays. Consequently, the regular salary increases paid to nurses fell and the number of nursing school candidates decreased, resulting in shortages.

Changes in the U.S. health-care system also create uncertainty. While the nursing needs for a growing population—especially the booming elderly population—is high, cost containment pressures will result in lowered nursing needs.

On the other hand, after a period of adjustment to the changing health-care situation, the job market may stabilize. At this point, while nursing positions will probably diminish in hospitals, they will be replaced by new openings in other settings. The aggressive use by HMOs of unlicensed nurses' aides instead of LPNs, however, may upset this positive employment prognosis.

For More Information

There are more than a thousand state-licensed practical nursing programs in various educational settings in the United States—far too many to list here. For information about a program in your area, contact the National Federation of Licensed Practical Nurses, Inc., P.O. Box 18088, Raleigh, NC 27619.

You can receive additional information from:

National Association for Practical Nurse Education
1400 Spring Street
Silver Spring, MD 20910

National League for Nursing
350 Hudson Street
New York, NY 10014

NURSE-MIDWIVES

Principal activity: Providing obstetrical care

Work commitment: Full- or part-time

Preprofessional education: Licensed RN

Program length: 9 months to 2 years

Work prerequisites: Certification and license

Career opportunities: Excellent

Income range: $45,000 to $60,000

Scope

Nurse-midwives are registered nurses who provide professional health care to women throughout pregnancy, labor, delivery, and for a short time after birth. They maintain consultative arrangements with obstetricians and other specialists to provide assistance when needed. Nurse-midwives serve only carefully screened women—those whose pregnancies and deliveries are not likely to present complications. Women with prior histories of pregnancy complications and those with existing health problems are referred to obstetricians or are cared for jointly. Currently about 5% of all births in the United States are attended by midwives, a relatively dramatic increase from the past which is expected to continue. Most midwife-attended births today take place in hospitals. The growing popularity of nurse-midwives is evidenced by the fact that federal health insurance (i.e., Medicaid) now reimburses them for their professional services. In addition, about 25 state legislatures require that insurance coverage must include services rendered by certified nurse-midwives associated with physicians or hospitals.

Activities

The nurse-midwife performs complete physical examinations of her pregnant patients and monitors and records the progress of each pregnancy. To help increase the well-being of the mother and future child, she provides education on proper nutrition, exercise, breast feeding, child care, and the baby's integration into the family. Family care during the birthing process is formulated with the parents. The nurse-midwife supervises the labor period, provides pain-relief medication when necessary, and performs normal deliveries. If unexpected complications arise, an obstetrician is called in promptly.

The nurse-midwife examines and evaluates the baby upon birth and notes its state of health. She also provides the initial follow-up care to the new mother and child, after which a pediatrician assumes responsibility for the infant.

In addition to their other duties, nurse-midwives advise their patients on family planning and perform routine gynecological care.

Work Settings

Nurse-midwives typically are self-employed. They also may work in hospitals, HMOs, clinics, and obstetricians' offices.

Advancement

Nurse-midwives who work for institutions may elect to move into private practice, thus arranging their own employment conditions.

Prerequisites

The basic requirement for undertaking a nurse-midwife certification program is being a registered nurse. Candidates must have a batchelor's degree in nursing before starting a master's degree program. RNs who want to become certified nurse-midwives should have some prior experience in obstetrical nursing.

Desirable personal attributes in this field include satisfaction with nursing, the desire for a more challenging and responsible position, sensitivity (especially in interpersonal relations), dexterity, and quick thinking.

Education/Training

There are three routes to becoming a certified nurse-midwife. The first two are open to those who are already registered nurses, and the third option is for those who do not have an RN degree.

Certificate program: This requires an intense period of 9 to 12 months of study and supervised clinical experience.

Master's degree program: This extends for 16 to 24 months and leads to the simultaneous awarding of a certificate in nurse-midwifery and a master's degree.

Combined RN/master's degree program: This is three-year program consists of two parts. The first year is devoted to general nursing education courses that prepare candidates to take the RN license examination. Upon electing nurse-midwifery as a specialty, candidates spend the next two years in a master's degree program, which includes information on the essential medical aspects of pregnancy, labor, childbirth, and infant care. Gaining admission into a nurse-midwife program can be difficult, as the number of candidates far exceeds the number of program openings annually.

Certification/Registration/Licensure

Graduates of accredited nurse-midwife programs are eligible to take the national certification examination.

Career Potential

Estimates are that the need for nurse-midwives will more than double in the next decade. This makes the outlook for jobs excellent. This attractive situation may be the result of changing views of the birth process in the United States. An increasing number of prospective mothers today view the process as a natural event that requires more educational and emotional support and less medical intervention. So they are choosing a more personalized and empathetic birthing experience at a lower cost.

For More Information

The professional organization for nurse-midwives is the American College of Nurse-Midwives, 818 Connecticut Avenue NW, Washington, DC 20006

Nurse-Midwife Programs

California

University of California, San Diego
9500 Gilman Drive, Dept. 0809
La Jolla, CA 92093
www.ucsf.edu/

Charles R. Drew University of Medicine and Science
1621 East 120th Street, Mail Point #22
Los Angeles, CA 90059
www.cdrewu.edu/

University of Southern California
1540 Alcazar Street, CHP 222
Los Angeles, CA 90033
www.usc.edu/hsc/ucnurse

University California
Los Angeles School of Nursing
Factor Building. Room 5934
Box 956919
Los Angeles, CA 90095
www.nursing.ucla.edu/

University of California–San Francisco
San Francisco General Hospital
1001 Potrero Avenue, SFGH, 6D21
San Francisco, CA 94110
www.ucsf.edu/

Colorado

University of Colorado
4200 East 9th Avenue
Box C288-14
Denver, CO 80262
http://freenet.uchsc.edu/son

Connecticut

Yale University School of Nursing
100 Church Street South
Box 9740
New Haven, CT 06536
http://info.med.edu/nursing

District of Columbia

Georgetown University
3700 Reservoir Road, NW
Washington, DC 20007
www.dml.georgetown.edu/schnurs/
midwife1.html

Florida

University of Miami
5801 Red Road, P.O. Box 248153
Coral Gables, FL 33124
www.miami.edu/

University of Florida
School of Nursing
653 West 8th Street, Bldg.1, 2nd Floor
Jacksonville, FL 32209
http://con.ufl.edu/

Georgia

Emory University
Woodruff School of Nursing
Atlanta, GA 30322
www.nurse.emory.edu/

Illinois

University of Illinois at Chicago
845 South Damen Avenue
Chicago, IL 60612
www.uic.edu/nursing/mcn.htm

Kentucky

Frontier School of Midwifery
P.O. Box 528
Hyden, KY 41749
www.midwives.org/

Maryland

University of Maryland
School of Nursing, Suite 575
655 W. Lombard Street
Baltimore, MD 21201
http://nursing.umaryland.edu/

Massachusetts

Boston University
School of Nursing
715 Albany Street
Boston, MA 02118
www.bumc.bu.edu/sph.mc

Baystate Medical Center
Nurse-Midwifery Education Program
Springfield, MA 01199
http://baystatehealth.com/

Michigan

University of Michigan
School of Nursing
400 North Ingalls, Room 3320
Ann Arbor, MI 48109
www.umich.edu/

Minnesota

University of Minnesota School of Nursing
308 Harvard Street, SE
6-101 Weaver-Densford Hall
Minneapolis, MN 55455
www.nursing.umn.edu/

Missouri

University of Missouri at Columbia
Sinclair School of Nursing
Columbia, MO 65211
www.health.missouri.edu/

New Jersey

University of Medicine and Dentistry
of New Jersey
65 Bergen Street
Newark, NJ 07107
www.umdnj.edu/

New Mexico

University of New Mexico
College of Nursing
Nursing/Pharmacy Building
Albuquerque, NM 87131
www.unm.edu/

New York

State University of New York
School of Nursing
450 Clarkson Avenue, Box 1227
Brooklyn, NY 11203
www.hscbklyn.edu/CHRP/Midwif/default.html

Columbia University
School of Nursing
630 W 168th Street
New York, NY 10032
www.columbia.edu/

New York University
429 Shimkin Hall
50 West 4th Street
New York, NY 10012
www.nyu.edu/pagea/nursing

State University of New York at Stony Brook
School of Nursing
Stony Brook, NY 11794
www.uhmc.sunyb.edu/nursing

North Carolina

East Carolina University
Nurse-Midwifery Program
Greenville, NC 27858
www.ecu.edu/

Ohio

Case Western Reserve University
School of Nursing
10900 Euclid Avenue
Cleveland, OH 44106
http://cwru4.nurs.cwru.edu/

University of Cincinnati
College of Nursing and Health
P.O. Box 210038
Cincinnati, OH 45221
www.uc.edu/www/nursing

Ohio State University
College of Nursing
1585 Neil Avenue
Columbus, OH 43210
www.con.ohio.state.edu/

Oregon

Oregon Health Sciences University
3181 SW Sam Jackson Park Road
Portland, OR 97201
www.ohsu.edu/

Pennsylvania

University of Pennsylvania
Nursing Education Building
420 Guardian Drive
Philadelphia, PA 19104
www.nursing.upenn.edu/midwifery

Institute of Midwifery, Women, and Health
Hayward Hall, Room 222
Schoolhouse Lane & Henry Ave.
Philadelphia, PA 19144
www.instituteofmidwifery.org/

Rhode Island

University of Rhode Island
College of Nursing
Kingston, RI 02881
www.uri.edu/

South Carolina

Medical University of South Carolina
Nurse-Midwife Program
99 Jonathan Lucas St.
Charleston, SC 29403
www.musc.edu/

Tennessee

Vanderbilt University
School of Nursing
102 Godchaux Hall
Nashville, TN 37240
www.vanderbilt.edu/nursing/

Texas

Parkland Memorial Hospital/
University of Texas Southwestern
Nurse-Midwife Program
5201 Harry Hines Boulevard
Dallas, TX 75235
www.swmed.edu/home_pages/parkland/
midwifery/midwifehome.html

Baylor College of Medicine
Nurse-Midwife Program
One Baylor Plaza
Houston, TX 77030
www.bcm.tmc.edu/midwifery

University of Texas at El Paso/
Texas Tech University
Nurse-Miwife Program
4800 Alberta Avenue
El Paso, TX 79905
www.ttuhsc.edu/

University of Texas Medical Branch at
Galveston
School of Nursing
1100 Mechanic
Galveston, TX 77555
www.utmb.edu/

Utah

University of Utah
College of Nursing
10 South 200 East Front
Salt Lake City, UT 84112
www-medlib.med.utah.edu/nmw

Virginia

Shenandoah University
School of Nursing
1775 North Sector Court
Winchester, VA 22601
www.su.edu/

Washington

University of Washington
School of Nursing
Box 357262
Seattle, WA 98195
w.son.washington.edu/~midwife/

West Virginia

Marshall University Medical Center
Nurse-Midwife Program
1600 Medical Center Drive
Huntington, WV 25701
www.marshall.edu/

Wisconsin

Marquette University
School of Nursing
P.O. Box 1881
Milwaukee, WI 53201
www.marquette.edu/

NURSE PRACTITIONERS

Principal activity: Providing primary care medical services under a doctor's supervision.

Work commitment: Full-time

Preprofessional education: B.S. in nursing

Program length: 1½ to 2 years

Work prerequisites: Master's degree and certification

Career opportunities: Favorable

Income range: $40,000 to $60,000

Scope

Nurse practitioners (NPs) offer health services that enable primary care physicians to provide care to more patients and to deliver services in areas where they are needed. Like physician assistants, they extend primary care physicians' potential by allowing them to focus their attention on treating more critically ill and complex cases. However, although they have similar training and responsibilities as physician assistants, nurse practitioners have greater autonomy. Some states allow them to practice independently and even to prescribe medications. Many have specialties in areas such as pediatric and geriatric care.

Activities

Nurse practitioners handle a wide range of problems. They take medical histories, conduct physical examinations, make diagnoses, and treat common minor injuries and illnesses. NPs can order and interpret laboratory tests, EKGs, and x-ray analyses. They also advise patients on health maintenance and perform such routine procedures as injections, immunizations, and wound care. They may help develop and implement patient treatment plans and write progress notes.

NPs assist physicians both in acute, short-term hospitals and in extended-care facilities. They educate families about disease prevention and family planning and refer them to other specialists and community health agencies.

Work Settings

Nuse practitioners work in clinics, nursing homes, hospitals, and their own offices.

Advancement

Nurse practitioners who work in hospitals and large clinics may be appointed to supervisory positions. Some open their own offices.

Prerequisites

To gain admission to a nurse-practitioner program one must be a registered nurse and hold a batchelor's degree in nursing from an accredited program.

Desirable personal attributes include an ability to use good judgment under stress, strong communication skills, manual dexterity, and a pleasant personality.

Education/Training

The program of study lasts from 18 months to 2 years and involves both classroom and clinical exposure. Because most nurse practitioners have a more limited background in the basic sciences, these are not so intensively emphasized during the first year of study as they are for PAs. Health maintenance subjects, including proper nutrition, are an important element of the curriculum. In the second year of study, candidates gain supervised clinical experience under a physician.

Certification/Registration/Licensure

Nurse practitioners must be nationally certified by the American Nurses' Association or a specialty nursing organization.

Career Potential

The employment outlook for nurse practitioners is quite favorable, because of the need for medical care in underserved areas, where they play an important role in providing primary care. In addition, growing HMOs will use more personnel like NPs, who provide cost-effective care. Today, NPs are gaining wider acceptance by the medical community, the public, and the government.

For More Information

More than 450 educational institutions offer nurse practitioner programs—far too many to list here. Most of them confer master's degrees.

To get more information about the field, contact the American College of Nurse Practitioners, 1090 Vermont Ave. NW, Washington, DC 20005.

The National Organization of Nurse Practitioner Faculties sells a National Directory of Nurse Practitioner Programs that is updated annualy. You can write to the organization at One Dupont Circle, Washington, DC 20036.

REGISTERED NURSES

Principal activity: Providing skilled nursing care for sick patients

Work commitment: Usually full-time

Preprofessional education: High school diploma

Program length: 2 to 4 years

Work prerequisites: Diploma/degree/license

Career opportunities: Probably favorable

Income range: $25,000 to $55,000

Scope

Patients often judge the quality of a hospital by the nursing care they receive. This demonstrates the importance of this strongly people-oriented profession, which focuses on health recovery and maintenance. The field provides an opportunity for service in a wide range of settings and specialties and for a high degree of career satisfaction. Registered nurses are directly responsible for carrying out treatment plans that have been ordered by physicians. This requires a combination of technical skills and knowledge of nursing procedures together with an understanding of expected results.

Activities

Because nursing covers a broad spectrum of situations, we'll discuss its activities in terms of both hospital and nonhospital work settings.

In Hospitals

Hospital nurses determine patients' care needs in light of a physician's medical treatment plan. Based on their assessments, nurses formulate care plans, then execute and evaluate their effectiveness. These plans must provide for both the medical and the physical needs of their patients. Nurses also lend emotional support that can facilitate the recovery and rehabilitation process. Because they are in close contact with patients for extended periods, they can provide valuable insights on their progress. Nurses document patients' charts and help prepare them for activities after discharge. A registered nurse may be assigned responsibility over the activities of LPNs and other junior nursing staff members.

Private duty nurses provide exclusive care of individual patients in a hospital or in their homes. These nurses are self-employed.

Operating room nurses provide care prior to, during, and immediately after surgery. They help prepare patients for surgery, directly assist surgeons and other team physicians by providing them with needed instruments and supplies, and check on the postoperative state of patients. There are various specialties in this area—for example, orthopedic, cardiac, and thoracic surgery nurses.

Critical care nurses care for patients who are in life-threatening states. Their special training qualifies them to provide complicated nursing support services, recognize physiological changes in patients' conditions, and operate sophisticated medical equipment.

Rehabilitation nurses serve both adults and children suffering a reduction in their optimal functional potential due to accidents, birth defects, or diseases. They provide a variety of treatments, exercises, and emotional support, which facilitates both regaining lost function and adapting to permanent disabilities. To prepare for this specialty, candidates must complete a post-RN course or a master's degree in rehabilitation nursing.

Clinical nurse specialists hold advanced degrees (usually a master's) with specialized training. Their areas of expertise may be cancer, cardiac, neonatal, or mental health care. They may be directly involved in the delivery of nursing services as well as in education, administrative, or consultative activities. They also work in non-hospital settings.

Advanced practice nurses are highly trained specialists with one of four professional titles: clinical nurse specialist (see above), nurse-anesthetist (p. 138), nurse practitioner (p. 152), and nurse-midwife (p. 147).

Ouside of Hospitals

Office nurses work for physicians in all specialties as well as for dental surgeons, nurse-midwives, and nurse practitioners. They may perform routine laboratory tests and administrative functions.

School nurses are engaged by boards of education to provide health and nursing services in individual schools or school districts. They provide emergency medical care, help administer physical exams, communicate with parents about students' physical or emotional problems, ensure that state health codes (especially regarding immunization) are implemented, and advise school constituencies on health issues.

Community health nurses provide services to patients in non-hospital settings such as clinics, schools, and private homes. They teach groups about maintaining a healthy environment, proper nutrition, and preventive health measures. They also carry out physicians' plans and provide care for ambulatory patients. In addition, they initiate public health programs that encourage immunization and provide information on alcohol, drugs, and infectious diseases.

Occupational health nurses are engaged by corporations, factories, and government agencies to provide nursing care for their employees. This care may include treating minor diseases and injuries, providing physical examinations, and educating workers about health issues.

Nurse educators typically are faculty members of nursing schools. They assist in the training of nurses and teach continuing education courses.

Advancement

With additional experience and training, a registered nurse may move into a supervisory, management, or administrative position such as head nurse. Other potential directions for advancement included specialty training, especially in one of the advanced practice nurse specialties.

Prerequisites

In order to gain admission to a nursing education program, candidates must have a high school diploma (or its equivalent) with a minimum C average.

Those entering this field should have good physical and emotional health, compassion, patience, being a team worker, and the ability to assume challenging medical responsibilities.

Education/Training

There are three educational routes to become a registered nurse:

Two-year associate degree programs offered by community, junior, and technical colleges.

Three-year diploma programs offered by hospitals.

Four-year bachelor's degree programs offered by colleges and universities. These usually award the bachelor's of science in nursing (BSN) degree.

All three of these programs involve both classroom course work and supervised nursing practice. The basic curriculum is the same for each, but the programs vary in depth and in scope, depending on the length of the program. The basic courses cover anatomy, physiology, sociology, English, psychology, philosophy, microbiology, and nursing concepts and techniques. Those pursuing a bachelor's degree must also take courses in precalculus mathematics, chemistry (both general and organic), biology, anthropology, epidemiology, and several advanced nursing courses. Within the bachelor's program there may be special tracks leading to specialty training, such as community health or school nursing. For some specialties, a master's degree is essential.

Certification/Registration/Licensure

A nursing license is required in every state. Candidates obtain their license by passing a written state board examination after graduating from an accredited nursing school.

Career Potential

Recent decades have seen fluctuations in job opportunities for nurses. Consequently, projecting future opportunities is difficult. The major factor is the change currently underway in the health-care system, especially in light of a growing population of elderly citizens. Most experts believe that, once the nature of health-care management is established, job opportunities probably will be favorable. (See the discussion for Licensed Practical Nurses.)

For More Information

There are more than a thousand different educational institutions offering diplomas and degrees (from batchelor's to doctorate) in nursing—far too many to list here.

For more information, contact the American Nurses' Association, 600 Maryland Avenue SW (Suite 100W), Washington, DC 20024; or the National League for Nursing, 350 Hudson Street, New York, NY 10014.

Specialty Nursing Organizations

American Academy of Nurse Practitioners
P.O. Box 12846
Austin, TX 78711
www.aanp.org/

American Association of Critical-Care Nurses
101 Columbia
Aliso Viejo, CA 92656
www.aacn.org/

American Association of Neuroscience Nurses
224 North Des Plaines, Suite 601
Chicago, IL 60661
www.aann.org/

American Association of Nurse Anesthetists
222 South Prospect Avenue
Park Ridge, IL 60068
www.aana.org/

American Association of Nurse Attorneys
720 Light Street
Baltimore, MD 21230
www.taana.org/

American Association of Occupational Health Nurses
50 Lenox Pointe
Atlanta, GA 30324
www.aaohn.org/

American Association of Spinal Cord Injury Nurses
75-20 Astoria Boulevard
Jackson Heights, NY 11370
www.aascin.org/

American College of Nurse-Midwives
1522 K Street, Suite 1000
Washington, DC 20005
www.midwife.org/

American Nephrology Nurses' Association
North Woodbury Road, Box 56
Pitman, NJ 08071
http://anna.inurse.com/

American Organization of Nurse Executives
840 North Lake Shore Drive
Chicago, IL 60611
www.aone.org/

American Society of Ophthalmic Registered Nurses
P.O. Box 193030
San Francisco, CA 94119
http://webeye.ophth.uiowa.edu/asogn/

American Society of Plastic and Reconstructive Surgical Nurses, Inc.
North Woodbury Road, Box 56
Pitman, NJ 08071
http://asprsn.inurse.com/

American Society of Post Anasthesia Nurses (ASPAN) Recovery Room Nurses
11512 Allecingie Parkway
Richmond, VA 23235
www.aspan.org/

American Urological Association Allied (for urological nurses)
11512 Allecingie Parkway
Richmond, VA 23235
www.auanet.org/

Association for Practitioners in Infection Control
505 East Hawley Street
Mundelein, IL 60060
www.apic.org/

Association of Operating Room Nurses, Inc.
2170 South Parker Road, Suite 300
Denver, CO 80231
www.aorn.org/

Association of Rehabilitation Nurses
5700 Old Orchard Road, First Floor
Skokie, IL 60077
www.rehabnurse.org/

Association of Women's Health, Obstetric,
and Neonatal Nurses
409 Twelfth Street SW, Suite 300
Washington, DC 20024
www.awhonn.org/

Council of Cardiovuscular Nursing
American Heart Association
7320 Greenville Avenue
Dallas, TX 75231
www.americanheart.org/

Dermatology Nurses' Association
North Woodbury Road, Box 56
Pitman, NJ 08071
http://dna.inurse.com/

Emergency Nurses' Association
216 Higgins Road
Park Ridge, IL 60068
www.ena.org/

National Association of Orthopedic Nurses
North Woodbury Road, Box 56
Pitman, NJ 08071
http://naon.inurse.com/

National Association of Pediatric Nurse
Associates and Practitioners
1101 Kings' Highway North, Suite 206
Cherry Hill, NJ 08034
www.napnap.org/

National Association of School Nurses, Inc.
P.O. Box 1300
Scarborough, ME 04074
http://ce.vrmedia.com/nurses/

National Flight Nurses' Association
6900 Grove Road
Thorofare, NJ 08086
www.astna.org/

National Nurses' Society on Addictions
5700 Old Orchard Road, First Floor
Skokie, IL 60077
www.nnsa.org/

Oncology Nursing Society
501 Holiday Drive
Pittsburgh, PA 15220
www.ons.org/

Society of Otorhinolaryngology and Head/
Neck Nurses
116 Canal Street, Suite A
New Smyrna Beach, FL 32168
www.entnet.org/sohu/

PHARMACISTS

Principal activity: Dispensing medications

Work commitment: Part- and full-time

Preprofessional education: High school diploma

Program length: 5 years

Work prerequisites: B.S. in pharmacy, license

Career opportunities: Good

Income range: $45,000 to $60,000

Scope

The pharmaceutical industry has made dramatic advances in recent decades, developing a wide variety of new drugs to enhance, extend, or even save lives. Once they have been developed, tested, and approved by the U. S. Food and Drug Administration, these medicines must made available to the public. This is the pharmacist's responsibility. While remarkable advances in manufacturing pharmaceuticals has dramatically reduced the need for pharmacists to compound medications, there are new, complex responsibilities associated with dispensing them. Community pharmacists are in the unique position of establishing personal relationships with the people in the neighborhoods they serve.

Activities

Pharmacists must carefully interpret and review prescriptions written by physicians and dentists. They have specialized knowledge of proper dosages, frequency of usage, and drug interactions, and they are qualified to discuss these issues with both doctors and patients. After securing the proper drugs, they must package them properly.

The elderly and young children are the largest consumers of medications. They frequently need guidance on the handling their medications beyond what is written on the label. Pharmacists may tell them what time of day to take a medication or what foods to avoid at the time of taking a medication. Elderly patients frequently take multiple drugs simultaneously, some of which may be incompatible. They may be under the care of several physicians who write prescriptions for them for various different ailments. With a computer, a pharmacist has ready access to a patient's prescription history and can warn the patient about possible drug interactions.

Pharmacists are also in a strategic position to provide advise on self-medication products (nonprescription items) that are used to prevent and treat a variety of common ailments, such as colds, flu, headaches, and muscle pains. They can offer comparative judgments on the effectiveness of medications. Some pharmacists also stock and sell surgical appliances.

While most don't employ full-time pharmacists, many nursing homes and extended-care facilities make arrangements with pharmacists to provide consultation services and various medications for their clients. In this way the institutions can provide for their patients' prescription needs in a reliable manner.

Work Settings

Pharmacists work in a variety of settings. Community pharmacies employ two-thirds of all pharmacists; and 25 percent of pharmacists who work in this venue actually own their own pharmacies. Other work settings are hospital pharmacies, which provide for inpatients and sometimes for outpatients. Hospital pharmacists are also responsible for preparing some special intravenous solutions in bulk and for providing medications and drug information within their institutions. In this setting, pharmacists come into professional contact with physicians, nurses, and nutritionists; therefore, their impact is felt in many parts of the hospital.

Although community and hospital pharmacies employ the majority of pharmacy school graduates, others are employed in the armed forces, V.A. hospitals, the U.S. Public Health Service, and Indian health programs. Positions are also available in pharmaceutical industry laboratories and research firms. Since such specialized work involves research and development, an advanced degree (an M.S., Pharm.D., or Ph.D.) is usually required. Teaching positions are also filled by pharmacists in schools offering such programs.

Advancement

In community and hospital pharmacies, pharmacists can advance to managerial positions. Pharmacists also can establish their own businesses. With an advanced degree (see below), pharmacists can enter administration, teaching, or research activities.

Prerequisites

A high school diploma or its equivalent is needed to apply for admission to an accredited pharmacy program.

Desirable personal attributes include an interest in science in general, and in the healing arts in particular; good communication and people skills; great attention to detail; and good math and business skills.

Education/Training

Currently there are two degree programs in pharmacy: the five-year bachelor of science in pharmacy (B.S. Pharmacy) and the six-year doctor of science in pharmacy (Pharm.D.). While there is a current drive in the United States to move all programs toward the doctoral level, this goal will take some time to achieve, and the overwhelming majority of schools still offer the bachelor's degree program.

The first two years (or prepharmacy phase) of all programs include courses in biology, anatomy, physiology, chemistry (both general and organic), physics, and mathematics. This phase can be completed at a campus branch of a university or at a community college. The professional phase of the program must be taken within a college of pharmacy. Studies there include learning about natural drugs (pharmacognosy), synthetic drugs (medicinal chemistry), the effects of drugs on the body (pharmacology), and the effects of dosage on drug activity (pharmaceutics). Students also study the social, psychological, administrative, and professional aspects of the practice of pharmacy.

Those interested in teaching, administrative work, or laboratory research probably should secure a master's of science (M.S.), doctor of pharmacy (Pharm.D.) or doctor of philosophy (Ph.D.) degree. These degrees require additional study time.

Certification/Registration/Licensure

In order to begin practice, graduates of accredited programs must complete an internship under a licensed community or hospital pharmacist and pass a qualifying examination. Internships usually last one year, although some states now recognize shorter-period "extern-ships" under the supervision of a school of pharmacy.

The exam, which is administered by a state board of pharmacy, takes three days and includes theoretical questions on pharmacy disciplines and a practical examination.

Most states offer reciprocity concerning licensure, which means if you've passed the exam in one state you can set up practice in another. But some states require all pharmacists to pass their own exam before setting up practice.

Career Potential

Since the elderly—who are the largest consumers of pharmaceuticals—constitute the fastest growing segment of the U.S. population, the demand for pharmacists is expected to be strong across the country.

For More Information

The following two organizations can provide useful additional information:

American Pharmaceutical Association
2215 Constitution Avenue NW
Washington DC, 20007
www.aphanet.org/

American Association of Colleges of Pharmacy
1426 Prince Street
Alexandria, Va 22314
www.aapa.org /

For licensure information, you can write to the National Association of Boards of Pharmacy, 200 Busse Highway, Park Ridge, IL 60068.

Colleges and Schools of Pharmacy

Alabama

Auburn University
Auburn University, AL 36849
http://pharmacy.auburn.edu/

Samford University
800 Lakeshore Drive
Birmingham, AL 35229
www.samford.edu/schools/pharmacy.html

Arizona

University of Arizona
College of Pharmacy
P.O. Box 21027
Tucson, AZ 85721
www.pharmacy.arizona.edu/

Arkansas

University of Arkansas for Medical Sciences
4301 West Markham Street
Little Rock, AR 72205
www.uams.edu/cop/default.htm

California

University of California in San Francisco
School of Pharmacy
513 Parnassus Avenue
San Francisco, CA 94143
www.ucsf.edu/campus/SchPhar.html

University of the Pacific
School of Pharmacy
Stockton, CA 95211
www.uop.edu/pharmacy/

University of Southern California
1985 Zonal Avenue
Los Angeles, CA 90089
www.usc.edu/pharmacy/index.html

Colorado

University of Colorado
4200 East 9th Avenue, C238
Denver, CO 80262
www.uchsc.edu/sp/sp

Connecticut

University of Connecticut
P.O. Box U-92
372 Fairfield Road
Storrs, CT 06269
www.ucc.ucon.edu/~wwwpharm/index.html

District of Columbia

Howard University
College of Pharmacy
2300 Fourth Street NW
Washington, DC 20059
www.howard.edu/hupage/schools/pharm.html

Florida

Florida A&M University
College of Pharmacy
P.O. Box 367
Tallahassee, FL 32307
www.famu.edu/dev/collegeofpharmacy.html

University of Florida
College of Pharmacy
Box 100495
Gainesville, FL 32610
http://nervm.nerdc.ufl.edu/~cop28/index.html

Georgia

Mercer University
Southern School of Pharmacy
3001 Mercer University Drive
Atlanta, GA 30341
www.mercer.edu/dean_phm.htm

University of Georgia
College of Pharmacy
Athens, GA 30602
www.rx.uga.edu/

Idaho

Idaho State University
College of Pharmacy
Box 8288
Pocatello, ID 83209
http://pharmacy.isu.edu/welcome.html

Illinois

University of Illinois at Chicago
College of Pharmacy
833 South Wood Street
Chicago, IL 60612
www.uic.edu/depts/pppr

Chicago College of Pharmacy/Midwestern
University
555 31st Street
Downers Grove, IL 60515
www.midwestern.edu/

Indiana

Butler University
College of Pharmacy
4600 Sunset Avenue
Indianapolis, IN 46208
www.butler.edu/www/cophs

Purdue University
School of Pharmacy
1330 Heine Pharmacy Building
West Lafayette, IN 47907
www.pharmacy.purdue.edu/

Iowa

Drake University
College of Pharmacy
2507 University Avenue
Des Moines, IA 50311
www.drake.edu/collegenews/pharm.html

University of Iowa
College of Pharmacy
Iowa City, IA 52242
www.uiowa.edu/~pharmacy/

Kansas

University of Kansas
School of Pharmacy
2056 Malcott Hall
Lawrence, KS 60045
www.pharm.ukans.edu/

Kentucky

University of Kentucky
College of Pharmacy
Rose Street / Pharmacy Building
Lexington, KY 40536
www.uky.edu/Pharmacy/welcome.html

Louisiana

Northeast Louisiana University
College of Pharmacy
700 University Avenue
Monroe, LA 71209
www.nlu.edu/Pharmacy&Health.html

Xavier University of Louisiana
College of Pharmacy
7325 Palmetto Street
New Orleans, LA 70125
www.xula.edu/

Maryland

University of Maryland
School of Pharmacy
20 North Pine Street
Baltimore, MD 21201
www.pharmacy.ab.umd.edu/

Massachusetts

Massachusetts College of Pharmacy and Allied
Health Sciences
179 Longwood Avenue
Boston, MA 02115
www.mcp.edu/

Northeastern University
Bouve College of Pharmacy
360 Huntington Avenue
Boston, MA 02115
www.dac.neu.edu/Units/Bouve/Pharmacy/

Michigan

Ferris State University
College of Pharmacy
220 Ferris Drive
Big Rapids, MI 49307
www.pharmacy.ferris.edu/

University of Michigan
College of Pharmacy
428 Church Street
Ann Arbor, MI 48109
www.umich.edu/!pharmacy/

Wayne State University
College of Pharmacy
105 Shapero Hall
Detroit, MI 48202
http://wizard.pharm.wayne.edu/pharmahp.html

Minnesota

University of Minnesota
College of Pharmacy
5-130 Health Sciences, Unit F
308 Harvard Street SE
Minneapolis, MN 55455
http://pharmacy.hsci.umn.edu/

Mississippi

University of Mississippi
School of Pharmacy
University, MS 339216
www.olemiss.edu/

Missouri

St. Louis College of Pharmacy
4588 Parkview Place
St. Louis, MO 63110
www.stlcop.edu/

University of Missouri–Kansas City
School of Pharmacy
5005 Rockhill Road
Kansas City, MO. 64110
www.umkc.edu/cctr/dept/pharmacy/index.html

Montana

University of Montana
School of Pharmacy & Allied Health Services
Missoula, MT 59812
www.umt.edu/deparmnt/pharm.htm

Nebraska

Creighton University
School of Pharmacy
2500 California Plaza
Omaha, NE 68178
www.creighton.edu/pharm.htm.

University of Nebraska
Medical Center College of Pharmacy
600 South 42nd / Box 98600
Omaha, NE 68198
www.unmc.edu/Pharmacy/college.html

New Jersey

State University of New Jersey–Rutgers
College of Pharmacy
P.O. Box 789
Piscataway, NJ 08855
http://pharmacy.rutgers.edu/

New Mexico

University of New Mexico
College of Pharmacy
2350 Alamo SE
Albuquerque, NM 87106
www.unm.edu/

New York

Long Island University
Arnold & Maria Schwartz College of Pharmacy
75 DeKalb Avenue at University Place
Brooklyn., NY 11201
www.ortge.ufl.edu/gradcat96/dept78.html

St. John's University
College of Pharmacy
8000 Utopia Parkway
Jamaica, NY 11439
www.stjohns.edu/

State University of New York at Buffalo
School of Pharmcy
C126 Cooke-Hochstetter Complex
Buffalo, NY 14260
www.buffalo.edu/

North Carolina

Campbell University
School of Pharmacy
P.O. Box 1090
Buies Creek, NC 27506
www.campbell.edu/~pharmacy/cuhome.html

University of North Carolina
School of Pharmacy
CB # 7360 Beard Hall
Chapel Hill, NC 27599
http://sunsite.unc.edu/pharmacy/
pharmacy.html

North Dakota

North Dakota State University
College of Pharmacy
P.O. Box 5055
Fargo, ND 58105
www.ndsu.nodak.edu/

Ohio

Ohio Northern University
College of Pharmacy
Ada, OH 45810
www.onu.edu/Pharmacy/

Ohio State University
College of Pharmacy
500 West 12th Avenue
Columbus, OH 43210
www.acs.ohio-state.edu/

University of Cincinnati Medical Center
College of Pharmacy
Mail Location #4, P.O. Box 67004
Cincinnati, OH 45267
www.ucmc.edu/

University of Toledo
College of Pharmacy
2801 West Bancroft Street
Toledo, OH 43606
www.utoledo.edu/

Oklahoma

Southwestern Oklahoma State University
School of Pharmacy
100 Campus Drive
Weatherford, OK 73096
www.swosu.edu/

University of Oklahoma
College of Pharmacy
P.O. Box 26901
Oklahoma City, OK 73190
www.cpb.uokhsc.edu/

Oregon

Oregon State University
College of Pharmacy
203 Pharmacy Building
Corvallis, OR 97331
http://osu.orst.edu/dept/cop

Pennsylvania

Duquesne University
Mylan School of Pharmacy
Pittsburgh, PA 15282
www.duquesne.edu/pharmacy/
PHARMACY.html

Philadelphia College of Pharmacy and Science
600 South 43rd Street
Philadelphia, PA 19104
www.pcps.edu/

University of Pittsburgh
School of Pharmacy
1106 Salk Hall
Pittsburgh, PA 15261
http://info.pitt.edu/~rxschool/

Temple University
School of Pharmacy
3307 North Broad Street
Philadelphia, PA 19140
www.temple.edu/departments/pharmacy/

Rhode Island

University of Rhode Island
College of Pharmacy
Kingston, RI 02881
www.uri.edu/pharm/

South Carolina

Medical University of South Carolina
College of Pharmacy
171 Ashley Avenue
Charleston, SC 29425
www.musc.edu/pharmacy/

University of South Carolina
College of Pharmacy
Five Richland Medical Park
Columbia, SC 29203
http://pharmwww.biol.sc.edu/index.html

South Dakota

South Dakota State University
College of Pharmacy
Box 2202 C
Brookings, SD 57007
www.sdstate.edu/

Tennessee

University of Tennessee
College of Pharmacy
847 Monroe Avenue, Suite 238
Memphis, TN 38163
www.utmem.edu/pharm/pharm.html

Texas

Texas Southern University
College of Pharmacy
3100 Cleburne Street
Houston, TX 77004
www.tsu.edu/Homepages/Pharmacy
index.html

University of Houston
College of Pharmacy
4800 Calhoun Boulevard
Houston, TX 77204
www.pharmacy.uh.edu/

University of Texas
College of Pharmacy
Austin, TX 78712
http://saklad.uthscsa.edu/

Utah

University of Utah
College of Pharmacy
201 Skaggs Hall
25 South Medical Drive
Salt Lake City, UT 84112
www.pharm.utah.edu/

Virginia

Virginia Commonwealth University
School of Pharmacy
MCV, P.O. Box 581
410 North 12th Street
Richmond, VA 23298
http://views.vcu.edu/pharmacy/

Washington

University of Washington
School of Pharmacy
P.O. Box 357631
Seattle, WA 98195
www.u.washington.edu/

Washington State University
College of Pharmacy
Pullman, WA 99164
www.wsu.edu:8080/~pharmacy/
pharmacy.html

West Virginia

West Virginia University
School of Pharmacy
P.O. Box 9500
Morgantown, WV 26506
www.hsc.wvu.edu/sop/index.html

Wisconsin

University of Wisconsin
School of Pharmacy
425 North Charter Street
Madison, WI 53706
www.wisc.edu/pharmacy

Wyoming

University of Wyoming
School of Pharmacy
P.O. Box 3375
Laramie, WY 82071
www.uwyo.edu/hs/pharmacy/pharmacy/htm

PHYSICIAN ASSISTANTS

Principal activity: Carrying out specific medical duties under a physician's supervision

Work commitment: Usually full-time

Preprofessional education: 2-year college-level program

Program length: 2 years

Work prerequisites: PA program, certificate, or degree

Career opportunities: Excellent

Income range: $40,000 to $70,000

Scope

Physician assistants (PAs) carry out diagnostic and treatment tasks that are assigned and supervised by physicians. These responsibilities must be consistent with the state's law. They perform many of the routine jobs previously handled by family or primary care physicians. Studies have shown that a significant number of patients visiting such doctors can be successfully cared for by physician assistants. PAs thus allow physicians to apply their knowledge and skills to more complex cases. PAs may work in consultation with physicians or may be of direct personal assistance.

Activities

PAs are involved in a wide variety of activities. These may include taking initial medical histories, performing physical examinations, ordering common laboratory tests, and arriving at preliminary diagnoses. PAs may also be involved in treating medical emergencies such as bruises, cuts, and minor burns. They may handle certain phases of pre- and post-operative patient care. When working for various specialists, PAs may administer injections, suture wounds, or apply casts.

Work Settings

With the wide acceptance of physician assistants by the medical community today, positions are available in hospitals, HMOs, clinics, and physicians' offices.

Advancement

By obtaining additional education and experience, PAs can secure more prestigious appointments with larger facilities. Additional specialized education can qualify them to become involved in specialty work.

Prerequisites

PA programs offer certificates or degrees (associate, bachelor's, or master's) upon completion of a prescribed course of studies. The prerequisites are determined by the nature of the program. To apply for admission to a four-year program, a candidate must have a high school diploma or its equivalent. Those seeking to enter two-year programs should have at least two years of college or already have a bachelor's degree. They should also have been involved in health-care work for several years.

Desirable personal attributes for work in this field include a logical thinking style, a strong sense of compassion, an ability to use good judgment, a willingness to follow instructions, and the ability to work well under and with others. Competition for admission to PA programs is intense. Thus, interested individuals should strive to earn good high school and college grades.

Education/Training

Most PA programs last two years. The educational program is divided into two parts. The first lasts 6 to 12 months and covers basic and advanced clinical sciences, including courses in anatomy, physiology, biochemistry, pharmacology, pathology, microbiology, physical diagnosis, radiology, and electrocardiography. The second part of the program lasts 9 to 15 months and includes clinical rotations and preceptorships in a variety of clinical disciplines, at hospitals, clinics, and physician's offices, with the most emphasis given to primary care.

Certification/Registration/Licensure

PA activities are regulated by individual states, and their requirements vary. In most states PAs must be certified by the National Commission on Certification of Physician Assistants. After completing an accredited program, candidates must pass an exam of written and skills assessment components. Those passing these tests are Physician Assistant-Certified. To retain this status, they must take at least 100 hours of continuing medical education every two years and retake the certification exam every six years.

Career Potential

Employment outlook for PAs is excellent as physicians and patients have become convinced they are effective health-care providers. Today, thousands of PAs are working throughout the United States, and a near 50-percent increase can be expected over the next decade.

For More Information

The professional organization for PAs is the American Academy of Physician Assistants, 950 North Washington Street, Alexandria, VA 22314.

For certification information, contact the National Commission on Certification of Physician Assistants, 6849-B2 Peachtree Road, Atlanta, GA 30320.

Physician Assistant Programs

California

Charles R Drew University of Medicine and Science
College of Allied Health
1621 East 120th Street
Los Angeles, CA 90059
www.cdrew.edu/

University of Southern California
School of Medicine
1975 Zonal Avenue, KAM B-29
Los Angeles, CA 90033
www.usc.edu/

Western University of Health Sciences
College Plaza
309 East Second Avenue
Pomona, CA 91766
www.westernu.edu/

University of California–Davis
Medical Center
Department of Family Practice
2525 Stockton Blvd., Suite 1025
Sacramento, CA 95817
www.ucdavis.edu/

Stanford University/Foothill College
School of Medicine
703 Welch Road, Suite F-1
Palo Alto, CA 94304
www.stanford.edu/

Colorado

University of Colorado School of Medicine
Box C-219
4200 East 9th Avenue
Denver, CO 80262
www.uchs.edu/

Connecticut

Yale University School of Medicine
47 College St., Suite 220
New Haven, CT 06510
www.yale.edu/

District of Columbia

George Washington University
2175 K Street NW, Suite 820
Washington, DC 20037
www.gwu.edu/

Howard University
College of Allied Health Sciences
Sixth Avenue & Bryant Street, Annex I
Washington, DC 20059
www.howard.edu/

Florida

University of Florida
Box 100176
Gainesville, FL 32610
www.ufl.edu/

Georgia

Emory University
School of Medicine
1462 Clifton Road NE, Suite 280
Atlanta, GA 30322
www.emory.edu/

Medical College of Georgia
Physician Assistant Department (B)
Kelly Administration Building 170
Augusta, GA 30912
www.mcg.edu/

Illinois

Cook County Hospital/Malcolm X College
1900 West Van Buren Street, Suite 3241
Chicago, IL 60612
www.ccc.edu/malcolmx/home.htm

Iowa

University of Iowa College of Medicine
5167 Westlawn
Iowa City, IA 52242
www.uiowa.edu/

University of Osteopathic Medicine
& Health Sciences
3200 Grand Avenue
Des Moines, IA 50312
www.uomhs.edu/

Kansas

Wichita State University
College of Health Professions
Campus Box 43
Wichita, KS 67260
www.twsu.edu/

Kentucky

University of Kentucky
PA Program
121 Washington Ave., Room 118
Lexington, KY 40536
www.uky.edu/

Maryland

Essex Community College
7201 Rossville Boulevard
Baltimore, MD 21237
www.essex.cc.md.us/

Massachusetts

Northeastern University
202 Robinson Hall
Boston, MA 02115
www.neu.edu/

Michigan

University of Detroit Mercy
8200 West Outer Drive
P.O. Box 19900
Detroit, MI 48219
www.udmercy.edu/

Western Michigan University
Kalamazoo, MI 49008
www.wmich.edu/

Missouri

Saint Louis University
School of Allied Health Professions
3437 Caroline Street
St. Louis, MO 63104
www.slu.edu/

Nebraska

University of Nebraska Medical Center
600 South 42nd Street
P.O. Box 984300
Omaha, NE 68198
www.unmc.edu/

New Jersey

University of Medicine & Dentistry of New
Jersey
R. Wood Johnson Medical School
675 Hoes Lane
Piscataway, NJ 08854
www.umdnj.edu/

New York

Albany-Hudson Valley Medical College
47 New Scotland Avenue
Albany, NY 12208
www.amc.edu/

The Brooklyn Hospital Center/Long Island
University
121 DeKalb Avenue
Brooklyn, NY 11201
www.liunet.edu/

Touro College of Health Sciences
27-33 West 23rd Street
New York, NY 11756
www.touro.edu/

CUNY Harlem Hospital Center
506 Lennox Avenue WP-Rm 619
New York, NY 10037
www.uhfnyc.org/

Bayley Seton Hospital
75 Vanderbilt Avenue
Staten Island, NY 10304
www.schsi.org/residency/physicians.html

HSC, The University at Stony Brook
School of Health Technology & Management
HSCL 2-052
Stony Brook, NY 11794
www.informatics.sunysb.edu/

State University of New York
Health Science Center at Brooklyn
450 Clarkson Avenue, Box 1222
Brooklyn, NY 11234
www.hscbklyn.edu/

North Carolina

Duke University Medical Center
P.O. Box 3848
Durham, NC 27710
www.duke.edu/

Wake Forest University School of Medicine
Medical Center Blvd.
Winston-Salem, NC 27157
www.wfu.edu/

North Dakota

University of North Dakota School of Medicine
Department of Community Medicine
501 North Columbia Road
P.O. Box 9037
Grand Forks, ND 58203
www.und.nodak.edu/

Ohio

Kettering College of Medical Arts
3737 Southern Boulevard
Kettering, OH 45429
www.ketthealth.com/kcma/

Cuyahoga Community College
PA Program
1100 Pleasant Valley Road
Parma, OH 44130
www.tri-c.cc.oh.us/

Oklahoma

University of Oklahoma
Health Sciences Center
P.O. Box 26901
Oklahoma City, OK 73190
www.ou.edu/

Pennsylvania

Gannon University
109 University Square
Erie, PA 16541
www.gannon.edu/

Saint Francis College
P.O. Box 600
Loretto, PA 15940
www.sfcpa.edu/

Hahnemann University
School of Health Professions
Broad & Vine Sts., Mail Stop 504
Philadelphia, Pa. 19102
www.mcphu.edu/

King's College
133 North River Street
Wilkes-Barre, PA 18711
www.kings.edu/

Tennessee

Trevecca Nazarene College
333 Murfreesboro Road
Nashville, TN 37210
www.trevecca.edu/

Texas

Southwestern Medical Center
University of Texas
6011 Harry Hines Boulevard
Dallas, TX 75235
www.utexas.edu/

University of Texas Medical Branch
School of Allied Services
301 University Blvd.
Galveston, TX 77550
www.sahs.utmb.edu/sahs/
physician_assistant_studies/

Baylor College of Medicine
Department of Community Medicine
One Baylor Plaza, Room 633E
Houston, TX 77030
www.bcm.tmc.edu/

Utah

University of Utah School of Medicine
50 North Medical Drive
Building 528
Salt Lake City, UT 84132
www.utah.edu/

Washington

University of Washington
Medex Northwest Physician Assistant Program
4245 Roosevelt Way NE
Seattle, WA 98105
www.washington.edu/

West Virginia

Alderson-Broaddus College
P.O. Box 578, College Hill
Philippi, WV 26416
http://ab.edu/

Wisconsin

University of Wisconsin–Madison
Medical Sciences Center, Room 1050
1300 University Avenue
Madison, WI 53706
www.wisc.edu/

Uniformed Services

U.S. Air Force
3790 MSTW/MSM
Sheppard AFB, TX 76311
www.sheppard.af.mil/

Interservice PA Program
Academy of Health Sciences
ATTN: MCCS-HMP (PA Branch)
3151 Scott Road
Fort Sam Houston, TX 78234
(210) 221-8004

Naval School of Health Sciences
8901 Wisconsin Ave.
Bethesda, MD 20889
http://nshs.med.navy.mil/

SURGEON ASSISTANTS

Principal activity: Assisting surgeons in various settings

Work commitment: Usually full-time

Preprofessional education: 2-year college-level program

Program length: 2 years

Work prerequisites: PA certification

Career opportunities: Favorable

Income range: $30,000 to $50,000

Scope

Surgeon assistants (SAs) are physician assistants with specialized training that qualifies them to work for and under the supervision of surgeons. SAs make up about 15 percent of all physician assistants and are usually identified as PAs.

The scope of their activities is determined by their training, the arrangement they have with their supervising surgeons, and the limitations imposed by state law. The basic responsibilities of the job include securing preliminary information from patients and assisting surgeons in providing therapy to patients.

Activities

Commonly, SAs secure patients' medical histories, carry out physical examinations, and perform (or order) standard laboratory tests. They then organize the data and make a preliminary interpretation to present to the surgeon. SAs also perform preoperative procedures, assist during surgery, and participate in patients' postoperative care. SAs may also treat minor injuries under a surgeon's guidance.

Work Settings

The SA's usual work setting is a surgical office, hospital, or clinic. In hospitals, they may work in the operating, recovery, or emergency rooms and in outpatient clinics.

Prerequisites

The prerequisites for SA training programs range from a high school diploma to certification as a physician assistant.

Desirable personal attributes for this profession include a pleasant personality, good oral and writing skills, the ability to make sound decisions under pressure, manual dexterity, and the capacity to work well with and under others.

Education/Training

There are three ways to secure training as an SA:

1. Those who have completed a physician assistant training program and have been certified can secure on-the-job training with a surgeon or at a hospital surgical service. Such training may last 3 to 6 months.

2. Those who have completed the prerequisites—namely, two years of basic science college work—should seek admission to a PA program. Once they have completed the program and been certified, they can get specialized training at a postgraduate program for surgeon assistants or with a sugeon or hospital.

3. Candidates can seek admission directly into one of several accredited SA programs (see below). Like PA programs, these require two years of basic science work. These programs are divided into didactic and clinical segments. The focus of the curriculum is to provide the clinical and technical skills relevant to surgical care in addition to basic medical training. The programs provide exposure to both general and specialized surgery and to emergency room traumatic surgery.

A certificate is awarded upon completion of any SA program. The competition for places in these SA programs is intense.

Certification/Registration/Licensure

Currently, there is no specific certification as an SA, but one may apply for certification as a physician assistant.

Career Potential

The need for SAs is growing as the demand for surgical services increases. With the changes currently taking place in health care, SAs should be readily integrated into the personnel needed by HMOs.

For More Information

The professional organization for SAs is the American Academy of Physician Assistants, 950 North Washington Street, Alexandria, VA 22314

Surgeon Assistant Programs

Alabama

University of Alabama at Birmingham
School of Health Related Professions
Webb Building Room 407
Birmingham, AL 35294
www.uab.edu/

New York

Cornell University Medical College
1300 New York Avenue
New York, NY 10021
www.cornell.edu/

Ohio

Cuyahoga Community College
11000 Pleasant Valley Road
Parma, OH 44130
www.tri-c.cc.oh.us/

Adjunctive Health Careers
Technologists, Technicians, and Assistants

Physicians, dentists, and other diagnosing and treating practitioners are assisted in their work by a wide variety of technologists, technicians, and assistants. These health-care workers provide invaluable service, performing complex laboratory tests and analyses, operating sophisticated equipment to monitor patients, and handling many routine duties. These people both directly or indirectly help save lives, ease pain, and improve patients' quality of life. Their activities are indispensable in maintaining an effective health-care system.

Most of the professions discussed in this chapter require an associate degree, while others need only about one year of training. A few even provide on-the-job training experience that counts toward qualification.

The 33 careers discussed here are quite varied, not only in the amount of education or training required, but also in terms of duties and responsibilities. Some careers are hospital-based, while others are based mainly in office or clinic settings. Some are devoted solely to patient care, be it physical or mental, while others are exclusively diagnostic in nature. Thus, a wide range of options is available to those prepared to invest several months to a few years in training.

ANESTHESIOLOGIST ASSISTANTS

Principal activity: Assisting anesthesiologists during surgery

Work commitment: Full-time

Preprofessional education: Bachelor's degree

Program length: 2 years

Work prerequisites: Master's degree, certification

Career opportunities: Relatively favorable, but uncertain

Income range: $55,000 to $75,000

Scope

Anesthesiologists' assistants (AAs) belong to a relatively new health-care profession that is not as yet widely known. They are members of a surgical team, working under a physician's supervision to administer anesthesia to patients. A formal training program in this field was initiated in the mid-1970s. Individuals with a strong interest in medicine will find this position both challenging and rewarding, intellectually and financially. This field is suitable for both men and women.

Activities

Principally AAs are involved in maintaining patients under anesthesia and monitoring vital signs during operations. The anesthesiologist, who is the AA's immediate supervisor, usually is available somewhere on the floor or in the hospital to provide guidance. The AA is present when the anesthesiologist induces sleep at the onset of surgery and also at the completion of the operation. AAs also help the anesthesiologist review medical and surgical data prior to procedures.

Work Settings

Obviously, most AAs work in the operating and recovery rooms of hospitals, but they may also be involved in pre-anesthetic evaluation of patients on the other floors. They also may find employment in clinics and outpatient surgical facilities. AAs are eligible to work in all states that permit the use of physician assistants, since they are considered specialist practitioners in that field. Currently most AAs are employed in Ohio and Georgia, since the two training programs for such personnel are located there.

Advancement

An anesthesiologist assistant who enjoys the work and has the academic potential, resources, and personal opportunity to do so may consider applying to medical school and becoming a physician.

Prerequisites

A college degree with a premedical, biology, or chemistry major is recommended. Applicants with backgrounds in other allied health fields such as nursing, medical technology, or respiratory therapy are also considered. Thus, some AA applicants may be just out of college, while others will have worked in a health-care field for some time.

Desirable personal attributes for those entering this field include a superior ability in science, an ability to function well under stress, and the capacity to assume enormous personal responsibilities.

Education/Training

The AA training program lasts two years and leads to a master's degree. The emphasis is on basic science studies in such areas as anatomy, physiology, and pharmacology, followed by clinical experience in various aspects of anesthesiology.

Certification/Registration/Licensure

A certification examination is given by the National Commission on the Certification of Anesthesiologist Assistants.

Career Potential

Current AA graduates are in high demand and receive attractive starting salaries. Future needs are uncertain and will depend on how widely this profession gains acceptance. The field also will depend on the impact of managed health care, where the use of AAs can lower costs. Some of those entering this field may wish to go on to medical school and eventually become anesthesiologists.

For More Information

The professional organization for this field is the American Academy of Anesthesiologist Assistants, P.O. Box 81362, Wellesley, MA 02481.

For certification information, contact the National Commission for Certification of Anesthesiologist Assistants, P.O. Box 15519, Atlanta, GA 30333.

Anesthesiology Assistant Programs

Georgia

Emory University
617 Woodruff Memorial Building
Atlanta, GA 30322
www.emory.edu

Ohio

University Hospitals of Cleveland
11100 Euclid
Cleveland, OH 44106
www.uhrad.com

BLOOD BANK TECHNOLOGISTS AND SPECIALISTS

Principal activity: Securing and processing donated blood for transfusions

Work commitment: Full-time

Preprofessional education: Bachelor's degree and certification as a medical technologist

Program length: 1 year for technologist; 2 years for specialist

Work prerequisites: Completion of accredited blood bank technology program

Career opportunities: Average

Income range: $35,000 to $45,000

Scope

Although the first human blood transfusion occurred in the early 1800s, reliable success with this life-saving technique was not assured until 1900. Then it was discovered that both the red blood cells and plasma of the donor must be compatible with those of the recipient. Over the years, blood transfusion has become a sophisticated technological activity. Blood bank technologists draw, process, and store blood that is used for accident victims, patients undergoing surgery, and those with chronic blood diseases such as hemophilia and leukemia.

Currently there are two kinds of personnel in this field: blood bank technologists and specialists in blood bank technology, and both are discussed in this section.

Activities

Blood bank technologists draw, process, test, type, and store donated blood. Those who acquire special education to become *specialists in blood bank technology* may be called upon to serve as administrators and educators, technical consultants, and researchers. Their special skills help them select appropriate donors, carry out pretransfusion testing, and detect possible dangerous blood conditions.

Work Settings

Blood bank technologists are employed by medical centers and hospitals, as well as by community blood bank transfusion services, private laboratories, and blood banks.

Advancement

With experience, a blood bank technologist can assume supervisory responsibilities over other personnel or be appointed to administrative control over the operations of a facility.

This is most likely for specialists in blood bank technology, since they have more education and training.

Prerequisites

There are two common routes to accredited programs in blood bank technology:

- being a certified medical technologist with bachelor's degree;

- having a bachelor's degree with a major in the biological or physical sciences plus one year of full-time clinical laboratory experience.

Desirable personal attributes include meticulous work habits, dependability, and the capacity to work under stress.

Education/Training

One-year accredited programs in blood bank technology are offered by many hospital and community blood banks, the American Red Cross, and many universities. These programs involve courses and training in immunology, genetics, serology, physiology, transfusion practices, and laboratory operations. In addition, students receive practical experience in a blood bank setting and training in immunohema/biological concepts. Some programs offer a master's degree, which makes one eligible to apply for certification as a specialist in blood bank technology.

Certification/Registration/Licensure

Certification in this field is offered by the American Society of Clinical Pathologists in conjunction with the American Association of Blood Banks.

Eligible candidates must satisfactorily complete a written generalist examination. Those passing are designated certified blood bank technologists (BB-ASCP).

Those with this designation who also have five years of experience or a master's or doctorate degree in immunohematology (or a related field) may take a more advanced examination to become a certified specialist in blood bank technology (SBB-ASCP).

Career Potential

Presently the demands for personnel in this field exceed the number of job candidates. However, most experts expect this imbalance to become stabilized in the next decade.

For More Information

The professional organization for the field is the American Society of Clinical Pathologists, P.O. Box 12277, Chicago, IL 60612.

Additional information can be secured from the American Association of Blood Banks, 8101 Glenbrook Road, Bethesda, MD 20814.

For certification or registration information, contact the Board of Registry, P.O. Box 12270, Chicago, IL 60612

Blood Bank Technologist/Specialist Programs

Alabama

University of Alabama at Birmingham
SBB Program
1714 9th Avenue, South
Birmingham, AL 35294
www.uab.edu/

California

Sacramento Medical Foundation
Specialist in Blood Banking Technology
1625 Stockton Blvd.
Sacramento, CA 95816
www.smfbc.org/

District of Columbia

U.S. Army Blood Bank Fellowship Program
Walter Reed Army Medical Center
6825 16th Street, NW
Washington, DC 20307
http://208.240.92.81.docs.

Florida

Central Florida Blood Bank, Inc.
32 W Gore Street
Orlando, FL 32806
www.cfbb.org/

Transfusion Medicine Academic Center
Florida Blood Services
Specialist in Blood Banking Program
445 31st Street North
St. Petersburg, FL 33713
www.fbsblood.org/

Georgia

American Red Cross Blood Services
Atlanta Specialist in Blood Bank Technology
Program
1925 Monroe Drive NE
Atlanta, GA 30030
www.redcross.org/atlanta/

Illinois

University of Illinois at Chicago
School of Biomedical & Health Information
Sciences
1919 W. Taylor St., Room 266
AHBP, MC 530
Chicago, IL 60612
www.bvis.uic.edu/

Louisiana

Medical Center of Louisiana
Charity Hospital
1532 Tulane Avenue
New Orleans, LA 70112
www.charity.trauma.com/

Maryland

Johns Hopkins Hospital SBB
Carnegie Building #667
600 North Wolfe Street
Baltimore, MD 21287
www.med.jhu.edu/

NIH Clinical Center Blood Bank
Specialist in BB Technology Program
NIH/CC/DTM, Building 10/1C711
10 Center Drive MSC 1184
Bethesda, MD 20892
www.nih.gov/

Massachusetts

Beth Israel Deaconess Medical Center
West Campus SBB Training Center
One Deaconess Road
Boston, MA 02215
www.bimdc.harvard.edu/

Ohio

The Ohio State University Medical Center
Blood Bank and American Red Cross
Blood Services-Central Ohio Region
995 East Broad Street
Columbus, OH 43205
www.med.ohio-state.edu/

American Red Cross Blood Services
Northern Ohio Region
3747 Euclid Avenue
Cleveland, OH 44115
www.arc-cleveland.org/

Hoxworth Blood Center
3130 Highland Avenue
P.O. Box 670055
Cincinnati, OH 45267
www.hoxworth.org/

Texas

Gulf Coast Regional Blood Center
100 La Concha Lane
Houston, TX 77054
www.giveblood.org/

University of Texas Southwestern Medical
Center
Blood Bank Technology Program
5323 Harry Hines Blvd.
Dallas, TX 75235
www.swmed.edu/

University of Texas Medical Branch
UTMB SBB Program
301 University Blvd.
Galveston, TX 77555
www.utmb.edu/

Wisconsin

The Blood Center of Southeast Wisconsin
638 North 18th Street
P.O. Box 2178
Milwaukee, WI 53201
www.cgschmidt.com/healthcare.htm/

CARDIOVASCULAR TECHNOLOGY PERSONNEL

Principal activity: Carrying out noninvasive and invasive cardiovascular procedures

Work commitment: Full time

Preprofessional education: High school diploma or equivalent

Program length: Usually on-the-job training (8 to 16 weeks)

Work prerequisites: Experience and/or schooling

Career opportunities: For technicians, below average; for specialists, higher

Income range: $20,000 to $35,000
  EKG technicians: $20,000 (average)
  Echocardiographers: $23,000 (average)
  Catheterization technologists: $30,000 (average)

Scope

Workers in this field record heart and circulatory function. They are also known as electrocardiograph (EKG) technicians and technologists. There are a number of specialized areas in this field, which includes the use of both noninvasive and invasive procedures.

Activities

Cardiovascular Technicians

Cardiovascular technicians are entry-level workers who usually perform their duties at a cardiologist's office or at a hospitalized patient's bedside. They use an EKG machine to detect and trace graphically the electrical impulses transmitted by the heart musculature. This instrument records the minute electrical changes taking place during and between the contractions of the heart chambers. The EKG technician readies the equipment, explains to the patient what the test procedure involves (i.e., attaching leads to appropriate body sites), and then makes a recording at various monitoring positions. The resulting cardiogram is used by the physician as a diagnostic indicator of the heart and circulatory system's state of health. Doctors routinely order EKGs before any significant surgery, upon hospitalization, as part of annual physical check-ups, and when monitoring patients with suspected or established cardiac or cardiovascular problems.

Specialized (Noninvasive) Cardiovascular Technicians

This category includes a variety of skilled EKG technicians who perform more sophisticated tests, including holter monitoring and stress testing. A *holter monitor* is a portable EKG unit that records electrical heart activity over an extended period (usually 24 hours). The technician fits the patient with the unit by placing the leads on designated sites on the chest and attaching the recording monitor to a belt around the patient's waist. When the patient returns in a day or so, the technician removes the cassette tape from the chest and either sends it out for analysis or places it in a scanner. After checking the tape's quality, the technician prints out the information from the tape so it can be evaluated by the cardiologist who ordered the test. For a *stress test*, the technician records a continuous EKG for a patient prior to and during treadmill exercise. This monitors and records the impact of increased exertion on the patient's heart function.

Other technicians who have special skills using ultrasound equipment such as echocardiographs, vectocardiographs, and cardiac Doppler units may devote all of their professional time to operating this equipment.

Cardiovascular Technologists

Cardiovascular technologists are involved in invasive studies of the heart. They work in coronary care or surgical intensive care units of hospitals, to assist physicians in introducing various dyes, probes, or catheters into patients' hearts or legs. This is done to determine if a blockage exists or for other diagnostic purposes. Such technologists may assist cardiac surgeons during angioplasties (balloon procedures performed to open clogged arteries) or when they insert pacemakers under the chest wall to help the heart maintain a normal rhythm of contraction.

Work Settings

Cardiovascular procedures that are noninvasive are carried out in cardiologists' offices as well as in hospitals. Invasive procedures are almost always hospital-based activities.

Advancement

With additional training and experience a cardiovascular technician can become a technologist and perhaps assume supervisory responsibilities. EKG technicians can attend school on a part-time basis and become technologists.

Prerequisites

A high school diploma or its equivalent is the essential starting point for securing a position in this field.

Desirable personal attributes for the field include manual dexterity, the ability to follow detailed instructions, dependability, and a pleasant and reassuring personality.

Education/Training

On-the-job training is the usual route to becoming an EKG technician. This training typically is given over a 6- to 16-week period by an EKG supervisor or cardiologist. Most hospitals prefer to train their own active hospital personnel. Many vocational-technical schools, junior and community colleges, and hospitals offer formal training programs. Programs for EKG technicians usually last one semester.

Prospective EKG technologists may secure on-the-job training (for one or two years), but they can also attend a formal program that usually lasts two years. In the latter case, the first year is devoted to academic instruction and the second to specialized training in noninvasive and invasive technology. Colleges award associate degrees to those who complete the program. Some qualified allied health personnel may receive credit for prior studies and thus shorten their training time.

Certification/Registration/Licensure

There is an accreditation process for this field, although it is not yet common. For further information, contact the Cardiovascular Credential International, 4456 Corporation Lane, Virginia Beach, VA 23463.

Career Potential

Employment opportunities for cardiovascular personnel are expected to grow more slowly than other fields over the next decade. This is due to the emphasis on cost containment by health benefits providers. Opportunities for skilled technicians and technologists are expected to be more favorable than those for EKG technicians trained only in routine cardiography.

For More Information

The professional organizations in this field are listed below:

Alliance of Cardiovascular Professionals, 910 Charles Street, Fredericksburg, VA 22401

Society of Vascular Technology, 401 President Drive, Lanham, MD 20706

American Society of Echocardiography, 4101 Lake Boone Trail, Raleigh, NC 27607

Cardiovascular Technologist Programs

Alabama

Community College of the AF/AYH
130 West Maxwell Boulevard
Maxwell AFB, AL 36122
www.maxwell.af.mil/

California

Grossmont College
8800 Grossmont College Drive
El Cajon, CA 92020
www.gccd.cc.ca.us/grossmont

Florida

Edison Community College
8099 College Parkway SW
P.O. Box 60210
Ft. Myers, FL 33906
www.edison.edu/

National School of Technology
16150 NE 17th Avenue
N Miami Beach, FL 33162
www.national-school-tech.edu/

Santa Fe Community College
3000 NW 83rd Street
Gainesville, FL 32606
http://santefe.cc.fl.us/

St. Joseph Hospital
3001 West Drive MLK Boulevard
Tampa, FL 33677
(813) 870-252

Ultrasound Diagnostic School
9950 Princess Palm Ave., Suite 120
Tampa, FL 33619
(813) 621-0072

Georgia

University Hospital / Georgia Heart Institute
Cardiovascular Technologist Program
1350 Walton Way
Augusta, GA 30901
www.augusta.tec.ga.us/

Illinois

Career Academy, Inc.
5 South Wabash Avenue, Suite 1505
Chicago, IL 60603
www.itt.edu/

Maine

Southern Maine Technical College
Fort Road
South Portland, ME 04106
www.ctech.smtc.tec.me.us/

Maryland

Howard Community College
10901 Little Patuxent Parkway
Columbia, MD 21044
www.howard.cc.edu/

Naval School of Health Sciences
8901 Wisconsin Ave.
Bethesda, MD 20889
http://nshs.med.navy.mil/

Massachusetts

Northeastern University
360 Huntington Avenue
Boston, MA 02116
www.northeastern.edu/

Michigan

Oakland Community College
7350 Cooley Lake Road
Waterford, MI 48237
www.occ.cc.mi.us/

Minnesota

Northwest Technical College–East Grand Forks
2022 Central Avenue UW
East Grand Forks, MN 56721
www.ntc-online.com/

New Jersey

Morristown Memorial Hospital
100 Madison Avenue
Morristown, NJ 07962
www.atlantichealth.org/hospitals/morristown/

University of Medicine & Dentistry of New Jersey
150 Bergen Street, D–447
Newark, NJ 07107
www.umdnj.edu/

New York

Mollow College
1000 Hempstead Avenue
Rockville Centre, NY 11571
222.molloy.edu/

Rochester General Hospital
1425 Portland Avenue
Rochester, NY 14621
http://arpc.com/rgh/

Ohio

Cuyahoga Community College
11000 Pleasant Valley Road
Parma, OH 44130
www.tri-c.cc.oh.us/

University of Toledo
Community and Technical College
2801 West Bancroft Street
Toledo, OH 43606
www.sp.utoledo.edu/index.htm/

Pennsylvania

American Center of Technical Arts & Sciences
1930 Chestnut Street, 1st Floor
Philadelphia, PA 19103
www.cts.com/

Geisinger Medical Center
Pennsylvania State University
100 North Academy Avenue
Danville, PA 17822
www.geisinger/edu

Eastern College
10 Fairview Drive
St. Davids, PA 19087
www.eastern.edu/

Gwynedd-Mercy College
Sumneytown Pike
Gwynedd Valley, PA 19437
www.gmc.edu/

Lancaster Institute for Health Education
555 North Duke Street
P.O. Box 3555
Lancaster, PA 17604
www.lha.org/lha-institute.html/

South Dakota

Southeast Technical Institute
Cardiovascular Technology Program
2301 Career Place
Sioux Falls, SD 57107
http://sti.tec.sd.us/

Texas

El Centro College
Main & Lamar Streets
Dallas, TX 75202
www.ecc.dcccd.edu/

Houston Community College
3100 Shenandoah
Houston, TX 77021
www.hccs.cc.tx.us/

Advanced Health Education Center
8502 Tybor Street
Houston, TX 77074
www.aheconline.com/

Virginia

Sentara Norfolk General Hospital
600 Gresham Drive
Norfolk, VA 23507
www.sentara.com/hospitals/sngh/sngh.html/

Washington

Spokane Community College
Cardiovascular Technology Program
North 1810 Green Street
Spokane, WA 99207
www.scc.spokane.cc.wa.us/

Canada

British Columbia Institute of Technology
3700 Willingdon Avenue
Burnaby, British Columbia
Canada V5G 3H2
www.bcit.bc.ca/~sohs/programs.htm

Burwin Institute
P O Box 1029
Lunenburg, Nova Scotia
Canada BOJ 2CO
www.burwin.com/

Career Canada College
385 Yonge Street
Toronto, Ontario
Canada M5B 1S1
www.careercanadacollege.com/

CLINICAL LABORATORY TECHNICIANS

Principal activity: Carrying out clinical tests ordered by physicians

Work commitment: Usually full-time

Preprofessional education: High school diploma

Program length: 2 years

Work prerequisites: Associate degree or certificate and certification

Career opportunities: Favorable

Income range: $20,000 to $33,000

   Phlebotomists: $18,000 (average)

Scope

In their office practices and while making hospital rounds, physicians order many different types of laboratory tests. These tests are used to determine a patient's state of health, for diagnostic purposes, and for determining treatment outcomes. In an average major hospital, these tests can number more than 2 million in a year. That's why clinical laboratory technicians, also known as medical laboratory technicians, are employed in such large numbers. They work under the supervision of certified laboratory technologists in a variety of settings to perform the thousands of lab tests required to treat patients.

Activities

Medical laboratory technicians perform the less complex tests and carry out the routine procedures that are assigned to laboratories. Technicians perform blood counts, microscopically examine specimens, and inoculate cultures. They may work in several areas of the clinical laboratory or specialize in just one.

For example, *histology technicians* (see p. 239) preserve and process tissue specimens obtained from patients, then cut and stain them for microscopic examination by pathologists. *Phlebotomists* are technicians who draw blood from patients for laboratory analysis. They are supervised by clinical laboratory technologists.

Work Settings

Clinical laboratory technicians may work in hospital or private laboratories, physicians' offices, HMOs, clinics, or commercial organizations such as pharmaceutical companies. Federal and local health agencies also employ medical laboratory technicians.

Advancement

By gaining experience or enrolling in a bachelor's degree program, a technician can become a clinical laboratory technologist (see p. 188) or attain a supervisory position.

Prerequisites

A high school diploma or its equivalent is essential for entry into a clinical laboratory technician training program.

Desirable attributes for this profession include solid abilities in biology and chemistry, excellent vision, organized and thorough work habits, maturity, a concern for details, and the ability to work under pressure and in association with others.

Education/Training

Clinical laboratory technicians generally have an associate degree from a junior or community college. This is the most common educational pathway to the field. Another approach is to secure a certificate from a hospital, medical school, vocational training institute, or the Armed Forces. A few technicians receive on-the-job training at a hospital.

The Clinical Laboratory Improvements Act requires those who perform certain highly complex tests to have at least an associate degree. There are two nationally recognized accrediting agencies for training programs in medical laboratory science. These are the Accrediting Bureau of Health Education Schools (ABHES) and the National Accrediting Agency for Clinical Laboratory Sciences (NAACLS).

Certification/Registration/Licensure

Clinical laboratory technicians can be certified by the National Certification Agency for Medical Laboratory Personnel, by the ABHES or the NAACLS, or by one of the agencies listed on page 190. Achieving such recognition can help you get a better-paying position and enhances your advancement potential.

Career Potential

The job outlook for clinical laboratory technicians is generally favorable. It is also, however, subject to continuing changes in the health-care industry.

For More Information

The professional organization for this field is the American Society of Cytopathology, 400 West Ninth Street, Wilmington, DE 19801.

Laboratory Technician Programs

There are hundreds of programs throughout the United States that train people to become clinical laboratory technicians—far too many to list here.

For information on an accredited training program in your area, write to either of the agencies listed below.

Secretary, ABHES
29689 V.S. 20
Elkhart, IN 41514

NAACLS
8410 W. Bryn Mar Avenue
Chicago, IL 60631

For information on certification, write to the National Certification Agency for Medical Laboratory Personnel, 2910 Woodmont Avenue, Bethesda, MD 20814.

You'll find more accrediting agencies listed under Clinical Laboratory Technologists.

 # CLINICAL LABORATORY TECHNOLOGISTS

Principal activity: Performing clinical laboratory tests ordered by physicians

Work commitment: Usually full-time

Preprofessional education: High school diploma or associate degree

Program length: 4 years

Work prerequisites: Bachelor's degree in medical technology and certification

Career opportunities: Positive

Income range: $25,000 to $40,000

Scope

The work of clinical laboratory technologists is vital in the detection, diagnosis, and treatment of many different diseases. Technologists perform tests on a wide variety of specimens, including body fluids, tissues, and cells.

Activities

Clinical laboratory technologists frequently use computer-automated equipment to perform large series of tests (24 to 40) simultaneously. Using microscopes, technologists seek to identify bacteria, parasites, and other microorganisms as well as abnormal cells in tissue fluids. They also analyze the chemical content of fluids and match blood types to determine the feasibility of transfusions. Cell counters are commonly used to determine into what numerical range specific types of cells fall. One of their key functions is to measure drug levels to judge how a patient is responding to a specific treatment. Their findings are relayed to physicians and become part of a patient's record. Thus, their laboratory services cover tests that fall into a variety of fields including cytology, histology, serology, bacteriology, and others.

Work Settings

Most clinical laboratory technologists are employed by hospitals, private laboratories, physicians' offices, or clinics. Some are employed by laboratory equipment manufacturers in product development, marketing, or sales.

Advancement

Clinical laboratory technologists with appropriate experience, graduate education, (see below), and managerial skills can advance to supervisory positions such as chief technologist or laboratory manager.

Prerequisites

A high school diploma or associate degree allows one to enroll in a bachelor's degree program in medical technology.

Desirable personal attributes for this field include a strong interest in and aptitude for the biological sciences, concern with precision and detail, superior vision, dependability, maturity, the capacity to work efficiently under pressure, and a desire to be part of a health-care team.

Education/Training

Two educational routes lead to a bachelor's degree in medical technology. One is a four-year program plus clinical experience at a college. The other involves three years of college course work followed by one year of practical training in a hospital setting. Course requirements in either program include biology, chemistry, microbiology, hematology, immunology, and clinical chemistry as well as clinical technology course work.

Graduate programs offering a master's degree in medical technology provide specialized training for careers in administration, teaching, and research.

Certification/Registration/Licensure

Certification, while voluntary, is a prerequisite for most jobs and is usually essential for advancement. There are four agencies that grant certification in this field (see below), and each has different requirements. Many clinical laboratory technologists are certified by more than one agency.

Career Potential

Certified licensed technologists should find favorable job opportunities as the U.S. population is grows larger and older. In addition, the number of available tests is always increasing and physicians are making greater use of them for diagnostic purposes. Restraining factors include the effort by HMOs to contain costs and the automation of testing procedures.

For More Information

The professional organizations in this field are listed below:

American Society for Clinical Laboratory Science
7910 Woodmont Avenue
Bethesda, MD 20814 a

American Medical Technologists
710 Higgin Road
Park Ridge, IL 60068.

Agencies that certify clinical laboratory technologists are listed below:

Board of Registry of the American Society of
Clinical Pathologists
P.O. Box 12277
Chicago, IL 60612
www.ascp.org/

American Medical Technologists
710 Higgins Road
Park Ridge, IL 60068
www.amt1.com/home.html

National Certification Agency for Medical
Laboratory Personnel
7910 Woodmont Ave., Suite 1301
Bethesda, MD 20814
www.app/meapro.com/nca/

Credentiating Commission of the International
Society for Clinical Laboratory Technology
818 Olive St.
St. Louis, MO 63101
http://voled.dodel.mil/dantes/cert/calendar/
ISCLT.HTM/

National Accrediting Agency for Clinical
Laboratory Sciences
8410 West Bryn Mawr,
Chicago, IL 60631
www.mcs.net/~naacls/

 # CYTOTECHNOLOGISTS

Principal activity: Preparing and studying cell smears for a microscopic evaluation

Work commitment: Full-time

Preprofessional education: 2 years of college; bachelor's degree preferred

Program length: Usually 1 year, but sometimes more

Work prerequisites: Graduating from an accredited cytotechnology program

Career opportunities: Favorable

Income range: $30,000 to $45,000

Scope

Our society is slowly coming to recognize the importance of preventive medicine. This is reflected in the campaigns to vaccinate children and to discourage smoking, excessive drinking, and substance abuse. It is also reflected in the push to test for early warning signs of cancer by means of mammography, colonoscopy, and pap smears. Cytotechnologists are especially trained to properly prepare specimens for examination and evaluation.

Activities

Cytotechnologists smear sample cells on slides and then stain them to enhance contrast and facilitate their evaluation. They are trained to identify abnormal cells on these slides, and they report their observations to pathologists, who review their work. More recently technologists have been using computers to help identify precancerous and cancerous cells. This technology will undoubtedly play a larger role in the future.

Work Settings

Cytotechnologists are employed by hospitals, private laboratories, and research institutes. Some teach in colleges and universities.

Advancement

In this profession, advancement comes by securing a degree and experience. Some employers identify three ascending ranks (I, II, III) of technologists.

Prerequisites

Completing two years of college is a minimum criterion for entering a cytotechnology training program, and some schools require even more credits. Undergraduates should take courses in biology, bacteriology, anatomy, physiology, genetics, and parasitology, as well as a year of basic chemistry.

   Desirable personal attributes for this field include superior vision, patience, dependability, precision, a strong sense of responsibility, and an interest in the biological sciences and in medical diagnosis.

Education/Training

To become a certified member of this profession, you must graduate from an accredited cytotechnology program. It is preferable to complete a bachelor's degree before studying cytotechnology. For those with a degree, the training program lasts one year; for others it takes longer.

   Accredited cytotechnology training programs include courses in clinical medicine, anatomy, histology, embryology, cytochemistry, cytophysiology, endocrinology, and cytology screening.

Certification/Registration/Licensure

Candidates must graduate from an accredited program before taking the certification exam administered by the American Society of Clinical Pathologists. After attaining certification and gaining three years of experience, cytotechnologists can be certified by the International Academy of Cytology. Several states require cytotechnologists to be licensed.

Career Potential

There will be many more openings in this field in the next decade. The employment prospects are presently quite favorable.

For More Information

The professional organization for this field is the American Society of Cytology, 900 West Ninth Street, Wilmington, DE 19801

For information on certification as a cytotechnologist, write to the Board of Registry, P.O. Box 12270, Chicago, IL 60612.

Cytotechnologist Programs

Alabama

Samford University
Birmingham, AL 35229
www.samford.edu/

University of Alabama at Birmingham
UAB Station
Birmingham, AL 35294
www.uab.edu/

Arkansas

Arkansas State University
Jonesboro, AR 72467
www.astate.edu/

University of Arkansas for Medicinal Science
4301 W. Markham
Little Rock, AR 72205
www.uams.edu/

California

California State University
1000 East Victoria Street
Carson, CA 90747
www.csudh.edu/

Charles R. Drew University of Medicine and Science
Los Angeles, CA 90059
www.cdrew.edu/

California State University
18111 Nordhoff Street
Northridge, CA 91330
www.csun.edu/

Connecticut

University of Connecticut
2131 Hillside Road U-88
Storrs, CT 06269
www.acon.edu/

District of Columbia

George Washington University
212 Eye Street NW
Washington, DC 20052
www.gwu.edu/

Howard University
2400 6th Street NW
Washington, DC 20059
www.howard.edu/

Florida

Barry University
Miami Shores, FL 33161
www.barry.edu/

Georgia

Columbus State University
4225 University Avenue
Columbus, GA 31907
www.pechnet.edu/columbus.htm

Armstrong Atlantic State University
11935 Abercorn Street
Savannah, GA 31419
www.peachnet.edu/armstrong.htm

Idaho

Boise State University
1910 University Drive
Boise, ID 83725
www.boisestate.edu/

Idaho State University
850 South Ninth
P.O. Box 8089
Pocatello, ID 83209
www.isu.edu/

Illinois

Roosevelt University
430 S. Michigan Avenue
Chicago, IL 60605
www.roosevelt.edu/

Illinois College
1101 W. College Avenue
Jacksonville, IL 62650
www.ic.edu/

Barat College
700 E. Westleigh Road
Lake Forest, IL 60045
www.barat.edu/

Augustana College
639 38th Street
Rock Island, IL 61201
www2.augustana.edu/

Indiana

Indiana University
300 North Jordan Avenue
Bloomington, IN 47405
www.indiana.edu/

Indiana University–Purdue University
2101 Coliseum Boulevard East
Fort Wayne, IN 46805
www.indianafw.edu/

Indiana University–Purdue University
Cavanaugh Hall, Room 129
Indianapolis, IN 46202
www.iupui.edu/

Iowa

University of Northern Iowa
1227 W. 27th Street
Cedar Falls, IA 50614
www.uni.edu/

Mount Saint Clare College
400 N. Bluff Road
Clinton, IA 52732
www.clre.edu/

Luther College
700 College Drive
Decorah, IA 52101
www.luther.edu/

Kansas

Fort Hays State University
600 Park Avenue
Hays, KS 67601
www.fhsu.edu/

University of Kansas
126 Strong Hall
Lawrence, KS 66045
www.ukans.edu/

Friends University
2100 W. University
Wichita, KS 67213
www.friends.edu/

Kansas Newman College
3100 McComick Avenue
Wichita, KS 67213
www.ksnewman.edu/

Kentucky

University of Louisville
2301 South 3rd Street
Louisville, KY 40292
www.louisville.edu/

Eastern Kentucky University
521 Lancaster Avenue
Richmond, KY 40475
www.edu.edu/

Louisiana

Northeast Louisiana University
700 University Avenue
Monroe, LA 71209
www.nlu.edu/

Maine

University of Maine
5713 Chadbourne Hall
Orono, ME 04469
www.umaine.edu/

Massachusetts

Suffolk University
8 Ashburton Place
Boston, MA 02108
www.suffolk.edu/

University of Massachusetts Dartmouth
285 Old Westport Road
North Dartmouth, MA 02747
www.umassd.edu/

Michigan

Andrews University
Halenz Hall, Room 326
Berrien Springs, MI 49104
www.andrews.edu/

Ferris State University
901 S. State Street
Big Rapids, MI 49307
www.ferris.edu/

Wayne State University
3 East, Helen Newberry Joy SSC
Detroit, MI 48202
www.wayne.edu/

Madonna University
36600 Schoolcraft Road
Livonia, MI 48150
www.munet.edu/

Northern Michigan University
1401 Presque Isle Avenue
Marquette, MI 49855
www.nmu.edu/

Baker College of Muskegon
1903 Marquette Avenue
Muskegon, MI 49442
www.baker.edu/

Baker College of Owosso
1020 S. Washington
Owasso, MI 48867
www.baker.edu/

Oakland University
101 North Foundation Hall
Rochester, MI 48309
www.acs.oakland.edu/

Minnesota

Moorehead State University
1104 7th Avenue South
Moorehead, MN 56563
www.moorhed.msus.edu/

Saint Mary's University of Minnesota
700 Terrace Heights
Winona, MN 55987
www.smun.edu/

Winona State University
Winona, MN 55987
www.winona.msus.edu/

Mississippi

University of Mississippi Medical Center
2500 North State Street
Jackson, MS 39216
www.olemiss.edu/

Missouri

University of Missouri–Columbia
230 Jesse Hall
Columbia, MO 65211
www.missouri.edu/

Avila College
11901 Wornall Road
Kansas City, MO 64145
www.avila.edu/

University of Missouri–St. Louis
8001 Natural Bridge Road
St. Louis, MO 63121
www.umsl.edu/

Nebraska

Dana College
2848 College Drive
Blair, NE 68008
www.dana.edu/

Clarkson College
101 South 42nd Street
Omaha, NE 68131
www.clarksoncollege.edu/

New Jersey

Bloomfield College
Park Place
Bloomfield, NJ 07003
www.bloomfield.edu/

Jersey City State College
2039 Kennedy Blvd.
Jersey City, NJ 07305
www.jcstate.edu/

St. Peter's College
1641 Kennedy Blvd.
Jersey City, NJ 07306
www.spc.edu/

Felician College
262 S. Main Street
Lodi, NJ 07644
www.felician.edu/

College of St. Elizabeth
2 Convent Road
Morristown, NJ 07960
www.st-elizabeth.edu/

Fairleigh Dickinson University
1000 River Road
Teaneck, NJ 07666
www.fdu.edu/

Kean College of New Jersey
1000 Morris Avenue
Union, NJ 07083
www.kean.edu/

New York

College of St. Rose
432 Western Avenue
Albany, NY 12203
www.strose.edu/

Long Island University
1 University Plaza
Brooklyn, NY 11201
www.brooklyn.liunet.edu/

Long Island University
CW Post Campus
700 Northern Blvd.
Brookville, NY 11548
www.liunet.edu/

State University at Stony Brook
Stony Brook, NY 11794
www.sunysb.edu/

State University of New York at Syracuse
201 Tolley Administration Bldg.
Syracuse, NY 13244
www.hscsyr.edu/

North Carolina

Greensboro College
815 West Market Street
Greensboro, NC 27401
www.gborocollege.edu/

East Carolina University
E 5th Street
Greenville, NC 27858
www.ecu.edu/

North Dakota

University of North Dakota
Box 8382
Grand Forks, ND 58202
www.und.nodak.edu/

Ohio

University of Akron
381 Buchtel Common
Akron, OH 44325
www.uakron.edu/

Mount Union College
Alliance, OH 44601
www.muc.edu/

Kent State University
161 Michael Schwartz Center
Kent, OH 44240
www.kent.edu/

Ursuline College
2550 Lander Road
Pepper Pike, OH 44124
www.ursuline.edu/

Notre Dame College of Ohio
South Euclid, OH 44121
www.ndc.edu/

Oklahoma

University of Oklahoma
Health Science Center
P.O. Box 26901
Oklahoma City, OK 73190
www.ou.edu/

Pennsylvania

Bloomsburg University
Ben Franklin Boulevard
Bloomsburg, PA 17815
www.bloomu.edu/

College Misericordia
301 Lake Street
Dallas, PA 18612
www.miseri.edu/

Elizabethtown College
One Alpha Drive
Elizabethtown, PA 17022
www.etown.edu/

Gannon University
University Square
Erie, PA 16541
www.gannon.edu/

Thiel College
75 College Avenue
Greenville, PA 16125
www.thiel.edu/

Gwynedd-Mercy College
1325 Sumneytown Pike
P.O. Box 901
Gwynedd Valley, PA 19437
www.gmc.edu/

Juaniata College
1700 Moore Street
Huntington, PA 16652
www.juniata.edu/

Mansfield University of Pennsylvania
Beecher House
Mansfield, PA 16933
www.mnsfld.edu/

Holy Family College
Grant & Frankford Avenues
Philadelphia, PA 19114
www.hfc.edu/

Thomas Jefferson University
130 South 9th Street
Philadelphia, PA 19107
www.tju.edu/

La Roche College
Babcock Boulevard
Pittsburgh, PA 15237
www.laroche.edu/

Slippery Rock University
Maltby Center
Slippery Rock, PA 16057
www.sru.edu/

Rhode Island

Salve Regina University
100 Ochre Point Avenue
Newport, RI 02840
www.salve.edu/

South Carolina

Charleston Southern University
P.O. Box 118087
Charleston, SC 29423
www.scuin.edu/

Medical University of South Carolina
171 Ashley Avenue
Charleston, SC 29425
www.musc.edu/

Francis Marion University
P.O. Box 100547
Florence, SC 29501
www.fmarion.edu/

Tennessee

Austin Peay State University
601 College Street
Clarksville, TN 37044
www.apsu.edu/

East Tennessee State University
P.O. Box 70717
Johnson City, TN 37614
www.etsu-tn.edu/

University of Tennessee–Knoxville
Knoxville, TN 37996
www.utk.edu/

University of Tennessee–Memphis
800 Madison Avenue
Memphis, TN 38163
www.utmem.edu/

Texas

Lamar University–Beaumont
P.O. Box 10009
Beaumont, TX 77710
www.lamar.edu/

University of North Texas
P.O. Box 13797
Denton, TX 76203
www.unt.edu/

University of Texas–Houston
P.O. Box 20036
Houston, TX 77225
www.uth.tmc.edu/

Utah

Weber State University
3750 Harrison Boulevard
Ogden, UT 84408
www.weber.edu/

Vermont

University of Vermont
Burlington, 05405
wsw.uvm.edu/

Trinity College Vermont
208 Colchester Avenue
Burlington, VT 05401
www.trinityvt.edu/

Virginia

Averett College
420 W. Main Street
Danville, VA 24541
www.averett.edu/

Old Dominion University
William B. Spong Hall
5215 Hampton Boulevard
Norfolk, VA 23529
www.odu.edu/

West Virginia

Marshall University
400 Hal Greer Boulevard
Huntington, WV 25755
www.marshall.edu/

Alderson-Broaddus College
500 College Hill
Phillipi, WV 26416
http://blue.ab.edu/

Wisconsin

Edgewood College
Madison, WI 53711
www.wedgewood.edu/

DENTAL ASSISTANTS

Principal activity: Directly assisting dentists in helping treat patients

Work commitment: Part- or full-time

Preprofessional education: High school diploma

Program length: 9 to 11 months

Work prerequisites: Certificate or degree

Career opportunities: Plentiful

Income range: $15,000 to $25,000

Scope

Dental assistants have a wide variety of responsibilities that require both technical and interpersonal skills. Their activities are critical to the success of a dental practice.

The job involves retrieving patients' records; preparing the necessary instruments for different procedures; preparing patients for treatment and making them comfortable prior, during, and after their treatment; and directly assisting the dentist during various procedures (e.g., clearing the mouth and handling instruments). In addition, dental assistants take and develop x-rays, make teeth impressions, remove sutures and surgical dressings, and perform a variety of office management tasks.

Work Settings

Dental assistants work in solo or group dental practices or in specialty offices such as orthodontics (teeth straightening) or endodontics (root canal treatment). Positions are also available in hospitals, clinics, schools and even insurance companies.

Advancement

With increased experience and superior ability, a dental assistant can be assigned greater responsibilities and secure an appointment as an office manager.

Prerequisites

A high school diploma or its equivalent is required to apply for admission to a dental assistant program.

Desirable personal attributes for a career in this field include good communication skills, an outgoing personality, good manual dexterity, and a desire to help people.

Education/Training

Dental assistants can finish their academic training in 9 to 11 months. Some schools even offer accelerated programs. Dental assistant programs are offered by colleges, community colleges, vocational-technical schools, and dental schools.

Education involves course work in the biomedical sciences and dental assisting techniques and procedures.

Certification/Registration/Licensure

Dental assistants become certified by passing an exam administered by the Dental Assisting National Board. Before taking the exam, candidates must complete an accredited dental assisting program. Those graduating from nonaccredited programs and those who have only on-the-job training may take the certifying exam only after attaining two years of full-time experience as dental assistants.

Some states require registration or licensure in addition to certification. These states offer their own tests for such licensure.

Career Potential

Dental assistant salaries are determined by their qualifications, experience, specific duties, and geographical location. Benefit packages may be provided.

The need for dental assistants has increased significantly in recent years, and long-term employment prospects are favorable. This is due to two factors: First, recent emphasis on preventive care has led to an increased need for dental services; second, most dentists today no longer work alone, but need an assistant who is an essential collaborator in treatment.

For More Information

The professional organization for this field is the American Dental Assistants Association, 293 North LaSalle Street, Chicago, IL 60601.

For more information, you can also speak with a dental assistant at your dentist's office and possibly arrange for an observational visit. An admissions officer at a school offering a program in this field will be glad to speak with you about the school's program and admissions issues.

Dental Assistant Programs

Alabama

James Faulkner State Community College
1900 Highway 31 South
Bay Minnette, AL 35607
www.faulkner.cc.al.us/

Bessemer State Technical College
P.O.Box 308
Bessemer, AL 35021
www.bstc.cc.al.us/

University of Alabama
UAB Station
Birmingham, AL 35294
www.uab.edu/

John C. Calhoun State Community College
Highway 31 North
P.O.Box 2216
Decatur, AL 35609
www.calhoun.cc.al.us/

Wallace State Community College
801 Main Street NW
Hanceville, AL 35077
www.wallacestatehanceville.edu/

Trenholm State Technical College
1225 Air Base Boulevard
Montgomery, AL 36108
www.embark.com/details/college/1/32/
d_2432.asp/

Alaska

University of Alaska
3211 Providence Drive
Anchorage, AK 99508
www.uaa.alaska.edu/

Arizona

Phoenix College
122 West Thomas Road
Phoenix, AZ 85013
www.pc.maricopa.edu/

Pima Community College
2202 West Anklam Road
Tucson, AZ 85709
www.pima.edu/

Arkansas

Cotton Boll Vocational Technical School
P.O. Box 36
Burdette, Arkansas 72321
www.cottonboll.org/

Pulaski Technical School
3000 West Scenic Road
North Little Rock, Ark 72118
www.ptc.tec.ar.us/

California

College of Alameda
555 Atlantic Avenue
Alameda, CA 94501
www.peralta.ccca.us/coa/coa.htm

Chaffey Community College
5885 Haven Avenue
Rancho Cucamonga, 91737
www.chaffey.cc.ca.us/

Citrus College
1000 Foothill Boulevard
Glendora, CA 91740
www.citrus.cc.ca.us/

Orange Coast College
2701 Fairview Road
Costa Mesa, CA 92626
www.occ.cccd.edu/

Cypress College
9200 Valley View
Cypress, CA 90630
www.cypress.cc.ca.us/

College of the Redwoods
7351 Tompkins Hill Road
Eureka, CA 95501
www.redwoods.cc.ca.us/

Chabot College
25555 Hesperian Boulevard
Hayward, CA 94545
www.clpccd.cc.ca.us/cc/

Hacienda–La Puente Adult Education
5959 East Gale Avenue
City of Industry, CA 91716
www.otan.dni.us/

College of Marin
835 College Avenue
Kentfield, CA 94904
www.marin.cc.ca.us/

Foothill College
12345 El Monte Road
Los Altos Hills, CA 94022
www.foothill.fhda.edu/

Modesto Junior College
435 College Avenue
Modesto, CA 95350
www.mjc.yosemite.cc.ca.us/

Monterey Peninsula College
980 Fremont Avenue
Monterey, CA 93940
www.mpc.edu/

Cerritos College
1110 East Alandra Boulevard
Norwalk, CA 90650
www.cerritos.edu/

Pasadena City College
1570 East Colorado Boulevard
Pasadena, CA 91106
www.paccd.cc.ca.us/

Diablo Valley College
321 Golf Club Road
Pleasant Hill, CA 94523
www.dvc.edu/

Kings River Community College
995 North Reed Avenue
Reedley, CA 93654
www.ecs.csus.edu/

Sacramento City College
3835 Freeport Boulevard
Sacramento, CA 95822
www.scc.losrios.cc.ca.us/

City College of San Francisco
50 Phelan Avenue
San Francisco, CA 94112
www.ccsf.cc.ca.us/

San Jose City College
2100 Moorpark Avenue
San Jose, CA 95128
www.sjcc.cc.ca.us/

College of San Mateo
1700 West Hillsdale Boulevard
San Mateo, CA 94402
www.smcccd.ca.us/

Palomar College
1140 West Mission Road
San Marcos, CA 92069
www.palomar.eduu/

Contra Costa College
2600 Mission Bell Drive
San Pablo, CA 94806
www.contracosta.cc.ca.us/

Santa Barbara City College
721 Cliff Drive
Santa Barbara, CA 93109
www.sbcc.cc.ca.us/

Santa Rosa Junior College
1501 Mendocino Avenue
Santa Rosa, CA 95401
www.santarosa.edu/

Colorado

T.H.Pickens Technical Center
500 Buckley Road
Aurora, CO 80011
www.aps.k12.co.us/41.htm

Pikes Peak Community College
5675 South Academy Boulevard
Colorado Springs, CO 80906
www.ppcc.ccoes.edu/

Emily Griffith Opportunity School
1250 Welton Street
Denver, CO 80204
www.egos-school.com/

Front Range Community College
P.O. Box 270490
Fort Collins, CO 80527
www.frcc.cc.co.us/

Connecticut

Tunxis Community-Technical College
271 Scott Swamp Road
Farmington, CT 06032
http://tunxis.commnet.edu/

Briarwood College
2279 Mount Vernon Road
Southington, CT 06489
www.briarwood.edu/

District of Columbia

Margaret Murray Washington Career High
School
27 "O" Street NW
Washington, DC 20001
(202) 673-7224

Florida

Manatee Technical Institute
5603 34th Street West
Bradenton, FL 34210
www.mcsb.org/school/mti/

Brevard Community College
1519 Clearlake Road
Cocoa, FL 32922
www.brevard.cc.fl.us/

Daytona Beach Community College
1200 W. International Speedway Blvd.
Daytona Beach, FL 32114
www.dbcc.cc.fl.us/

Broward Community College
225 E. Las Olas Blvd.
Fort Lauderdale, FL 33301
www.broward.cc.fl.us/

Indian River Community College
3209 Virginia Avenue
Ft. Pierce, FL 33981
www.ircc.cc.fl.us/

Santa Fe Community College
3000 Northwest 83rd Street
Gainesville, FL 32606
ww.santefe.cc.fl.us/

Florida Community College
4501 Capper Road
Jacksonville, FL 32218
www.fccj.cc.fl.us/

Palm Beach Community College
4200 Congress Avenue
Lake Worth, FL 33461
www.pbcc.cc.fl.us/

Lindsey Hopkins Technical Educational Center
750 Northwest 20th Street
Miami, FL 33127
www.oatace.org/school_directory/
lindsey_avc.html

Robert Morgan Vocational-Technical Institute
18180 SW 122 Avenue
Miami, FL 33177
www.oatace.org/school_directory/
robtmorgan_avc.html

Southern College
111 Hollingsworth Drive
Lakeland, FL 33801
www.flsouthern.edu/

Gulf Coast Community College
5230 West Highway 98
Panama City, FL 32401
www.gc.cc.fl.us/

Pensacola Junior College
1000 College Blvd.
Pensacola, FL 32507
www.pjc.cc.fl.us/

Charlotte County Vocational-Technical Center
18300 Toledo Blade Blvd.
Port Charlotte, FL 33948
http://tarpon.ccps.k12.fl.us/Schools/
TechCenter/program.htm

Pinellas Technical Education Center
901 34th Street
St. Petersburg, FL 33711
www.ptecs.pinellas.k12.fl.us/bustec.htm

Georgia

Albany Technical Institute
1021 Lowe Road
Albany, GA 31701
www.albanytec.org/

Augusta Technical Institute
3116 Deans Bridge Road
Augusta, GA 30906
www.august.tec.ga.us/

Gwinnett Technical Institute
5150 Sugarloaf Pkwy.
Lawrenceville, GA 30043
www.gwinnet-tech.org/

Medix School
2108 Cobb Pkwy.
Smyrna, GA 30080
www.medixschool.com/

Lanier Technical Institute
P.O. Box 58
Oakwood, GA 30566
www.lanier.tec.ga.us/

Savannah Technical Institute
5717 White Bluff Road
Savannah, GA 31499
www.savannah.tec.ga.us/

Idaho

Boise State University
1910 University Drive
Boise, Idaho 83725
www.boisestate.edu/

Illinois

John A. Logan College
700 Logan College Road
Carterville, IL 62918
www.jal.cc.il.us/

Parkland College
2400 West Bradley
Champaign, IL 61821
www.parkland.cc.il.us/

Morton College
3801 South Central Avenue
Cicero, IL 60804
www.morton.cc.il.us/

Illinois Central College
1 College Drive
East Peoria, IL 61635
www.icc.cc.il.us/

Lewis and Clark Community College
5800 Godfrey Road
Godfrey, IL 62035
www.lc.cc.il.us/

Lake Land College
South Route 45
Mattoon, IL 61938
www.lakeland.cc.il.us/

Illinois Valley Community College
815 n. Orlando Smith Avenue
Oglesby, IL 61348
www.ivcc.cc.il.us/

Indiana

University of Southern Indiana
8600 University Boulevard
Evansville, IN 47712
www.usi.edu/

Indiana University–Purdue University
2101 Coliseum Boulevard
Fort Wayne, IN 46805
www.ipfw.indiana.edu/

Indiana University Northwest
3400 Broadway
Gary, IN 46408
www.iun.indiana.edu/

Indiana University Medical Center
1121 West Michigan Street
Indianapolis, IN 46202
www.iupui.edu/home/medcentr.html

Professional Careers Institute
2611 Waterfront Parkway
Indianapolis, IN 46214
(317) 299-6001

Ivy Tech State College
1170 South Creasy Lane
Lafayette, IN 47905
www.ivy.tec.in.us/Lafayette/

Indiana University–South Bend
1700 Mishawaka Avenue
South Bend, IN 46615
www.indiana.edu/campus/
iu-south-bend.html

Iowa

Des Moines Area Community College
2006 Ankeny Boulevard
Ankeny, IA 50021
www.dmacc.cc.ia.us/

Kirkwood Community College
6301 Kirkwood Road, SW
P.O. Box 2068
Cedar Rapids, IA 52406
www.kirkwood.cc.ia.us/

Iowa Western Community College
2700 College Road, Box 4-C
Council Bluffs, IA 51502
www.iwcc.cc.ia.us/

Marshalltown Community College
3700 South Center Street
Marshalltown, IA 50158
www.iavalley.cc.ia.us/mcc/

Northeast Iowa Community College
10250 Sundown Road
Peosta, IA 52068
www.nicc.cc.ia.us/

Western Iowa Technical Community College
4647 Stone Avenue
P.O.Box 5199
Sioux City, IA 51102
www.cw.witcc.cc.ia.us/

Hawkeye Community College
1501 East Orange Road, Box 8015
Waterloo, IA 50704
www.hawkeye.cc.ia.us/

Kansas

Flint Hills Technical School
3301 West 18th Avenue
Emporia, KS 66801
www.fhtc.kansas.net/

Kentucky

Kentucky Tech–Bowling Green
1845 Loop Drive
Bowling Green, KY 42101
(270) 746-7467

Kentucky Tech–Lexington
359 Vo-Tech Road
Lexington, KY 40511
(270) 246-2444

Kentucky Tech–Paducah
2400 Adams Street
Paducah, KY 42003
(270) 443-6592

Maine

University of Maine
5713 Chdbourne Hall
Orono, ME 04469
www.umaine.edu/

Maryland

Allegany College
12401 Willowbrook Road
Cumberland, MD 21502
www.ac.cc.md.us/

Medix School
1017 York Road
Towson, MD 21204
www.medixschool.com/medlocal.htm

Massachusetts

Middlesex Community College
Springs Road
Bedford, MA 01730
www.middlesex.cc.ma.us/

Massasoit Community College
900 Randolph Street
Canton, MA 02021
www.massasoit.mass.edu/canton.htm

Northern Essex Community College
Elliott Way
Haverhill, MA 01830
www.necc.mass.edu/

Mount Ida College
777 Dedham Street
Newton Center, MA 02459
www.mountida.edu/

Charles H. McCann Technical School
Hodges Cross Roads
North Adams, MA 01247
www.berkshire.net/mccanntech.index.html

Springfield Technical Community College
One Armory Square
Springfield, MA 01105
www.stcc.mass.edu/

Worcester Polytechnic Institute
251 Belmont Street
Worcester, MA 01605
www.wpi.edu/

Michigan

Washtenaw Community College
P.O. Box D-1
Ann Arbor, MI 48106
www.washtenaw.cc.mi.us/

Kellogg Community College
450 North Avenue
Battle Creek, MI 49017
www.kellogg.cc.mi.us/

Lake Michigan College
2755 East Napier Avenue
Benton Harbor, MI 49002
http://lmc.cc.mi.us/

Wayne County Community College
801 West Fort Street
Detroit, MI 48226
www.wccc.edu/

Mott Community College
1401 East Court Street–CC114
Flint, MI 48053
www.mcc.edu/

Grand Rapids Community College
143 Bostwick Avenue NE
Grand Rapids, MI 49503
www.grcc.cc.mi.us/

Lansing Community College
P.O. B 40010
Lansing, MI 48901
www.lansing.cc.mi.us/

Northwestern Michigan College
1701 East Front Street
Traverse City, MI 49686
www.nmc.edu/

Delta College
University Center, MI 48710
www.delt.edu/

Minnesota

Bemidji Technical College
905 Grant Avenue, SE
Bemidji, MN 56601
www.ntc-online.com/

Normandale Community College
9700 France Avenue South
Bloomington, MN 55431
http://198.174.185.2501

Central Lakes College
501 West College Drive
Brainerd, MN 56401
www.clc.mnscu.edu/

Hennepin College
9000 Brooklyn Boulevard
Brooklyn, Park, MN 55445
(612) 425-3800

Hibbing Community College
1515 Est 25th Street
Hibbing, MN 55746
www.hcc.mnscu.edu/

Lakeland Medical-Dental Academy
1402 West Lake Street
Minneapolis, MN 55408
(612) 827-5656

Minneapolis Community & Technical College
1501 Hennepin Avenue South
Minneapolis, MN 55403
www.mctc.mnscu.edu/

Northwest Technical College
1900 28th Avenue South
Moorhead, MN 56560
www.ntc-online.com/

Rochester Community & Technical College
851 30th Avenue SE
Rochester, MN 55904
www.rctc.mnscu.edu/

St Cloud Technical College
1540 Northway Drive
St. Cloud, MN 56302
http://20.77.32.123/

Northeast Metro Secondary Technical Center
Century Community & Technical College
3300 Century Avenue North
White Bear Lake, MN 55110
www.mneta.net~nemetro/stw/sectc.html

Mississippi

Pearl River Community College
5448 US HWY 49 South
Hattiesburg, MS 39401
www.prcc.cc.ms.us/

Hinds Community College
3925 Sunset Drive
Jackson, MS 39213
www.hinds.cc.ms.us/

Missouri

Mineral Area College
P.O. Box 1000
Park Hills, MO 63601
www.mac.cc.mo.us/

Nichols Career Center
609 Union Street
Jefferson City, MO 65101
(573) 659-3100

East Central College
P.O. Box 529
Highway 50 and Prairie Dell
Union, MO 63084
www.ecc.mo.us/

Montana

MSU College of Tech–Great Falls
2100 16th Avenue South
Great Falls, MT 59405
http://msuco.tgf.montana.edu/

Salish Kootenai College
52000 Highway 93
P.O. Box 117
Pablo, MT 59855
www.skc.edu/

Nebraska

Central Community College
P.O. Box 1024
Hastings, NE 68902
www.cccneb.edu/

Southeast Community College
1111 O Street, Suite 111
Lincoln, NE 68508
www.college.sccm.cc.ne.us/

Metropolitan Community College
P.O. Box 3777
Omaha, NE 68103
www.mccneb.edu/

Omaha College of Health Careers
225 North 80th Street
Omaha, NE 68114
(402) 392-1300

Mid-Plains Community College
1101 Halligan Drive
North Platte, NE 69101
http://164.119.202.40/mpcc/index.html

Nevada

Truckee Meadows Community College
7000 Dandini Boulevard
Reno, NV 89512
www.wiche.edu/sep/Nevada/
truckee_meadows.cc.htm

New Hampshire

New Hampshire Technical Institute
11 Institute Drive
Concord, NH 03301
www.conc.tec.nh.us/

New Jersey

Camden County College
College Drive
P.O. Box 200
Blackwood, NJ 08012
www.camden.cc.edu/

Atlantic Cape Community College
5100 Black Horse Pike
Mays Landing, NJ 08330
www.atlantic.edu/

University of Medicine and Dentistry of New
Jersey
School of Health Professions
65 Bergen Street
Newark, NJ 07107
www.umdnj.edu/

Technical Institute of Camden County
343 Berlin-Cross Keys Road
Sicklerville, NJ 08081
www.ccts.tec.nj.us/TIHP.html

Berdan Institute
265 Route 46 West
Totowa, NJ 07512
www.arragon.com/schools/school-1204.asp

New York

State University of New York at Buffalo
465 Washington Street
Buffalo, NY 14203
www.buffalo.edu/

New York University Dental Center
345 East 24 Street
New York, NY 10010
www.nyu.edu/Dental/

North Carolina

Asheville-Buncombe Technical Community
College
340 Victoria Road
Asheville, NC 28801
www.asheville.cc.nc.us/

University of North Carolina
One University Heights
Asheville, NC 28801
www.unca.edu/

University of North Carolina
Old Dental Building
Chapel Hill, NC 27599
www.unc.edu/

Central Piedmont Community College
P.O. Box 35009
Charlotte, NC 28235
www.cpcc.cc.nc.us/

Fayetteville Technical Community College
2201 Hull Road
P.O. Box 35236
Fayetteville, NC 28303
www.faytech.cc.nc.us/

Wayne Community College
3000 Wayne Memorial Drive
Goldsboro, NC 27530
www.wayne.cc.nc.us/

Alamance Community College
1247 Jimmie Kerr Road
P.O. Box 8000
Graham, NC 27253
www.alamance.cc.nc.us/

Guilford Technical Community College
P.O. Box 309
Jamestown, NC 27282
http://technet.gtcc.cc.nc.us/

Wake Technical Community College
9101 Fayetteville Road
Raleigh, NC 27603
www.wake.tec.nc.us/

Rowan-Cabarrus Community College
P.O. Box 1595
Salisbury, NC 28145
www.rccc.cc.nc.us/

Wilkes Community College
P.O. Box 120
Wilkesboro, NC 28697
www.wilkes.cc.nc.us/

Cape Fear Community College
411 North Front Street
Wilmington, NC 28401
www.wilmington.net.cfcc/

North Dakota

Interstate Business College
520 East Maine Avenue
Bismarck, ND 58501
(701) 255-0779

North Dakota State College of Science
Department of Dental Auxiliaries
800 North Sixth Street
Wahpeton, ND 58076
www.ndscs.nodak.edu/

Ohio

Cuyahoga Community College
2900 Community College Avenue
Cleveland, OH 44115
www.tri-c.cc.oh.us/

Jefferson Community College
4000 Sunset Boulevard
Steubenville, OH 43952
(740) 264-5591

Oklahoma

Rose State College
6420 Southeast 15th Street
Midwest City, OK 73110
www.rose.cc.ok.us/

Oregon

Linn-Benton Community College
6500 Pacific Boulevard Southwest
Albany, OR 97321
www.lbcc.cc.or.us/

Lane Community College
4000 East 30th Avenue
Eugene, OR 97405
http://lanecc.edu/

Blue Mountain Community College
2411 Northwest Carden Avenue
Pendleton, OR 97801
www.bmcc.cc.or.us/

Portland Community Center
P.O. Box 19000
Portland, OR 97280
www.pcc.edu/

Chemeketa Community College
4000 Lancaster Drive NE
Salem, OR 97309
www.chemek.cc.or.us/

Pennsylvania

Harcum College
750 Montgomery Avenue
Bryn Mawr, PA 19010
www.harcum.edu/

Harrisburg Area Community College
1 HACC Drive
Harrisburg, PA 17110
www.hacc.edu/

Manor Junior College
710 Fox Chase Road
Fox Chase, PA 19046
http://manor.edu/

Luzerne County Community College
1333 South Prospect Street
Nanticoke, PA 18634
www.luzerne.edu/

Community College of Pennsylvania
1700 Spring Garden Street
Philadelphia, PA 19130
http://inet.ccp.cc.pa.us/

Murrell Dobbins Vocational-Technical School
22nd Street and Lehigh Avenue
Philadelphia, PA 19132
www.phila.k12.p.us/schools/dobbins/

Median School of Allied Health Careers
125 7th Street
Pittsburgh, PA 15222
http://chc.hcwp.org/medmshc.htm

Rhode Island

Community College of Rhode Island
1762 Louisquisset Pike
Lincoln, RI 02865
www.ccri.cc.ri.us/

South Carolina

Aiken Technical College
P.O. Box 696
Aiken, SC 29802
www.aik.tec.sc.us/

Midlands Technical College
P.O. Box 2408
Columbia, SC 29202
www.mid.tec.sc.us/

Florence-Darlington Technical College
P.O. Box 100548
Florence, SC 29501
www.flo.tec.sc.us/

Greenville Technical College
P.O. Box 5616 Station B
Greenville, SC 29606
www.greenvilletech.com/

TriCountry Technical College
P.O. Box 587
Pendleton, SC 29670
www.tricounty.tec.sc.us/

York Technical College
452 South Anderson Road
Rock Hill, SC 29730
www.yorktech.com/

Spartanburg Technical College
Highway I-85 P.O Box 4386
Spartanburg, SC 29305
http://199.5.204.101/

South Dakota

University of South Dakota
414 E. Clark Street
Vermillion, SD 57069
www.usd.edu/

Lake Area Technical Institute
230 11th Street NE
Watertown, SD 57201
www.lati.tec.sd.us/

Tennessee

Chattanooga State Technical Community
College
4501 Amnicola Highway
Chattanooga, TN 36406
www.cstcc.cc.tn.us/

East Tennessee State University
P.O. Box 70717
Johnson City, TN 37614
www.etsu-tn.edu/

Volunteer State Community College
1480 Nashville Pike
Gallatin, TN 37066
www.vscc.cc.tn.us/

Tennessee Technology Center–Knoxville
1100 Liberty Street
Knoxville, TN 37919
(615) 546-5567

Tennessee Technology Center–Memphis
550 Alabama
Memphis, TN 38105
(901) 543-6100

Roane State Community College
Oak Ridge, TN 38730
www.rscc.cc.tn.us/

Texas

Del Mar College
101 Baldwin Blvd.
Corpus Christi, TX 78404
www.delmar.edu/

Grayson County College
6101 Grayson Drive
Denison, TX 75020
www.grayson.edu/

El Paso Community College
P.O. Box 20500
El Paso, TX 79998
www.epcc.edu/

Houston Community College Southeast
3100 Shenandoah
Houston, TX 77021
www.hccs.cc.tx.us/

Tarrant County Junior College
828 Harwood Road
Hurst, TX 76054
www.tcjc.cc.tx.us/campus_ne/

San Antonio College
1300 San Pedro Avenue
San Antonio, TX 78212
www.accd.edu/sac/sacmain/sac.htm

School of Health Care Sciences
Dental Training Squadron
Sheppard AFB, TX 76311
www.shepprd.af.mil/

Texas State Technical College
3820 Campus Drive
Waco, TX 76705
http://waco.tstc.edu/waco.html

Utah

Provo College
1275 North University Avenue 1&2
Provo, UH 84604
www.byu.edu/health/

Bryman School
1144 West 3300 South
Salt Lake, UH 84119
(800) 456-2139

Virginia

Old Dominion University
G.H. Hirschfield School
Hampton Blvd.
Norfolk, VA 23529
www.odu.edu/

J. Sargeant Reynolds Community College
P.O. Box 85622
Richmond, VA 23285
www.jrs.cc.va.us/

Wytheville Community College
1000 East Main Street
Wytheville, VA 24382
www.wc.cc.va.us/

Washington

Bellingham Technical College
3028 Lindbergh Avenue
Bellingham, WA 98225
www.ctc.edu/~belltc/

Highline Community College
P.O. Box 98000
Des Moines, WA 98198
www.highline.ctc.edu/highline/home.htm

Lake Washington Technical College
11605 132nd Avenue NE
Kirkland, WA 98034
www.wtc.ctc.edu/

South Puget Sound Community College
2011 Mottman Road SW
Olympia, WA 98512
www.spscc.ctc.edu/

Renton Technical College
3000 NE 4th Street
Renton, WA 98056
www.renton-tc.ctc.edu/

Spokane Community College
1810 North Green Street
Spokane, WA 99217
www.scc.spokane.cc.wa.us/

Bates Technical College
1101 South Yakima Avenue
Tacoma, WA 98405
www.bates.ctc.edu/

Clover Park Technical College
4500 Steilacoom Boulevard SW
Lakewood, WA 98499
www.cptc.ctc.edu/cptc/

Wisconsin

Fox Valley Technical Institute
1825 Bluemound Drive
P.O. Box 2277
Appleton, WI 54913
www.foxvlley.tec.wi.us/

Lakeshore Technical Institute
1290 North Avenue
Cleveland, WI 53015
www.ltc.tec.wi.us/main.html

Northeast Wisconsin Technical College
2740 West Mason Street
P.O. Box 19042
Green Bay, WI 54307
www.twct.tec.wi.us/

Gateway Technical College
3520 30th Avenue
Kenosha, WI 53144
www.gateway.tec.wi.us/

Western Wisconsin Technical College
306 Sixth Street North
La Crosse, WI 54601
www.western.tec.wi.us/

Madison Area Technical College
3550 Anderson Street
Madison, WI 53704
http://twister.madison.tec.wi.us/

Wyoming

Sheridan College
3059 Coffeen Avenue
P.O. box 1500
Sheridan, WY 82801
www.sc.whecn.edu/

DENTAL LABORATORY TECHNICIANS

Principal activity: Preparing teeth replacement appliances such as crowns and bridges

Work commitment: Usually full-time

Preprofessional education: High school diploma

Program length: 2 years

Work prerequisites: Degree or certification

Career opportunities: Average to favorable

Income range: $20,000 to $30,000

Scope

Dental technicians hold a responsible position in dental health care. They serve patients indirectly and dentists directly by providing them with prostheses—that is, replacement units for missing natural teeth. Being a dental laboratory technician means holding a position that requires creative skill, sound judgment, and manual dexterity.

Activities

Dental technicians receive impressions (molds) and written, detailed instructions from dentists on the prostheses they need to prepare. They design these prostheses in the form of full dentures, for those lacking all of their teeth; removable partial dentures or fixed bridges, for those having one or several missing teeth; crowns, which are caps for teeth that need to be restored to their original shape and size; and orthodontics, to help straighten teeth. The prostheses are prepared using a variety of materials, including precious metals and alloys.

Work Settings

Dental technicians work for commercial dental labs, which may employ a few to over a hundred individuals. On average, such labs employ five full-time technicians. Laboratories generally prepare the full range of prostheses, but some specialize in one kind.

Additional opportunities exist for work in dental schools and training institutions, hospitals, and companies that manufacture prosthetic materials.

Advancement

With some experience and management skills, a technician can attain a supervisory position. In addition, technicians who have business acumen can start their own laboratories or become salespeople, marketing instruments, equipment, and materials used in the profession.

Prerequisites

A high school diploma or its equivalent is needed in order to apply to an accredited dental technology program. One should contact the specific school to learn about its individual requirements.

Desirable personal attributes for work in this field include superior manual dexterity, originality, and thoroughness.

Education/Training

On-the-job training is the route used by many prospective dental technicians. It usually takes several years to become highly skilled. Alternatively, two-year dental technology programs are offered by community colleges, technical-vocational schools, and even dental schools. Classroom and laboratory work is provided in subjects such as oral anatomy, dental materials science, and fabrication procedures. At the completion of the program, an associate degree is awarded.

Certification/Registration/Licensure

Certification is optional. Those with degrees in dental laboratory technology from an accredited program can become certified by passing an examination administered by the National Board for Certification in Dental Laboratory Technology. This exam evaluates both technical skills and knowledge. Two years of work experience is the prerequisite mandated for degree holders, and five years is required for nondegreed individuals with on-the-job training to be eligible for the certification exam.

Career Potential

Dental technicians may receive benefit packages and are paid on an hourly basis, with trainees receiving near the minimum scale. Increases in salary come with experience.

Although there has been a dramatic decline in the need for artificial dentures and an increase in ondodintic (root-canal) therapy that prolongs the usefulness of teeth, a strong demand for crowns and partials remains. Also, since the salaries of trainees are low, employers often have problems filling positions.

For More Information

For more information, write to one of these organizations:

American Dental Association
211 East Chicago Avenue
Chicago, IL 60611

The National Association of Dental Labs
8201 Greensboro Drive
Mclean, VA 22102

A useful means of gaining valuable personal insight into this career is visiting one or more dental laboratories and observing their technicians at work. Your observations can give you with a better understanding of the issues involved and can facilitate your career decisions.

Dental Laboratory Technician Programs

Alabama

Trenholm State Technical College
1225 Air Base Boulevard
Montgomery, AL 36108
(334) 832-9000

Arizona

Pima Community College
2202 West Anklam Road
Tucson, AZ 85709
www.pima.edu/

California

Los Angeles City College
855 North Vermont Avenue
Los Angeles, CA 90029
http://citywww.lacc.cc.ca.us/

Merced College
3600 M Street
Merced, CA 95348
http://merced.cc.ca.us/

Pasadena City College
1570 East Colorado Boulevard
Pasadena, CA 91106
www.paccd.cc.ca.us/

Diablo Valley College
321 Golf Club Road
Pleasant Hill, CA 94523
www.dvc.edu/

Naval School of Dental Technology
Box 368147, 32 St. Naval Street
San Diego, CA 92136
http://nshs.med.navy.mil/

City College of San Francisco
50 Phelan Avenue
San Francisco, CA 94112
www.ccsf.cc.ca.us/

Florida

Wm. T. McFatter Vocational- Technical Center
6500 Nova Drive
Davie, FL 33317
www.gate.net/~mcfatter/

Indian River Community College
3209 Virginia Avenue
Fort Pierce, FL 33450
www.ircc.cc.fl.us/

Lindsey Hopkins Technical Educational Center
750 NW 20th Street
Miami, FL 33127
www.oatace.org/school_directory/
lindsey_avc.html

Florida Southern College
111 Lake Hollingsworth Drive
Lakeland, FL 33801
www.flsouthern.edu/

Pensacola Junior College
1000 West College Blvd.
Pensacola, FL 32504
www.pjc.cc.fl.us/

Georgia

Atlanta Area Technical School
1560 Metropolitan Parkway SW
Atlanta, GA 30310
(404) 756-3700

Augusta Technical Institute
3116 Deans Bridge Road
Augusta, GA 30906
www.augusta.tec.ga.us/

Gwinnett Technical Institutel
5150 Sugarlof Parkway
Lawrenceville, GA 30043
www.gwinnett-tech.org/

Idaho

Idaho State University
RFC Building, Box 8380
Potacello, ID 83209
www.isu.edu/

Illinois

Southern Illinois University
College of Technical Careers
Carbondale, IL. 62901
www.siu.edu/

Triton College
2000 North Fifth Avenue
River Grove, IL 60171
www.triton.cc.il.us/

Indiana

Indiana University–Purdue University
2101 Coliseum Boulevard E
Fort Wayne, IN 46805
www.ipfw.indiana.edu/

Iowa

Kirkwood Community College
6301 Kirkwood Road SW
P.O. Box 2068
Cedar Rapids, Iowa 52406
www.kirkwood.cc.il.us/

Kentucky

University of Kentucky
Lexington Community College
Cooper Drive.
Lexington, KY 40506
www.uky.edu/LCC

Louisiana

Louisiana State University
1100 Florida Avenue
New Orleans, LA 70119
www.lsumc.edu/

Massachusetts

Middlesex Community College
Springs Road
Bedford, MA 01730
www.middlesex.cc.ma.us/

Michigan

Ferris State University
901 South State Street
Big Rapids, MI 49307
www.ferris.edu/

Minnesota

Northeast Metro Technical College
3300 Century Avenue North
White Bear Lake, MN 55110
(612) 779-5768

Missouri

St. Louis Community College Meramec
11333 Big Bend Boulevard
St. Louis, MO 63122
www.stlcc.cc.mo.us/

Nebraska

Central Community College
P.O. Box 1024
Hastings, NE 69802
www.cccneb.edu/

New Jersey

Union County College
1033 Springfield Avenue
Cranford, NJ 07016
www.ucc.edu/

New York

New York City Technical College
300 Jay Street
Brooklyn, NY 11201
www.nyctc.cuny.edu/

Erie Community College
4041 Southwestern Boulevard
Orchard Park, NY 14127
www.sunyerie.edu/

North Carolina

Durham Technical Community College
1637 Lawson Street
Durham, NC 27703
www.dtcc.cc.nc.us/

Ohio

Colombus State Community College
550 East Spring Street
Columbus, OH 43215
www.cscc.edu/

Cuyahoga Community College
2900 Community College Avenue
Cleveland, OH 44115
www.tri-c.cc.oh.us/

Oregon

Portland Community College
P.O. Box 19000
Portland, OR 97219
www.pcc.edu/

Tennessee

Chattanooga State Technical Community
College
4501 Amnicola Highway
Chattanooga, TN 37406
www.cstcc.cc.tn.us/

East Tennessee State University
P.O. Box 70717
Johnson City, TN 37614
www.etsu-tn.edu/

Texas

School of Health Care Sciences
Dental Training Squadron
Sheppard AFB, TX 76311
www.sheppard.af.mil/

University of Texas Health Sciences
7703 Floyd Curl Drive
San Antonio, TX 78229
www.uthsca.edu/

DIAGNOSTIC MEDICAL SONOGRAPHERS

Principal activity: Securing ultrasound images of body organs for diagnostic purposes

Preprofessional education: High school diploma

Work commitment: Full-time

Program length: 1 to 4 years

Work prerequisites: Diploma or degree in ultrasound

Career opportunities: Excellent

Income range: $25,000 to $50,000

Scope

Using sound waves, ultrasound can provide doctors with critical visual information about the size, contour, and in some cases even the action of various body organs. Physicians use ultrasound to study the brain, the heart, blood vessels, eyes, and abdominal and pelvic organs. It is also useful in detecting sites of fluid accumulation and tumors. It is a noninvasive procedure that is attractive because it provides clinical data without patient discomfort or risk.

Ultrasound is especially useful in obstetric practices, providing physicians with a view of the developing fetus, which allows for assessment of its development and position. The latter is important when doctors are considering such procedures as amniocentesis or delivery by C-section. This procedure also establishes or confirms the presence of multiple fetuses.

Activities

Before initiating the procedure, the sonographer explains the procedure to the patient, then smears the skin surface to be scanned with a gel to ensure that the transducer is in direct contact with the skin without an intervening layer of air. After positioning the patient, the sonographer views the screen as the scanning proceeds. Evaluating the quality of the image is critical to securing the essential information for the physician. This is achieved by appropriately recording the visual data. Working in this field requires special education and training. Sonographers also file results of sonography, evaluate new equipment, and maintain a reference library on ultrasound information.

Work Settings

Sonographers are employed by hospitals, clinics, obstetricians' offices, radiologists' offices, and research facilities.

Advancement

With experience and education, a sonographer can move into a supervisory position. Sonographers may specialize, using ultrasound in such areas as neurosonology (for brain examination), obstetrical/gynecological sonography (examination of the uterus), ophthalmic sonography (examination of the eye), or doppler sonography (examination of near surface arteries, such as carotids).

Prerequisites

The basic requirement for entering a training program is a high school diploma or its equivalent. Some programs require candidates to have an allied health science background.

Desirable personal attributes include attention to detail, patience, good rapport with patients and health professionals, good physical health, and excellent vision.

Education/Training

There are two routes you can follow to become a diagnostic medical sonographer: informal and formal. The first route, on-the-job training, is usually secured by people already working in the health-care field, such as registered nurses or radiological and medical technologists. Their prior educational backgrounds qualify them for many in-hospital training programs.

Formal training can be secured at various sites depending on the length of the program, award granted and students background.

Three different kinds of formal training programs lead to different kinds of degrees, depening on their length and scope:

Diploma programs typically last one year and are based in a hospital. These programs are best for those with a prior background in the health professions.

Associate degree programs typically last two years and are offered by community colleges.

Bachelor's degree programs last four years and are offered by colleges and universities.

Since the number of openings in most of these programs is limited, competition to secure admission is quite competitive.

The educational program consists of work in the classroom and supervised clinical experience that is usually concerned with human anatomy and physiology, histology, major relevant clinical diseases, pathological anatomy, physics, principles of ultrasound, imaging and display techniques, instrumentation maintenance, ultrasound characteristics, image evaluation, patient psychology and medical ethics.

Certification/Registration/Licensure

Candidates become certified as registered diagnostic medical sonographers by taking a two-day comprehensive written examination. There are five ways to become eligible for the exam. You can find more information on these different ways by writing to the Society of Diagnostic Medical Sonographers, whose address is listed below.

Career Potential

Currently the demand for sonographers is excellent in both the short- and long-term. This high demand results from the expansion of health care and the aging of the U.S. population.

As more institutions introduce sonography as a clinical diagnostic tool and significant advances are made in this field, its potential will be enhanced and it will become an even more challenging and rewarding field.

For More Information

The professional organization for this field is the Society of Diagnostic Medical Sonographers, 12770 Coit Road, Dallas, TX 75251.

The agency handling certification is the American Registry of Diagnostic Medical Sonographers, 600 Jefferson Plaza, Rockville, MD 20852.

Diagnostic Medical Sonography Programs

California

Loma Linda University
School of Allied Health Professionals
Loma Linda, CA 92350
www.llu.edu/

Colorado

Penrose Hospital School of Sonography
2215 N. Cascade Avenue
P.O. Box 80933
Colorado Springs, CO 80933
www.centura.org/services/
school_of_sonography/index.html

Florida

Broward Community College
3501 SW Davie Road
Davie, FL 33314
www.broward.cc.fl.us/

University of Miami–Jackson
Memorial Medical Center
1611 NW 12th Avenue
Miami, FL 33136
www.ir.miami.edu/

Hillsborough Community College
P.O. Box 30030
Tampa, FL 33630
www.hcc.cc.fl.us/

Georgia

Medical College of Georgia
Department of Radiologic Sciences
Building AE–1003
Augusta, GA 30912
www.mcg.edu/

Illinois

Wilbur Wright College
3400 North Austin
Chicago, IL 60634
www.ccc.edu/wright/

Triton College
2000 North Fifth Avenue
River Grove, IL 60171
www.triton.c..il.us/

Iowa

University of Iowa Hospitals and Clinics
Newton Road
Iowa City, IA 52242
www.uiowa.edu/

Kentucky

West Kennedy State Vocational Technical
5200 Blandville Road
Paducah, KY 42001
www.wkytech.com/

Louisiana

Alton Ochsner Medical Foundation
1514 Jefferson Highway
New Orleans, LA 70121
www.ochsner.org/education

Maryland

Maryland Institute of Ultrasound Technology
UMBC Office of Continuing Education
1000 Hilltop Circle
Baltimore, MD 21250
www.umbc.edu/

Massachusetts

Middlesex Community College
Springs Road
Bedford, MA 01730
www.middlesex.cc.ma.us/

Michigan

Henry Ford Hospital
2799 West Grand Blvd.
Detroit, MI 48202
www.henryfordhealth.org/

Marygrove College
8425 West McNichols Road
Detroit, MI 48221
http://209.41.12.52/

Jackson Community College
2111 Emmons Road
Jackson, MI 49201
www.jackson.cc.mi.us/

Oakland Community College
22322 Rutland Drive
Southfield, MI 48075
www.occ.cc.mi.us/

Minnesota

Mayo Foundation
200 First Street SW
Rochester, MN 55905
www.mayo.edu/

Missouri

St. Louis Community College at Forest Park
5600 Oakland Avenue
St. Louis, MO 63110
www.stlcc.cc.mo.us/fp/

New Jersey

University of Medicine and Dentistry of New Jersey
School of Health-Related Professions
65 Bergen Street
Newark, NJ 07107
www.umdnj.edu/

Bergen County Community College
400 Paramus Road
Paramus, NJ 07652
www.bergen.cc.nj.us/

New York

SUNY Health Science Center at Brooklyn
450 Clarkson Avenue
Brooklyn, NY 11203
www.hscbklyn.edu/

New York University Medical Center
342 East 26th Street
New York, NY 10016
www.nyu.edu/

Rochester Institute of Technology
1 Lomb Memorial Drive
P.O. Box 9887
Rochester, NY 14623
www.rit.edu/

North Carolina

Pitt Community College
Highway 11 South
Greenville, NC 27835
www.pitt.cc.nc.us/

Caldwell Community College & Technical Institute
2855 Hickory Boulevard
Hudson, NC 28638
www.caldwell.cc.nc.us/

Ohio

Kettering College of Medical Arts
3737 Southern Boulevard
Kettering, OH 45429
www.kcma.edu/

Central Ohio Technical College
1179 University Drive
Newark, OH 43055
www.cotc.tec.oh.us/

Owens Community College
Oregon Road
Toledo, OH 43699
www.owens.cc.oh.us/

Oklahoma

University of Oklahoma
Health Sciences Center
1100 N. Lindsey
Oklahoma City, OK 73104
www.ouhsc.edu/

Pennsylvania

Polyclinic Medical Center
2601 North Third Street
Harrisburg, PA 17110
www.pcom.edu/clinicaled/
pinnacle_health_system.htm

Community College of Allegheny County
Boyce Campus
595 Beatty Road
Monroeville, PA 15146
www.ccac.edu/

Thomas Jefferson University
1020 Walnut Street
Philadelphia, PA 19107
www.tju.edu/

Texas

Austin Community College
5930 Middle Fiskville Road
Austin, TX 78752
www.austin.cc.tx.us/

Del Mar College
101 Baldwin Blvd.
Corpus Christi, TX 78404
www.delmar.edu/

El Centro College
Main & Lamar
Dallas, TX 75202
www.ecc.dcccd.edu/

El Paso Community College
P.O. Box 20500
El Paso, TX 79998
www.epcc.edu/

Utah

Weber State University
Ogden, UT 84408
www.weber.edu/

Washington

Bellevue Community College
3000 Landherholm Circle
S.E. Bellevue, WA 98007
www.bcc.ctc.edu/

Seattle University
900 Broadway
Seattle, WA 98122
www.seattleu.edu/

West Virginia

West Virginia University Hospital
Robert C. Byrd Health Sciences Center
P.O. Box 6401
Morgantown, WV 26506
www.wvu.edu/

Wisconsin

Chippewa Valley Technical College
620 West Claremont Avenue
Eau Claire, WI 54701
www.chippewa.tec.wi.us/

University of Wisconsin Hospital and Clinics
600 Highland Avenue
Madison, WI 53792
www.rwhc.com/

St. Francis Hospital
3237 South 16th Street
Milwaukee, WI 53215
www.covhealth.org/affiliat/sfh.htm

St. Luke's Medical Center
2900 West Oklahoma Avenue
Milwaukee, WI 53215
www.aurorahealthcare.org/

DIETETIC TECHNICIANS

Principal activity: Helping dietitians meet the food needs of their employers' facilities

Work commitment: Full-time

Preprofessional education: High school diploma or its equivalent

Program length: 2 years

Work prerequisites: Associate degree

Career opportunities: Very favorable

Income range: $20,000 to $45,000

Scope

The job of a dietetic technician depends on the nature and size of his or her employer. It can cover a broad range of activities.

Activities

In small institutions, a dietetic technician can attain a management position under the supervision of a consultant dietitian.

At large hospitals or medical centers, dietetic technicians often work directly under a registered dietitian. Professionals are qualified to create recipes, prepare menus, enforce safety and sanitary standards, train and manage dietary and clerical workers. and manage cafeterias.

Work Settings

Dietary technicians often work in large health-care facilities—such as medical centers, hospitals, and nursing homes—or in smaller facilities (either health-related or not) such as cafeterias or diners.

Advancement

With experience, dietetic technicians may be promoted to supervisory positions However, it is difficult to transfer credits from a dietary technician program to a dietitian degree program, unless one does so at the same institution.

Prerequisites

A high school diploma or its equivalent is essential for entry to a dietetic technician's program. Courses in home economics and business practices are recommended.

Desirable personal attributes for those entering this field include an ability to work under pressure and superior decision-making skills.

Education/Training

Many junior and community colleges offer two-year associate degree programs for dietetic technicians. Course work includes classes in biology and chemistry, nutrition, diet therapy, and food services management.

Certification/Registration/Licensure

Graduates of accredited programs can take the National Registration Examination for Dietetic Technicians, which is offered by the Commission on Dietetic Registration. To maintain status as a registered dietetic technician (DTR), one must accumulate at least 50 hours of approved continuing education every five years.

Career Potential

The job outlook for dietetic technicians in the coming decade is quite favorable because of the aging population in the United States. Consequently, more facilities for senior citizens (such as nursing homes) will require the services of dietetic technicians.

For More Information

The professional organization for this field is the American Dietetic Association, 216 West Jackson Blvd., Chicago, IL 60606.

Dietetic Technician Programs

Arizona

Black River Technical College
P.O. Box 468
Pocahontas, AZ 72455
www.brtc.tec.ar.us/

Central Arizona College
8470 N. Overfield Road
Coolidge, AZ 85228
www.cac.cc.az.us/

California

Orange Coast College
2701 Fairview Road
Costa Mesa, CA 92628
www.occ.cccd.edu/

Grossmont College
8800 Grossmont College Drive
El Cajon, CA 92020
www.gcccd.cc.ca.us/

Long Beach City College
Family & Consumer Studies Division
4901 East Carson Street
Long Beach, CA 90808
(562) 938-4550

Los Angeles City College
855 North Vermont Avenue
Los Angeles, CA 90029
http://citywww.lacc.cc.ca.us/

Chaffey College
5885 Haven Avenue
Rancho Cucamonga, CA 91737
www.chaffey.cc.ca.us/

Colorado

Front Range Community College
3645 West 112th Avenue, #23
Westminster, CO 80030
www.wfrcc.cc.co.us/

Connecticut

Gateway Community Technical College
88 Bassett Road
New Haven, CT 06473
www.commnet.edu/gwctc/

Briarwood College
2279 Mount Vernon Road
Southington, CT 06489
www.briarwood.edu/

Florida

Palm Beach Community College
4200 Congress Avenue
Mail Station 32
Lake Worth, FL 33461
www.pbcc.cc.fl.us/

Miami-Dade Community College
300 NE 2nd Avenue, Suite 3704-30
Miami, FL 33132
www.mdcc.edu/

Illinois

City College of Chicago
Malcolm X College
1900 West Van Buren Street
Chicago, IL 60612
www.ccc.edu/malcolmx/home.htm

William Rainey Harper College
1200 West Algonquin Road
Palatine, IL 60067
www.harper.cc.il.us/

Louisiana

Delgado Community College
450 S. Clairborne Avenue
New Orleans, LA 70012
www.dcc.edu/

Maine

Southern Maine Technical College
Fort Road
South Portland, ME 04106
www.smtc.net/

Maryland

Baltimore City Community College
2901 Liberty Heights Avenue
Baltimore, MD 21215
www.bccc.state.md.us/

Massachusetts

Laboure College
2120 Dorchester Avenue
Boston, MA 02124
www.labourecollege.org/

Michigan

Wayne County Community College
Vocational & Career Education
8551 Greenfield
Detroit, MI 48228
www.wccc.edu/

Minnesota

Normandale Community College
9700 France Avenue South
Bloomington, MN 55431
www.nr.cc.mn.us/

University of Minnesota–Crookston
Center for Health & Human Services
2900 University Avenue
Crookston, MN 56716
www.crk.umn.edu/

Missouri

St. Louis Community College
3400 Pershall Road
St. Louis, MO 63135
www.stlcc.cc.mo.us/

Nebraska

Southeast Community College
8800 O Street
Lincoln, NE 68520
www.sccm.cc.ne.us/

New Hampshire

University of New Hampshire
Thompson School of Applied Science
Cole Hall
Durham, NH 03824
www.unh.edu/

New Jersey

Camden County College
P.O. Box 200
College Drive
Blackwood, NJ 08012
(609) 227-7200

Middlesex County College
P.O. Box 3050
Edison, NJ 08818
www.middlesex.cc.nj.us/

New York

LaGuardia Community College
31-10 Thomson Avenue
Long Island City, NY 11101
www.lagcc.cuny.edu/

Suffolk County Community College
121 Speonk–Riverhead Road
Riverhead, NY 11901
www.suny.suffolk.edu/

Rockland Community College
145 College Road
Suffern, NY 10901
(914) 574-4130

Westchester Community College
75 Grasslands Road
Valhalla, NY 10595
www.wcc.co.westchester.ny.us/

Erie Community College
6305 Main Street
Williamsville, NY 14221
www.sunyerie.edu/

Ohio

Cincinnati State Technical
and Community College
Health Technology Center
3520 Central Parkway
Cincinnati, OH 45223
www.cinstate.cc.oh.us/

Cuyohoga Community College
2900 Community College Avenue
Cleveland, OH 44115
www.tri-c.cc.oh.us/

Columbus State Community College
Box 1609
550 East Spring Street
Columbus, OH 443216
www.cscc.edu/

Sinclair Community College
444 West 3rd Street
Dayton, OH 45402
www.sinclair.edu/

Lima Technical College
4240 Campus Drive
Lima, OH 45804
www.ltc.tec.oh.us/

Hocking Technical College
3301 Hocking Parkway
Nelsonville, OH 45764
www.hocking.edu/

Owens Community College
P.O. Box 10000
Toledo, OH 43699
www.owens.cc.oh.us/

Muskingum Area Technical College
1555 Newark Road
Zanesville, OH 43701
www.matc.tec.oh.us/

Oklahoma

Oklahoma State University, Okmulgee
1801 East Fourth Street
Okmulgee, OK 74447
www.osu-okmulgee/edu/hosp

Oregon

Portland Community College
P.O. Box 19000
12000 S.W. 49th
Portland, OR 97280
www.pcc.edu/

Pennsylvania

Community College of Philadelphia
1700 Spring Garden Street
Philadelphia, PA 19130
www.ccp.cc.pa.us/

Community College of Allegheny County
808 RIdge Avenue
Pittsburgh, PA 15212
www.cacc.edu/

Westmoreland County Community College
Commissioners Hall
400 Armbrust Road
Youngwood, PA 15697
www.westmoreland.cc.pa.us/

South Carolina

Greenville Technical College
P.O. Box 5616
Greenville, SC 29606
www.gvltec.edu/

Tennessee

Shelby State Community College
P.O. Box 40568
Memphis, TN 38174
www.sscc.cc.tn.us/

Texas

El Paso Community College
100 West Rio Grande Avenue
El Paso, TX 79902
www.epcc.edu/

Tarrant County College
2100 TCJC Parkway
Ft. Worth, TX 76018
www.tcjc.cc.tx.us/

San Jacinto College
8060 Spencer Highway
Pasadena, TX 77501
www.sjcd.cc.tx.us/

St. Philip's College
1801 Martin Luther King
San Antonio, TX 78203
www.accd.edu/

Virginia

Northern Virginia Community College
HRI/DIT McDiarmid Building
8333 Little River Turnpike
Annandale, VA 22003
www.nvcc.cc.va.us/

J. Sargeant Reynolds Community College
P.O. Box 85622
Richmond, VA 23285
www.jsr.cc.va.us/

Tidewater Community College
1700 College Crescent
Portsmouth, VA 23456
www.tc.cc.va.us/

Washington

Shoreline Community College
16101 Greenwood Avenue North
Seattle, WA 98133
http://shoreline.ctc.edu/

Spokane Community College
North 1810 Greene Street, MS 2090
Spokane, WA 99217
www.scc.spokane.cc.wa.us/

Wisconsin

Madison Area Technical College
3550 Anderson Street
Madison, WI 53704
http://madison.tec.wi.us/

Milwaukee Area Technical College
1200 South 71st Street
Milwaukee, WI 53214
www.milwaukee.tec.wi.us/

ELECTROENCEPHALOGRAPHIC TECHNICIANS

Principal activity: Obtaining electroencephalograms from patients

Work commitment: Full-time

Preprofessional education: High school diploma

Program length: Several months of on-the-job training

Work prerequisites: On-the-job training

Career opportunities: Very good

Income range: $15,000 to $25,000

Scope

The scope of an EEG technician's work is the same as that of an EEG technologist (see p. 225). The training is shorter, however, so the EEG technician's depth of theoretical knowledge lower, as is his or her salary.

The title *EEG technician* is being phased out by ASET, the professional organization, but it will probably continue to be used by some institutions for the time being. EEG technologists will be the essential providers of services in this area.

Activities

EEG technicians secure accurate electroencephalograms for evaluation by the physician. Working under the supervision of an EEG technologist, they can readily obtain guidance to meet any challenging situations that may arise during the course of their work.

Work Settings

Most EEG technicians work in hospitals or HMOs, but employment opportunities also exist in the offices of neurologists and neurosurgeons.

Advancement

With added education and training, a technician can become a senior technician or an EEG technologist.

Prerequisites

A high school diploma is necessary for entry into this field.

Education/Training

EEG technicians are trained on-the-job in hospitals and clinics. The training involves the fundamentals of basic sciences, a survey of neurological diseases, electronics, and basic techniques of clinical electroencephalography.

Certification/Registration/Licensure

Neither licensure nor certification is required or available for work at this level.

Career Potential

Employment prospects for EEG technicians are very favorable, especially if they can advance to the status of technologist.

For More Information

Sources of additional information are the same as those for EEG technologists (below).

EEEG Technician Programs.

See programs listed under EEG technologists (pp. 227–228).

ELECTROENCEPHOLOGRAPHIC TECHNOLOGISTS

Principal activity: Obtaining electrocepholograms from patients

Work commitment: Full-time

Preprofessional education: High school diploma

Program length: 1 to 2 years

Work prerequisites: A formal or informal training program

Career opportunities: Very good

Income range: $18,000 to $35,000

Scope

The brain of a living human exhibits electrical activity that reflects its functional state. An encephalograph is an instrument that can sense and record the minute electrical impulses emitted by the brain. The brain wave record of electrical activity is called an *encephalogram* (*EEG*). The EEG technologist's responsibility is to obtain this record from patients. Such a tracing is used by neurologists and other doctors to diagnose and evaluate strokes, head injuries, brain tumors, epilepsy, and even learning disabilities.

The EEG identifies brain damage and reveals its site and extent. This instrument also is used to determine whether a patient is clinically alive.

Activities

Initially the EEG technologist (also known as an *electroneurodiagnostic technologist*) must ensure that the equipment is in optimal operational condition. The technologist briefs the patient about the procedure, then applies small electrodes to the patient's scalp. These electrodes are connected to the EEG machine. Using the desirable settings for the particular patient, the technologist then makes the recording. During the procedure, the technologist also monitors the patient's condition and behavior.

Work Settings

Most EEG technologists work in medical centers, hospitals, the offices of neurologists and neurosurgeons, HMOs, free standing emergency clinics, and psychiatric facilities.

Advancement

With experience, an EEG technologist can move to a supervisory or instructional position.

Prerequisites

Those entering this field need a high school diploma and a demonstrated interest and abilities in the biological sciences.

Desirable personal attributes include skill with electronics, manual dexterity, good vision, strong communication skills, and a favorable personality. Compassion and tact are also valuable assets that facilitate working with very sick people and those who may be brain damaged.

Experience/Training

There are two routes to becoming an EEG technologist: gratuating from a formal training program and securing on-the-job training. The latter usually entails two six-months educational phases that include didactic instruction and supervised practice. One can expect to receive a stipend during the training period.

A variety of institutions offer formal training programs, including community and senior colleges, universities, medical schools, and hospitals. Studies involve gross and neuroanatomy, physiology, neurology, neurophysiology, electronics, and instrumentation. The program usually lasts one to two years, and a certificate or associate degree may be awarded upon completion.

EEG technologists learn to identify normal and abnormal brain activity shown on a tracing, and how best to secure the desired information. They also become familiar with the diseases for which the EEG is a valuable diagnostic tool and with the operational characteristics of the equipment.

Certification/Registration/Licensure

Currently there are no licensing requirements for EEG technologists, but one can secure the status of *registered EEG technologist* from the American Board of Registration for Electroencephalographic and Evoked Potential Technologists. This registration follows a one-year training program and examination.

Career Potential

The employment outlook is highly favorable for those entering this field, because of the aging U.S. population and a greater use of EEGs in clinical medicine and research.

For More Information

The professional organization for this field is the American Society for Electro-neurodiagnostic Technologists, Inc., 204 West 7th Street, Carroll, IA 51401.

You can get information on registration from the American Board of Registration of Electroencephalographic and Evoked Potential Technologists, P.O. Box 916633, Longwood, FL 32791.

EEG Technologist Programs

California

Orange Coast College
2701 Fairview Road,
P O Box 5005
Costa Mesa, CA 92626
www.occ.cccd.edu/

Florida

Erwin Technical College
2010 East Hillsborough Avenue
Tampa, FL 33610
(813) 231-1800

Illinois

East-West University
816 South Michigan Avenue
Chicago, IL 60605
www.eastwest.edu/

St. John's Hospital
800 East Carpenter Street
Springfield, IL 62769
www.st-johns.org/public/

Loyola University Medical Center
2160 South First Avenue
Maywood, IL 60153
www.meddean.luc.edu/

Indiana

Indiana University–Purdue University
702 Barnhill Drive
Indianapolis, IN 46202
www.iupui.edu/

Iowa

Kirkwood Community College
P.O. Box 2068
Iowa City, IA 52406
www.kirkwood.cc.ia.us/healthscience.eeg.html

Maryland

Naval School Of Health Sciences
8901 Wisconsin Avenue
Bethesda, MD 20889
(301) 319-4760

Massachusetts

Children's Hospital Medical Center
300 Longwood Avenue
Boston, Ma 02115
www.childrenshospital.org/

Laboure College
2120 Dorchester Avenue
Boston, Ma 02124
www.labourecollege.org/

New York

Niagara City Community College
3111 Saunders Settlement Road
Sandborn, NY 14132
(716) 731-3271

North Carolina

Southwestern Community College
447 College Drive
Sylvia, NC 28779
www.southwest.cc.nc.us/

Pennsylvania

Crozier-Chester Medical Center
One Medical Center Boulevard
Chester, PA 19013
(610) 447-2691

Carlow College
Children's Hospital Of Pittsburgh
3705 Fifth Avenue
Pittsburgh, PA 15213
www.carlow.edu/

Wisconsin

Western Wisconsin Technical College
304 North 6th Street
P.O. Box 908
LaCrosse, WI 54602
(608) 785-9200

Canada

British Columbia Institute of Technology
3700 Willingdon Avenue
Burnaby, British Columbia
Canada, V5G 3H2
www.bcit.cc.ca/

EMERGENCY MEDICAL TECHNICIANS

Principal activity: Providing emergency medical care

Work commitment: Part- or full-time

Preprofessional education: High school diploma

Program length: 64 to 1,200 hours, depending on the level

Work prerequisites: Completion of an EMT course

Career opportunities: Average

Income range: $25,000 to $40,000 (grade-dependent)

Scope

As the name indicates, emergency medical technicians (EMTs) respond to calls by or for people in medical distress. They are trained in a wide range of lifesaving techniques and may respond to a wide range of emergencies, including vehicle or industrial accidents, heart attacks, bodily injuries due to accidents or violence, cases of poison or drug overdose, unscheduled childbirths, drownings, and situations involving emotionally disturbed individuals. EMTs function in the prehospital phase as the first medical responders to traumatic injuries and acute illnesses.

Activities

EMTs are directed to the scenes of medical emergencies by a police or fire-department, a hospital, or an emergency services dispatcher. They are given preliminary information about the medical problem(s) they will face so they can prepare the necessary equipment.

Upon arriving at the scene, the EMTs assess the situation, note the patient's vital signs, and determine if hospitalization is required. If it is not, they prioritize the emergency treatment needed and initiate therapeutic activities.

If the situation is life-threatening, they may call for back-up medical help or seek guidance from the local hospital emergency room physician. Following the advice of the physician (and subject to the EMTs' level of competence and their state's legal guidelines), they may perform a wide variety of procedures, both on the scene and on the way to the hospital.

When appropriate, the EMTs drive the patient to a hospital's emergency room. Once there, they report their findings and the emergency treatment they provided. They may also remain to assist the emergency staff in treating the patient.

Work Settings

EMTs are employed by medical centers and hospitals, police and fire departments, rescue agencies, and private ambulance companies. They also serve with volunteer corps that help meet emergencies in their communities.

Advancement

Three levels are EMTs are recognized, based on the training they have received and the procedures they are permitted to perform:

An **EMT–Basic** is qualified to carry out fundamental procedures such as cardiovascular resuscitation, fracture care (bandaging and splinting), bleeding control, childbirth assistance, and treatment for shock. This category is also known as *EMT–Ambulance.*

An **EMT–Intermediate** is qualified to perform all the above procedures, and to assess trauma, open an intravenous line, introduce fluids, provide airway management techniques, and use anti-shock garments.

An **EMT–Paramedic** is trained in advanced life support techniques, including interpreting electrocardiograms, administering medications, and providing defibrillation when a person's heart has stopped beating. Those especially qualified in the latter technique may also be designated as *EMT–Defibrillator.*

With continuing education, training, experience, and qualifying examinations, an EMT can advance from one level to another.

Prerequisites

Those entering this field must be at least 18 years old and have a high school diploma and a valid driver's license.

Desirable personal attributes include good physical health and strength, good vision, manual dexterity, the ability to use good judgment under stress, and a desire to help others in need.

Education/Training

EMT–Basic

The basic course requires 110 hours of training in emergency medical care techniques. Instruction covers handling emergencies associated with bleeding, fractures, shock, soft tissue trauma, cardiac arrest, internal injuries, childbirth, and the ingestion of toxic substances. Trainees learn how to use standard emergency equipment, communication skills, and vehicle operation and maintenance. They also gain familiarity with the legal aspects of hospitalization.

EMT–Intermediate

Trainees take courses in patient assessment, shock management, advanced airway maintenance, and intravenous fluid provision.

EMT–Paramedic

Training for this level requires EMT–Basic or higher status plus 700 to 1,000 hours of course work as well as hospital clinical practice and a supervised field internship. The training program usually lasts about nine months.

Certification/Registration/Licensure

EMTs at every level can register with the National Registry of Emergency Medical Technicians, if the meet the specific requirements for training, field experience, and examinations. Each individual state may have its own certifying agency. To maintain certification EMTs must register every two years.

Career Potential

The job market for EMTs in the foreseeable future is average. The most attractive positions are those with police, fire, and rescue squads. However, most of the opportunities in the future will be with hospitals and private ambulance services.

While the demand for emergency medical assistance is increasing due to the growing elderly population, budgetary difficulties are forcing cutbacks in EMT staffing at many hospitals and public safety departments.

For More Information

The professional EMT organization is the National Association of Emergency Medical Technicians, 102 West Lake Street, Clinton, ME 39056.

For information on certification and licensure, write to the National Registry of Emergency Medical Technicians, Box 2923, 6610 Busch Boulevard, Columbus, OH 43229.

EMT–Paramedic Programs

Alabama

University of Alabama at Birmingham
UAB Station
Birmingham, AL 35294
www.uab.edu/

Wallace Community College
Department of Emergency Medicine
Route 6, Box 62
Dothan, AL 36303
www.wallace.edu/wccpages/

University of South Alabama
Alpha E
Mobile, AL 36688
www.usouthal.edu/

University of Alabama at Tuscaloosa
College of Community Health Services
P.O. Box 870326
Tuscaloosa, AL 35487
www.ua.edu/

Arizona

St. Mary's Hospital
1601 West St. Mary's Road
Tucson, AZ 85745
www.mercyhealthnwa.smhs.com/

California

Daniel Freeman Memorial Hospital
333 North Prairie Avenue
Inglewood, CA 90301
www.danielfreeman.org/

Crafton Hills College
11711 Sand Canyon Road
Yucaipa, CA 92399
www.sbccd.cc.ca.us/chc/index.htm

Colorado

St. Anthony Central Hospital
4231 West 16th Avenue
Denver, CO. 80204
www.centura.org/

Swedish Medical Center
501 East Hampden Avenue
Englewood, CO. 80110
www.swedishhospital.com/

Florida

Manatee Technical Institute
5603 34th Street West
Bradenton, FL 34210
www.mcsb.org/school/mti/

Brevard Community College
1519 Clearlake Road
Cocoa, FL 32922
www.brevard.cc.fl.us/

Daytona Beach Community College
1200 W. International Speedway Blvd.
Daytona Beach, FL 32114
www.dbcc.cc.fl.us/

Lake County Vocational Technical College
2001 Kurt Street
Eustis, FL 32726
(352) 742-6486

Broward Community College
225 East Las Olas Blvd.
Ft. Lauderdale, FL 33301
www.broward.cc.fl.us/

Edison Community College
8099 College Parkway, SW
P.O. Box 06210
Ft. Myers, FL 33906
www.edison.edu/

Indian River Community College
3209 Virginia Avenue
Ft. Pierce, FL 34981
www.ircc.cc.fl.us/

Santa Fe Community College
3000 NW 83rd Street
Gainesville, FL 32602
http://santafe.cc.fl.us/

Florida Community College
4501 Capper Road
Jacksonville, FL 32218
www.fccj.cc.fl.us/

Lake City Community College
Route 19, Box 1030
Lake City, FL 32025
www.lakecity.cc.fl.us/

Palm Beach Community College
4200 Congress Avenue
Lake Worth, FL 33461
www.pbcc.cc.fl.us/

Maimi-Dade Community College
Medical Center Campus
950 NW 20th Street
Miami, FL 33127
www.mdcc.edu/medical/

Pasco-Hernando Community College
36727 Blanton Road
Dade City, FL 33525
(352) 567-6701

Central Florida Community College
3001 SW College Blvd.
Ocala, FL 34474
www.cfcc.cc.fl.us/

Valencia Community College
190 South Orange Street
Orlando, FL 32801
www.valencia.cc.fl.us/

Gulf Coast Community College
5230 West Highway 98
Panama City, FL 32401
www.gc.cc.fl.us/

Pensacola Junior College
1000 College Blvd.
Pensacola, FL 32504
www.pjc.cc.fl.us/

St. Petersburg Junior College
P.O. Box 13489
Pinellas Park, FL 33733
www.spjc.cc.fl.us/

Sarasota County Technical Institute
4748 Beneva Road
Sarasota, FL 34233
http://careerscape.org/scti/sctipg1.html

Fort Collins Technical Institute
2980 Collins Avenue
St. Augustine, FL 32095
www.fcti.stjohns.k12.fl.us/

Tallahassee Community College
444 Appleyard Drive
Tallahassee, FL 32304
www.tallahassee.cc.fl.us/

Hillsborough Community College
Dale Mabry Campus
P.O. Box 30030
Tampa, FL 33630
www.hcc.cc.fl.us/

Polk Community College
999 Avenue "H" NE
Winter Haven, FL 33881
www.polk.cc.fl.us/

Indiana

Methodist Hospital of Indiana
1701 North Senate Boulevard
Indianapolis, IN 46206
www.clarian.com/

Iowa

Mercy Medical Center
1111 Sixth Avenue
Des Moines, IA 50314
www.mercydesmoines.org/

Kansas

Johnson County Community College
12345 College Blvd.
Overland Park, KS 66210
www.johnco.cc.ks.us/

Kentucky

Eastern Kentucky University
521 Lancaster Avenue
Richmond, KY 40475
www.eku.edu/

Michigan

Lansing Community College
P.O. Box 40010
Lansing, MI 48901
www.lansing.cc.mi.us/

Minnesota

Northeast Metro Technical College
3300 Century Avenue North
White Bear Lake, MN 55110
(218) 779-5783

Nebraska

Creighton University
2500 California Place
Omaha, NE 68178
www.creighton.edu/

New Hampshire

New Hampshire Technical Institute
11 Institute Drive
Concord, NH 03001
www.conc.tec.nh.us/

New Mexico

University of New Mexico
Health Sciences Center, Suite 302
2500 Marble, NE
Albuquerque, NM 87131
www.unm.edu/

North Carolina

Western Carolina University
201 HFR Administration Building
Cullowhee, NC 28723
www.wcu.edu/

Catawba Valley Community College
2550 Highway 70 SE
Hickory, NC 28602
www.cvcc.cc.nc.us/

Ohio

Columbus State Community College
550 East Spring Street
Columbus, OH 43215
www.cscc.edu/

Youngstown State University
One University Plaza
Youngstown, OH 44555
www.ysu.edu/

Oregon

Oregon Health Sciences University
3181 SW Sam Jackson Park Road
Portland, OR 97201
www.ohsu.edu/

Pennsylvania

Harrisburg Area Community College
One HACC Drive
Harrisburg, PA 17110
www.hacc.edu/

St. Joseph Hospital & Health Care Center
250 College Avenue
Lancaster, PA 17603
(717) 291-8211

Williamsport Hospital
777 Rural Avenue
Williamsport, PA 17701
www.shscares.org/

South Carolina

Greenville Technical College
P.O. Box 5616, Station B
Greenville, SC 29606
www.greenvilletech.com/

Tennessee

Volunteer State Community College
1480 Nashville Pike
Gallatin, TN 37066
www.vscc.cc.tn.us/

Roane State Community College
Harrison, TN 37748
www.rscc.cc.tn.us/

Jackson State Community College
2046 North Parkway
Jackson, TN 38301
www.jscc.cc.tn.us/

Shelby State Community College
737 Union Avenue
P.O. Box 40568
Memphis, TN 38174
www.sscc.cc.tn.us/

Texas

Austin Community College
5930 Middle Fiskville Road
Austin, TX 78752
http://ella.austin.cc.tx.us/

University of Texas
Southwestern Medical Center at Dallas
5323 Harry Hines Boulevard
Dallas, TX 75235
www.swmed.edu/

Texas Technical University
Health Sciences Center
3601 Fourth Street
Lubbock, TX 79430
www.ttu.edu/

University of Texas Health Sciences Center
7703 Floyd Curl Drive
San Antonio, TX 78229
www.ut.edu/

Utah

Weber State University
Ogden, UT 84408
www.weber.edu/

Virginia

Northern Virginia Community College
8333 Little River Turnpike
Annandale, VA 22003
www.nv.cc.va.us/

College of Health Sciences
Community Hospital of Roanoke Valley
920 South Jefferson Street
Roanoke, VA 24016
www.chs.edu/

Washington

Institute of Prehospital Medicine
Bellingham Technical College
3028 Lindbergh Avenue
Bellingham, WA 98225
www.beltc.ctc.edu/

Central Washington University
Health Education and Leisure Services
1400 East Eight Avenue
Ellensburg, WA 98926
www.cwu.edu/

Harborview Medical Center
University of Washington
325 Ninth Avenue
Seattle, WA 98104
www.washington.edu/medical/hmc/

Spokane Community College
1810 North Greene Street
Spokane, WA 99217
www.scc.spokane.cc.wa.us/

Tacoma Community College
6501 South 19th Street
Tacoma, WA 98466
www.tacoma.ctc.edu/

FOOD TECHNOLOGISTS

Principal activity: Providing nourishing and safe food for public consumption

Work commitment: Full-time

Preprofessional education: High school diploma

Program length: 4 years

Work prerequisites: Bachelor's degree required; master's degree preferred

Career opportunities: Stable

Income range: $30,000 to $65,000

Scope

Food technologists are involved in a wide variety of activities associated with providing the public with sanitary and nutritious food. They help with the selection, processing, packaging, preservation, and distribution of food.

To achieve the goal of manufacturing food that is beneficial, tasteful, good looking, and lasting, the food production industry employs technologists in food laboratories, food testing kitchens, and production facilities. Technologists also help develop new products.

Activities

Food technologists are commonly employed in industrial settings. They work in research and development, pilot testing of new food processes, equipment, and packaging systems. They supervise plant safety, quality control, and waste disposal. Technologists are also responsible for the chemical analysis of food composition.

Work Settings

The major employers of food technologists are the three categories of companies belonging to the food industry.

1. food processors, which convert raw foods into food products,

2. food manufacturers, including those that create entirely new food products, and

3. food ingredient makers, including those that produce spices, vitamins, and food supplements.

Many food technologists work for the federal government, including the Food and Drug Administration, the Environmental Protection Agency, and NASA. State agencies that monitor the handling of foods in restaurants, hotels, and other retail food distribution businesses are also source for employment. Technologists are also employed by such organizations as the United Nations and the World Health Organization, as well as by colleges, universities, and health foundations.

Advancement

Candidates with advanced degrees (such as a master's or doctorate) can secure professional advancement.

Prerequisites

Desirable personal attributes for those entering the field include a solid interest in science and food, an organized manner of thinking and working, patience, and good communication and team-working skills.

Education/Training

A bachelor's degree is the minimum requirement for employment int his field. The preferred major is food technology, but related areas such as nutrition may be acceptable. Course work should include food processing analysis and engineering, chemistry, microbiology, physics, mathematics, and statistics.

Those interested in the business aspects of the food industry should take economics and business administration courses. In addition, the traditional humanities and social science courses should be taken.

Many schools with undergraduate food technology programs also offer advanced degrees. Almost half of food technologists employed in the United States have master's or doctorate degrees.

Junior colleges, community vocational schools, and technical training schools offer two-year programs and award associate degrees. Graduates of such programs are known as *food technicians* and, with further education, may become technologists.

Certification/Registration/Licensure

No certification or licensure currently is available in this field. Those with at least a bachelor's degree in food technology and five years of professional experience can apply for professional membership in the Institute of Food Technology.

Career Potential

This employment outlook in this field should remain stable in the foreseeable future. However, changes in climate, economic conditions, and public policy may have unpredictable effects on job opportunities.

For More Information

The professional organization in this field is the Institute of Food Technology, 221 North LaSalle Street, Chicago, IL 606015.

Food Technologist Programs

Alabama

Auburn University
328 Spidle Hall
Auburn, AL 36849
www.auburn.edu/

Alabama A&M University
P.O. Box 264
Normal, AL 35762
http://alpha1.aamu.edu/

Arkansas

University of Arkansas
272 Young Avenue
Fayetteville, AR 72701
www.uark.edu/

California

Chapman University
One University Drive
Orange, CA 92866
www.chapman.edu/

San Jose State University
One Washington Square
San Jose, CA 95192
www.sjsu.edu/

California Polytechnic State University
San Luis Obispo, CA 93407
www.calpoly.edu/

Colorado

Colorado State University
Fort Collins, CO 80523
www.colostate.edu/

Delaware

University of Delaware
College of Health & Nursing Sciences
345 McDowell Hall
Newark, DE 19716
www.udel.edu/

Florida

University of Florida
P.O. Box 110370
Gainesville, FL 32611
www.ufl.edu/

Georgia

University of Georgia
Athens, GA 30602
www.uga.edu/

Hawaii

University of Hawaii
2444 Dole Street
Honolulu, HI 96822
www.hawaii.edu/

Idaho

University of Idaho
Holm Research Center
Moscow, ID 83844
www.uidaho.edu/

Illinois

University of Illinois
905 South Goodwin Avenue
Urbana, IL 61801
www.uiuc.edu/

Indiana

Purdue University
1160 Smith Hall
West Lafayette, IN 47907
www.purdue.edu/

Iowa

Iowa State University
Ames, IA 50011
www.iastate.edu/

Kansas

Kansas State University
Manhattan, KS 66506
www.ksu.edu/

Kentucky

University of Kentucky
Lexington, KY 40506
www.uky.edu/

Maine

University of Maine
Orono, ME 04469
www.umaine.edu/

Maryland

University of Maryland
College Park, MD 20742
www.umcp.edu/

Massachusetts

University of Massachusetts
Massachusetts Avenue
Amherst, MA 01003
www.umass.edu/

Michigan

Michigan State University
East Lansing, MI 48824
www.msu.edu/

Minneapolis

University of Minnesota
277 Coffey Hall
1420 Eckles Avenue
St. Paul, MN 55108
www.coafes.umn.edu/

Missouri

University of Missouri–Columbia
230 Jesse Hall
Columbia, MO 65211
www.missouri.edu/

Nebraska

University of Nebraska–Lincoln
103 Ag Hall
Lincoln, NE 68583
www.unl.edu/

New Jersey

Rutgers State University of New JErsey
Cook College
59 Biel Road
New Brunswick, NJ 08901
http://aesop.rutgers.edu/

New York

Cornell University
College of Agriculture & Life Sciences
273 Roberts Hall
Ithaca, NY 14853
www.cals.cornell.edu/

North Carolina

North Carolina State University
College of Agriculture & Life Sciences
Raleigh, NC 27695
www.cals.ncsu.edu/

North Dakota

North Dakota State University
1301 North University
Fargo, ND 58105
www.ndsu.nodak.edu/

Ohio

Ohio State University
2121 Fyffe Road
Columbus, OH 43210
www.acs.ohio-state.edu/

Oklahoma

Oklahoma State University
103 Whitehurst
Stillwater, OK 74078
http://osu.okstate.edu/

Oregon

Oregon State University
Corvallis, OR 97331
www.orst.edu/

Pennsylvania

Delaware Valley College
700 East Butler Avenue
Doylestown, PA 18901
www.delvalcol.edu/foodscience/index.htm

Pennsylvania State University
111 Borland Laboratory
University Park, PA 16802
www.psu.edu/

Rhode Island

University of Rhode Island
Woodward Hall
9 Alumni Avenue
West Kingston, RI 02881
www.uri.edu/cels/fsn/

South Carolina

Clemson University
224 Poole Agricultural Center
P.O. Box 340371
Clemson, SC 29634
www.clemson.edu/

Tennessee

University of Tennessee
P.O. Box 1071
Knoxville, TN 37901
www.utk.edu/

Texas

Texas A & M University
College Station, TX 77843
www.tamu.edu/

Utah

Utah State University
Logan, UH 84332
www.usu.edu/

Brigham Young University
Provo, UH 84602
www.byu.edu/

Virginia

Virginia Polytechnic Institute
and State University
Blacksburg, VA 24061
www.vt.edu/

Washington

Washington State University
Department of Food Science
Pullman, WA 99164
www.wsu.edu/

University of Washington
Box 355680
Seattle, WA 98105
www.washington.edu/

Wisconsin

University of Wisconsin–Madison
103 Babcock Hall
1605 Linden Dr.
Madison, WI 53706
www.wisc.edu/foodsci/

University of Wisconsin–River Falls
410 South Third Street
River Falls, WI 54022
www.uwrf.edu/

Canada

Acadia University
Wolfville, Nova Scotia
Canada B0P 1X0
www.acadiau.ca/

University of Alberta
Edmonton, Alberta
Canada T6G 2P5
www.ualberta.ca/

University of British Columbia
2329 West Mall
Vancouver, British Columbia
Canada V6T 1Z4
www.ubc.ca/

University of Guelph
Guelph, Ontario
Canada N1G 2W1
www.uoguelph.ca/

University of Manitoba
Winnipeg, Manitoba
Canada R3T 2N2
www.umanitoba.ca/

Universite Laval
1312 Building Paul–Comtois
Ste-Foy, Quebec
Canada B1K 7P4
www.ulabal.ca/

McGill University
845 Sherbrooke Street West
Montreal, Quebec
Canada H3A 2T5
www.mcgill.ca/

HISTOLOGY TECHNICIANS

Principal activity: Preparing histological slides for microscopic examination by pathologists

Work commitment: Full-time

Preprofessional education: High school diploma

Program length: 6 months to 2 years

Work prerequisites: On-the-job training or formal education

Career opportunities: Stable

Income range: $20,000 to $35,000

Scope

Anatomy, which is one of the biomedical sciences, has many subdivisions. One of these is *histology*, or the microscopic study of tissues. To study tissues, the material must be especially prepared and be suitable for analysis under a standard microscope. The tissues may be used for diagnostic, research, or educational purposes. Because of the critical nature of their work, these technicians and their supervisors, who are known as *histotechnologists*, are essential to the proper functioning of hospitals, research, and teaching institutions.

Activities

For routine microscopic examination, histologic technicians preserve, dehydrate, and embed tissue samples in wax sections. The specimens are then mounted on glass slides. Next, they are dehydrated and stained. This reveals the internal structure, with different elements of the cells revealed in contrasting colors.

The procedure that is routinely used in tissue preparation is time consuming, often taking several days. However, sometimes it is medically essential to obtain sections immediately for pathological evaluation. For example, when a biopsy is taken of suspected malignant tissue while a patient is under anesthesia on the operating table, the surgeon needs to have a pathologist's opinion and advice within a matter of minutes in order to determine how to proceed. In these cases the biopsied material is treated by a technician using a quick-freeze method and then sectioned for prompt pathological review.

Work Settings

Most histological technicians work in medical centers and hospitals. Others work in research and teaching institutions.

Advancement

With experience, additional education and evidence of managerial skills, advancement to histological technologist is possible.

Prerequisites

A high school diploma or its equivalent is essential for entry to this field. Studies in biology and chemistry are important.

Desirable personal attributes for workers in the field include a genuine interest in the biomedical sciences, superior vision, manual dexterity, patience, the ability to do routine work in a responsible manner, and an exacting nature.

Education/Training

Currently there are two training routes in this field: (1) on-the-job training and (2) formal preparation. The latter is becoming increasingly commonplace. Formal educational programs are offered by medical centers and hospitals as well as community and junior colleges. From the former, one can secure a certificate or diploma; from the latter, one may be granted an associate degree. These programs can extend from six months to two years, depending on where they are undertaken.

In accredited programs the curriculum usually consists of classroom instruction and practical laboratory work. Courses include human anatomy, histology, histochemistry, chemistry, mathematics, processing techniques, and medical technology. Record keeping and administrative procedures are also taught.

Certification/Registration/Licensure

Certification in this field is available through the Board of Registry of the American Society of Clinical Pathology or other organizations (see below). A variety of different prerequisites for persons with different background are available, and an examination must be passed. Histological technologists can obtain certification, but a bachelor's degree is required.

Career Potential

Demand for professionals in this field should remain stable for the foreseeable future. However, changing health-care reimbursement and coverage plans may significantly impact professional needs in the field.

For More Information

The professional organization in this field is the National Society for Histotechnology, 4201 Northview Drive, Bowie, MD 20716.

Certification is available through the following agencies:

National Accrediting Agency for Clinical Laboratory Sciences
8410 West Bryn Mawr Avenue
Chicago, IL 60631

The National Certification Agency for Medical Laboratory Personnel
Bethesda, MD 20814

Board of Registry of the American Society of Clinical Pathologists
P.O. Box 12277
Chicago, IL 60612.

MEDICAL ASSISTANTS

Principal activity: Serving as an office assistant for health-care practitioners

Work commitment: Full- or part-time

Preprofessional education: High school diploma

Program length: 1 to 2 years

Work prerequisites: Diploma, certificate, or associate degree

Career opportunities: Excellent

Income range: $15,000 to $25,000

Scope

A medical assistant is a multiskilled professional who is qualified to function in both clinical and administrative areas. They work under the supervision of a licensed health-care practitioner. The medical assistant also serves as a liaison between patient and doctor. He or she provides guidance and personal attention to the patient to relieve anxiety. The efficiency of a medical office depends, in large measure, on the ability and efficiency of the medical assistant.

Activities

The range of a medical assistant's clinical duties is determined by state law. These duties may include preparing the exam room, taking a preliminary medical history from patients, measuring and noting their height and weight, securing and recording their vital signs (e.g., pulse, blood pressure, and temperature), preparing patients for and assisting in examinations and treatment processes, applying dressings, drawing blood, performing routine blood tests and electrocardiograms, preparing and administering medications under the physician's direction, cleaning and sterilizing instruments, disposing of used supplies, maintaining the stock of standard supplies used, and ordering replacements.

The administrative responsibilities of medical assistants involve secretarial, clerical, and receptionist duties along with book and record keeping. These responsibilities include scheduling patient appointments, receiving patients upon their arrival, securing and updating patient records, coding procedures and diagnoses, preparing correspondence, and arranging for pharmacy prescriptions or hospital admissions when necessary. Additional duties may involve responding to phone calls, maintaining accounts, and dealing with insurance carriers.

The ratio of clinical to administrative work usually is determined by the size of the practice. In a small office, the medical assistant typically handles both, while in a larger one, there may be a separation of duties.

Medical assistants working for specialists are responsible for special procedures relevant to their specialty. Thus, each major specialty may have its own medical assistants. (See, for example, the discussion of ophthalmic medical assistants.)

Work Settings

The majority of medical assistants work in the offices of practicing physicians, for individual practitioners or medical groups, or for HMOs, hospitals, clinics, and nursing homes.

Advancement

Securing additional experience and training can enhance the status of a medical assistant, who can move into supervisory or specialty work areas.

Prerequisites

A high school diploma is needed both as a prerequisite for formal education and for on-the-job training. Courses in biology, computers, and book keeping are an asset.

Desirable personal attributes for medical assistant include a pleasant personality and disposition, strong oral and written communication skills, a service orientation, organized work habits, and a respect for individual privacy.

Education/Training

While some medical assistants simply secure on-the-job training, most are graduates of formal educational programs. Such programs are offered by community and junior colleges and by vocational schools. Programs include courses in biology, anatomy, physiology, medical terminology, computers, accounting, record keeping, transcription, and office management. Clinical aspects are covered in courses dealing with laboratory techniques, clinical procedures, and patient care.

Training programs vary in length. Most vocational school programs take one year, while those at community colleges take two years of course work and supervised clinical experience.

Finally, there are two medical assistant program accrediting agencies: the Commission for the Accreditation of Allied Health Education Programs (CAAHEP) and the Accrediting Bureau of Health Education Schools (ABHES). Programs accredited by the former agency are listed below.

Certification/Registration/Licensure

The two professional organizations in this field provide certification or registration to those who meet their requirements. Those meeting the standards set by the American Association of Medical Assistants are designated *Certified Medical Assistants* (*CMAs*), while those meeting the standards set by the American Medical Technologists are designated *Registered Medical Assistants* (*RMAs*).

Career Potential

Experts foresee a highly favorable outlook for employment in this field over the next decade. This is especially true for those having formal training. Both the size of the U.S. population and the number of physicians is increasing. Consequently, the demand for medical services is greater and the need for medical assistants is accelerating.

For More Information

The two professional organizations in this field are listed below:

American Association of Medical Assistants
20 North Wacker Drive
Chicago, IL 60606

Registered Medical Assistants of the American Medical Technologists
710 Higgins Road
Park Ridge, IL 60068

Medical Assistant Programs

Alabama

Wallace Community College
Route 6, Box 62
Dothan, AL 36303
www.wallace.edu/

Trenholm State Technical College
1225 Air Base Boulevard
P.O. Box 9000
Montgomery, AL 36108
(334) 240-9726

Alaska

University of Alaska Anchorage
3211 Providence Drive
Anchorage, AK 99508
www.uaa.alaska.edu/

Arizona

Phoenix College
1202 West Thomas Road
Phoenix, AZ 85013
www.pc.maricopa.edu/

Arkansas

Capital City Junior College
7723 Asher Avenue, Box 4818
Little Rock, AR 72214
(501) 562-0700

Colorado

Boulder Valley Area Vo-Tech Center
6600 East Arapahoe
Boulder, CO 80303
(303) 447-1010

Emily Griffith Opportunity School
1250 Welton Street
Denver, CO 80204
www.egos-school.com/

Connecticut

Morse School of Business
275 Asylum Street
Hartford, CT 06103
(860) 522-2261

Northwestern Connecticut Community College
Park Place East
Winstead, CT 06098
www.nwctc.edu/

Stone Academy
1315 Dixwell Avenue
Hamden, CT 06514
(203) 288-7474

Florida

David G. Erwin Technical Center
2010 East Hillborough Avenue
Tampa, FL 33610
(813) 231-1800

Pensacola Junior College
1000 College Blvd.
Pensacola, FL 32504
www.pjc.cc.fl.us/netscape.html

Pinellas Technical Educational Center
901 34th Street South
St. Petersburg, FL 33711
http://168.213.60.5/PTEC2.htm

Sarasota County Technical Institute
4748 Beneva Road
Sarasota, FL 34233
www.careerscape.org/

South College
1760 North Congress Avenue
W Palm Beach, FL 33409
(561) 697-9200

Georgia

Atlanta Technical Institute
1560 Metropolitan Parkway SW
Atlanta, GA 30310
(404) 758-3700

Columbus Technical Institute
928 Manchester Expressway
Columbus, GA 31904
www.columbus.tec.ga.us/

Medix School
2108 Cobb Parkway
Smyrna, GA 30080
www.medixschool.com/

Savannah Technical Institute
5717 White Bluff Road
Savannah, GA 31405
(912) 351-4562

South College
709 Mall Boulevard
Savannah, GA 31406
(912) 691-6000

Thomas Technical Institute
15689 US Highway 19 North
Thomasville, GA 31792
www.thomas-tech.com/

Valdosta Technical Institute
4089 Val Tech Road
P.O. Box 928
Valdosta, GA 31602
www.valdosta.tec.ga.us/

Idaho

College of Southern Idaho
315 Falls Avenue
Twin Falls, ID 83303
www.csi.cc.id.us/

Illinois

Midstate College
411 West Northmoor Road
Peoria, IL 61614
www.midstate.edu/

Northwestern Business College
4829 North Lipps Avenue
Chicago, IL 60630
www.cl.ais.net/

Indiana

Ivy Tech State College, Columbus
4475 Central Avenue
Columbus, IN 47203
www.ivy.tec.in.us/columbus

Ivy Tech State College, Northwest
2401 Valley Drive
Valparaiso, IN 46383
http://gar.ivy.tech.in.us/valparaiso.html

International Business College
3811 Old Illinois Road
Ft. Wayne, IN 46804
(219) 432-8702

International Business College
7205 Shadeland Station
Indianapolis, IN 46256
(317) 841-6400

Michiana College
1030 East Jefferson Boulevard
South Bend, IN 46617
www.michianacollege.com

Iowa

American Institute of Commerce
1801 East Kimberley Road
Davenport, IA 52807
www.aiccf.com/

Southeastern Community College
1015 South Gear Aveneu, Drawer F
West Burlington, IA 52655
www.secc.cc.ia.us/

Iowa Lakes Community College
1900 North Grand
Spencer, IA 51301
(712) 262-7141

Kentucky

Kentucky Technical Institute
800 West Chestnut Street
Louisville, KY 40203
(502) 595-4275

West Kentucky Technical College
P.O. Box 7408
Paducah, KY 42002
www.wkytech.com/

Louisiana

Bossier Parish Community College
2719 Airline Drive
Bossier City. LA 71111
www.bpcc.cc.la.us/

Bryman College
2322 Canal Street
New Orleans, LA 70119
(504) 822-4500

Massachusetts

Southeastern Technical Institute
250 Foundry Street
S. Easton, MA 02375
(508) 238-1860

Michigan

Baker College of Muskegon
1903 Marquette Avenue
Muskegon, MI 49442
www.baker.edu/

Baker College of Owasso
1020 South Washington Street
Owasso, MI 48867
www.baker.edu/

Davenport College
415 East Fulton Street
Grand Rapids, MI 49503
www.davenport.edu/grandrapids/

Henry Ford Community College
5101 Evergreen Road
Dearborn, MI 48128
www.henryford.cc.mi.us/

Macomb Community College
Warren, MI 48093
www.macomb.cc.mi.us/

Oakland Community College
7350 Cooley Lake Road
Waterford, MI 48327
www.occ.cc.mi.us/

Minnesota

Anoka-Hennepin Technical College
1355 West Highway 10
Anoka, MN 55303
www.ank.tec.mn.us/

Medical Institute of Minnesota
5503 Green Valley Drive
Bloomington, MN 55437
www.mim.tec.mn.us/

Minneapolis Business College
1711 W County Road B
Roseville, MN 55113
www.bradfordschools.com/rose/index.html

Duluth Business University
Minneapolis School of Business
412 West Superior Street
Duluth, MN 55802
http://dbumn.com

Rochester Community & Technical College
851 30 Avenue SE
Highway 14 East
Rochester, MN 55904
www.roch.edu/

Northwest Technical College
2022 Central Avenue NE
East Grand Fork, MN 56721
www.ntc-online.com/

Mississippi

Hinds Community College
3805 Highway 80 East
Pearl, MS 39208
www.hinds.cc.ms.us/

Missouri

Springfield College
1010 West Sunshine Street
Springfield, MO 65807
(417) 864-7220

Nebraska

Central Community College
P.O. Box 1024
Hastings, NE 68902
www.cccneb.edu/

Grand Island College
410 West Second
Grand Island, NE 68801
www.kdsi.net/gicollege/general.htm

New Hampshire

New Hampshire Community Technical College
One College Drive
Claremont, NH 03743
www.nhctc.tec.nh.us/clare.htm

New Jersey

Berdan Institute
265 Rt. 46 West
Totowa, NJ 07512
www.berdaninstitute.com/ceu.htm

Hudson County Community College
2039 Kennedy Boulevard / Science 330
Jersey City, NJ 07305
www.hudson.cc.nj.us/

New York

Bryant & Stratton Business Institute
953 James Street
Syracuse, NY 13203
(315) 472-6603

Bryant & Stratton Business Institute
1225 Jefferson Road
Rochester, NY 14623
(716) 292-5627

Bryant & Stratton Business Institute
465 Main Street, Suite 400
Buffalo, NY 14203
(716) 884-9120

Erie Community College
121 Ellicott Street
Buffalo, NY 14202
www.sunyerie.edu/

North Carolina

Carteret Community College
3505 Arendell Street
Morehead City, NC 28557
http://gofish.cartaret.cc.nc.us/

Gaston College
201 Highway 321 South
Dallas, NC 28034
www.gaston.cc.nc.us/

Guilford Technical Community College
P.O. Box 309
Jamestown, NC 27282
http://technet.gtcc.cc.nc.us/

Haywood Community College
185 Freedlander Drive
Clyde, NC 28721
http://w3.haywood.cc.nc.us/

King's College
322 Lamar Avenue
Charlotte, NC 28204
www.bradfordschools.com/char/index.html

Pitt Community College
Highway 11 South, Drawer 7007
Greenville, NC 27835
www.pitt.cc.nc.us/

Wake Technical Community College
9101 Fayetteville Road
Raleigh, NC 27603
www.wake.tec.nc.us/

Wingate University
P.O. Box 3024
Wingate, NC 28174
www.wingate.edu/

Ohio

Southern Ohio College NE
2791 Mogadore Road
Akron, OH 44312
(330) 733-8766

Akron Medical-Dental Institute
1625 Portage Trail
Akron, OH 44303
(330) 928-3400

Belmont Technical College
120 Fox-Shannon Place
St. Clairsville, OH 43950
www.belmont.cc.oh.us/

Bradford School
6170 Busch Boulevard
Columbus, OH 43229
www.bradfordschools.com/

Davis Junior College of Business
4747 Monroe Street
Toledo, OH 43623
(419) 473-2700

Knox County Career Center
306 Martinsburg Rd.
Mt. Vernon, OH 43050
www.treca.ohio.gov/schools/kccc/index.htm

Medina County Career Center
1101 West Liberty Street
Medina, OH 44256
www.medina.lib.oh.us/

Ohio Valley Business College
16808 St. Clair Avenue
E Liverpool, OH 43920
(330) 330-1070

University of Toledo
Community and Technical College
12801 West Bancroft Street
Toledo, OH 43606
www.utoledo.edu/

Oklahoma

Tulsa Community College
909 South Boston Avenue
Tulsa, OK 74119
www.tulsa.cc.ok.us/metro/campme.html

Oregon

Mt. Hood Community College
26000 SE Stark Street
Gresham, OR 97030
www.mhcc.cc.or.us/

Pennsylvania

Delaware County Community College
Rt. 252 & Media Line Road
Media, PA 19063
www.dccc.edu/

Duffs Business Institute
110 9th Street
Pittsburgh, PA 15222
(412) 261-4530

Harcum College
750 Montgomery Avenue
Bryn Mawr, PA 19010
www.harcum.edu/

Mt. Aloysius College
7373 Admiral Peary Hwy.
Cresson, PA 16630
(814) 886-6388

Sawyer School
717 Liberty Avenue
Pittsburg, PA 15222
www.sawyer.edu/

South Carolina

Trident Technical College
P.O. Box 11807
Charleston, SC 29423
www.trident.tec.sc.us/

South Dakota

Lake Area Technical Institute
230 11ᵗʰ Street NE
Watertown, SD 57201a
www.lati.tec.sd.us/

Tennessee

Knoxville Business College
720 North Fifth Avenue
Knoxville, TN 37917
(423) 524-3043

Miller-Motte Business College
1820 Business Park Drive
Clarksville, TN 37040
(615) 553-0071

Utah

American Institute of Medical & Dental
Technology
1675 North Freedom Boulevard, Bldg. 5A
Provo, UT 84604
(801) 377-2900

Latter Day Saints Business College
411 East South Temple
Salt Lake City, UT 84111
www.ldsbc.edu/

Salt Lake City Community College
4600 S Redwood RD/
P.O. Box 30808
Salt Lake City, UT 84130
www.slcc.edu/

Virginia

National Business College of the Roanoke
Valley
1813 East Main Street
Salem, VA 24153
(540) 986-1800

Wisconsin

Blackhawk Technical College
6004 Prairie Road
P.O. Box 5009
Janesville, WI 53547
www.blackhawk.tec.wi.us/

Bryant & Stratton College
1300 North Jackson Street
Milwaukee, WI 53202
www.bryantstratton.edu/

MENTAL HEALTH ASSISTANTS

Principal activity: Assisting in the care of the mentally disabled

Work commitment: Full-time

Preprofessional education: Usually a high school diploma

Program length: Several months to 2 years

Work prerequisites: On-the-job training possible; usually an associate degree is necessary

Career opportunities: Increasing

Income range: $15,000 to $30,000

Scope

Mental health assistants perform a variety of services for those who are emotionally and mentally handicapped. They provide therapeutic, supportive, and preventive care. The population served is wide-ranging, extending from children to the aged, both acutely and chronically sick, and those suffering from mental retardation and alcohol or drug dependencies. These workers are supervised by psychiatrists, psychologists, social workers, and most directly by registered nurses.

Activities

Mental health assistants initially interview and evaluate clients (patients), keep records, teach new skills, help motivate clients to learn, carry out therapeutic activities, provide behavior modification counseling, act as client advocates, help clients make the transition back to their homes, prepare their families for their care, follow up and report on client progress, and serve as a community resource for clients and their families.

These workers also take vital signs and participate in physical treatments and personal care. Their general goal should be to contribute to maximizing clients' opportunities for achieving their highest potential.

Work Settings

Mental health assistants work in state and private in-patient mental health facilities such as hospitals, schools for the mentally retarded, clinics, and community health centers. They also work in crisis and emergency centers, halfway houses, sheltered workshops, nursing homes, rehabilitation centers, and educational institutions.

Advancement

With increased experience and responsibility, these workers can receive salary gains. Some advancement is possible for those who develop specialty capabilities, such as working with children, substance abuse clients, crisis intervention clients, or the developmentally disabled.

Prerequisites

A high school diploma or its equivalent is desirable. Where an associate degree is sought, such a diploma is essential.

Desirable personal attributes for these workers include a strong sense of compassion, a great deal of patience, solid emotional stability, an outgoing and cheerful personality, tactfulness, and a genuine desire to help the emotionally ill.

Education/Training

Most openings in this field require an associate degree in mental health. Many community colleges offer programs in this field at this level. The curriculum in a mental health program involves courses in basic and psychiatric nursing, general and abnormal psychology, the theory of personality and social development, child development, group dynamics, and mental health technology.

Most training programs also offer the opportunity for students to perform supervised mental health work with clients.

Certification/Registration/Licensure

Only a few states require licensure, but their number is expected to increase.

Career Potential

In recent years, increased opportunities for workers in mental health have been created. This is the result of a greater awareness of the cost effectiveness of workers in this field. The increased number of clients being located in community settings rather than in inpatient facilities—together with the strong public demand for mental health services to cope with social problems such as substance abuse and an aging population—has contributed to this growth.

For More Information

Several hundred programs offer training in this field—far too many to list here.

Currently, there is no professional organization in this field. For more information, write to the Center for Mental Health Services, Human Resource Planning and Development Branch, Room 15C18, Rockville, MD 20857

NUCLEAR MEDICINE TECHNOLOGISTS

Principal activity: Securing nuclear medicine images of patients for physicians

Work commitment: Full-time

Preprofessional education: A high school diploma

Program length: 1 to 4 years

Work prerequisites: A certificate or degree/license

Career opportunities: Fair

Income range: $28,000 to $40,000

Scope

Doctors use many diagnostic techniques to uncover the causes of disease. One especially useful approach is to administer radioactive compounds, whose unstable atoms omit radiation spontaneously, and then to monitor their uptake in organs and tissues in which they localize. Abnormal areas show lower or higher concentrations of radioactivity than normal ones. To accomplish this, a special camera is placed over the body area of interest, and the radioactivity concentrated there is translated into light spots that expose the camera's film. The developed film—or *scan*—can show doctors a variety of functional or structural abnormalities.

Under a doctor's supervision, nuclear medicine technologists carry out the procedures that provide the data required to formulate a diagnosis of a possible structural or functional abnormality.

Nuclear medicine is used to detect diseases of the brain, the heart, the liver, the thyroid and other organs.

Activities

Nuclear medical technologists explain the procedure to patients, position them, then calculate the needed radioactive dose. Under a physician's supervision, they then administer the drugs for the test. Next, they operate the gamma ray detecting equipment, check the image quality, and arrange for recording of the data and development the film.

Nuclear medicine technologists also perform the laboratory procedure known as *radio assay*. This involves adding radioactive materials to specimens such as blood serum to determine hormone levels, for example.

Technologists also are responsible for ordering, handling, and properly disposing of radioactive drugs and for maintaining records of radionuclides and patient data.

Work Settings

Most nuclear medical technologists work in hospitals, but some are employed in radiologist's offices, in public health facilities, and in research and teaching institutions.

Advancement

With experience and education, a nuclear medical technologist can advance to a position as chief technologist department administrator, or director of a lab.

Prerequisites

A high school diploma or its equivalent is necessary for admission into most training programs.

Desirable personal attributes for workers in this field include physical stamina, strong verbal and numerical skills, attention to details, and the ability to work well with other professionals and with patients.

Education/Training

There are three programs of training in this field:

Certificate programs. These one-year programs are designed for health professionals seeking to changes careers. Typically, they are offered in hospitals and medical centers.

Associate degree programs. These two-year program usually are offered by community colleges.

Bachelor's degree programs. These four-year programs are offered by colleges and universities.

In a formal program of studies, courses include statistics, instrumentation, biochemistry, immunology, radionuclide chemistry and therapy, radiopharmacy administration, radiology, clinical nuclear medicine, and computer application and operation.

Most formal training programs in the field are accredited by the Joint Review Committee on Education Programs in Nuclear Medicine Technology Certification Board.

Certification/Registration/Licensure

About half of all states require nuclear medicine technologists to be licensed, and most employers prefer to hire registered or certified technologists.

Attaining certification is achieved by meeting the requirements of the American Registry of Radiologic Technologists or of the Nuclear Medicine Technology Certification Board.

Career Potential

The demand for nuclear medicine technologists is expected to be average in the coming years, but future openings may become more limited. As the U.S. population ages, the demand for this diagnostic technique will increase. However, the use of less invasive diagnostic techniques may negatively affect the field.

For More Information

For more information, write to one of the agencies listed below:

Society of Nuclear Medicine Technologists
1850 Samuel Morse Drive
Reston, VA 20090

American Society of Radiological Technologists
15000 Central Avenue, SE
Albuquerque NM 87123

Joint Review Committee on Educational Programs in Nuclear Medicine Technology
1144 West 3500 South
Salt Lake City, Utah 84119

Nuclear Medicine Technology Certification Board
2970 Clairmont Road
Atlanta, GA 30329

Nuclear Medicine Technologist Programs

Alabama

University of Alabama at Birmingham
School of Health-Related Professions
UAB Station, SHRP 214
Birmingham, AL 35294
www.uab.edu/

Arizona

Gateway Community College
108 North 40th Street
Phoenix, AZ 85034
www.gwc.maricopa.edu/

Arkansas

Baptist Medical System
11900 Colonel Glenn Road
Little Rock, AR 72210
www.baptist-health.com/

St. Vincent Infirmary Medical Ctr.
2 St. Vincent Circle
Little Rock, AR 72205
www.stvincenthealth.org/

University of Arkansas for Medical Sciences
4301 W Markam, Slot 714
Little Rock, AR 72205
www.uams.edu/

California

California State University, Dominguez Hills
1000 E Victoria Street
Carson, CA 90747
www.csudh.edu/

Loma Linda University
Office of the Dean
Loma Linda, CA 92350
www.llu.edu/

Charles R. Drew University of
Medicine and Science
1731 East 120th Street
Los Angeles, CA 90059
www.cdrewu.edu/

Los Angeles County–USC Medical Center
1200 North State Street
Los Angeles, CA 90033
www.usc.edu/

West Los Angeles Veterans'
Ambulatory Care Center
11301 Wilshire Boulevard
Los Angeles, CA 90073
(301) 268-3526

University of California–San Francisco
505 Parnassus Avenue
San Francisco, CA 94143
www.ucsf.edu/

Cancer Foundation of Santa Barbara
300 West Pueblo Street
Santa Barbara, CA 93105
www.ccsb.org/

Colorado

Community College of Denver
P.O. Box 173363
Denver, CO 80217
www.ccd.rightchoice.org/

Connecticut

St. Vincent's Medical Center
2800 Main Street
Bridgeport, CT 06606
www.stvincents.org/

Gateway Community Technical College
60 Sargeant Drive
New Haven, CT 06511
www.gwctc.commnet.edu/

Delaware

Delaware Technical Community College
333 Shipley Street
Wilmington, DE 19801
www.dtcc.edu/

District of Columbia

George Washington University Medical Center
2300 Eye Street, NW
Washington, DC 20037
www.gwumc.edu/

Florida

Santa Fe Community College
3000 NW 83rd Street
Gainesville, FL 32606
www.santefe.cc.fl.us/

University of Miami–Jackson
Memorial Medical Center
1611 NW 12th Avenue
Miami, FL 33136
www.ir.miami.edu/health-sciences/

Mt. Sinai Medical Center of Greater Miami
4300 Alton Road
Miami Beach, FL 33140
www.MountSinaiMiami.org/

Hillsborough Community College
P.O. Box 30030
Tampa, FL 33630
www.hcc.cc.fl.us/

Georgia

Medical College of Georgia
Augusta, GA 30912
www.mcg.edu/

Illinois

College of DuPage
425 22nd Street
Glen Ellyn, IL 60137
www.cod.edu/

Edward Hines Jr., Veterans
Administration Hospital
Fifth Avenue & Roosevelt RD
Hines, IL 60141
(708) 202-8387

St. Francis Medical Center
530 N.E. Glen Oak Avenue
Peoria, IL 61637
www.osfsaintfrancis.org/

Triton College
2000 North Fifth Avenue
River Grove, IL 60171
www.triton.cc.il.us/

Indiana

Ball State University
Methodist Hospital of Indiana
1701 N Senate Boulevard
Indianapolis, IN 46202
www.clarian.com/

Indiana University School of Medicine
425 University Blvd.
Cavanaugh Hall, Room 129
Indianapolis, IN 46202
www.indiana.edu/campus/iupui.htm.

Iowa

University of Iowa College of Medicine
120 CMAB
Iowa City, IA 52242
www.uiowa.edu/

Kentucky

Lexington Community College
Cooper Drive
Oswald Building
Lexington, KY 40506
www.uky.edu/LCC/

University of Louisville
Health Science Center
Louisville, KY 40292
www.louisville.edu/

Louisiana

Alton Ochsner Medical Foundation
1514 Jefferson Highway
New Orleans, LA 70121
www.ochnser.org/education/

Delgado Community College
615 City Park Avenue
New Orleans, LA 70119
www.dcc.edu/

Shreveport Veterans' Medical Center
510 East Stoner Avenue
Shreveport, LA 71101
(318) 221-8411

Maryland

Essex Community College
7201 Rossville Boulevard
Baltimore, MD 21237
www.ccbc.cc.md.us/

Naval School of Health Sciences
8901 WIsconsin Avenue
Bethesda, MD 20889
www.nshs.med.navy.mil/

Prince George's Community College
301 Largo Road
Largo, MD 20774
www.pg.cc.md.us/

Massachusetts

Bunker Hill Community College
250 New Rutherford Avenue
Boston, MA 02129
www.bhcc.state.ma.us/

Massachusetts College of Pharmacy & Health
Sciences
179 Longwood Avenue
Boston, MA 02215
www.mcp.edu/

Salem State College
352 Lafayette Street
Salem, MA 01970
www.salem-ma.edu/

Springfield Technical Community College
One Armory Square
Springfield, MA 01105
www.stcc.mass.edu/

University of Massachusetts Medical Center
55 Lake Avenue North
Worcester, MA 01655
www.umass.med.edu/

Michigan

Ferris State University
901 South State Street
Big Rapids, MI 49307
www.ferris.edu/

St. John's Hospital & Medical Center
22101 Moross Road
Detroit, MI 48236
www.stjohn.org/

William Beaumont Hospital
3601 West Thirteen Mile Road
Royal Oak, MI 48073
www.beaumont.edu/

Minnesota

Mayo Foundation
200 First Street SW
Rochester, MN 55905
www.mayo.edu/

St. Mary's University
700 Terrace Heights
Winnona, MN 55987
www.smumn.edu/

Mississippi

University of Mississippi Medical Center
2500 North State Street
Jackson, MS 39216
www.umc.edu/

Missouri

Univerisity of Missouri–Columbia
One Hospital Drive
Columbia, MO 65211
www.missouri.edu/

Research Medical Center
2316 East Meyer Boulevard
Kansas City, MO 64132
www.healthmidwest.org/hospitals/rmc.shtml

St. Luke's Hospital of Kansas City
4400 Wornall Road
Kansas City, MO 64111
www.sdint-lukes.org/about/stlukes.html

St. Louis University
Allied Health Building, Room 3113
3437 Caroline Mall
St. Louis, MO 63104
www.slu.edu/

Nebraska

University of Nebraska Medical Center
600 South 42nd Street
Omaha, NE 68198
www.unmc.edu/

Nevada

University of Nevada
4505 Maryland Parkway
Las Vegas, NV 89154
www.unlv.edu/

New Jersey

John F. Kennedy Medical Center
65 James Street
Edison, NJ 08818
http://jfkmc.org/index.htm

University of Medicine & Dentistry
of New Jersey
65 Bergen Street
Newark, NJ 07107
www.umdnj.edu/

Gloucester County College
1400 Tanyard Road
Sewell, NJ 08080
www.gccnj.edu/

Overlook Hospital
99 Beauvoir Avenue
Summit, NJ 07902
www.atlantichealth.org/hospitals/overlook/

New Mexico

University of New Mexico
School of Medicine
Albuquerque, NM 87131
www.unm.edu/

New York

CUNY Bronx Community College
University Avenue & W 181 St.
The Bronx, NY 10453
www.bcc.cuny.edu/

SUNY Health Science Center–Brooklyn
450 Clarkson Avenue
Brooklyn, NY 11203
www.hscbklyn.edu/

SUNY Health Science Center at Buffalo
105 Parker Hall
Buffalo, NY 14260
http://wings.buffalo.edu/

Institute of Allied Medical Professions
405 Park Avenue
New York, NY 10022
(212) 758-1410

New York University Medical Center
550 First Avenue
New York, NY 10016
www.med.njy.edu/som/

St. Vincent's Hospital and
Medical Center of New York
153 W 11th Street #840
New York, NY 10011
(212) 604-7000

Northport VA Medical Center
79 Middleville Road
Northport, NY 11768
(516) 261-4400

Manhattan College
Manhattan College Parkway
Riverdale, NY 10471
www.mancol.edu/

Rochester Institute of Technology
One Lamb Memorial Drive
Rochester, NY 14623
www.rit.edu/

Wagner College
One Campus Road
Staten Island, NY 10301
www.wagner.edu/

North Carolina

University of North Carolina Hospitals
101 Manning Drive
Chapel Hill, NC 27514
(919) 966-4131

Forsyth Technical Community College
2100 Silas Creek Parkway
Winston-Salem, NC 27103
www.forsyth.tec.nc.us/

Ohio

Aultman Hospital
2600 Sixth Street SW
Canton, OH 44710
www.aultman.com/education/

University Hospital
234 Goodman Street
Cincinnati, OH 45219
www.health-alliance.com/univ_control.html

Ohio State University Medical Center
410 W Tenth Avenue
Columbus, OH 43210
www.osumedcenter.edu/

The University of Findlay
1000 N Main Street
Findley, OH 45840
www.findlay.edu/

St. Elizabeth Hospital Medical Center
1044 Belmont Avenue
Youngstown, OH 44501
(330) 746-7211

Oklahoma

University of Oklahoma
Health Sciences Center
1100 North Lindsay
Oklahoma City, OK 73104
www.ou.edu/

Oregon

Portland VA Medical Center
P.O. Box 1034
3710 SW US Veterans Hospital Road
Portland, OR 97207
(503) 220-8262

Pennsylvania

Cedar Crest College
100 College Drive
Allentown, PA 18104
www.cedarcrest.edu/

Harrisburg Hospital
111 South Front Street
Harrisburg, PA 17101
www.pinnaclehealth.org/

Hospital of the University of Pennsylvania
3400 Spruce Street
Philadelphia, PA 19104
www.med.upenn.edu/health/

Temple University
College of Allied Health Professions
3307 North Broad Street
Philadelphia, PA 19140
www.temple.edu/CAHP/

Community College of Allegheny County
808 Ridge Avenue
Pittsburgh, PA 15212
www.ccac.edu/

Wilkes-Barre General Hospital
North River & Auburn Streets
Wilkes-Barre, PA 18764
(570) 829-8111

Rhode Island

Rhode Island Hospital
593 Eddy Street
Providence, RI 02902
www.brown.edu/

South Carolina

Midlands Technical College
P.O. Box 2408
Columbia SC 29202
www.mid.tec.sc.us/edu/home.html

Tennessee

University of Tennessee Medical Center
1924 Alcoa Highway
Knoxville, TN 37920
www.utmck.edu/homens4.htm

Baptist Memorial Hospital
899 Madison Avenue
Memphis, TN 38146
www.bmhcc.org/services/hospitals/
MedCenter.asp

Vanderbilt University Medical Center
Radiology Department–RM R1317 MCN
21st and Garland
Nashville, TN 37232
www.mc.vanderbilt.edu/

Texas

University of Texas Medical Branch
School of Allied Health Services
301 University Blvd.
Galveston, TX 77555
www.sahs.utmb.edu/

Baylor College of Medicine
One Baylor Plaza
Houston, TX 77030
www.bcm.tmc.edu/

Houston Community College System
Eastwood Health Sciences Center
3100 Shenandoah
Houston, TX 77021
www.hccs.cc.tx.us/

University of the Incarnate Word
4301 Broadway
San Antonio, TX 78209
www.uiw.edu/

Utah

Weber State University
Ogden, UT 84408
www.weber.edu/

University of Utah Health Sciences Center
50 North Medical Drive
Salt Lake City, UT 84132
WWW.uutah.edu/

Vermont

University of Vermont
004 Rowell Building
Brulington, VT 05405
www.uvm.edu/

Virginia

University of Virginia Health Science Center
Jefferson Park Avenue/Box 486
Charlottesville, VA 22908
www.uva.edu/

Old Dominion University
Hampton Blvd.
Norfolk, VA 23529
http://web.odu/edu/

Virginia Commonwealth University
Department of Radiation Sciences
West Hospital
1200 East Broad Street
Richmond, VA 23298
www.vcu.edu/

Carilion Health Systems
Roanoke Memorial Hospitals
P.O. Box 13367
Roanoke, VA 24033
www.carilion.com/hospitals/crmh.html

Washington

Bellevue Community College
3000 Landerholm Circle SE
P.O. Box 92700
Bellevue, WA 98807
www.bcc.ctc.edu/

West Virginia

West Virginia State College
P.O. Box 1000
Institute, WV 25112
www.wvsc.edu/

West Virginia University
Robert C. Byrd Health Sciences Center
Morgantown, WV 26506
www.hsc.wvu.edu/

Wheeling Jesuit University
316 Washington Avenue
Wheeling, WV 26003
www.wju.edu/

Wisconsin

St. Joseph's Hospital
611 St. Joseph Avenue
Marshfield, WI 54449
www.stjosephs-marshfield.org/

Milwaukee County Medical Complex
9455 West Watertown Plank Road
Milwaukee, WI 53226
(414) 257-6995

St. Luke's Medical Center
2900 West Oklahoma Avenue
Milwaukee, WI 53215
(414) 649-6000

St. Mary's Hospital of Milwaukee
2323 North Lake Drive
Milwaukee, WI 53211
(404) 291-1039

Nursing and Psychiatric Aides

Principal activity: Assisting with routine patient care in medical and psychiatric hospitals

Work commitment: Usually full-time

Preprofessional education: High school diploma

Program length: 6 weeks to 3 months

Work prerequisites: On-the-job training

Career opportunities: Good

Income range: $12,000 to $25,000

Scope

Nursing and psychiatric aides help in the routine daily care of physically or mentally ill or impaired patients in a variety of settings. Although not involving sophisticated equipment or cutting-edge procedures, their work is vital in helping people recover or remain at least physically or emotionally stable and as comfortable as possible in an environment outside of their homes.

Activities

Nursing aides, also known as *nursing assistants* or *hospital attendants*, work under the direct supervision of the nursing staff in facilitating routine activities and enhancing patients' well-being. They make beds; help patients eat, bathe, dress, and walk; take readings of vital signs (e.g., temperature, pulse, and respiration); help secure meals; provide massages (to maintain skin health); and respond to calls by patients for assistance. When necessary, they transport patients to specific sites for treatment, therapy, or recreation. They also help maintain the condition of their patients' rooms and report to their supervisors any significant changes in patients' conditions.

    Psychiatric aides, also known as *psychiatric nursing or mental health assistants*, provide help with daily personal care for mentally impaired or emotionally disturbed individuals. Their work is supervised by psychiatric nurses. In addition, when necessary they help patients eat, bathe, and dress. These aides also socialize with patients and participate in their recreational and educational programs. This may involve playing games or going on field trips. They accompany patients to therapy sites and report any unusual changes in patient behavior to their supervisors.

Work Settings

About half of all nursing aides are employed in nursing homes, where they are frequently known as *geriatric aides*. One-quarter work in acute-care or chronic care-hospitals, and the rest work in residential facilities or private households.

    Most psychiatric aides render their services in hospitals (state, country, private, and acute care), residential facilities, and community mental health centers. A few are employed in nursing homes.

Prerequisites

No formal education is needed for either position, but a high school diploma is helpful.

    Desirable personal attributes for either job include good physical and emotional health, the ability to follow instructions and use good judgment, dependability, and a strong sense of compassion.

Education/Training

Formal nursing aide training, which varies in length and depth, is offered by some high schools, vocational-technical institutes, community colleges, and nursing homes. Courses cover body mechanics, nutrition, anatomy, physiology, infection control, communication skills, personal care skills, and resident rights.

    Many facilities rely exclusively on informal, on-the-job training provided by a nurse or an experienced aide. This training may last several days or a few months.

Certification/Registration/Licensure

While professional accreditation is uncommon, some nursing homes require aides to successfully complete state-mandated programs. Others require aides to take a minimum of 75 hours of training and pass a competency exam within four months. Successful candidates receive certificates and are placed on a State Registry of Nursing Aides.

Career Potential

Employment prospects for nurses aides will be good over the next decade. The expanding older population in the U.S. will result in an increase of nursing homes and long-time care facilities.

There will also be a strong demand for psychiatric aides, as the large pool of elderly needs more mental health services. In addition, private psychiatric facilities and community health centers will have increased need for their services.

For More Information

There is no professional organization in this field. For more information, write to the American Health Care Association, 1201 L Street NW, Washington, DC 20005.

 # OPHTHALMIC ASSISTANTS

Principal activity: Assisting ophthalmologists

Work commitment: Usually full-time

Preprofessional education: High school diploma

Program length: 1 to 2 years

Work prerequisites: Certification preferred

Career opportunities: Very favorable

Income range: $15,000 to $20,000

Scope

The ophthalmic assistant is the lowest of three ranks of para-ophthalmic personnel. These workers perform various support services to help eye doctors diagnose and treat their patients. The other two levels are *ophthalmic technician* (p. 263) and *ophthalmic technologist* (p. 265).

Activities

The major function of an ophthalmic assistant is to secure information about patients' overall medical conditions and specific details about their ocular history, as well as any current problems; to measure their visual acuity (both with and without glasses); to secure other ocular measurements; to administer medications; to handle minor adjustments and repairs of eye glasses; to maintain ophthalmologic equipment; and to sterilize the doctor's instruments.

Work Settings

Most ophthalmic assistants are employed in ophthalmologists' offices. Others secure positions in medical centers, hospitals, clinics, and research facilities.

Advancement

With additional experience and training, an ophthalmic assistant can become a technician or technologist.

Prerequisites

A high school diploma or its equivalent is necessary to enter this field.

Desirable personal attributes include excellent vision, a commitment to accuracy, manual dexterity, good communication skills, a pleasant personality, and a great deal of patience.

Education/Training

There are two routes to becoming an ophthalmic assistant. One is securing on-the-job training and experience. The other is an educational program completed at a hospital or teaching institution. Courses include anatomy (especially of the eye), physiology, psychology, medical terminology, microbiology, optics, eye testing, diagnostic treatment methods, and ophthalmic instruments.

Certification/Registration/Licensure

Certification is voluntary but does facilitate career advancement. Meeting certain educational requirements and having a set amount of experience qualifies a candidate to take the written certification exam.

Career Potential

The job outlook for this profession is very favorable, because of the increase in the U.S. population, and especially of elderly individuals, who are those most frequently in need of eye care.

For More Information

The certification organization is the Joint Commission on Allied Personnel of Ophthalmology, 2025 Woodlawn Drive, St. Paul, MN 55125.

Ophthalmic Assistant Programs

Arizona

Pima Medical Institute
3350 East Grant Road
Tucson, AZ 85716
(520) 326-1600

Colorado

Pima Medical Institute
1701 West 72nd Avenue
Denver, CO 80221
(303) 426-1800

District of Columbia

Georgetown University Medical Center
3800 Reservoir Road NW
Washington, DC 20007
www.gumc.edu/

Louisiana

Tulane University Medical Center
1430 Tulane Avenue
New Orleans, LA 70112
www.tmc.tulane.edu/

Delgado Community College
615 City Park Avenue
New Orleans, LA 70119
www.dcc.edu/cpark.html

Massachusetts

Boston University School of Medicine
715 Albany Street, L-124
Boston, MA 02118
www.bumc.bu.edu/

Michigan

Detroit Institute of Ophthalmology
15415 East Jefferson Avenue
Grosse Pointe Park, MI 48230
http://rush.brophy.com/DIO_web/html/
main01.htm

New Jersey

Uuniversity of Medicine & Dentistry
90 Bergen Street, Room 6157
Newark, NJ 07103
www.umdnj.edu/

New York

Lighthouse International
111 East 59th Street
New York, NY 10022
www.lighthouse.org/

Ohio

Stark State College of Technology
6200 Frank Avenue NW
Canton, OH 44720
www.stark.cc.oh.us/

Pennsylvania

Westmoreland County Community College
Armbrust Road
Youngwood, PA 15697
www.westmoreland.cc.pa.us/

Texas

AMEDD Center and School
2751 McIndoe Road
Fort Sam Houston, TX 78234
http://fshtx.cs.amedd.army.mil/AMEDDCS/
default.htm

Washington

Pima Medical Institute
1627 Eastlake Avenue
Seattle, WA 98102
(206) 322-6100

West Virginia

Carver Career & Technical Educational Center
4700 Midland Drive
Charleston, WV 25306
www.wvonline.com/carver/aboutus.htm

Canada

Centennial College
Box 631, Station A
Scarborough, Ontario
Canada M1K 5E9
www.cencol.on.ca/

OPHTHALMIC TECHNICIANS

Principal activity: Assisting an ophthalmologist

Work commitment: Usually full-time

Preprofessional education: High school diploma

Program length: 1 to 2 years

Work prerequisites: Certification preferred

Career opportunities: Very favorable

Income range: $17,500 to $22,500

Scope

The ophthalmic technician is the middle of the three ranks of paramedical eye care personnel. Their support services for the ophthalmologist are more sophisticated and thus demand a higher degree of training and skill.

Activities

Ophthalmic technicians perform the same tasks as ophthalmic assistants (see p. 260). Additionally, they are qualified to evaluate ocular mobility, measure for contact lenses and instruct patients in their use and care, secure eye samples for cultures, ensure that optical instruments are aligned and calibrated, change dressings, and provide other direct patient care.

Work Settings

Most ophthalmic technicians work in the offices of ophthalmologists. Others work in patient treatment facilities such as medical centers, hospitals, and clinics.

Advancement

With experience and training, an ophthalmic technician can become an ophthalmic technologist. Supervisory responsibilities also are possible.

Prerequisites

A high school diploma or its equivalent is needed to work int his field.

Desirable personal attributes for people entering the field include high visual acuity, meticulous work habits, strong interpersonal skills, manual dexterity, and a strong sense of responsibility.

Education/Training

Both informal, on-the-job training and formal training programs are available. Formal programs include courses in anatomy, physiology, pharmacology, microbiology, pathology, optics, diseases of the eye, visual field testing, and supervised clinical practice.

Certification/Registration/Licensure

Certification is not mandatory, but it can be helpful in advancing one's career. With a set length of experience, candidates can take the certification exam.

Career Potential

The job potential for ophthalmic technicians is very favorable due to the increasing demands for ophthalmological services.

For More Information

The certifying body is the Joint Commission of Allied Health Personnel in Ophthalmology, 2025 Woodlane Drive, St. Paul, MN 55125.

Ophthalmic Technician Programs

District of Columbia

Georgetown University Medical Center
Department of Ophthalmology
3800 Reservoir Road NW
Washington, DC 20007
www.gwumc.edu/

Illinois

Triton College
2000 North Fifth Avenue
River Grove, IL 60171
www.triton.cc.il.us/

Massachusetts

Boston University Medical Center
Department of Ophthalmology
715 Albany Street, L-124
Boston, MA 02118
www.bumc.bu.edu/

Michigan

Detroit Institute of Ophthalmology
15415 East Jefferson Avenue
Grosse Point Park, MI 48230
http://rush.brophy.com/DIO_web/html/
main01.htm

Minnesota

Regions Hospital
School of Ophthalmic Technology
640 Jackson Street
St. Paul, MN 55101
www.healthpartners.com/regions/

North Carolina

Duke University School of Medicine
Ophthalmic Medical Technician Program
Box 3802
Durham, NC 27710
www2.duke.edu/som/bulopt.thml

Oregon

Portland Community College
705 North Killingsworth Street
Portland, OR 97217
www.pcc.edu/cascade/index.htm

OPHTHALMIC TECHNOLOGISTS

Principal activity: Assisting ophthalmologists

Work commitment: Usually full-time

Preprofessional education: High school diploma

Program length: 1 to 2 years

Work prerequisites: Certification preferred

Career opportunities: Very favorable

Income range: $20,000 to $25,000

Scope

The ophthalmic technologist is the highest level of three ranks of para-ophthalmic personnel. Technologists are qualified to provide the most advanced type of assistance to ophthalmologists. They are involved in the widest array of activities, carry the greatest responsibilities, and are receive the highest salaries.

Activities

Ophthalmic technologists provide a wide range of patient services. They take patient histories, perform routine tests and measurements, fit patients for contact lenses, and maintain sophisticated ophthalmological equipmen. They also perform vital measurements and tests with sophisticated equipment and assist in surgery (both in the doctor's office and in hospitals).

Work Settings

For the most part, ophthalmic technologists are employed in private practice offices of ophthalmologists. They may also work in medical centers, hospitals, and clinics.

Advancement

An ophthalmic technologist may secure a supervisory position in a larger office.

Prerequisites

A high school diploma or its equivalent is necessary for this profession.

Desirable personal attributes for technologists include superior vision, the ability to perform highly detailed work, above-average manual dexterity, strong oral communication abilities, a positive personality, strong organization skills, and supervisory ability.

Education/Training

On-the-job training is available, but securing a formal education will help one secure a better position. Formal programs include courses in the basic biomedical sciences, ophthalmic pharmacology, toxicology, optics, eye diseases and their diagnosis and treatment, visual testing and measurements, optical instrument care, and ophthalmic surgical procedures. Supervised practice is obligatory.

Certification/Registration/Licensure

Certification certainly helps in the employment search. Candidates who have completed a formal education program and have the required experience can take a written certification exam. They also must pass a hands-on test.

Career Potential

Job opportunities in this profession are very favorable. This is the result of the high demand for the services of ophthalmologists, especially by the elderly. In addition, public awareness of the need for quality eye care is increasing.

For More Information

The certifying body in the field is the Joint Commission of Allied Health in Ophthalmology, 2025 Woodlane Drive, St. Paul, MN 35125.

Ophthalmic Technologist Programs

District of Columbia

Georgetown University Medical Center
3800 Reservoir Road NW
Washington, DC 20007
www.gwumc.edu/

Florida

University of Florida
Box 100284
Gainesville, FL 32661
www.ufl.edu/

Louisiana

Louisiana State University Medical Center
433 Bolivar Street
New Orleans, LA 70112
www.lsumc.edu/

Massachusetts

Boston University Medical Center
715 Albany Street, L-124
Boston, MA 02118
www.bumc.edu/

Michigan

Detroit Institute of Ophthalmology
15415 East Jefferson Avenue
Grosse Pointe, MI 48230
http://rush.brophy.com/

Minnesota

Regions Hospital
640 Jackson Street
St. Paul, MN 55101
www.healthpartners.com/regions/

New York

New York Eye & Ear Infirmary
310 East 14th Street
New York, NY 10003
www.nyee.edu/

Virginia

Old Dominion University/
Eastern Virginia Medical School
600 Gresham Drive
Norfolk, VA 23507
www.odu.edu/

Canada
Stanton Yellowknife Hospital
Box 10
Yellowknife, Ontario
Canada X1A 2NI
(807) 920-4111

Dalhousie Medical School
5849 University Avenue
Halifax, Nova Scotia
Canada B3H 4H7
www.mcms.dal.ca/

OPTICIANS

Principal activity: Dispensing eyeglasses and contact lenses

Work commitment: Usually full-time, but part-time is possible

Preprofessional education: High school diploma

Program length: 2- to 4-year apprenticeship; 6-month to 2-year educational program

Work prerequisites: Completion of apprenticeship or formal program with certificate or diploma

Career opportunities: Good

Income range: $20,000 (entry level) to $60,000 (self-employed).

Scope

Most people recognize the importance of proper eye care and periodically visit an *ophthalmologist* (a medical doctor specializing in eye diseases) or an optometrist. Children may have their eyes routinely checked in school, where some will find they have problems such as near-sightedness.

Like optometrists, opticians fit, adjust, and dispense glasses and contact lenses (but do not prescribe them). Many people, especially those at the onset of middle age, find their eyes no longer retain visual acuity and they need corrective lenses to adjust to the change. They are given prescriptions for eue glasses or contact lenses to overcome this limitation.

Activities

Opticians first evaluate the prescriptions presented to them and measure the distance between the centers of the customers' pupils to determine positioning of the lenses. Next, they help customers choose frames that accommodate the thickness and weight of the lenses they need and that complement their facial characteristics.

Once the selection is made, the optician orders the frames as well as the appropriate lenses. The latter are usually prepared by an ophthalmic laboratory technician (see p. 263), who receives a work order specifying the lens prescriptions, size, material, color, and style.

The optician may place the ground lenses in the selected frame, but often the lenses are already inserted. The glasses are properly adjusted so they are comfortable and properly positioned.

Opticians may also be called upon to duplicate glasses. The prescriptions may be on file, obtained from an ophthalmologist, or determined by use of a *lensometer*. Opticians also repair broken lenses and frames.

Some opticians are also qualified to fit contact lenses. To do so, they must be trained to measure eye shape and size. Fitting contact lenses requires considerable care, skill, and patience. The selected lenses are then checked to see if they fit and the customer is taught how to use them to avoid damaging the lens or infecting the eyes.

Some opticians are also skilled in dispensing cosmetic shells that conceal defects in the appearance of an eye or in fitting artificial eyes.

Work Settings

Opticians may work for ophthalmologists or optometrists or in hospital eye clinics. Most commonly they are employed by optical stores or chains. Many are self-employed.

Advancement

Opticians can advance by moving to a larger facility or by opening their own business. Others become managers in stores or sales representatives.

Prerequisites

A high school diploma or its equivalent is essential for this field. Recommended courses include basic anatomy, physics, algebra, geometry, and mechanical drawing.

Desirable personal attributes include an ability to deal with the public in a tactful and courteous manner, good communication skills, manual dexterity, superior vision, and a desire to help people.

Education/Training

Training is usually secured in an on-the-job apprenticeship, but formal programs do exist. Large employers generally offer structured training programs, and small employers provide more informal training that can last two to four years. Apprenticeship programs involve instruction in optical mathematics, optical physics, usage of precision instruments for measurement, other equipment, office management, and sales.

Some community colleges offer two-year associate degree programs in optical fabrication and dispensing. Shorter formal educational programs are offered by vocational-technical institutes, trade schools, and manufacturers. These programs last six months to two years and award a diploma or certificate at completion.

Certification/Registration/Licensure

Opticians may apply to the Commission on Optical Accreditation and the National Contact Lens Examiners for certification of their skills. Certification must be renewd every three years through continuing education.

Many states require a license dispense eyeglasses. Candidates must meet certain educational standards and pass a written or practical examination.

Career Potential

Job opportunities in this field should be quite favorable, due to the again of the U.S. population. Improvements in lenses and changes in frame styles also enhance prospective business needs.

For More Information

The professional organization in this field is the Opticians' Association of America, 10341 Democracy Lane, Fairfax, VA 22030.

An additional source of information is the National Academy of Opticianry, 10111 Martin Luther King Jr. Highway, Bowie, MD 20720.

Opticianry Programs

Connecticut

Middlesex Community-Technical College
100 Training Hill Road.
Middletown, CT 06457
www.mxctc.commnet.edu/mxhome/
mxhome.htm

Florida

Hillsborough Community College
Dale Mabry Campus
P.O. Box 30030
Tampa, FL 33630
www.hcc.cc.fl.us/dalemabry/dalemabry.htm

Miami-Dade Community College
950 NW 20th Street
Miami, FL 33127
www.mdcc.edu/medical/

Georgia

DeKalb Technical Institute
495 North Indian Creek Drive
Clarkston, GA 30021
www.dekalb.tec.ga.us/

Massachusetts

Holyoke Community College
303 Homestead Avenue
Holyoke, MA 01040
www.hcc.mass.edu/

Mount Ida College
777 Dedham Street
Newton Centre, MA 02459
www.mountida.edu/

Worcester Polytechnic Institute
100 Institute Road
Worcester, MA 01609
www.wpi.edu/

Michigan

Ferris State University
901 South State Street
Big Rapids, MI 49307
www.ferris.edu/

Minnesota

Anoka-Hennepin Technical College
1355 West Highway 10
Anoka, MN 55303
www.ank.tec.mn.us/

New Hampshire

New Hampshire Community Technical College
505 Amherst Street
Nashua, NH 03061
www.nashua.tec.nh.us/

New Jersey

Camden County College
P.O. Box 200
College Drive
Blackwood, NJ 08012
www.camdencc.edu/

Essex County College
303 University Avenue
Newark, NJ 07102
www.essex.edu/

Raritan Valley Community College
P.O. Box 3300
Somerville, NJ 08876
www.raritanval.edu/

New Mexico

Southwestern Indian Polytechnic Institute
9169 Coors Road NW
P.O. Box 10146
Albuquerque, NM 87196
http://kafka.sipi.tec.nm.us/

New York

Erie Community College
6205 Main Street
Williamsville, NY 14221
www.sunyerie.edu/

Interboro Institute
450 West 56th Street
New York, NY 10019
www.arragon.com/schools/school-1051.asp

Mater Dei College
5428 State Highway 37
Ogdensburg, NY 13669
www.materdei.net

New York City Technical College
300 Jay Street
Brooklyn, NY 11201
www.nyctc.cuny.edu/

Tennessee

Roane State Community College
276 Patton Lane
Harriman, TN 37748
www.rscc.cc.tn.us/

Texas

El Paso Community College
P.O. Box 20500
El Paso, TX 79998
www.epcc.edu/

Virginia

J. Sargeant Reynolds Community College
P.O. Box 85622
Richmond, VA 23285
www.jsrcc.cc.va.us/

Naval Ophthalmic Support & Training Activity
P.O. Box 350
Yorktown, VA 23691
http://nostra.med.navy.mil/command.html

Thomas Nelson Community College
P.O. Box 9407
Hampton, VA 23670
www.tncc.cc.va.us/

Washington

Seattle Central Community College
1701 Broadway
Seattle, WA 98122
http://edison.sccd.ctc.edu/sccc.html

OPTOMETRIC ASSISTANTS

Principal activity: Assisting optometrists

Work commitment: Full- and part-time

Preprofessional training: High school diploma

Program length: 1 year

Work prerequisites: Registered status preferred

Career opportunities: Favorable

Income range: $16,000 to $19,000

Scope

Optometric assistants facilitate the professional activities of optometrists. They are categorized as *para-optometrists* or *eye care paramedics*. Their various but routine activities are essential to the effective functioning of an optometrist's office.

Activities

Optometric assistants perform office and record-keeping duties and act as a patient receptionist. They take medical histories, prepare patients for eye examinations, order lenses prescribed by the optometrist, obtain facial and frame measurements, and help patients choose their frames. They also may record the data an optometrist secures during an examination.

Work Settings

The usual work setting is an optometrist's office, which may be a private practice or part of a chain. HMOs, health-care clinics, and government agencies also employ optometric assistants.

Advancement

Becoming a registered assistant and working in a large establishment offer the possibility of a supervisory appointment. With additional training , an optometric assistant can become a technician.

Prerequisites

A high school diploma or its equivalent is required for work in this field.

Desirable personal attributes for optometric assistants include the ability to work well with people, organized work habits, and accuracy.

Education/Training

Most people seeking to become optometric assistants get on-the-job training. Increasingly, however, a formal education is becoming more common.

One-year courses are offered by vocational-technical schools and community colleges. The program covers office procedures and secretarial skills in addition to courses in anatomy and physiology of the eye and other vision-related topics. Students do classroom, and laboratory work as well as supervised clinical experience.

Certification/ Registration/Licensure

After completing a training program and gaining some experience, an optometric assistant can gain registration by passing the Optometric Assistant Registry Examination. This allows one to be designated as an *Opt.A.R.*, an attribute that can increase one's employment opportunities.

Career Potential

The job outlook for optometric assistants is favorable. Two major considerations lead to this positive forecast. The first is that the overall population of the United States is increasing, especially the elderly, who have the highest need for optometric services. Second, today's graduating optometrists are trained to use the services of para-optometric personnel, to whom they delegate many routine responsibilities.

For More Information

There is no professional organization for optometric assistants, but additional information is available from the America Optometric Association (AOA), Paraoptometric Section, 243 North Lindbergh Boulevard, St. Louis, MO 63141.

The list of optometric assistant programs that follows was prepared by the AOA.

Optometric Assistant Programs

Colorado

Colorado Mountain College
Timberline Campus
901 South Highway 24
Leadville, Co. 80461
www.coloradomtn.edu/

Florida

Erwin Technical Center
2010 East Hillsborough Avenue
Tampa, FL 33610
(813) 231-1815

McFatter Technical Center
6500 Nova Drive
Davie, FL 33317
www.mcfatter.com/

Traviss Technical Center
3225 Winter Lake Road
Lakeland, FL 33803
www.curriculum.inst.pcsb.k12.fl.us/

Iowa

North Iowa Area Community College
500 College Drive
Mason City, IA 50401
www.niacc.cc.ia.us/

Minnesota

Minnesota West Community College
Highway 212 West
Granite Falls, MN 52641
www.mnwest.mnscu.edu/granitefalls.html

St. Cloud Technical College
1540 Northway Drive
St. Cloud, MN 56303
wwww.mrwa.com/sctc.htm

Nebraska

Mid-Plains Community College
1101 Halligan Drive
North Platte, NE 69101
http://164.119.202.40/mpcc/index.html

South Carolina

Greenville Technical College
P.O. Box 5616, Station B
Greenville, SC 29606
www.greenvilletech.com/

Wisconsin

Lakeshore Technical College
1290 North Avenue
Cleveland, WI 53105
www.ltc.tec.wi.us/main.html

Madison Area Technical College
3550 Anderson Street
Madison, WI 53704
www.madison.tec.wi.us/

OPTOMETRIC TECHNICIANS

Principal activity: Assisting optometrists

Work commitment: Full- or part-time

Preprofessional education: High school diploma

Program length: 2 years

Work prerequisites: Associate degree preferred

Career opportunities: Favorable

Income ranges: $18,000 to $25,000

Scope

Optometric technicians are also called *para-optometric workers* or *eye care paramedics*. They facilitate the professional activities of the offices in which they work.

Activities

The activities of the optometric technician include those of the assistant, but also incorporate more complex tasks that are vital to good eye care. They may determine the power of lenses and perform vision tests to determine acuity in color discrimination and field pattern. They may even record ocular pressure. Their work is more sophisticated than that of other para-optometrics.

Work Settings

The principal work setting for optometric technicians is the optometrist's office, but opportunities also exist in HMOs, health clinics, and government agencies. The armed forces also employs optometric technicians.

Advancement

Becoming registered and for working for a large establishment offer the possibility of a supervisory appointment.

Prerequisites

A high school diploma or its equivalent is essential for entering this field.

Desirable personal attributes for optometric technicians include good communication skills, organized work habits, manual dexterity, a neat, presentable appearance, and a desire to help others.

Education/Training

One can gain on-the-job training from optometrists and then get experience while working. Formal training programs are offered by hospitals, optometry colleges, and medical schools. These programs extend last two years and can lead to an associate degree. In addition to the basic ocular anatomy and physiology, courses are provided in vision training, contact lens theory and practice, and supervised field experience.

Certification/Registration/Licensure

After securing the necessary training and experience and passing the Optometric Technician Registry Examination, the technician becomes eligible for registration and use of the designation *Oph.T.R.* One's employment potential is significantly enhanced with these credentials.

Career Potential

The demand for optometric technicians is strong. Experts predict there will be an increased need for their services by optometrists as the U.S. population increases and gets older. Becoming a registered technician improves one's employability and advancement prospects.

For More Information

There is no professional organization for optometric technicians. For more information, write to the American Optometric Association, Paraoptometric Section, 243 N. Lindbergh Boulevard, St. Louis, MO 63141.

Optometric Technician Programs

Florida

Miami-Dade Community College
950 NW 20th Street
Miami, FL 33127
www.mdcc.edu/medical/

Indiana

Indiana University
300 North Jordan Avenue
Bloomington, IN 47405
www.indiana.edu/

Michigan

Ferris State University
901 South State Street
Big Rapids, MI 49307
www.ferris.edu/

Ohio

Owens Community College
Oregon Road
P.O. Box 10000
Toledo, OH 43699
www.owens.cc.oh.us/

Washington

Spokane Community College
N 1810 Greene Street
Spoakane, WA 99207
www.scc.spokane.cc.wa.us/

ORTHOPTISTS

Principal activity: Providing muscle therapy for eye motion disorders

Work commitment: Part- or full-time

Preprofessional education: High school diploma

Program length: 2 years

Work prerequisites: Certification after training

Career opportunities: Improving

Income range: $25,000 to $50,000

Scope

An orthoptist is a professional who, working under the supervision of an ophthalmologist, treats problems of eye movement and the inability to focus both eyes simultaneously. These problems are due to eye misalignment, a condition called *strabismus*, which occurs in about 3 percent of young children. If left untreated, it results in what is commonly called being "cross-eyed." The consequences of this situation may be both physical and psychological discomfort.

Activities

There are three therapeutic approaches to correcting strabismus. Using prescribed eye glasses to correct the misalignment is the most straightforward. If that is unsuccessful, another alternative is surgery, in which eye muscle is repaired. A third and noninvasive approach is *orthopic therapy*, in which the patient is taught to perform special exercises that gradually improve eye movement to overcome problems with vision and appearance. Orthoptists, many of whom are also *ophthalmic technologists*, may also be involved in carrying out special eye tests.

Work Settings

Orthoptists work in the offices of ophthalmologists as well as in hospitals, eye clinics, and teaching institutions.

Advancement

Salary increases come with experience and perhaps a move to a larger facility.

Prerequisites

A bachelor's degree is mandatory to undertake study in this field. Students should major in a subject that is relevant, such as biology or psychology, and take courses in biology, chemistry, physics, anatomy, and psychology.

Desirable personal attributes include the ability to work with children, patience, a sense of humor, and an outgoing personality.

Education/Training

After completing a bachelor's degree, a candidate must complete a two-year training program in one of the centers approved by the American Orthoptic Council. Graduate-level programs also are offered in this field.

Certification/Registration/Licensure

Those who have completed an accredited orthoptic program and who pass written, oral, and practical examinations are awarded certification. Certification is essential for employment in the field.

For More Information

The professional organization in this field is the American Orthoptic Council, 3914 Nakoma Road, Madison, WI 53711.

Orthoptic Programs

Florida

University of Florida
J-393 Shands Hospital
1600 SW Archer Road
Gainesville, FL 32608
www.hsc.ufl.edu/

Iowa

University of Iowa Hospitals
100 Hawkins Drive
Iowa City, IA 52242
www.medicine.uiowa.edu/uhs/

Michigan

University of Michigan
W.K. Kellogg Eye Center
1000 Wall Street
Ann Arbor, MI 48105
www.kellogg.umich.edu/

Minnesota

University of Minnesota
516 Delaware Street SE
P.O.Box 493
Minneapolis, MN 55455
www.umn.edu/

Missouri

St. Louis University Medical Center
1755 Grand Blvd.
St. Louis, MO 63104
www.slu.edu/health_sciences.html

St. Louis Children's Hospital
Washington University
One Children's Place, 2 South 89
St. Louis, MO 63110
www.bjc.org/slch.html

New York

New York Eye & Ear Infirmary
310 East 14th Street
New York, NY 10003
www.nyee.edu/

Texas

Hermann Eye Center
University of Texas Medical School–Houston
6431 Fannin Street
Houston, TX 77030
www.med.uth.tmc.edu/

Virginia

Eastern Virginia Medical School
P.O. Box 1980
Norfolk, VA 23501
www.evms.edu/

Wisconsin

University of Wisconsin Hospital
600 Highland Avenue
Madison, WI 53705
www.uwhospital.org/

Canada

Hospital for Sick Children
555 University Avenue
Toronto, Ont. Canada M5G 1X8
www.sickkids.on.ca/

University of Saskatchewan
Royal University Hospital
Saskatoon, Saskatchewan
Canada S7N 4L3
www.usask.ca/

ORTHOTISTS AND PROSTHETISTS

Principal activity: Designing, fabricating, and fitting braces and artificial limbs for patients

Work commitment: Full-time

Preprofessional education: High school diploma

Program length: 2 years

Work prerequisites: Certificate or bachelor's degree

Career opportunities: Very favorable

Income range: $30,000 to $40,000

Scope

A variety of medical problems can result in weakened limbs or a spinal column that needs artificial support. Stroke victims, those who have had spinal cord or bone damage, and patients with congenital muskuloskeletal disorders such as muscular dystrophy belong to this group. They may need a device to support and help straighten their limbs or spine. *Orthotists* help these patients by designing, making, and fitting the braces or other supportive devices they need.

Patients who have lost one or more limbs due to illnesses such as diabetes, an accident, or a congenital defect need artificial limbs (prosthesis) to help them cope with their handicaps. *Prosthetists* design, fabricate, and fit artificial limbs using a variety of materials.

The fields of orthotics and prosthetics are interrelated; professionals in one field also study the other and many are skilled in both.

Activities

To make braces, orthotists use a wide variety of materials, including wood, plastic, metals, carbon, and leather. They make the necessary measurements and casts, then modify the model, perform fittings, and evaluate the finished product. They must also teach patients how to use and care for their braces. All the work is initiated on the basis of a prescription written by a physician, often after consultation with an orthotist.

Prosthetists design artificial limbs, select the most suitable material for them, take measurements, make casts and models, and perform adjustments. They also teach patients to use and care for the prostheses.

Artificial limbs are designed on the basis of a physician's prescription, often written in consultation with the prosthetist.

Prosthetists not only make traditional artificial limbs, they may incorporate advanced microelectronics and computer technology into the design of electromechanical units. Thus, when electrodes detect a weak signal resulting from muscular contraction, the mechanism amplifies and processes the signal to stimulate a motor within the prosthesis, thereby activating a body part.

Computers are being used to design and manufacture artificial limbs today. The measurements taken by a prosthetist are coded into a computer, which is programmed to develop a three-dimensional image of the most appropriate design. This image is then fed into the operating system of the manufacturing machine that produces the limb.

Orthotists and prosthetists also supervise the work of orthotic-prosthetic technicians (see below).

Work Settings

Orthotists and prosthetists are employed in hospital laboratories, rehabilitation centers, privately owned facilities, and research agencies (both private and governmental).

Advancement

Advancement typically comes with certification and increased experience and education. Developing expertise in both fields improves one's chances of advancement.

Prerequisites

A high school diploma or its equivalent is needed for entry to a training program. Courses in biology, chemistry, physics, and mathematics as well as workshops in metal, wood, and plastics are helpful.

Desirable personal attributes include mechanical ability, manual dexterity, patience, an ability to grasp and resolve manipulative problems, tact, solid communication skills, and a sincere desire to help disabled people.

Education/Training

There are three educational routes for careers in these two fields:

1. One can earn a bachelor's degree with a major in orthotics or prosthetics at an undergraduate school having an accredited program. Undergraduate preparation involves courses in biology, chemistry, physics, anatomy, physiology, mathematics, biostatistics, mechanics, biomechanics, mechanical drawing, properties of materials, metal working, orthotic and prosthetic techniques, orthopedic and neuromuscular disorders, upper and lower limb orthotics and prosthetics, and spinal orthotics.

2. Those with a bachelor's degree in a field other than orthotics or prosthetics can complete an accredited postgraduate certificate program that takes one to two years.

3. The third route is to have a special combination of relevant educational background, clinical experience, and professional training that meets the requirements for certification.

Orthotic and prosthetic technicians

These professionals also work in laboratories, under the supervision of an orthotist or prosthetist, fabricating and maintaining braces, surgical supports, and artificial limbs. Such technicians can also be certified by having a high school diploma, completing a formal program in either field (or both), and passing a technical examination. Many junior or community colleges offer training for such technicians.

Certification/Registration/Licensure

Those completing an accredited program in orthotics or prosthetics or an accredited certificate program, and those meeting the special requirements who also have one year of clinical experience, are eligible to take the American Board for Certification in Orthotics and Prosthetics Practitioners Certification Examination. If qualified, one can became certified in both fields by passing the three-part exam given in each field.

Career Potential

Employment prospects are very favorable, and there is a growing demand for qualified personnel in this field. The introduction of new materials and fabrication techniques have made the work more interesting and challenging.

For More Information

The professional organization in the field is the American Orthotic and Prosthetic Association, 1650 King Street, Alexandria, VA 22314.

Orthotics and Prosthetics Programs

California

Rancho Los Amigos Medical Center
7450 Leeds Street
Downey, CA 90242
www.rancho.org/

Connecticut

Newington Certificate Program
181 East Cedar Street
Newington, CT 06111
www.oandp.com.educatio/ucon/phindex.html

Illinois

Northwestern University
633 Clark Street
Chicago, IL 60208
www.nwu.edu/

Minnesota

Century College
3300 Century Ave. North
White Bear Lake, MN 55110
www.century.cc.mn.us/

New Jersey

Rutgers University
P.O. Box 909
Piscataway, NJ 08855
www.rutgers.edu/

Texas

University of Texas
Southwestern Medical Center
5323 Harry Hines Boulevard
Dallas, TX 75235
www.swmed.edu/

Washington

University of Washington
School of Medicine
A-300 Health Sciences Center, Box 356340
Seattle, WA 98195
www.washington.edu/

Perfusionists

Principal activity: Operating heart-lung bypass equipment during surgery

Work commitment: Full-time

Preprofessional education: Bachelor's degree

Program length: 1 to 2 years

Work prerequisites: Certification after formal education

Career opportunities: Very attractive

Income range: $40,000 to $60,000

Scope

One of the major medical technological breakthroughs of the last 50 years is the development of the heart-lung machine. This was devised to maintain the human body in a living state even when such vital organs as the heart and lungs are not functioning. Removal of carbon dioxide from and the addition of oxygen to the blood takes place as the blood passes through the machine and is then returned to the anesthetized patient. Thus, surgeons now are able to make necessary repairs.

The professional who operates the heart-lung machine during surgery is the *perfusionist*. These workers are also involved in acquiring patients' blood for temporary storage before surgery. With coronary bypass surgery becoming commonplace, the current focus of advancement in this field involves organ transplantation.

Activities

Perfusionist are trained to carry out a complex, challenging, and extremely responsible job. They use complex, specialized instruments and life-support techniques. Constant monitoring of vital signs is essential to properly managing the physiologic functions of the patient. The perfusionist must be prepared to respond quickly and appropriately to instructions from the surgeon or anesthesiologist.

Work Settings

Most perfusionists work in medical centers and hospitals, and they may be involved in securing and properly transporting organs for transplantation between institutions.

Advancement

Salary increases come with experience. One's status may be enhanced by developing expertise in a specialized areas in the field.

Prerequisites

Most formal education programs require a bachelor's degree. Some also prefer applicants, with backgrounds in respiratory therapy, medical technology, or nursing.

Desirable personal attributes include superior intelligence, quick response ability, manual dexterity, mechanical ability, emotionally stability, being able to work as part of a team, the ability to function well under stress over prolonged periods, a long attention span, and a strong desire to help people who are seriously ill.

Education/Training

Training is provided at community colleges, hospitals, and increasingly at universities. Course work includes anatomy, physiology, chemistry, pharmacology, and pathology. Training is provided in the operation of heart-lung bypass equipment for adults, children, and even infants; long-term life support; and perfusion of transplant organs. Clinical experience covering a variety of procedures is an essential part of the program.

Certification/Registration/Licensure

Certification can be secured through the American Board of Cardiovascular Perfusion.

To secure certification, candidates must have the stipulated educational and clinical experience and pass a demanding oral and written examination. Certification is essential for employment.

Career Potential

There is a shortage of perfusionists today, so opportunities are good for those planning to enter the field. New technology and attractive salaries enhance this field's appeal to those seeking a challenging and demanding career.

For More Information

The professional organization in the field is the American Society of Extra-Corporal Technology, 11480 Sunset Hills Road, Reston, VA 22090

For more information, write to the American Academy of Cardiovascular Perfusion, P.O. Box 468, Pell City, AL 35125.

For information on certification, contact one of the agencies listed below:

American Board of Cardiovascular Perfusion
207 North 25th Avenue
Hattiesburg, MS 39401

Accreditation Committee for Perfusion Education
7108-C at South Alton Way
Englewood, CO 30112.

Perfusionist Programs

Arizona

University of Arizona
Gittings Building, Room 102
P.O. Box 210093
Tucson, AZ 85271
www.arizona.edu/

Connecticut

Quinnipiac College
275 Mt. Carmel Avenue
Hamden, CT 06518
www.quinnipiac.edu/

District of Columbia

Walter Reed Army Medical Center
6900 Georgia Avenue NW
Washington, DC 20307
www.wramc.amedd.army.mil/

Florida

Barry University
11300 N.E. Second Avenue
Miami Shores, FL 33161
www2.barry.edu/

Illinois

Rush–Presbyterian–St. Luke Medical Center
1653 West Congress Pkwy
Chicago, IL 60612
www.rpslmc.edu/

Iowa

University of Iowa Hospitals and Clinics
200 Hawkins Drive
Iowa City, IA 52242
www.uihc.uiowa.edu/

Kansas

Via Christi Regional Medical Center
3600 East Harry
Wichita, KS 67218
www.via-christi.org/vcrmc.nsf/

Maryland

John Hopkins Bayview Medical Center
4940 Eastern Avenue
Baltimore, MD 21224
www.johnshopkins.edu/

Massachusetts

Northeastern University
360 Huntington Avenue
Boston, MA 02116
www.northeastern.edu/

Minnesota

University of Minnesota Heart & Lung Institute
425 East River Road
Minneapolis, MN 55455
www.med.umn.edu/

Nebraska

University of Nebraska Medical Center
600 South 42nd Street
Omaha, NE 68198
www.unmc.edu/

New Jersey

Cooper Hospital/University Medical Center
One Cooper Plaza
Camden, NJ 08103
www.cooperhealth.org/

General Hospital Center at Passaic
350 Boulevard
Passaic, NJ 07055
www.atlantichealth.org/hospitals/passaic

New York

SUNY Health Science Center at Syracuse
750 East Adams Street
Syracuse, NY 13210
www.hscsyr.edu/

Ohio

Ohio State University
1583 Perry Street
Columbus, OH 43210
www.acs.ohio-state.edu/

Christ Hospital
2139 Auburn Avenue
Cincinnati, OH 45219
www.health-alliance.com/christ_control.html

Cleveland Clinic Foundation
9500 Euclid Avenue G33
Cleveland, OH 44195
www.clevelandclinic.org/

Oregon

St. Vincent Providence Medical Center
2205 SW Barnes Road
Portland, OR 97225
www.providence.org/portland/education/
DEFAULT/HTM

Pennsylvania

MCP Hahnemann University
Broad & Vine Streets, Mail Stop 472
Philadelphia, PA 19102
www.auhs.edu/

Duquesne University
600 Forbes Avenue
Pittsburgh, PA 15282
www.duq.edu/

M.S. Hershey Medical Center/
Penn State University
P.O. Box 850
Hershey, PA 17033
www.psu.edu/

Shadyside Hospital
5230 Centre Avenue
Pittsburgh, PA 15232
www.upmc.edu/SHADYSIDE/

South Carolina

Medical University of South Carolina
171 Ashley Avenue
Charleston, SC 29425
www.musc.edu/

Tennessee

Vanderbilt University Medical Center
2986 Vanderbilt Clinic
Nashville, TN 37232
www.mc.vanderbilt.edu/

Texas

Texas Heart Institute
P O Box 20345
Houston, TX 77225
www.tmc.edu/thi/

Wisconsin

Milwaukee School of Engineering
1025 North Broadway Street
Milwaukee, WI 53202
www.msoe.edu/

PULMONARY FUNCTION TECHNOLOGISTS

Principal activity: Administering and evaluating pulmonary function tests

Work commitment: Usually full-time

Preprofessional education: High school diploma required; associate or bachelor's degree preferred

Program length: 6 months to 4 years

Work prerequisites: On-the-job training possible; formal education preferred

Career opportunities: Favorable

Income range: $20,000 to $ 35,000

Scope

Increasingly, the medical profession is stressing the importance of preventive health care. This approach involves maintaining a good diet, having a regular exercise regime, and undergoing periodic check-ups by a physician. Some medical screening tests have become a routine part of the check-up procedure. Patients with the potential for lung problems are encouraged to have pulmonary function tests. Pulmonary technologists operate the machines and evaluate the data they provide.

Activities

Technologists contribute to the evaluation of a patient's lung health by running several types to tests, including exercise tolerance, bronchial challenge studies, blood gas studies, gas diffusion studies, and sleep studies. The pulmonary technologist selects and readies the test equipment to be employed and then explains the procedure to the patient before carrying out. The technologist performs the test while monitoring the patient's response, then evaluates the results and their reliability. A composite of different test results provides the physician with the information needed to establish a diagnosis and, when necessary, to provide appropriate therapeutic management for problems.

Work Settings

Pulmonary technologists are employed by hospitals and clinics as well as in private practice offices, rehabilitation facilities, and diagnostic centers.

Advancement

Advancement comes with experience and further education, such as a bachelor's degree. Specialization in specific diagnostic procedures will enhance a technologist's status.

Prerequisites

A high school diploma is a minimum requirement, but to enroll in most programs an associate or bachelor's degree is necessary.

Desirable personal attributes include patience, good communication skills, dependability, and manual dexterity.

Education/Training

There are several ways to get training for this field:

1. One can earn a bachelor's degree in pulmonary technology from a college or university with an accredited program.

2. One can earn an associate degree in pulmonary technology from a community college with an accredited program.

3. One can attend a post-college program in pulmonary technology offered at medical center or hospital.

4. One can obtain on-the-job training in the field.

Certification/Registration/Licensure

Certification is offered by the National Board for Respiratory Care upon satisfactory completion of a written examination. To be eligible to take the exam, candidates must have graduated from an accredited pulmonary technology or respiratory therapy program and have at least six months of experience in the field. Alternately, one could have a high school diploma and two years of experience.

At present licensure is not required, and even certification is voluntary.

Career Potential

Currently there is a shortage of trained personnel in this field, and increased openings are anticipated as more medical facilities establish cardiopulmonary laboratories. Thus, prospects for employment opportunities are favorable.

For More Information

The professional organization in the field is the National Society for Pulmonary Technology, 120 Falcon Drive, Fredericksburg, Va 22408.

For information on accredited educational programs, write to the Joint Review Committee for Respiratory Therapy Education, 1701 Euless Boulevard, Euless, TX 76040.

RADIATION THERAPY TECHNOLOGISTS

Principal activity: Helping to administer therapeutic radiation

Work commitment: Full-time

Preprofessional education: High school diploma

Program length: 1 to 4 years

Work prerequisites: Certificate or diploma; associate or bachelor's degree and certification

Career opportunities: Favorable

Income range: $25,000 to $40,000

Scope

One of the biggest killers in the United States today is cancer. In treating those who have been diagnosed with this disease, three approaches are typically used: surgery, chemotherapy, and radiation. These treatments are used either alone or in combination. Depending on the nature of the tumor and how much it has spread, these techniques can extend and even save lives and reduce pain.

Radiation sources in use today include high-energy x-rays, electron beams, and gamma rays. The goal is to pinpoint the tumor site, so that it can be exclusively targeted by the radiation beam while minimizing as far as possible distraction of healthy cells. A variety of techniques are used to locate the position and extent of tumors. Once this is done, a physician, the *radiation oncologist*, determines the best treatment plan. Doctors often use computers for this process, which results in the preparation of a radiation prescription and treatment plan. This plan is then put into effect by the radiation technologist.

Activities

Using sophisticated equipment, the radiation technologist helps program the control panel so that exactly proscribed doses of radiation are omitted. Using lead shields, the technologist ensures that exposure is restricted to the exact body site being targeted. Working with the radiation physicist, technologists also help prepare, maintain, and calibrate the radiation equipment to ensure its safe and effective usage.

Technologists help prepare and handle the radioactive materials used in the tests. They must keep detailed, accurate records of radiation treatments. Throughout all activities, they must work to ensure the safety of patients and attending medical personnel. Thus, they must be able to identify the location of any radiation hazards and take appropriate action. They must deal with their patients with sensitivity and tact during very stressful times.

Work Settings

Most radiation technologists work in medical centers and hospitals. A few work in commercial sales and as educators, instructing new professionals.

Advancement

With increased experience and education, upward career movement is possible. At larger institutions, one may become a supervisor.

Prerequisites

A high school diploma or its equivalent the minimum requirement for those seeking professional training.

Desirable personal attributes include detail-oriented work habits, strong ability in mathematics, a sense of compassion, and a desire to help others.

Education/Training

There are several training paths in this field:

1. One can attend a four-year bachelor's degree program.

2. One can attend a two-year associate degree program.

3. One can get a two-year certificate (or diploma) from a hospital program.

4. One can earn a one-year certificate (or diploma) from a hospital program.

The goal is to phase out all but the bachelor's programs over the next few years.

Education in this field involves classroom and laboratory work and supervised clinical experience. Courses include anatomy, physiology, mathematics, pathology, clinical radiation oncology, radiation physics, radiology, radiation protection, technical radiation oncology, medical imaging, introduction to computers, venipuncture, methods of patient care, and medical ethics.

Certification/Registration/Licensure

Certification, which is required for employment in this field, is provided by the American Registry of Radiological Technologists (ARRT). To become certified, one must graduate from an accredited radiation therapy program and pass a four-hour competency examination. Some states accept ARRT certification in lieu of taking a state licensure exam.

Career Potential

The existing shortage of registered radiation technologists is expected to continue in the next decade. This is due to the growing population, the increased number of senior citizens, and the expanded use of radiological technology.

For More Information

The professional organization is the American Society of Radiological Technologists, 15000 Central Avenue SE, Albuquerque, NM 87123.

For information about certification, write to the American Registry of Radiologic Technologists, 1255 Northland Drive, Mendota Heights, MN 55120.

RADIOLOGICAL TECHNOLOGISTS

Principal activity: Securing radiographs using varied radiological instruments

Work commitment: Part- and full-time

Preprofessional education: High school diploma

Program length: 1 to 4 years

Work prerequisites: Certificate, diploma, associate, or bachelor's degree

Career opportunities: Satisfactory

Income range: $20,000 to $30,000

Scope

The use of x-rays, or *radiography*, to reveal the internal organization of the body has enormously expanded in the past few decades. It is now possible to not only study the state of a body's bones and joints, but also organs, tissues, and vessels as well as the functional status of the digestive, circulatory, and urinary systems. This remarkable capacity results from the development of such sophisticated equipment as *CT scanning* (*computerized tomography*), *MRI* (*magnate resonance imaging*), and *digital subtraction angiography*.

Today, in addition to standard flat films, images are recorded on video tape and motion picture film. It is the radiological technologist or *radiographer* who is responsible for obtaining these images.

Activities

To obtain the standard radiographs that are commonly ordered, technologists prepare patients by explaining the procedure, ensuring that they carry no accessories that will be impervious to the x-rays, and properly positioning them to provide exposure of the correct area. They shield sensitive areas of the body with lead-containing covers, so that they are not exposed to radiation. Then they focus the x-ray source at the proper height and angle for the body area being filmed, place the film holder in the correct position under the patient's body, and expose that part of the body to the beam. Finally, the radiographer sets the controls of the instrument to make sure that the film is adequately exposed to provide an image with the right density, contrast, and detail. The film is then removed, quickly developed, checked, and passed on to the physician.

Experienced radiographers may be called upon to carry out more complex imaging procedures, such *fluoroscopy*. In this procedure, radiographs are taken while or shortly after a patient drinks or is infused with a contrast medium (usually containing barium), which provides images of different parts of the digestive tract. In addition to taking the x-rays, the technologist prepares the contrast medium and makes sure that the required amount enters the body.

Some specialized radiographers, called *CT scanners*, are trained in the use of machines that produce cross-sectional views of a patient's body. Others may be called *MRI technologists*. They are trained to operate machines using giant magnets and radiowaves to create an image of both hard and soft body tissues.

Work Settings

Radiological technologists work primarily in hospitals, usually as members of a radiology department. They may use mobile x-ray units to take bedside, operating room or emergency room x-rays. Some radiographers are employed in private practice settings, clinics, educational institutions, and industry.

Advancement

With experience and training, a staff technologist may be elevated to chief supervisor, chief technologist, or even department manager. Others may advance by specializing, becoming CT or MRI scanners or angiographers. Those who teach can advance through the academic ranks, while others may move up in a corporate sales setting.

Prerequisites

A high school diploma or its equivalent is required for entry to a training program. Recommended high school courses include biology, chemistry, physics, algebra, trigonometry, and psychology.

Desirable personal attributes include attention to detail, good communication skills, careful work habits (to avoid radiation exposure), a sense of compassion, and a desire to help people.

Education/Training

Radiographer programs are offered by several kinds of institutions, thus their awards upon completion are varied. Consequently, there are multiple routes to completing a radiography program:

- Hospitals account for more than 50 percent of accredited programs in the U.S. These are two-year certificate or diploma programs.

- Junior and community colleges offer 40 percent of accredited programs These are two-year associate degree programs.

- Universities offer less than 5 percent of accredited programs. These are four-year bachelor or two-year master's degree programs and are best for those who want teaching or supervisory positions.

- Some vocational-technical institutes offer one-year programs for those with a background in the allied health sciences, such as medical technologists or registered nurses. These provide certificates or diplomas at completion.

It should be noted that some institutions offer all three levels of educational preparation, leaving the option up to the individual. This is because employment opportunities are available to those who complete an accredited program at any level. The programs are both didactic and practical. Classroom-lab work and training involve courses in anatomy, physiology, radiation physics, radiation protection, medical terminology, medical imaging and processing, positioning of patients, medical ethics and the use of computers in radiological science.

Certification/Registration/Licensure

Certification is essential for work in this field. Graduates from accredited programs can take a four-hour examination administered by the American Registry of Radiological Technologists to become certified.

Career Potential

The employment outlook is satisfactory for the time being, with more openings than candidates in many places. The job market may not be as attractive as it was in the past, however, as many people are entering the field. With a growing demand for health care and an older population, opportunities should remain stable for the foreseeable future.

For More Information

The professional organization for the field is the American Society of Radiologic Technologists, 15000 Central Avenue SE, Albuquerque, NM 87123.

For information on certification, write to the American Registry of Radiologic Technologists 1255 Northland Drive, Mendota, MN 55120.

Almost all radiography students receive their education by attending programs accredited by the Joint Review Committee on Education in Radiological Technology. There are at least 700 such programs in North America—far too many to list here.

For a complete list of accredited programs, write to the Joint Review Committee on Education in Radiologic Technology, 20 N. Wacker Drive, Chicago, IL 60606.

SURGICAL TECHNOLOGISTS

Principal activity: Performing vital operating room services

Work commitment: Full-time

Preprofessional education: High school diploma

Program length: 9 months to 2 years

Work prerequisites: Certificate, diploma, or associate degree

Career opportunities: Very favorable

Income range: $20,000 to $35,000

Scope

Surgical technologists used to be known as *operating room technicians*. During surgical operations, they work under the direction of surgeons and the supervision of registered nurses to help maintain the sterile atmosphere and contribute to the efficiency of the operating room. Their services facilitate a successful surgical outcome.

Activities

Prior to surgery, technologists prepare the sterile instruments to be used as well as sterile drapings and solutions. They may also check if necessary nonsterile equipment is available and in proper working order. Surgical technologists also see that patients have been properly prepared. They help place patients on and secure them to the operating table and help the surgical team to dress with gowns and gloves for the operation.

During surgery a *scrub (sterile) technologist* passes sterile instruments and other supplies to the surgeon or assistant surgeon. He or she may thread needles, hold retractors, cut sutures, count sponges, and generally tries to anticipate the surgeons' needs during the procedure. A *circulating (nonsterile) technologist* stands by to provide needed supplies, adjust lighting, and bring in any necessary diagnostic machines. After the operation, this technologist arranges for excised specimens to be sent to the pathology lab and assists in transporting the patient to the recovery room. In the meantime, the scrub technologist cleans the area, ensuring that instruments are placed in appropriate sites for sterilization. Technologists also make sure that the operating facility is adequately stocked with supplies that are in common use.

Work Settings

Surgical technologists typically work in hospital surgical facilities (either inpatient or outpatient), delivery rooms, emergency rooms, and private specialized surgical centers. Some work for a physician or a group of physicians.

Advancement

With experience certification, and supervisory skills, a surgical technologist can become an assistant operating room supervisor. In the position one directs the activities of other surgical technologists and reports to the O.R. supervisor, who is usually a registered nurse.

Alternately, a technician can become an assistant operating room administrator, who is responsible for ordering supplies and helps arrange the work schedule.

Advancement can also occur by specialization in such areas as open-heart or neurosurgery, for which special skills are needed.

Prerequisites

A high school diploma is essential for entry to a surgical technologist training program.

Desirable personal qualities include intelligence, manual dexterity, stamina, and the capacity to work effectively with other professionals. Candidates should also be able to exercise quick, calm, and sound judgment,

Education/Training

Formal training programs for surgical technologists are offered by vocational schools, junior and community colleges, universities, hospitals, and the military. Programs last from nine months to two years. The shorter programs award certificates or diplomas, while the two-year programs award associate degrees. More than 150 accredited programs are available nationwide.

Formal programs consist of classroom education and supervised clinical experience. Courses are offered in anatomy, physiology, microbiology, pharmacology, medical terminology, and professional ethics. Others cover the care of patients during surgery, aseptic techniques, and surgical procedures. During clinical training, which varies from 500 to 1,000 hours, students learn about common surgical procedures and about those used in various specialties.

Another educational route is open to hospital personnel such as nurses' aides or practical nurses. They can simply transfer to surgery departments, where they receive on-the-job training. This may extend from six weeks to one year. Such technologists are ineligible for certification.

Certification/Registration/Licensure

Surgical technologists can apply for certification from the Liaison Council on Certification for Surgical Technologists, whose address is listed on page 292. Prerequisites include graduating from an accredited program and successfully completing a national certification examination. To retain certification, candidates must take continuing education and periodically retake the exam.

Career Potential

The employment outlook for surgical technologists is quite favorable because the number of surgical procedures is generally increasing as the population can better afford it and is living longer. Cost containment also favors the use of surgical technologists, especially where HMO coverage is a consideration.

For More Information

The professional organization for the field is the Association of Surgical Technologists (AST), 7108-C South Alton Way, Englewood, CO 80112.

For information on certification, contact the Liason Council of the AST.

VETERINARY ASSISTANTS

Principal activity: Helping veterinarians care for animals

Work commitment: Full-time

Preprofessional education: High school diploma

Program length: 3 months to 2 years

Work prerequisites: Adequate training and experience

Career opportunities: Good

Income range: $15,000 to $30,000

Scope

The activities of a veterinary assistant (or technician) are comparable to those of a primary care nurse. They observe the status of animals placed in a veterinarian's care and help in the operations of the facility.

Activities

Veterinary assistants ready animals for surgery, help anesthetize them, and watch them post-operatively. They ensure that medications are given on schedule and change dressings periodically. They also are responsible for maintaining sanitary conditions in the facility. They make sure that sterile instruments and adequate supplies are available. They may also be required to perform certain laboratory tests and obtain specimens. Routinely weighing animals and record keeping are additional responsibilities.

Work Settings

Veterinary assistants work in private offices, veterinary hospitals, boarding kennels, animal shelters, zoos, grooming shops, research centers, and private stables. Some are employed by various government agencies.

Advancement

In larger facilities, a veterinarian assistant with the right training, experience, and management abilities can assume administrative responsibilities.

Prerequisites

A high school diploma is necessary for entry into this field.

Desirable personal attributes include a love for animals, good physical health and strength, patience, emotional stability, responsibility, and dependability.

Education/Training

Many veterinary assistants receive on-the-job training, while others get postsecondary education at trade schools and junior, technical, or community colleges. Those attending the latter receive associate degrees.

Certification/Registration/Licensure

These awards of recognition are not required, but can be earned from one of the organizations listed below.

Career Potential

Employment prospects for veterinary assistants are favorable for the foreseeable future. With the current strong economy, the number of pet owners significantly increases. Consequently, more caretakers are needed to provide services for maintenance and medical treatment.

For More Information

There is no professional organization for this field, but information is available from the agencies listed below:

American Veterinary Association
1931 North Moacham Road
Schaumburg, IL 60173

Humane Society of the United States
210 O Street NW
Washington, DC 20037

For information on certification, write to the American Association for Laboratory Animal Science, 70 Timber Creek Drive, Cordova, TN 93018.

Rehabilitation Careers

 ## THERAPISTS AND THERAPIST ASSISTANTS

The health-care field includes many rehabilitation careers. Their goal is helping individuals with impairments to achieve a higher level of functioning and fulfillment. These careers require direct and often close contact with patients. Practice locations vary and include hospitals, nursing homes, outpatient facilities, and in-home services.

Therapists evaluate patients' levels of functioning. With other members of the treatment team, they plan therapeutic activities and exercise programs for patients with physical, emotional, social, or education impairments.

An activities program may include creative skills (art, dance, music, poetry, or psychodrama), manual skills (crafts or industrial arts), educational skills (writing, reading, or perceptual training), daily living skills (self-care or homemaking), functional skills (use of prostheses or adaptive equipment), or recreational skills (either individual or group).

When necessary, therapists design treatment plans involving more than one approach. They set goals in light of the existing problems and the patient's motivation, and conduct periodic assessments to determine progress and see if the established goals have been met. Then they modify the treatment plan accordingly. When a patient transfers home or to another facility, the therapist provides needed information to make sure that there is continuity of therapy.

ART THERAPISTS

Principal activity: Using art therapeutically to improve clients' physical and emotional states

Work commitment: Part- or full-time

Preprofessional education: High school diploma

Program length: 4 to 6 years

Work prerequisites: Bachelor's degree acceptable; master's degree preferred

Career opportunities: Favorable

Income range: $20,000 to $40,000

Scope

Art therapy is a means of communication provided to mentally and physically impaired people who are unable to communicate verbally. By using drawn patterns and pictures, such patients can express themselves, providing an opportunity to help improve their self-image and personal growth.

Activities

Art therapists encourage their patients to express their feelings about themselves, their families, and their homes. The therapist analyzes the content of the drawn material in terms of perspective, proportions, detail (or lack of it), technique, colors, nature of the subject selected, and general aesthetic quality. He or she then attempts to interpret the thoughts, feelings, fears, and hopes reflected in the drawing and seeks to uncover the meaning of the illustrations.

Commonly, the art therapist participates with others in the health-care team—psychiatrists, psychologists, and other therapists—to formulate a diagnosis and overall treatment plan. The therapist then designs specific art activities to be carried out in an individual or group context. Using various types of arts and crafts, the therapist provides instruction, then observes and notes what occurs during therapy sessions and reports the degree of progress to the health-care team so that the treatment plan can be modified to better meet the client's needs.

When provided in a group setting, art therapy can stimulate socialization among participants. Expressing themselves through art and other creative outlets also gives patients a sense of satisfaction, relaxes them, and enhances their self-esteem. Thus, art therapy can benefit victims of trauma and violence and those with learning or sensory disabilities.

Half of those treated by art therapists annually are adults, and the other half are adolescents and children.

This profession makes a significant contribution to the rehabilitation of emotionally disabled and handicapped people.

Work Settings

Art therapists work in psychiatric clinics, community centers, nursing homes, schools, and group homes. Some work as private practitioners. The largest employment sites are short- and long-term psychiatric hospitals.

Advancement

Advancement is available by securing a master's degree and obtaining certification.

Prerequisites

A high school diploma is a prerequisite for admission to college. In addition, natural skills in creative art are essential.

Desirable personal attributes for art therapists include patience, a strong sense of compassion, an ability to communicate well, and emotional stability.

Education/Training

The educational backgrounds of art therapists vary, with programs offered by universities, hospitals, and art institutes. These may be entry-level undergraduate, certificate/diploma, or master's degree programs. Most are not approved by the American Art Therapy Association, which has accredited more than 25 graduate programs.

At the undergraduate level, one should major or minor in creative or commercial art or art education. Preparing an art portfolio is also a good idea. Courses in the behavioral and social sciences are desirable.

While some job opportunities are open to those with a bachelor's degree and clinical experience, completing a one-year certificate/diploma program or a two-year master's degree program is very desirable. The latter forms the basis for securing certification.

Master's degree programs usually include art-related courses in normal and pathological art expression; art therapy for children, adolescents, and the aged; therapeutic ability through art; art therapy and communication; and art therapy for the disabled. Behaviorally oriented courses include normal and abnormal psychological development, dynamics and group practice, and diagnosis and treatment approaches. Experience in a variety of clinical settings is required.

Certification/Registration/Licensure

Certification may be secured through the American Art Therapy Association. To gain certification, one must satisfy the association's educational, internship, and paid-work experience requirements and provide letters of recommendation and a portfolio of slides. Securing registered status as an art therapist (ATR), while not essential, can help in securing employment at higher salary levels. To work in public schools, state licensure is needed.

Career Potential

There is optimism about the employment prospects in this field, and this is reflected in the increasing number of graduate programs that now offer training in art therapy. The optimism is based on the validation of art therapy as a therapeutic modality, a view which has gained federal recognition and support. In addition, there has been a significant increase in the number of therapists seeking certification as registered art therapists. This bodes well for raising the status of the profession to a higher level.

For More Information

The professional organization in this field is the American Art Therapy Association (AARTA), 1202 Allanson Road, Mundelheim, IL 60060.

Art Therapy Programs

The master's degree programs listed below are accredited by the AATA. Many more institutions offer bachelor's degrees or certificates/diplomas in the field.

Master's Degree Programs

California

College of Notre Dame
1500 Ralston Avenue
Belmont, CA 94002
www.cnd.edu/

Sonoma State University
1801 East Cotati Avenue
Rohnert Park, CA 94928
www.sonoma.edu/

Loyola Marymount University
7900 Loyola Blvd.
Los Angeles, CA 90045
www.lmu.edu/

Colorado

Naropa Institute
2130 Arapahoe Avenue
Boulder, CO 80302
www.naropa.edu/

District of Columbia

George Washington University
2129 G Street NW, Building L
Washington, DC 20052
www.gwu.edu/

Florida

Florida State University
126 Carothers Hall B-171
Tallahassee, FL 32306
www.fsu.edu/

Illinois

Adler School of Professional Psychology
65 East Wacker Parkway
Chicago, IL 60601
www.adler.edu/

Art Institute of Chicago
112 South Michigan Avenue
Chicago, IL 60603
www.artic.edu/

Southern Illinois University
Box 1764
Edwardsville, IL 62026
www.siue.edu/

Illinois State University
Normal, IL 61761
www.istu.edu/

University of Illinois at Chicago
929 West Harrison Street
Chicago, IL 60607I
www.uic.edu/

Kansas

Emporia State University
1200 Commercial
Emporia, KS 66801
www.emporia.edu/

Kentucky

University of Louisville
Gardiner Hall 331
Louisville, KY 40292
www.louisville.edu/

Massachusetts

Lesley College
29 Everett Street
Cambridge, MA 02138
www.lesley.edu/

Springfield College
263 Alden Street
Springfield, MA 01109
www.spfldcol.edu/

Michigan

Wayne State University
Community Arts Building
Detroit, MI 48202
www.wayne.edu/

Missouri

St. Louis Institute of Art Psychotherapy
308-A North Euclid
St. Louis, MO 63108
www.macbhe.gov/institutions/propriet/
propschools/P0260.thm

New Mexico

University of New Mexico
Albuquerque, NM 87131
www.unm.edu/

Southwestern College
RR 20, Box 29-D
P.O. Box 4788
Santa Fe, NM 87502
www.swc.edu/

New York

Pratt Institute
East 3200 Willoughby Avenue
Brooklyn, NY 11205
www.pratt.edu/

Long Island University
CW Post Campus
Northern Boulevard
Brookville, NY 11548
www.liunet.edu/

College of New Rochelle
New Rochelle, NY 10805
http://cnr.edu/

Hillside Children's Center
1183 Monroe Avenue
Rochester, NY 14620
www.cayuganet.org/hsc/hillside.html

Nazareth College of Rochester
4245 East Avenue
Rochester, NY 14618
www.naz.edu/

Hofstra University
212 Mason Hall
Hempstead, NY 11550
www.hofstra.edu/

New York University
70 Washington Square South
New York, NY 10012
www.nyu.edu/

Ohio

Ursuline College
2550 Lander Road
Pepper Pike, Ohio 44124
www.ursuline.edu/

Oregon

Marylhurst University
P.O. Box 261
Marylhurst, OR 97036
www.marylhurst.edu/

Pennsylvania

MCP Hahnemann University
905 Broad Vine Street
Philadelphia, PA 19102
www.auhs.edu/

Marywood College
2300 Adams Avenue
Scranton, PA 18509
www.marywood.edu/

Vermont

Vermont College
Norwich University
Montpelier, Vt. 05602
www.norwich.edu/

Virginia

Eastern Virginia Medical School
P.O. Box 1980
Norfolk, VA 23501
www.evms.edu/

Wisconsin

University of Wisconsin–Superior
1800 Grand Avenue
Superior, WI 54880
www.uwsuper.edu/

Canada

Concordia University
1455 de Maisonneuve Boulevard West
Montreal, Que. Canada H3G 1M8
www.concordia.ca/

Certificate Programs
California

College of Notre Dame
1500 Ralston
Belmont, CA 94002
www.cnd.edu/

Louisiana

Greater New Orleans Creative Arts Therapies
Institute
5500 Prytania Street
New Orleans, LA 70115
www.tec.uno.edu/nocca/

Massachusetts

New England Art Therapy Institute
216-T Silver Lane
Sunderland, MA 01375
http://javanet.com/~cccneati/

New York

New School for Social Research
66 West 12th Street
New York, NY 10011
www.newschool.edu/

Oklahoma

University of Oklahoma
1700 ASP Avenue #202
Norman, OK 73037
www.occe.ou.edu/

Texas

University of Houston–Clear Lake
2700 Bay Area Blvd.
Houston, TX 77058
www.cl.uh.edu/

Canada

The University of Western Ontario
Stevenson-Lawson Building
London, Ont. N6A 5B8
www.uwo.ca/

Bachelor's Degree Programs
Alabama

Spring Hill College
4000 Dauphin Street
Mobile, AL 36608
www.shc.edu/

Illinois

Barat College
700 Westleigh Road
Lake Forest, IL 60045
www.barat.edu/

Indiana

University of Indianapolis
1400 E Hanna Avenue
Indianapolis, IN 46227
www.uindy.edu/

Kansas

Pittsburgh State University
1701 S Broadway
Pittsburgh, KS 66762
www.pittstate.edu/

Massachusetts

Anna Maria College
Sunset Lane
Paxton, MA 01612
www.annamaria.edu/

Our Lady of the Elms College
291 Springfield Street
Chicopee, MA 01013
www.elms.edu/

Springfield College
263 Alden Street
Springfield, MA 01109
www.spfldcol.edu/

New Jersey

Caldwell College
9 Ryerson Avenue
Caldwell, NJ 07006
www.caldwell.edu/

New York

St. Thomas Aquinas College
123 Route 240
Sparkill, NY 10976
www.stac.edu/

Ohio

Bowling Green State University
Bowling Green, OH 43403
www.bgsu.edu/

Pennsylvania

Mercyhurst College
Glenwood Hills
Erie, PA 16546
www.eden.mercy.edu/

University of the Arts
Philadelphia College of Arts
320 South Broad Street
Philadelphia, PA 19102
www.uarts.edu/

South Carolina

Converse College
580 East Main Street
Spartanburg, SC 29302
www.converse.edu/

Wisconsin

Edgewood College
855 Woodrow Street
Madison, WI 53711
www.edgewood.edu/

Alverno College
3401 South 39 Street
P.O. Box 34922
Milwaukee, WI 53534
www.alverno.edu/

Mt. Mary College
2900 North Menomonee River Pkwy
Milwaukee, WI 53222
www.mtmary.edu/

University of Wisconsin–Superior
1800 Grand Avenue
Superior, WI 54880
www.uwsuper.edu/

DANCE/MOVEMENT THERAPISTS

Principal activity: Improving clients' mental and physical states

Work commitment: Part- or full-time

Preprofessional education: Bachlor's degree

Program length: 4 to 6 years

Work prerequisites: Master's degree

Career opportunities: Limited

Income range: $20,000 to $50,000

Scope

Dance therapy is a means of using movement to improve the emotional and physical condition of individuals. It facilitates the diagnosis and treatment of persons with such mental illnesses as schizophrenia and psychotic depression, and also those with personality disorders. People with brain damage and learning disabilities and those with hearing, visual, and physical disabilities also can benefit from this type of therapy. Others who can be helped are those who have suffered physical and emotional trauma from variety of sources.

The basic concept of dance therapy is based on the premise that there is a constant interaction between the mind and the body. Those two components register both pain and pleasure. Conversely, emotional pain as experienced during anxiety and depression can be expressed outwardly, involuntarily, through posture, movements, muscle tension, and breathing patterns. In other words motion provides a pathway to express one's feelings. In addition, dance can divert patients' attention from their inner concerns and uplift their spirits.

Dance therapists work with physicians and other therapists to help restore the health of their patients.

Activities

Initially, the therapist observes and interprets the patient's outward physical expressions and seeks to establish meaningful contact. Then, using dance movement exercises either individually or in groups, the therapist seeks to improve communication, enhance the patients' self-image and self-confidence.

Activities that require touching and rhythmic motion can help reconnect severely disturbed individuals with their social environments. Working through their feelings, even in a nonverbal form such as motion, can facilitate the recovery process.

Similarly, dance and movement can be applied to a wide variety of disabilities faced by both children and adults and can improve their ability to function.

Work Settings

Dance therapists are employed by short- and long-term residential facilities, nursing homes, and psychiatric institutions. Some are in private practice, contracting with such facilities to provide services on an hourly basis. Others teach, either full- or part-time, at dance studios or educational institutions.

Advancement

Because this is a relatively new profession, advancement opportunities are limited. They include entering the teaching profession to develop dance/motion training programs at educational institutions as well as promotion to supervisory appointments in a variety of settings.

Prerequisites

A person who wants to enter this field must first secure a bachelor's degree. Most applicants take courses or major in psychology, dance, or physical education as part of a broad liberal arts program. Experience as a dance instructor for youngsters and adults, in choreography, in *kinesiology* (study of human muscle movement) is also recommended.

Desirable personal attributes include a love of dance, a great deal of patience, good dance skills, physical strength, a strong sense of compassion, and a desire to work with disabled people.

Education/Training

A dance therapist must secure a master's degree from a college or university program that is accredited by the American Dance Therapy Association (ADTA). Graduate work includes courses in psychopathology, human development, dance/movement theory and practice, and observation and research skills, as well as a supervised internship in a clinical setting. The program usually takes two years. Two master's degrees are offered in this field: a Master of Arts in movement theory and a Master of Arts in creative arts therapy.

Certification/Registration/Licensure

At present there are no state licensing requirements for dance therapists, but professional competence is identified through registered status from the ADTA. Two different levels of registration exist. To be qualified to work in a professional treatment system, one needs a master's degree plus 700 supervised clinical internship hours. Additional requirements and more experience are needed to be registered to teach, supervise, and engage in private practice.

Career Potential

Dance therapy is relatively new, but it has become accepted in its own right. The state of the economy, however, will have a significant impact on employment prospects.

The field (along with art and music therapy) has been recognized as beneficial in working with elderly citizens, and some governmental funding for this has been provided. With the growing pool of older Americans, the prospective need for dance/movement therapists should increase.

For More Information

The professional organization for this field is the American Dance Therapy Association, Inc., 2000 Century Plaza, Suite 108, Columbia, MD 21044.

Dance/Movement Therapy Programs

Master's Degree Programs
Arizona

Arizona State University
Tempe, AZ 85287
www.asu.edu/

California

California State University, Hayward
25800 Carlos Bee Blvd.
Hayward, CA 94542
www.csuhayward.edu/

University of California, Los Angeles
P.O. Box 951369
Los Angeles, CA 90095
www.ucla.edu/

California Institute of Integral Studies
765 Ashbury
San Franciso, CA 94117
www.ciis.edu/

Colorado

Naropa Institute
2130 Arapahoe Avenue
Boulder, CO 80302
www.naropa.edu/

Connecticut

Wesleyan University
Middletown, CT 06459
www.wesleyan.edu/

Massachusetts

Lesley College
29 Everett Street
Cambridge, MA 02138
www.lesley.edu/

New Hampshire

Antioch New England Graduate School
40 Avon Street
Keene, NH 03431
www.antiochne.edu/

New York

State University of New York at Brockport
Brockport, NY 14420
www.brockport.edu/

New York University
70 Washington Square South
New York, NY 10012

Southampton College
Long Island University
Southampton, NY 11968
www.liunet.edu/

Oregon

Marylhurst College
P.O. Box 261
Marylhurst, OR 97036
www.marylhurst.edu/

Pennsylvania

MCP Hahnemann University
905 Broad Street
Philadelphia, PA 19102
www.auhs.edu/

Bachelor's Degree Programs
California

Loyola Marymount University
7900 Loyola Blvd.
Los Angeles, CA 90045
www.lmu.edu/

Illinois

Barat College
700 Westleigh Road
Lake Forest, IL 60045
www.barat.edu/

Maryland

Goucher College
1021 Dulaney Valley Road
Baltimore, MD 21204
www.goucher.edu/

Michigan

Hope College
Dow Center
Holland, MI 49423
www.hope.edu/

Minnesota

Metropolitan State University
121 Seventh Place East, Metro Square
St. Paul, MN 55101
www.metrostate.edu/

New Jersey

Brookdale Community College
765 Newman Springs Road
Lincroft, NJ 07738
www2.brookdale.cc.ny.us/

New York

Hunter College
425 E 25th Street
New York, NY 10010
www.hunter.cuny.edu/

Marymount College
Tarrytown, NY 10591
www.marymt.edu/

HOME HEALTH AIDES

Principal activity: Helping the elderly and disabled meet their daily needs

Work commitment: Part- and full-time

Preprofessional education: High school diploma

Program length: 75 hours recommended

Work prerequisites: Formal training recommended

Career opportunities: Very favorable

Income range: $15,000 to $23,000

Scope

Most people in our society can take care of their own personal needs. There is, however, a significant number of people who, for one of several reasons, are unable to meet their personal needs and require assistance. The underlying problem may be due to injury, illness, emotional problems, or a social disadvantage (e.g., language impairment). Frequently, however, the sole cause is the weakness that sometimes comes with old age. Home health aides help all these people meet their daily needs.

Activities

Home health aides provide a broad spectrum of personal care services. They may help with personal hygiene, walking and voluntary or prescribed exercises, shopping and preparing meals (while seeing that special dietary restrictions are met), and maintaining an orderly and clean home. They also make sure their clients take the proper medications on schedule, change surgical dressings, and check vital signs. These helpers also provide companionship for clients and report on their progress to the family or a supervisor (typically, a registered nurse or social worker). By providing these services, home health aides allow their clients to remain in their own homes, which is less costly and less traumatic than custodial care.

Work Settings

Home health aides are employed by many kinds of agencies to work in clients homes. They may be referred by local welfare departments, hospitals, community agencies, or private health care agencies. Some aides also find work helping clients in nursing homes.

Advancement

Working for more affluent clients over extended periods can result in gradual increases in salary (which is usually on an hourly basis).

The Home Care Aide Association of America has proposed a three-level career ladder for aides. If this plan is accepted, it will provide for formal advancement possibilities.

Prerequisites

A high school diploma or its equivalent is recommended for work in this field.

Desirable personal attributes include good health, physical stamina, maturity and good judgment, a desire to help others, a great deal of patience, and a positive, outgoing personality.

Education/Training

While definitive standards have not yet been established nationwide, two basic avenues are currently available to prepare for becoming an aide.

1. Many employment agencies offer a very short training program, followed by on-the-job experience.

2. Currently, about half the states require a formal program that involves about 60 hours of training, followed by 15 hours of practical experience.

The National Home Caring Council is trying to establish training standards for the profession.

Training programs are offered by community colleges, state programs for the aged, adult education programs, and private agencies. In these programs, a prospective aide is taught how to meet a client's personal hygiene needs, plan and prepare nutritious meals, ensure comfort, monitor the client's health, administer medications, and cope with the types of problems commonly faced in the job.

Certification/Registration/Licensure

Currently certification is not available, and no license is required to serve as a home care aide.

Career Potential

Very favorable employment prospects in the home care field are the result of a rapidly growing population of elderly people. Many need only part-time assistance, but others are too feeble to care for themselves. In addition, there are many who are chronically ill or disabled. Over time, specialization in this area should occur, which will increase career potential and advancement possibilities.

For More Information

The professional organization for the field is the Home Care Aide Association of America, 519 C Street NE, Washington, DC 20002.

HORTICULTURAL THERAPISTS

Principal activity: Using gardening as therapy for appropriate patients

Work commitment: Part- or full-time

Preprofessional education: High school diploma

Program length: 4 years

Work prerequisites: Bachelor's degree in horticulture

Career opportunities: Improving

Income range: $25,000 to $32,000

Scope

This is a unique profession, using nature for therapeutic purposes. Two premises serve as the basis of horticultural therapy, which seeks to improve the well-being of persons with mental, physical, and social disabilities. The first is that seeing the beauty of nature—expressed in the form of flowers, plants, and shrubs—generates inner pleasure. This seems to be an innate human response. Thus, for example, flowers are a common gift for those we seek to please. The colors and aroma of flowers stimulate happiness and contentment, which may be especially meaningful to those deprived of their full capabilities. The second premise is that the work associated with growing flowers, fruits, vegetables, and shrubs can be beneficial in itself. Gathering the products of one's own labor from the soil can give the individual a unique sense of accomplishment.

Activities

Horticultural therapists encourage and support disabled clients to participate in all phases of gardening, from planting to selling their produce. They help their clients improve their self-esteem, confidence, attitudes, motor and problem-solving skills, sociability, and communication skills. In conjunction with other therapies, this kind of activity can generate a new sense of independence and purpose and helps prepare clients for a return to their homes. This type of therapy can have a significant impact on the recovery of clients to a functional state.

Work Settings

Horticultural therapists are employed in hospitals (both general and psychiatric), convalescent centers, nursing homes, rehabilitation centers, and correctional facilities.

Advancement

With additional experience, therapists can move to a larger facility of go into private practice, offering their services on a contract basis.

Prerequisites

A high school diploma or its equivalent is essential for work in this field. It's also a good idea to get experience working for greenhouses, nurseries, or landscape companies during summers. Volunteer work with disabled people also is helpful.

Desirable personal attributes include a genuine desire to help the disabled, manual dexterity, a love of gardening, and patience.

Education/Training

A bachelor's degree in horticulture is the basic requirement for employment. Degree programs are offered by at least 15 colleges and universities in the U.S. Courses include agriculture, psychology, sociology, horticultural therapy, and a supervised internship.

Certification/Registration/Licensure

Currently there are no state licensing laws in this profession. However, horticultural therapists can voluntarily register with the American Horticultural Therapy Association. This organization has established two classifications for horticultural therapists based education and experience. A *registered horticultural therapist* holds a bachelor's degree and has had at least one year of paid employment; a *master horticultural therapist* holds a master's degree and four years of paid employment.

Career Potential

This is one of the emerging health-care fields that has growth potential. Increased awareness of the therapeutic effects of gardening and the expending population of senior citizens are generating a need for horticultural therapists.

For More Information

The professional organization is the American Horticultural Therapy Association, 326-A Christopher Avenue, Gaithorsburg, MD 20879.

Horticultural Therapy Programs

The notations below denote the type of program offered:

a = associate degree	b = batchelor's degree	m = master's degree
o = one-year program	e = elective courses	

Illinois

College of DuPage (e)
22nd Street and Lambert Road
Glen Ellyn, IL 60137
www.cod.edu/

Iowa

Hawkeye Community College (a)
1501 East Orange Road
Waterloo, IA 50704
www.hawkeye.cc.ia.us/

Kansas

Kansas State University (b, m)
2021 Throckmorton Hall
Manhattan, KS 66506
www.ksu.edu/

Massachusetts

University of Massachusetts (e)
French Hall
Amherst, MA 01002
www.umass.edu/

New York

New York Botanical Garden (c)
200th Street and Kazimiroff Boulevard
Bronx, NY 10458
www.nybg.org/

SUNY Cobleskill (e)
Cobleskill, NY 12043
www.cobleskill.edu/

Rockland Community College (e)
145 College Road
Suffern, NY 10901
www.sunyrockland.edu/

Oklahoma

Tulsa Community College (a)
3727 East Apache
Tulsa, OK 74115
www.tulsa.cc.ok.us/

Pennsylvania

Temple University (e)
580 Meeting House Road
Ambler, PA 19002
www.temple.edu/

Rhode Island

University of Rhode Island (a)
Kingston, RI 02881
www.uri.edu/

Tennessee

Tennessee Technological University (e)
Box 5034
Cookeville, TN 38505
www.tntech.edu/

Texas

Texas A & M University (a)
College Station, TX 77843
www.tamu.edu/

Virginia

Virginia Tech (a)
Blacksburgh, VA 24061
www.vt.edu/

Northern Virginia Community College (c)
1000 Harry Flood Byrd Highway
Sterling, VA 20164
www.nv.cc.va.us/

Washington

Edmonds Community College (o)
20000 68th Avenue, West
Lynnwood, WA 98036
www.edcc.edu/

MUSIC THERAPISTS

Principal activity: Using music therapeutically for a variety of disorders.

Work commitment: Part- or full-time

Preprofessional education: High school diploma

Program length: 4 years

Work prerequisites: Bachelor's degree in music therapy

Career opportunities: Good

Income range: $20,000 to $30,000

Scope

Humans seem to have a natural positive reaction to music, whether vocal or instrumental. Infants respond to lullabies by falling asleep; adolescents respond to hard rock by getting "pumped up." Music can change a person's mood, and this forms the basis of music therapy. This therapy is used as part of a treatment plan to help change patients' behavior. Music is helpful in treating a variety of behavioral, physical, and learning disorders. Music therapy can improve patients' self-control and self-image, enhance their attention spans, reduce depression, and facilitate their integration to their surroundings.

Activities

Music therapists plan and execute musical activities as part of a rehabilitation program for disabled people. They coordinate their work with other health care professionals such as physicians, nurses, teachers, social workers, psychiatrists, psychologists, and other therapists. They provide their services to emotionally and socially maladjusted or mentally disabled children, adolescents, and adults. Others who can benefit are those with learning disabilities, geriatric patients, and those with physical impairments such as vision or hearing loss. The activities can be done individually or in a group and may be used in combination with dance therapy. The therapist may teach patients new tunes or play tapes to help withdrawn patients recall their pasts, reminisce, and participate with others in social activities.

Work Settings

Music therapists work in a wide variety of settings, including hospitals (both general and psychiatric), rehabilitation centers, nursing homes, extended care facilities, hospices, schools, and correctional facilities.

Advancement

Music therapists can advance by securing a master's or doctoral degree and obtaining an administrative or supervisory position. Teaching or private practice are other options.

Prerequisites

A high school diploma is required to gain admission to a college or university offering a music therapy program.

In addition to genuine musical skills, desirable personal attributes include patience, emotional stability, creativity, compassion, and a desire to help people.

Education/Training

Those seeking to enter this field should earn a bachelor's degree in music theory. This program includes courses in music, music theory, voice, and instrument lessons. These classes are supplemented by courses in psychology, sociology, biology, and liberal arts. Those wishing to work in a school also need education courses.

Most institutions with programs in this field offer batchelor's degrees, but a few offer master's and even doctoral programs.

Certification/Registration/Licensure

Certification is available from the Certification Board of Musical Therapists. Those seeking certification must pass a standard exam and maintaining continuing education requirements. Registration is available from the National Association of Music Therapists and the American Association for Music Therapy.

Career Potential

Music therapists will find favorable employment prospects in the coming decade. In addition to public and medical acceptance of the field, the U.S. Congress has recognized its significance and approved financial grants for the elderly in this area.

However, the state of the economy and the impact of health-care system changes will significantly influence employment prospects.

For More Information

The professional organizations in this area are listed below:

The American Association for Music Therapy
P.O. Box 60012
Valley Forge, PA 19484

National Association for Music Therapy
8455 Cotesville Road
Silver Spring, MD 20910

Music Therapy Programs

Alabama

University of Alabama at Birmingham
1714 Ninth Avenue South
Birmingham, AL 35294
www.uab.edu/

Arizona

Arizona State University
School of Music
Tempe, AZ 85287
www.asu.edu/

California

California State University–Northridge
18111 Nordhoff Street
Northridge, CA 91330
www.csun.edu/

Chapman University
One University Drive
Orange, CA 92866
www.chapman.edu/

University of the Pacific
3601 Pacific Avenue
Stockton, CA 95211
www.uop.edu/

Colorado

Colorado State University
Fort Collins, CO 80523
www.colostate.edu/

District of Columbia

Howard University
6th and Bryant Streets, NW
Washington, DC 20059
www.howard.edu/

Florida

Florida State University
Department of Music
Tallahassee, FL 32306
www.fsu.edu/

University of Miami
5801 Red Road
Coral Gables, FL 33124
www.ir.miami.edu/

Georgia

Georgia College
P.O. Box 023
Milledgville, GA 31061
www.gac.peachnet.edu/

Illinois

Western Illinois University
Department of Music
Macomb, IL 61415
www.wiu.edu/

Illinois State University
Music Department
Normal, IL 61761
www.ilstu.edu/

Indiana

University of Evansville
1800 Lincoln Avenue
Evansville, IN 47721
www.evansville.edu/

Indiana University/Purdue University
2101 Coliseum Boulevard
Fort Wayne, IN 46805
www.ipfw.edu/

Iowa

University of Iowa
Division of Music Education
Iowa City, IA 52242
www.uiowa.edu/

Wartburg College
P.O. Box 1003
Waverly, IA 50677
www.wartburg.edu/

Kansas

University of Kansas
126 Strong Hall
Lawrence, KS 66045
www.ukans.edu/

Louisiana

Loyola University of New Orleans
6363 St. Charles Avenue
New Orleans, LA 70118
www.loyno.edu/

Massachusetts

Anna Maria College
Box 78
Paxton, MA 01612
www.annamaria.edu/

Michigan

Michigan State University
Department of Music
East Lansing, MI 48824
www.msu.edu/

Western Michigan University
West Michigan Avenue
Kalamazoo, MI 49008
www.wmich.edu/

Eastern Michigan University
Department of Music
Ypsilanti, MI 48197
www.emich.edu/

Minnesota

Augsburg College
2211 Riverside Avenue South
Minneapolis, MN 55454
www.augsburg.edu/

University of Minnesota–Twin Cities
240 Williamson
Minneapolis, MN 55455
www.umn.edu/tc/

Missouri

University of Missouri, Kansas City
650 East 25th Street
Kansas City, MO 64108
www.umkc.edu/

Maryville University, St. Louis
13550 Conway Road
St. Louis, MO 63141
www.maryville.edu/

New Jersey

Montclair State University
Department of Music
Upper Montclair, NJ 07043
www.montclair.edu/

New Mexico

Eastern New Mexico University
Station #5, ENMU
Portales, NM 88130
www.enmu.edu/

New York

State University of New York at Fredonia
Fredonia, NY 14063
www.fredonia.edu/

State University or New York at New Paltz
Music Department
New Paltz, NY 12561
www.newpaltz.edu/

Nazareth College
4245 East Avenue
Rochester, NY 14618
www.naz.edu/

North Carolina

Queens College of Charlotte
Department of Music
Charlotte, NC 28274
www.queens.edu/

East Carolina University
East 5th Street
Greenville, NC 27858
www.ecu.edu/

Ohio

Ohio University
416 Tower
Athens, OH 45701
www.ohiou.edu/

Baldwin Wallace College
Department of Music
Berea, OH 44017
www.baldwinw.edu/

College of Mt. Saint Joseph
5701 Delhi Road
Cincinnati, OH 45233
www.msj.edu/

Cleveland Institute of Music
11021 East Boulevard
Cleveland, OH 44106
www.cwru.edu/CIM/cimhome.html

University of Dayton
300 College Park
Dayton, OH 45469
www.udayton.edu/

College of Wooster
Department of Music
Wooster, OH 44691
www.wooster.edu/

Oklahoma

Southwestern Oklahoma State University
Weatherford, OK 73096
www.swosu.edu/

Oregon

Willamette University
900 State Street
Salem, OR 93701
www.willamette.edu/

Pennsylvania

Elizabethtown College
Department of Music
Elizabethtown, PA 17022
www.etown.edu/

Mansfield University
Beecher House
Mansfield, PA 16933
www.mansfield.edu/

Duquesue University
600 Forbes Avenue
Pittsburgh, PA 15282
www.duq.edu/

MCP Hahnemann University
905 Broad Street
Philadelphia, PA 19101
www.auhs.edu/

Temple University
Broad St. & Montgomery Avenue
Philadelphia, PA 19122
www.temple.edu/

Marywood College
2300 Adams Avenue
Scranton, PA 18509
www.marywood.edu/

Slippery Rock University
Department of Music
Slippery Rock, PA 16057
www.sru.edu/

South Carolina

Charleston Southern University
Music Department
Charleston, SC 29411
http://csuniv.edu/

Tennessee

Tennessee Technological University
TTU Box 5006
Cookeville, TN 38505
www.tntech.edu/

Texas

West Texas A&M University
2501 Fourth Avenue
Canyon, TX 79016
www.wtamu.edu/

Southern Methodist University
Division of Music
Dallas, TX 75275
www.smu.edu/

Texas Women's University
P O Box 425648
Denton, TX 76204
www.twu.edu/

Sam Houston State University
Department of Music
Huntsville, TX 77341
www.shsu.edu/

Utah

Utah State University
University Hall
Logan, UT 84322
www.usu.edu/

Virginia

Radford University
P.O. Box 6903
Radford, VA 24142
www.runet.edu/

Shenandoah University
Music Therapy Department
Winchester, VA 22601
www.su.edu/

Wisconsin

Alverno College
3401 South 39th Street
Milwaukee, WI 53534
www.alverno.edu/

University of Wisconsin–Eau Claire
P.O. Box 4004
Eau Claire, WI 54701
www.uwec.edu/

University of Wisconsin–Oshkosh
Department of Music
Oshkosh, WI 54901
www.uwosh.edu/

OCCUPATIONAL THERAPISTS

Principal activity: Helping disabled people improve their quality of life

Work commitment: Part- and full-time

Preprofessional education: High school diploma

Program length: 4 years

Work requirements: Bachelor's degree, certification, and license

Career opportunities: Very favorable

Income range: $30,000 to $60,000

Scope

Occupational therapists (OTs) use a variety of activities to improve the lives of their patients, who may have mental, emotional, developmental, or physical disabilities. These therapists use educational, vocational, and rehabilitational techniques to improve their clients' ability to meet the daily tasks of living as well as to recover and maintain their work skills. They help patients improve their basic motor functions and reasoning capacities, and teach them how to compensate for a permanent loss of function. The ultimate goal of the occupational therapist is to help a patient achieve the most independent, productive, and satisfying lifestyle possible.

Activities

Occupational therapists train temporarily or permanently disabled patients to perform a variety of activities. They may use physical exercises to increase strength and manual dexterity. They may use pencil-and-paper games, list-making games, and eye-hand coordination activities to help various patients gain coordination and memory abilities. They also use computer programs to help patients improve their decision-making, abstract reasoning, perceptual, memory, sequencing, and coordination skills.

For those with permanent disabilities—such as spinal cord injuries, muscular dystrophy, or cerebral palsy—therapists teach them how to use adaptive equipment, including wheelchairs, splints, and devices that help with dressing and eating.

Work Settings

Occupational therapists provide services in a variety of settings. Most work in hospitals and nursing homes. Others work in rehabilitation centers, clinics, retirement communities, senior citizen centers, and special camps.

Advancement

With increased experience, an occupational therapist can become a senior therapist or specialized therapist. With a master's degree, one can be promoted to a supervisory of administration position.

Prerequisites

A high school diploma or its equivalent is needed undertake a college program of studies.

Desirable personal attributes include an abundance of patience, physical stamina, manual dexterity, compassion, the ability to improvise, and a genuine desire to help people.

Education/Training

There are several ways to get your education in this field; all involve completing an accredited program.

1. One can complete two years of liberal arts and science, then entering an OT program for the last two years of undergraduate studies.

2. One can complete a four-year bachelor's degree program in occupational therapy.

3. Those holding a bachelor's degree in another field can enroll in a graduate program and secure a certificate or master's degree in occupational therapy.

The standard OT curriculum involves courses in anatomy, neuroanatomy, physiology, neurophysiology, kinesiology, psychology, psychobiology, pediatrics, gerontology, and home economics. Manual and industrial arts, self-care activities, vocational and rehabilitational skills are also included. Students must also complete six to nine months of practical experience.

Certification/Registration/Licensure

Graduates of accredited occupational therapy programs can take a certification examination administered by the American Occupational Therapy Association. After passing it, one becomes a *registered occupational therapist (OTR)*. Most states require therapists to be licensed, as well.

Career Potential

Occupational therapists are in high demand and enjoy very favorable employment options, because of the current interest in sports and a rapidly aging population.

For More Information

The professional organization in this field is the American Occupational Therapy Association, 4720 Montgomery Lane, Bethesda, MD 20854.

Occupational Therapy Programs

Alabama

Jefferson State Community College
22601 Carson Road
Birmingham, AL 35215
www.jscc.cc.al.us/

Wallace State College
P.O. Box 2000
Hanceville, AL 35077
www.wallacestatehanceville.edu/

Arizona

Apollo College
630 West Southern Avenue
Mesa, AZ 85210
www.ApolloCollege.com/

California

Grossmont College
8800 Grossmont College Drive
El Cajon, CA 92020
www.gcccd.cc.ca.us/grossmont/

Loma Linda University
SAHP–Nichol Hall
Loma Linda, CA 92350
www.llu.edu/

Mount St. Mary's College
10 Chester Place
Los Angeles, CA 90007
www.msmc.la.edu/

Sacramento City College
3835 Freeport Boulevard
Sacramento, CA 95822
www.scc.losrios.cc.ca.us/

Colorado

Arapahoe Community College
2500 West College Drive
Littleton, CO 80160
www.arapahoe.edu/

Denver Technical College
925 South Niagara Street
Denver, CO 80224
www.dtc.edu/

Morgan Community College
17800 Road 20
Fort Morgan, CO 80701
www.mcc.cc.co.us/

Pueblo Community College
900 West Orman Avenue
Pueblo, CO 81004
www.pcc.cccoes.edu/

Connecticut

Briarwood College
2279 Mount Vernon Road
Southington, CT 06489
www.briarwood.edu/

Delaware

Delaware Technical & Community College
P.O. Box 610
Georgetown, DE 19947
www.terry.dtcc.edu/

Florida

Central Florida Community College
3001 Southwest College Road
Ocala, FL 34478
www.cfcc.cc.fl.us/

Daytona Beach Community College
1200 International Speedway Boulevard
Daytona Beach, FL 32114
www.dbcc.cc.fl.us/

Hillsborough Community College
P.O. Box 33030
Tampa, FL 33630
www.hcc.cc.fl.us/

Palm Beach Community College
4200 South Congress Avenue
Lake Worth, FL 33461
www.pbcc.cc.fl.us/

Georgia

Medical College of Georgia
Augusta, GA 30912
www.mcg.edu/

Middle Georgia College
1100 Second Street, S. E.
Cochran, GA 31014
www.mgc.peachnet.edu/

Hawaii

Kapi'olani Community College
4303 Diamond Head Road
Honolulu, HI 96816
www.kcc.hawaii.edu/

Illinois

College of DuPage
22nd Street and Lambert Road
Glen Ellyn, IL 60137
www.cod.edu/

Illinois Central College
201 SW Adams
Peoria, IL 61635
www.icc.cc.il.us/

Parkland College
2400 West Bradley Avenue
Champaign, IL 61821
www.parkland.cc.il.us/

South Suburban College of Cook Country
15800 South State Street
South Holland, IL 60473
www.ssc.cc.il.us/

WIlbur Wright College
4300 North Naragansett Avenue
Chicago, IL 60634
www.ccc.edu/wright/

Indiana

Ivy Tech State College
1 West 26th Street
Indianapolis, IN 46206
www.ivy.tec.in.us/

Iowa

Kirkwood Community College
6301 Kirkwood Boulevard, SW
Cedar Rapids, IA 52406
www.kirkwood.cc.ia.us/

Western Iowa Tech Community College
4647 Stone Avenue
Sioux City, IA 51102
www.witcc.cc.ia.us/

Kansas

Barton County Community College
R.R. 3, Box 136Z
Great Bend, KS 67530
www/barton.cc.ks.us/

Louisiana

Delgado Community College
615 City Park Avenue
New Orleans, LA 70119
www.dcc.edu/

Northeast Louisiana University
Monroe, LA 71209
www.nlu.edu/

Maine

Kennebec Valley Technical College
92 Western Avenue
Fairfield, ME 04937
www.kvtc.mtcs.tec.me.us/

Maryland

Allegany Community College
Willowbrook Road
Cumberland, MD 21502
www.ac.cc.md.us/

Catonsville Community College
800 South Rolling Road
Catonsville, MD 21228
www.ccbc.cc.md.us/

Massachusetts

Bay Path College
588 Longmeadow Street
Longmeadow, MA 01106
www.baypath.edu/

Bay State College
122 Commonwealth Avenue
Boston, MA 01615
www.baystate.edu/

Becker College
61 Sever Street, Box 15071
Worcester, MA 01615
www.becker.edu/

Bristol Community College
777 Elsbree Street
Fall River, MA 02720
http://bullwinkle.bristol.mass.edu/

Greenfield Community College
270 Main Streer
Greenfield, MA 01301
www.bcc.mass.edu/

Lasell College
1844 Commonwealth Avenue
Auburndale, MA 02166
www.lasell.edu/

Massachusetts Bay Community College
50 Oakland Street
Wellesley Hills, MA 02181
www.mbcc.mass.edu/

Mount Ida College
777 Dedham Street
Newton Centre, MA 02159
www.mountida.edu/

North Shore Community College
1 Ferncroft Road
Danvers, MA 01923
www.nscc.cc.ma.us/

Quinsigamond Community College
670 West Boylston Street
Worcester, MA 01606
www.qcc.mass.edu/

Springfield Technical Community College
One Armory Square
Springfield, MA 01101
www.stcc.mass.edu/

Michigan

Baker College of Muskegon
123 Apple Avenue
Muskegon, MI 49442
www.baker.edu/

Charles Stuart Mott Community College
2100 West Thompson Road
Fenton, MI 48430
www.mcc.edu/

Grand Rapids Community College
143 Bostwick, NE
Grand Rapids, MI 49503
www.grcc.cc.mi.us/

Lake Michigan College
111 Spruce Street
Niles, MI 49120
http://lmc.cc.mi.us/

Macomb Community College
44575 Garfield Road
Clinton Township, MI 48038
www.macomb.cc.mi.us/

Schoolcraft College
1751 Radcliff Street
Garden City, MI 48135
www.schoolcraft.cc.mi.us/

Minnesota

Anoka-Hennepin Technical College
1355 West Highway 10
Anoka, MN 55303
www.ank.tec.mn.us/

Lake Superior College
2101 Trinity Road
Duluth, MN 55811
www.lsc.cc.mn.us/

Northwest Technical College–East Grand Forks
Highway 220 North
East Grand Forks, MN 56721
www.ntc-online.com/

The College of St. Catherine
601 25th Avenue South
Minneapolis, MN 55454
www.stkate.edu/

Mississippi

Pearl River Community College
5448 US Highway 49 South
Hattiesburgh, MS 39401
www.prcc.cc.ms.us/

Missouri

Penn Valley Community College
3201 Southwest Trafficway
Kansas City, MO 64111
www.kcmetro.cc.mo.us/pennvalley/

St. Louis Community College of Meramec
11333 Big Bend Boulevard
St. Louis, MO 63122
www.stlcc.cc.mo.us/mcl

Sanford-Brown College
368 Brookes Drive
Hazelwood, MO 63042
(314) 965-6606

Montana

Montana State University
2100 16th Avenue, South
Great Falls, MT 58405
http://msucotgf.montana.edu/

Nebraska

Clarkson College
101 South 42nd Street
Omaha, NE 68131
www.clarksoncollege.edu/

New Jersey

Atlantic Cape Community College
5100 Black Horse Pike
Mays Landing, NJ 08330
www.atlantic.edu/

Union County College
232 East Second Street
Plainfield, NJ 07060
www.ucc.edu/

New Mexico

Eastern New Mexico University
52 University Boulevard
Roswell, NM 88202
www.enmu.edu/

Western New Mexico University
P.O. Box 680
Silver City, NM 88062
www.wnmu.edu/

New York

Erie Community College
6205 Main Street
Williamsville, NY 14221
www.sunyerie.edu/

Genesee Community College
One College Road
Batavia, NY 14020
www.sunygenessee.cc.ny.us/

Herkimer County Community College
Reservoir Road
Herkimer, NY 13350
www.hccc.ntcnet.com/

LaGuardia Community College
31-10 Thomson Avenue
Long Island City, NY 11101
www.lagcc.cuny.edu/

Orange County Community College
115 South Street
Middletown, NY 10940
www.orange.cc.ny.us/

Rockland Community College
145 College Road
Suffern, NY 10901
www.sunyrockland.edu/

Suffolk County Community College
Crooked Hill Road
Brentwood, NY 11717
www.sunysuffolk.edu/

Touro College
27-33 West 23rd Street
New York, NY 10010
www.touro.edu/

North Carolina

Caldwell Community College
2855 Hickory Boulevard
Hudson, NC 28638
www.caldwell.cc.nc.us/

Pitt Community College
Drawer 7007
Highway 11, South
Greenville, NC 27835
www.pitt.cc.nc.us/

Southwestern Community College
275 Webster Road
Sylva, NC 28779
www.southwest.cc.nc.us/

Stanly Community College
141 College Drive
Albemarle, NC 28001
www.stanly.cc.nc.us/

North Dakota

North Dakota State College of Science
Hektner Hall
Wahpeton, ND 58076
www.ndscs.nodak.edu/

Ohio

Cincinnati State Technical & Community College
3520 Central Parkway
Cincinnati, OH 45223
www.cinstate.cc.oh.us/

Cuyahoga Community College
2900 Community College Avenue
Cleveland, OH 44115
www.tri-c.cc.oh.us/

Kent State University
400 East Fourth Street
East Liverpool, OH 43920
www.kenteliv.kent.edu/

Lourdes College
6832 Convent Boulevard
Sylvania, OH 43560
www.lourdes.edu/

Muskingum College
1555 Newark Road
Zanesville, OH 43701
www.muskingum.edu/

Shawnee State University
940 Second Street
Portsmouth, OH 45662
www.shawnee.edu/

Sinclair Community College
444 West Third Street
Dayton, OH 45402
www.sinclair.edu/

Stark Technical College
6200 Frank Avenue NW
Canton, OH 44720
(216) 494-6170

Oklahoma

Oklahoma City Community College
7777 South May Avenue
Oklahoma City, OK 73159
www.okc.cc.ok.us/

Southwestern Oklahoma State University
P.O. Box 190
Fort Cobb, OK 73038
www.swosu.edu/

Tulsa Community College
3727 East Apache
Tulsa, OK 74115
www.tulsa.cc.ok.us/

Oregon

Mt. Hood Community College
26000 SE Stark Street
Gresham, OR 97030
www.mhcc.cc.or.us/

Pennsylvania

Community College of Allegheny County
595 Beatty Road
Monroeville, PA 15146
www.cacc.edu/

Clarion University of Pennsylvania
Clarion, PA 16214
www.clarion.edu

Harcum College
Bryn Mawr, PA 19010
www.harcum.edu/

Lehigh Carbon Community College
4525 Education Park Drive
Schnecksville, PA 18078
www.lccc.edu/

Mount Aloysius College
Cresson, PA 16630
http://ntweb.mtaloy.edu/

Pennsylvania College of Technology
One College Avenue
Williamsport, PA 17701
www.pct.edu/

Pennsylvania State University
Campus Drive
Mont Alto, PA 17237
www.psu.edu/

South Carolina

Trident Technical College
P.O. Box 118067
Charleston, SC 29423
www.trident.tec.edu/

Tennessee

Nashville State Technical Institute
120 White Bridge Road
Nashville, TN 37209
www.ntsi.tec.tn.us/

Roane State Community College
276 Patton Lane
Harriman, TN 37748
www.rscc.cc.tn.us/

Texas

Amarillo College
6222 West 9th Street
Amarillo, TX 79178
www.actx.edu/

Army Medical Department Center & School
3141 Binz Engelman
Fort Sam Houston, TX 78234
www.cs.amedd.army.mil/

Austin Community College
3100 Shenandoah
Houston, TX 77021
www.austin.cc.tx.us/

Navarro College
3200 West 7th Avenue
Corsicana, TX 75110
www.nav.cc.tx.us/

North Central Texas College
601 East Hickory Street
Denton, TX 76201
www.nctc.cc.tx.us/

St. Philip's College
1801 Martin Luther King Street
San Antonio, TX 78203
www.accd.edu/spc/spcmain/spc.htm

San Jacinto College South
13735 Beamer Road
Houston, TX 77089
www.sjcd.cc.tx.us/

Utah

Salt Lake Community College
4600 South Redwood Road
Salt Lake City, UT 84130
www.slcc.edu/

Virginia

College of Health Sciences
920 South Jefferson Street
Roanoke, VA 24016
www.chs.edu/

J .Sargeant Reynolds Community College
P.O. Box 85622
Richmond, VA 23285
www.jsr.cc.va.us/

Washington

Green River Community College
12401 SE 320th Street
Auburn, WA 98002
www.greenriver.ctc.edu/beta/

Yakima Valley Community College
Sixteenth Avenue & Nob Hill Boulevard
P.O. Box 1647
Yakima, WA 98907
www.rfttc.org/

Wisconsin

Fox Valley Technical College
1825 North Bluemond Drive
Appleton, WI 54913
www.foxvalley.tec.wi.us/

Madison Area Technical College
211 North Carroll Street
Madison, WI 53233
http://twister.madison.tec.wi.us/

Milwaukee Area Technical College
700 West State Street
Milwaukee, WI 53233
www.matc.edu/

Western Wisconsin Technical College
304 North Sixth Street
LaCrosse, WI 54602
www.western.tec.wi.us/

OCCUPATIONAL THERAPY ASSISTANTS

Principal activity: Helping occupational therapists

Work commitment: Full-time

Preprofessional education: High school diploma

Program length: 1 to 2 years

Work prerequisites: Certificate or associate degree

Career opportunities: Favorable

Income range: $23,000 to $32,000

Scope

Occupational therapy assistants carry out most of the routine activities designed by occupational therapists, who supervise their activities.

Activities

Occupational therapy assistants select or construct equipment to help patients, individually and in groups, move toward independent living. They also help with the planning and are major participants in implementing treatment programs. As part of their routine responsibilities, they lay out materials needed for treatment, make sure that adequate materials are on hand, order them when necessary. They also see to it that equipment is properly maintained.

Work Settings

Nearly half of all occupational therapy assistants work in hospitals, and a small portion in nursing homes. Other work settings include senior citizen residences and mental health facilities.

Advancement

With experience and professional success, a motivated assistent may return to school to become a fully trained therapist. However, it is preferable to follow the direct route to this career, if one is interested from the outset.

Prerequisites

A high school diploma or its equivalent is needed to enroll in an occupational therapy assistant program.

Desirable personal attributes include manual dexterity, patience, maturity, an ability to work with and under people, and a sense of compassion.

Education/Training

There are two routes to getting the training for a position in this field:

1. One-year certificate programs are offered by many vocational and technical schools.

2. Two-year associate degree programs are offered by some community colleges.

The curriculum includes anatomy, physiology, and occupational therapy theory and skills, plus several months of supervised practical experience.

Certification/Registration/Licensure

Upon completion of an accredited program and passing the certification examination of the American Occupational Therapy Certification Board, one is entitled to be designated at Certified Occupational Therapy Assistant (COTA).

Career Potential

The outlook for job opportunities in the field is favorable. This is consistent with the need for occupational therapists and the increaseing population of elderly individuals needing such services.

For More Information

The American Occupational Therapy Association, 4720 Montgomery Lane, Bethesda, MD 20824 is the professional organization for both therapists and assistants.

Occupational Therapy Assistants Programs

Alabama

University of Alabama, Birmingham
University Station
Birmingham, AL 36088
www.uab.edu/

California

Los Angeles City College
855 North Vermont Avenue
Los Angeles, CA 90029
http://citywww.lacc.cc.ca.us/

Connecticut

Manchester Community-Technical College
P.O. Box 1046
Manchester, CT 06040
www.mctc.commnet.edu/

Florida

Palm Beach Junior College
4200 South Congress Avenue
Lake Worth, FL 33461
www.pbcc.cc.ufl.us/

Hawaii

Kapi'olani Community College
4303 Diamond Head Road
Honolulu, HI 96816
www.kcc.hawaii.edu/

Illinois

Chicago City-Wide College/
Cook County Hospital
1900 West Polk Street
Chicago, IL 60612
www.cookcountyhospital.edu/

Illinois Central College
201 SW Adams
Peoria, IL 61635
www.icc.cc.il.us/

Indiana

Indiana University School of Medicine
1140 West Michigan Street
Indianapolis, IN 46223
www.indiana.edu/

Iowa

Kirkwood Community College
6301 Kirkwood Boulevard, SW
P.O. Box 2068
Cedar Rapids, IA 52406
www.kirkwood.cc.ia.us/

Kansas

Barton County Community College
R.R. 3, Box 136Z
Great Bend, KS 67530
www.barton.cc.ks.us/

University of Kansas
318 Blake Hall
Lawrence, KS 66045
www.ukans.edu/

Louisiana

Northeast Louisiana University
Monroe, LA 71209
www.nlu.edu/

Massachusetts

North Shore Community College
1 Ferncroft Road
Danvers, MA 01923
www.nscc.cc.ma.us/

Becker College
61 Sever Street
Worcester, MA 01605
www.becker.edu/

Quinsigamond Community College
670 West Boylston Street
Worcester, MA 01606
www.qcc.mass.edu/

Michigan

Grand Rapids Community College
143 Boswick, NE
Grand Rapids, MI 49503
www.grcc.cc.mi.us/

Schoolcraft College
18600 Haggerty Road
Livonia, MI 48152
www.schoolcraft.cc.mi.us/

Minnesota

Anoka-Hennepin Technical College
1355 West Highway 10
Anoka, MN 55303
www.ank.tec.mn.us/

Duluth Area Vocational
Technical Institute
2101 Trinity Road
Duluth, MN 55811

St. Mary's University
2500 Park Avenue
Minneapolis, MN 55404
www.stmary.edu/

New Jersey

Union County College
232 East Second Street
Plainfield, NJ 07606
www.ucc.edu/

Atlantic Cape Community College
5100 Black Horse Pike
Mays Landing, NJ 08330
www.atlantic.edu/

New York

Erie Community College
6205 Main Street
Buffalo, NY 14221
www.sunyerie.edu/

Herkimer County Community College
Reservoir Road
Herkimer, NY 13350
www.hccc.ntcnet.com/

LaGuardia Community College
31-10 Thomson Avenue
Long Island City, NY 11101
www.lagcc.cuny.edu/

Orange County Community College
115 South Street
Middletown, NY 10940
www.orange.cc.ny.us/

Rockland Community College
145 College Road
Suffern, NY 10901
www.sunyrockland.edu/

North Carolina

Stanly Community College
141 College Drive
Albemarle, NC 28001
www.stanly.cc.nc.us/

Caldwell Community College
1000 Hickory Boulevard
Hudson, NC 29638
www.caldwell.cc.nc.us/

North Dakota

North Dakota State College of Science
Wahpeton, ND 58075
www.ndscs.nodak.edu/

Ohio

Cuyahoga Community College
2900 Community College Avenue
Cleveland, OH 44115
www.tri-c.cc.oh.us/

Lourdes College
6832 Convent Boulevard
Sylvania, OH 43560
www.lourdes.edu/

Oklahoma

Oklahoma City Community College
7777 South May Avenue
Oklahoma City, OK 73159
www.okc.cc.ok.us/

Oregon

Mount Hood Community College
26000 SE Stark Street
Gresham, OR 97030
www.mhcc.cc.or.us/

Pennsylvania

Mount Aloysius Junior College
Cresson, PA 16630
http://ntweb.mtaloy.edu/

Lehigh County Community College
2370 Main Street
Schnecksville, PA 18078
www.lccc.edu/

Tennessee

Nashville State Technical Institute
120 White Bridge Road
Nashville, TN 37209
www.nsti.tec.tn.us/

Texas

Houston Community College
3100 Shenandoah
Houston, TX 77021
www.hccs.edu/

St. Philip's College
2111 Nevada Street
San Antonio, TX 78203
www.accd.edu/spc/spcmain/spc.htm

Washington

Green River Community College
12401 SE 320th Street
Auburn, WA 98002
www.greenriver.ctc.edu/beta/

Wisconsin

Fox Valley Technical Institute
1825 North Bluemond Drive,
P.O. Box 2277
Appleton, WI 54913
www.foxvalley.tec.wi.us/

Madison Area Technical College
211 North Carroll Street
Madison, WI 53703
http://twister.madison.tec.wi.us/

Milwaukee Area Technical College
700 West State Street
Milwaukee, WI 53203
www.matc.edu/

PATIENT REPRESENTATIVES

Principal activity: Helping to resolve patients' problems while they are hospitalized

Work commitment: Part- or full-time

Preprofessional education: High school diploma

Program length: Varies

Work prerequisites: Bachelor's degree preferred

Career opportunities: Improving

Income range: $30,000 to $50,000

Scope

Hospitalization results in major changes in an individual's lifestyle. People experience a loss of independence and are often uncertain about their options and rights. This unstable situation can lead to a sense of confusion, which is more profound for aged, disadvantaged, and language-limited individuals. To enhance the quality of patients' hospital stays and to facilitate their recovery, most hospitals employ a patient representative, who acts as the advocate for those who are hospitalized. This service goes a long way toward helping with the nonmedical stresses of a hospital stay.

Activities

Patient representatives help to resolve problems between hospitals and patients. They must be attentive to patient concerns, even if they seem trivial, since they may be significant in the patient's mind. By ascertaining exactly what the problem is, determining if it is genuine, giving clarification on hospital procedures, and explaining the need for certain actions, they can help resolve difficulties before they escalate into major problems.

Representatives may find information on a patient's treatment plan and then explain it to the patient's family. Where a genuine complaint has been voiced by a patient, representatives may intercede with the appropriate authorities to seek a solution.

Hospitals have vested interest in their patients' satisfaction. In today's marketplace, they often must compete for patients. The efforts of the patient representative can contribute significantly to this goal.

Work Settings

Most patient representatives work in hospitals, but some are employed by HMOs, nursing homes, and health centers.

Advancement

With experience and education, a patient representative can move to a larger institution or gain supervisory status.

Prerequisites

A high school diploma or its equivalent is the minimum prerequisite. Employers establish their own educational and work experience requirements, so other requirements may vary.

Desirable personal attributes include sound judgment, an ability to view situations objectively, the capacity to work with a diverse group of people, a personality that generates a sense of trust, and an ability to work under emotionally stressful conditions.

Education/Training

Since no formal educational standards exist employers establish their own guidelines. These may include prior work in health-related areas and college courses in biology, medical terminology, social sciences, and a foreign language (especially Spanish).

Many employers now require a bachelor's degree, and one school offers a master's degree program in the field.

Certification/Registration/Licensure

At present, there are no certification or licensing requirements in this field.

Career Potential

The outlook for employment in this field is favorable, but this assessment is based on the assumption that positive factors outweigh negative ones. Thus, as health-care institutions realize the benefits of services in this field and as consumer advocates become more vocal, the pressure to appoint patient representatives increases. On the other hand, cost-cutting measures will serve as a deterrent to expansion of the field. The positive forces seem to have an upper hand at present, but an economic downturn could change the situation.

For More Information

For more information, write to the National Society for Patient Representation and Consumer Affairs of the American Hospital Association, 840 North Lake Shore Drive, Chicago, IL 60611.

Patient Representative Program

Sarah Lawrence College
1 Mead Way
Bronxville, NY 10708
www.slc.edu/

PHYSICAL THERAPISTS

Principal activity: Helping patients overcome physical limitations

Work commitment: Part- or full-time

Preprofessional education: High school diploma, plus 200 to 300 volunteer hours

Program length: 4 years for a bachelor's degree; 2 for a master's degree

Work prerequisites: Bachelor's degree plus certification and licensure required; master's degree preferred

Career opportunities: Leveling off

Income range: $35,000 to $75,000

Scope

Physical therapists help to relieve pain, restore function, promote healing, and prevent permanent disability. To achieve these goals, they may use a variety of treatments, including exercise, water, heat, cold, electricity, ultrasound, and massage. Physical therapy provides benefits to joints, bones, muscles, and nerves that have been impaired because of disease or injury. When healing or function restoration is not possible, physical therapists teach patients how to adapt to their limitations.

Physical therapy is applicable in a wide range of medical specialties, including orthopedics, neurology, neurosurgery, geriatrics, pediatrics, rheumatology, obstetrics-gynecology, sports medicine, internal medicine, and even psychiatry.

Patients who benefit most from physical therapy include victims of strokes and brain, spinal cord, burn, or sports injuries; postoperative patients; cerebral palsy and muscular dystrophy patients; arthritis sufferers; and newborns with physical defects.

Activities

Physical therapists evaluate a patient's current status using various diagnostic procedures, then establish a treatment plan and arrange for its implementation.

A patient treatment plan depends on the nature of the illness or injury. Thus, for a paraplegic, the therapist might recomment exercises to maintain lower limb joint motion and strengthen the muscles of the shoulder and upper limb. He or she will also teach the patient to use a wheelchair or crutches properly. Physical therapists work with arthritis sufferers, burn victims, open-heart surgery patients, and even newborns. Because the field is growing, some therapists today are specializing in one field, such as pediatrics or orthopedics.

Work Settings

Physical therapists work in many different settings. About a third work in hospitals. Others work in rehabilitation centers, institutions for the disabled, community centers, private offices, nursing homes, and even private residences. Some hold teaching or administration positions at colleges and universities.

Advancement

With experience, a physical therapist can become a senior therapist, department supervisor, coordinator of rehabilitation services, or even facility administrator. Along with such increases in responsibility come substantial pay increases.

Prerequisites

A high school diploma or its equivalent is needed to begin a college program in physical therapy.

Desirable personal attributes include patience, manual dexterity, physical strength, strong communication skills, endurance, and an optimistic personality.

Education/Training

High school students who are interested in becoming physical therapists should take courses in biology, chemistry, physics, mathematics, and social studies. After securing a high school diploma or its equivalent, they should attend a bachelor's degree program in physical therapy (more than 100 are offered in United States).

Those already holding a bachelor's degree in a different area can pursue one of two routes:

1. They can earn an additional bachelor's degree in physical therapy (with advanced standing credits).

2. They can apply to a master's degree program (after completing the required science and other course prerequisites). There are about 25 such programs

in the United States, and most take two years to complete. (Many physical therapists secure master's degrees, and some even pursue doctorates to enhance their status.)

The typical program of studies includes basic courses in human anatomy, physiology, and neuroanatomy, and clinical courses in medicine, tests and measurements, and therapeutic exercises. Students then must have a supervised clinical experience.

Certification/Registration/Licensure

All states require physical therapists to be licensed in order to practice. Some even require continuing education.

Career Potential

Because of the increase in the elderly population and the number of those participating in physical activities, the demand for physical therapists today is very high. In fact, physical therapy consistently ranks as one of the fastest growing fields in the United States. Competition to gain admission to educational programs is also intense.

Experts anticipate that the demand will level off in the coming decade, and there will be a surplus of therapists in the next few years.

For More Information

The professional organization for this field is the American Physical Therapy Association, 1111 North Fairfax Street, Alexandria, VA 22314.

Physical Therapy Programs

Alabama

University of Alabama at Birmingham
900 19th Street
UAB Station, AL 35294
www.uab.edu/

University of South Alabama
1504 Spring Hill Avenue
Mobile, AL 36604
www.usouthal.edu/

Arizona

Northern Arizona University
C.U. Box 15105
Flagstaff, AZ 86011
www.nau.edu/

Arkansas

University of Central Arkansas
201 Donaghey Avenue
Conway, AR 72035
www.uca.edu/

California

California State University, Fresno
2345 East San Ramon Avenue
Fresno, CA 93740
www.fansonly.com/schools/fres/

Loma Linda University
Loma Linda, CA 92350
www.llu.edu/

California State University, Long Beach
1250 Bellflower Boulevard
Long Beach, CA 90840
www.acs.csulb.edu/

Mount St. Mary's College
12001 Chalon Road
Los Angeles, CA 90049
www.msmc.la.edu/

University of Southern California
1540 East Alcazar Street
Los Angeles, CA 90033
www.usc.edu/

California State University, Northridge
Northridge, CA 91330
www.csun.edu/

Samuel Merritt College
370 Hawthorne Avenue
Oakland, CA 94609
www.samuelmerritt.edu/

Chapman University
333 North Glassel
Orange, CA 92666
www.chapman.edu/

California State University, Sacramento
Sacramento, CA 95819
www.csus.edu/

San Francisco State University
374 Parnassus
San Francisco, CA 94143
www.fansonly.com/schools.sdsu/

University of the Pacific
Stockton, CA 95211
www.uop.edu/

Colorado

Regis University
3333 Regis Boulevard
Denver, CO 80221
www.regis.edu/

University of Colorado
4200 East Ninth Avenue, Box C244
Denver, CO 80262
www.cudenver.edu/

Connecticut

Quinnipiac College
Mount Carmel Avenue
Hamden, CT 06518
www.quinnipiac.edu/

University of Connecticut
358 Mansfield Road, U-101
Storrs, CT 06269
www.uconn.edu/

University of Hartford
200 Bloomfield Avenue
West Hartford, CT 06117
www.hardfield.edu/

Delaware

University of Delaware
303 McKinley Laboratory
Newark, DE 19716
www.udel.edu/

District of Columbia

Howard University
6th and Bryant Streets, NW
Washington, DC 20059
www.howard.edu/

Florida

University of Miami School of Medicine
5915 Ponce de Leon Boulevard
Coral Gables, FL 33146
www.ir.miami.edu/

Nova Southeastern University
3200 South University Drive
Ft. Lauderdale, FL 33328
www.nova.edu/

University of Florida
Box 100154 HSC
Gainesville, FL 32610
www.ufl.edu/

University of North Florida
4567 St. Johns Bluff Road South
Jacksonville, FL 32224
www.unf.edu/

Florida International University
Miami, FL 33199
www.fiu.edu/

University of Central Florida
4000 Central Florida Boulevard
Orlando, FL 32816
www.ucf.edu/

University of St. Augustine for Health Sciences
1690 US Route 1 South
St. Augustine, FL 32086
www.usa.edu/

Florida A & M University
Ware-Rhaney Building
Tallahassee, FL 32307
www.famu.edu/

Georgia

Emory University
1441 Clinton Road NE
Atlanta, GA 30322
www.emory.edu/

Georgia State University
University Plaza
Atlanta, GA 30303
www.gsu.edu/

Medical College of Georgia
Augusta, GA 30912
www.mcg.edu/

North Georgia College and State University
Barnes Hall
Dahlonega, GA 30597
www.ngc.peachnet.edu/

Armstrong Atlantic State University
11935 Abercorn Street
Savannah, GA 31419
www.armstrong.edu/

Idaho

Idaho State University
Box 8002
Pocatello, ID 83209
www.isu.edu/

Illinois

Northwestern University Medical School
645 North Michigan Avenue
Chicago, IL 60611
www.nwu.edu/

University of Illinois at Chicago
1919 West Taylor Street
Chicago, IL 60612
www.uic.edu/

Northern Illinois University
DeKalb, IL 60115
www.niu.edu/

Midwestern University
555 31st Street
Downers Grove, IL 60515
www.midwestern.edu/

University of Chicago Medical School
3333 Green Bay Road
North Chicago, IL 60064
www.uchicgo.edu/

Bradley University
1501 West Bradley Avenue
Peoria, IL 61625
www.bradley.edu/

Indiana

University of Evansville
1800 Lincoln Avenue
Evansville, IN 47722
www.evansville.edu/

Indiana University
1226 West Michigan Street
Indianapolis, IN 46202
www.indiana.edu/

University of Indianapolis
1400 East Hanna Avenue
Indianapolis, IN 46227
www.uindy.edu/

Iowa

University of Osteopathic Medicine & Health Sciences
3200 Grand Avenue
Des Moines, IA 50312
www.uomhs.edu/

University of Iowa
2600 Steindler Building
Iowa City, IA 52242
www.uiowa.edu/

Kansas

University of Kansas Medical Center
3901 Rainbow Boulevard
Kansas City, KS 66170
www.ukans.edu/

Wichita State University
1845 Fairmont
Wichita, KS 67260
www.wichita.edu/

Kentucky

University of Kentucky
121 Washington Avenue
Lexington, KY 40506
www.uky.edu/

University of Louisville
525 East Madison Street
Louisville, KY 40292
www.louisville.edu/

Louisiana

Louisiana State University
500 Kings Highway, P O Box 33932
Shreveport, LA 71130
www.lsus.edu/

Maine

University of New England
11 Hills Beach Road
Biddeford, ME 04005
www.une.edu/

Maryland

University of Maryland School of Medicine
100 Penn Street
Baltimore, MD 21201
www.ab.umd.edu/

University of Maryland, Eastern Shore
Kiah Hall
Princess Anne, MD 21853
www.umes.umd.edu/

Massachusetts

Boston University
635 Commonwealth Avenue
Boston, MA 02215
http://web.bu.edu/

Northeastern University
360 Huntington Avenue
Boston, MA 02115
www.northeastern.edu/

Simmons College
300 The Fenway
Boston, MA 02115
www.simmons.edu/

University of Massachusetts Lowell
1 University Avenue
Lowell, MA 02115
www.uml.edu/

Springfield College
263 Alden Street
Springfield, MA 01109
www.spfldcol.edu/

Michigan

Grand Valley State University
328 Henry Hall
Allendale, MI 49401
www.gvsu.edu/

Andrews University
Berrien Springs, MI 49104
www.andrews.edu/

Wayne State University
439 Shapero Hall
Detroit, MI 48202
www.wayne.edu/

University of Michigan–Flint
Flint, MI 48502
www.flint.umich.edu/

Central Michigan University
134 Pearce Hall
Mt. Pleasant, MI 48859
www.cmich.edu/

Oakland University
Rochester, MI 48309
www.acs.oakland.edu/

Minnesota

College of St. Scholastica
1200 Kenwood Avenue
Duluth, MN 55811
www.css.edu/

College of St. Catherine
601 15th Avenue South
Minneapolis, MN 55454
www.skate.edu/

University of Minnesota
Box 388 UMHC
Minneapolis, MN 55455
www.umn.edu/tc/

Mayo School of Health Related Sciences
1104 Siebens Building
Rochester, MN 55905
www.mayo.edu/

Mississippi

University of Mississippi Medical Center
2500 North State Street
Jackson, MS 39216
www.olemiss.edu/

Missouri

University of Missouri
106 Lewis Hall
Columbia, MO 65211
www.missouri.edu/

Rockhurst University
1100 Rockhurst Road
Kansas City, MO 64110
www.rockhurst.edu/

Maryville University of St. Louis
13550 Conway Road
St. Louis, MO 63141
www.maryville.edu/

St. Louis University
1504 South Grand Boulevard
St. Louis, MO 63104
www.slu.edu/

Washington University
School of Medicine
4444 Forest Park Boulevard
St. Louis, MO 63108
www.wustl.edu/

Montana

University of Montana–Missoula
Missoula, MT 59812
www.umt.edu/

Nebraska

Creighton University
2500 California Plaza
Omaha, NE 68178
www.creighton.edu/

University of Nebraska Medical Center
600 South 42nd
Omaha, NE 68198
www.unomaha.edu/

New Jersey

Kean College
65 Bergen Street
Newark, NJ 07107
www.kean.edu/

Richard Stockton College of New Jersey
Jim Leeds Road
Pomona, NJ 08240
http://loki.stockton.edu/

Rutgers–State University of New Jersey
40 East Laurel Road
Stratford, NJ 08084
www.rugers.edu/

New Mexico

University of New Mexico
Albuquerque, NM 87131
www.unm.edu/

New York

Daemen College
4380 Main Street
Amherst, NY 14226
www.daemen.edu/

Long Island University
University Plaza
Brooklyn, NY 11201
www.liunet.edu/

SUNY Health Science Center at Brooklyn
450 Clarkson Avenue
Brooklyn, NY 11203
www.hscbklyn.edu/

D'Youville College
1 D'Youville Square
320 Porter Avenue
Buffalo, NY 14201
www.dyc.edu/

SUNY at Buffalo
405 Kimball Tower
Buffalo, NY 14214
www.buffalo.edu/

Touro College
135 Carman Road
Dix Hills, NY 11746
www.touro.edu/

Ithaca College
335 Smiddy Hall
Ithaca, NY 14850
www.ithaca.edu/

Columbia University
710 W 168th Street, 8th Floor
New York, NY 10032
www.columbia.edu/

Hunter College
425 East 25th Street
New York, NY 10010
www.hunter.cuny.edu/

New York University
345 East 24th Street
Weissman Building
New York, NY 10010
www.nyu.edu/

College of Staten Island, CUNY
2800 Victory Boulevard
Staten Island, NY 10314
www.csi.cuny.edu/

SUNY at Stony Brook
Health Science Center
Stony Brook, NY 11794
www.sunysb.edu/

SUNY Health Science Center at Syracuse
750 East Adams Street
Syracuse, NY13210
www.esf.edu/

The Sage Colleges
Troy, NY 12180
www.sage.edu/

Utica College of Syracuse University
1600 Burstone Road
Utica, NY 13502
www.syr.edu/

New York Medical College
Valhalla, NY 10595
www.nymc.edu/

North Carolina

University of North Carolina at Chapel Hill
Medical School Wing CB #7135
Chapel Hill, NC 27599
www.unc.edu/

Duke University
P.O. Box 3965
Durham, NC 27710
www.duke.edu/

East Carolina University
Greenville, NC 27858
www.edu.edu/

Winston-Salem State University
601 MLK Jr Drive
Winston-Salem, NC 27110
www.wssu.edu/

North Dakota

University of North Dakota School of Medicine
P.O. Box 9037
501 North Columbia Road
Grand Forks, ND 58502
www.und.nodak.edu/

Ohio

Ohio University
Convocation Center
Athens, OH 45701
www.ohio.edu/

University of Cincinnati
P.O. Box 210038
Cincinnati, OH 45221
www.uc.edu/

Cleveland State University
1983 East 24th Street
Cleveland, OH 44115
www.csuohio.edu/

Ohio State University
1583 Perry Street
Columbus, OH 43210
www.acs.ohio-state.edu/

University of Findlay
1000 North Main Street
Findlay, OH 45840
www.findlay.edu/

Oklahoma

Langston University
Langston, OK 73050
www.lunet.edu/

University of Oklahoma
P.O. Box 26901
Oklahoma City, OK 73190
www.ou.edu/

Oregon

Pacific University
2043 College Way
Forest Grove, OR 97116
www.pacificu.edu/

Pennsylvania

Widener University
1 University Place
Chester, PA 19013
www.widener.edu/

College Misericordia
301 Lake Street
Dallas, PA 18612
www.miseri.edu/

Gannon University
AJ Palumbo Academic Center
109 University Square
Erie, PA 16541
www.gannon.edu/

Beaver College
450 South Easton Road
Glenside, PA 19038
www.beaver.edu/

Philadelphia College of Pharmacy and Science
600 South 43rd Street
Philadelphia, PA 19104
www.pcps.edu/

Temple University
3307 North Broad Street
Philadelphia, PA 19140
www.temple.edu/

Thomas Jefferson University
130 South 9th Street
Philadelphia, PA 19107
www.tju.edu/

Duquesne University
111 Health Science Building
Pittsburgh, PA 15282
www.duq.edu/

Chatham College
Woodland Road
Pittsburgh, PA 15232
www.chatham.edu/

University of Pittsburgh
4019 Forbes Tower
Pittsburgh, PA 15260
www.pitt.edu/

University of Scranton
800 Linden Street
Scranton, PA 18510
www.uofs.edu/

Slippery Rock University
North Road
Slippery Rock, PA 16057
www.sru.edu/

Rhode Island

University of Rhode Island
113 Keaney
Kingston, R I 02881
www.uri.edu/

South Carolina

Medical University of South Carolina
171 Ashley Avenue
Charleston, SC 29425
www.musc.edu/

South Dakota

University of South Dakota
414 East Clark
Vermillion, SD 57069
www.usd.edu/

Tennessee

University of Tennessee at Chattanooga
615 Mc Callie Avenue
Chattanooga, TN 37403
www.utc.edu/

East Tennessee State University
P.O. Box 70624
Johnson City, TN 37601
www.etsu-tn.edu/

University of Tennessee
822 Beale Street
Memphis, TN 38163
www.utmem.edu/

Tennessee State University
3500 John A. Merritt Boulevard
Nashville, TN 37209
www.tnstate.edu/

Texas

Hardin-Simmons University
2200 Hickory, Box 16065
Abilene, TX 79698
www.hsutx.edu/

University of Texas Southwestern
Medical Center at Dallas
5323 Harry Hines Boulevard
Dallas, TX 75235

Texas Woman's University
425766 TWU Station
Denton, TX 76204a
www.twu.edu/

Baylor University
U.S. Army Medicine and Surgery Division
3151 Scott Road
Ft. Sam Houston, TX 78234
www.baylor.edu/

University of Texas Medical Branch–Galveston
301 University Boulevard
Galveston, TX 77550
www.utmb.edu/

Texas Tech University
Health Science Center
3601 4th Street
Lubbock, TX 79430
www.ttu.edu/

University of Texas
Health Science Center at San Antonio
7703 Floyd Curl Drive
San Antonio, TX 78284
www.uthscsa.edu/

Southwest Texas State University
Health Science Center
601 University Drive
San Marcos, TX 78666
www.swt.edu/

Utah

University of Utah
1130 Annex, Wing B
Salt Lake City, UT 84112
www.utah.edu/

Vermont

University of Vermont
305 Rowell Building
Burlington, VT 05405
www.uvm.edu/

Virginia

Old Dominion University
Health Science Building
Norfolk, VA 23529
www.odu/edu/

Virginia Commonwealth University
Box 980224
Richmond, VA 23298
http://griffin.vcu.edu/

Shenandoah University
333 West Cork Street
Winchester, VA 22601
www.su.edu/

Washington

Eastern Washington University
526 Fifth Street, MS 4
Cheney, WA 99004
www.ewu.edu/

University of Washington
1959 NE Pacific Street, Box 356490
Seattle, WA 98195
www.washington.edu/

University of Puget Sound
1500 North Warner
Tacoma, WA 98416
www.ups.edu/

West Virginia

West Virginia University School of Medicine
P.O. Box 9226
Morgantown, WV 26506
www.wvu.edu/

Wheeling Jesuit University
316 Washington Avenue
Wheeling, WV 26003
www.wju.edu/

Wisconsin

University of Wisconsin, LaCrosse
2032 Cowley Hall
LaCrosse, WI 54601
www.uwlax.edu/

University of Wisconsin, Madison
1300 University Avenue
Madison, WI 53706
www.wisc.edu/

Concordia University Wisconsin
12800 North Lake Shore Drive
Mequon, WI 53092
www.cuw.edu/

Marquette University
P.O. Box 1881
Milwaukee, WI 53201
www.mu.edu/

Canada

University of Alberta
Corbett Hall
Edmonton, Alberta
Canada T6G 2G4
www.ualberta.ca/

Queens University
Kingston, Ontario
Canada K7L 3N6
www.queensu.ca/

McGill University
3654 Drummond Street
Montreal, Quebec
Canada H3G 1Y5
www.mcgill.ca/

Universite de Montreal
CP 6128-Succursale Centre-Ville
Montreal, Quebec
Canada H3C 3J7
www.umontreal.ca/

University of Western Ontario
Elborn College
London, Ontario
Canada N6G 1H1
www.uwo.ca/

University of Saskatchewan
1121 College Drive
Saskatoon, Saskatchewan
Canada S7N OW3
www.usask.ca/

University of British Columbia
2211 Wesbrook Mall
Vancouver, British Columbia
Canada V6T 2B5
www.ubc.ca/

University of Manitoba
770 Bannatyne Avenue
Winnipeg, Manitoba
Canada R3E OW3
www.umanitoba.ca/

PHYSICAL THERAPY ASSISTANTS

Principal activity: Helping physical therapists to execute treatment plans

Work commitment: Usually full-time

Preprofessional education: High school diploma

Program length: 2 years

Work prerequisites: Associate degree

Career opportunities: Very favorable

Income range: $22,000 to $28,000

Scope

Physical therapy assistants work under the direction of a licensed physical therapist to help in the treatment of patients. Their specific activities are regulated by state law and are determined by the policies of the facility at which they work and by their supervising therapist.

Activities

The guiding program for the physical therapy assistant is the treatment plan developed by the therapist. The assistant helps teach disabled patients to carry out daily life activities (e.g., dressing), assists in their prescribed exercises, carries out tests, administers treatments (e.g., heat and hydrotherapy), notes and reports on patient progress, teaches patients how to use and care for assisting devices, and helps with variety of routine office chores.

Work Settings

Physical therapy assistants work in hospitals, rehabilitation centers, nursing homes, and in the offices of private practitioners.

Advancement

Some physical therapy assistants go back to school to pursue their physical therapy degree. Their prior experience is an asset in seeking a place in a program.

Prerequisites

A high school diploma is needed for admission into a physical therapy assistant program. Those seeking to enter the field should be physically strong and prepared to work closely with and under the supervision of others. They should also have a pleasant personality and a sincere desire to help others.

Education/Training

Physical therapy assistants must complete an accredited two-year program, leading to an associate degree. The program includes classes in anatomy and physiology and a year of technical courses in treatment modalities (e.g., massage, exercises, heat, and ultrasound) and clinical experience.

Certification/Registration/Licensure

Licensure is required in some states. Where there is no licensure requirement, a specific educational background and exam may be specified by the state licensing board.

Career Potential

The field of physical therapy has become much in demand because of advances in orthopedics (e.g., knee and hip replacements), sports medicine, and personal fitness programs. Simultaneously, the pool of elderly citizens is steadily increasing. Thus, the demand for physical therapy assistants is high and career prospects are very attractive.

For More Information

The professional organization for this field is the American Physical Therapy Association, 1111 North Fairfax Street, Alexandria, VA 22514.

Physical Therapy Assistant Programs

There are hundreds of physical therapy assistant programs in the United States—too many to include here. For a complete list of accredited programs, contact the American Physical Therapy Association at the address listed above.

RECREATIONAL THERAPISTS

Principal activity: Using recreational activities to enhance rehabilitation

Work commitment: Full-time

Preprofessional education: High school diploma

Program length: 4 years

Work prerequisites: Bachelor's degree

Career opportunities: Fair

Income range: $25,000 to $40,000

Scope

Recreational therapists work with mentally, emotionally, and physically disabled patients, helping them recover from or adjust to illnesses, disabilities, or social problems. The therapist's observations of patients' physical, mental, and social progress contributes to a fuller understanding of their treatment goals.

Activities

Recreational therapists plan and carry out programs that may involve athletics, art, dancing, music, gardening, or camping. These activities help patients get needed exercise, develop social relationships, diminish anxiety and tension, and increase self-esteem. Recreational therapists also help their clients to use the recreational activities their communities offer. They may train volunteers and help institutions develop courses in this field.

Work Settings

Recreational therapists are employed by a variety of public and private institutions, including mental and VA hospitals, residences for the mentally disabled, prisons, juvenile detention homes, senior citizen residences, and rehabilitation centers.

Advancement

Advancement comes with experience and education. For governmental positions, recreational therapists can take the civil service exam.

Moving from a certificate or associate degree to a bachelor's degree, or from a batchelor's to a master's degree also facilitates upward mobility.

Prerequisites

A high school diploma or its equivalent is necessary to enter a degree program.

Desirable personal attributes include patience, a pleasant personality, working well with others, creativity, and a desire to help people.

Education/Training

For some entry-level positions, a certificate or associate degree is sufficient. However, to get a professional appointment, one needs a bachelor's degree in recreation, with an emphasis on rehabilitation or therapeutic recreation. Additionally, recreational therapists must complete 400 hours of training at a university- or college-affiliated hospital.

Certification/Registration/Licensure

One can secure registration through the American Association for Rehabilitation Therapy (AART). While not mandatory, registration can help in the job search process.

To become registered, you must be a member of the AART, get two years of experience in a health-care facility, and submit a transcript of your college records and two letters of recommendation.

Career Potential

The employment outlook for this field is uncertain. Budget cuts by government agencies have imposed serious restraints on organizations that employ recreational therapists.

For More Information

The professional organization for the field is the National Recreation and Park Association, 22377 Belmont Ridge Road, Asburn, VA 20148.

Recreational Therapy Programs

California

California State University, Northridge
18111 Nordhoff Street
Northridge, CA 91330
www.csun.edu/

Indiana

Indiana University
300 North Jordan Avenue
Bloomington, IN 47405
www.indiana.edu/

Indiana Institute of Technology
1600 East Washington Boulevard
Fort Wayne, IN 46803
www.indtech.edu/

Iowa

University of Iowa
Recreational Therapy Dept.
Cedar Falls, IA 50614
www.uiowa.edu/

Maine

University of Southern Maine
Portland, ME 04103
www.usm.maine.edu/

Massachusetts

Northeastern University
360 Huntington Avenue
Boston, MA 02115
www.northeastern.edu/

Springfield College
Springfield, MA 01109
www.spfldcol.edu/

Michigan

Lake Superior State University
Sault Sainte Marie, MI 49783
www.lssu.edu/

New York

SUNY College at Cortland
Cortland, NY 13045
www.cortland.edu/

Utica College of Syracuse University
Utica, NY 13502
www.syr.edu/

North Carolina

Belmont Abbey College
Belmont, NC 28012
www.bac.edu/

Catawba College
Salisbury, NC 28144
www.catawba.edu/

Ohio

Defiance College
Defiance, OH 43512
www.defiance.edu/

Oklahoma

Southwestern Oklahoma State University
Weatherford, OK 73096
www.swosu.edu/

Pennsylvania

Lincoln University
Recreational Therapy Program
Lincoln University, PA 19352
www.lincoln.edu/

Vermont

Green Mountain College
Poultney, VT 05764
www.greenmtn.edu/

Virginia

Virginia Wesleyan College
Wesleyan Drive
Norfolk, VA 23502
www.vwc.edu/

Washington

Eastern Washington University
EWU MS-148
Cheney, WA 99004
www.ewu.edu/

West Virginia

West Virginia State College
Institute, WV 25112
www.wvsc.edu/

Wisconsin

University of Wisconsin, La Crosse
La Crosse, WI 54601
www.uslax.edu/

RESPIRATORY THERAPISTS

Principal activity: Treating patients with breathing disorders

Work commitment: Full-time

Preprofessional education: High school diploma

Program length: 2 to 4 years

Work prerequisites: Associate or bachelor's degree

Career opportunities: Good to excellent

Income range: $23,000 to $50,000 therapists

Scope

Respiratory therapists provide treatment for patients suffering from cardiorespiratory problems., including asthma, bronchitis, emphysema, and pneumonia. They also treat postoperative patients, accident victims, and patients suffering from heart failure, drowning, electric shock, drug overdose, and strokes. Their patients range from premature babies to older people with chronic lung diseases.

Activities

Respiratory therapists participate in both the evaluation and treatment phases of patient care. They may test patients' lung capacity and analyze the oxygen, carbon dioxide, and PH levels of patients' blood. These therapists work under a physician's supervision to administer therapy, monitor and record patient progress, and teach patients about respiratory exercises and equipment use. They also are responsible for maintaining equipment such as mechanical ventilators, resuscitators, and blood-gas analyzers.

Work Settings

Most respiratory therapists are employed by hospitals or medical centers, where they may work night or weekend hours. Others work in the offices of pulmonary medicine specialists, in nursing homes, or for companies that rent equipment to home-bound patients.

Advancement

One way to get a promotion is to move from caring for general patients to caring for critical patients. Those with a bachelor's degree may advance to supervisory or managerial positions at a hospital or commercial company.

Prerequisites

A high school diploma or its equivalent is necessary, since formal training for this field is offered at a post-secondary level.

Desirable personal attributes for the field include good judgment, mechanical ability, physical stamina, the capacity to function under stressful conditions, and a desire to help those who are gravely ill.

Education/Training

There are two programs available to prepare for a career in this field:

1. One can earn a two-year associate degree, offered by junior colleges and vocational technical institutes.

2. One can pursue a four-year bachelor's degree, offered by colleges, universities, medical schools, and hospitals.

The standard educational program includes courses in anatomy, physiology (with special emphasis on the cardiopulmonary aspect), microbiology, pharmacology, respiratory and cardiovascular diseases, anesthesiology, patient psychology, and respiratory therapy technique (e.g., airway management, blood-gas analysis, mechanical ventilation, cardiopulmonary resuscitation, and pulmonary function testing).

Certification/Registration/Licensure

To become a registered respiratory therapist, one must graduate from an accredited program and pass a three-hour certification exam, a two-part written exam, and a clinical examination. Twenty states have their own licensing requirements .

Career Potential

The growing number of elderly people in the United States implies a strong demand for respiratory therapists. This makes for a favorable job outlook in this profession. Advances in medical treatment for heart attacks, premature births, accident victims, and AIDS patients further increase the need for professionals in this field.

For More Information

The professional organization is the American Association for Respiratory Care. For more information on certification and registration, write to the National Board for Respiratory Care.

Respiratory Therapy Programs

Hundreds of colleges, community colleges, and technical institutes offer training for respiratory therapists—far too many to list here. For a list of educational programs in your area, contact one of the agencies listed here:

American Association for Respiratory Care
11030 Abeles
Dallas, TX 75229

National Board for Respiratory Care
8510 North Nierman Road
Lencza, KS 66214

RESPIRATORY THERAPIST TECHNICIANS

Principle activity: Helping treat patients with breating disorders

Work commitment: Full-time

Preprofessional education: High school diploma

Program length: 2 years

Work prerequisites: Associate degree

Career opportunities: Good to excellent

Income range: $20,000 to $30,000

Scope

Respiratory therapy technicians perform many of the same functions as respiratory therapists (see p. 343), but their education and training level is lower. Thus, they do not perform the more complex respiratory procedures.

Activities

See the activities listed under Respiratory Therapists.

Work Settings

See the section listed under Respiratory Therapists.

Career Advancement

See the section listed under Respiratory Therapists.

Prerequisites

See the section listed under Respiratory Therapists.

Education/Training

Respiratory therapist technicians undergo the same kind of training as respiratory therapists, but in a shorter, less-intensive program.

Certification/Registration/Licensure

The National Board for Respiratory Care has established criteria for certified respiratory therapy technicians. Candidates must graduate from an accredited program and pass a three-hour examination.

Career Potential

See the section listed under Respiratory Therapists

For More Information

See the section listed under Respiratory Therapists

 # RESPIRATORY THERAPY AIDES

Principal activity: Helping respiratory therapists and technicians to meet their professional responsibilities.

Work commitment: Full-time

Preprofessional education: High school diploma

Program length: Several months

Work prerequisites: Experience

Career opportunities: Good to excellent

Income range: $12,000 to $15,000

Scope

Respiratory therapy aides differ significantly from respiratory therapists and technicians. They have little patient contact and are not directly involved in the therapeutic process.

Activities

Respiratory therapy aides maintain the equipment used by respiratory therapists and technicians. This includes cleaning, sterilizing, and storing equipment. In addition, they are responsible for record-keeping.

Work Settings

See the section under Respiratory Therapists.

Advancement

See the section under Respiratory Therapists.

Prerequisites

See the section under Respiratory Therapists.

Education/Training

On-the-job training is provided in appropriate facilities.

Certification/Registration/Licensure

Certification is not available or necessary for this field.

Career Potential

See the section under Respiratory Therapists.

For More Information

See the section under Respiratory Therapists.

SPEECH-LANGUAGE PATHOLOGISTS AND AUDIOLOGISTS

Principal activity: Helping people with speech and hearing disorders

Work commitment: Part- or full-time

Preprofessional education: Bachelor's degree

Program length: 4 to 6 years

Work prerequisites: Master's degree

Career opportunities: Above average

Income range: $30,000 to $60,000

Scope

Tens of millions of Americans have speech or hearing disorders. *Speech pathologists* evaluate and treat people with speech, language, voice, and fluency defects. *Audiologists* evaluate and treat people with hearing impairments.

These problems of speech and language may be due to hearing loss, brain damage, stroke, cleft palate, mental disability, or emotional difficulties.

Activities

Speech-language pathologists evaluate and diagnose patients using instruments as well as written and oral examinations. This allows them to determine the nature and extent of impairments as well as record and analyze speech abnormalities. These professionals then plan and implement treatment programs to restore or improve communication skills. They teach patients how to make sounds, improve their voices, and increase their language skills. For clients with severe impairments, they may provide automated devices or offer sign language instruction.

Audiologists evaluate hearing-impaired persons, determining the type and extent of their loss. They use audiometers and other testing instruments. These tests provide data on the nature and extent of a patient's hearing loss and ability to distinguish between sounds. When necessary, audiologists secure relevant information from other professionals to arrive at an accurate diagnosis and proper course of treatment. Treatment may include cleaning the ear canal, fitting of appropriate hearing aides, and providing instruction in speech or lip reading.

Work Settings

Most professionals in this field are employed in medical centers, hospitals, rehabilitation centers, or schools.

Advancement

Both speech pathologists and audiologists can, with experience, advance to administrative or teaching positions.

Prerequisites

A bachelor's degree in speech-pathology and audiology is necessary. As part of such a program, a student learns biology, anatomy, physiology, sociology, linguistics, semantics, phonetics, and psychology.

Desirable personal attributes include a friendly personality, a desire to help people, and patience.

Education/Training

A master's degree in speech pathology or audiology is necessary to practice in this field. Studies include advanced work in anatomy, physiology, physics, speech, language and hearing disorders, and psychology.

Courses in the evaluation and treatment of disorders in this field are taught in clinical settings.

A master's degree permits one to be certified and makes one eligible for federal (Medicare and Medicaid) reimbursement.

Certification/Registration/Licensure

Speech pathologists and audiologists who hold a master's degree and have completed a one-year internship at an approved setting are eligible to sit for a certification examination administered by the American Speech-Language-Hearing Association. Certification is an asset in gaining advancement.

Many states require a Certificate of Clinical Competence (CCC), which allows one to work in public schools.

Career Potential

Opportunities are expected to be above average in this field, because of the growing pool of older citizens, a significant number of whom have or will develop hearing impairments. In addition, there is a greater emphasis on detecting and remedying speech disorders at an early age.

For More Information

The professional organization in this field is the American Speech-Language-Hearing Association, 10801 Rockville Pike, Rockville, MD 20852.

Speech-Language Pathologist & Audiologist Programs

Alabama

Alabama Agricultural & Mechanical University
P.O. Box 580
Normal, AL 35762
www.aamu.edu/

Auburn University at Montgomery
1199 Haley Center
Auburn, AL 36849
www.auburn.edu/

University of Alabama
P.O. Box 870242
Tuscaloosa, AL 35487
www.ua.edu/

University of Montevallo
Station 6720
Montevallo, AL 35115
www.montevallo.edu/

University of South Alabama
2000 University Commons
Mobile, AL 36688
www.usouthal.edu/

Arizona

Northern Arizona University
P.O. Box 15045
Flagstaff, AZ 86011
www.nau.edu/

Arizona State University
P.O. Box 870102
Tempe, AZ 85287
www.asu.edu/

University of Arizona
P.O. Box 210071
Tucson, AZ 85721
www.arizona.edu/

Arkansas

University of Central Arkansas
210 Donaghey, Box 4985
Conway, AR 72035
www.uca.edu/

University of Arkansas, Fayetteville
410 Arkansas Avenue
Fayetteville, AR 72701
www.uark.edu/

University of Arkansas at Little Rock
2801 South University
Little Rock, AR 72204
www.ualr.edu/

Arkansas State University
P.O. Box 1450
State University, AR 72467
www.astate.edu/

California

California State University, Chico
Chico, CA 95929
www.csuchico.edu/

California State University, Fresno
5048 North Jackson Avenue
Fresno, CA 93740
www.fansonly.com/schools/fres/

California State University, Fullerton
800 North State College Boulevard
Fullerton, CA 92634
www.fullerton.edu/

California State University, Hayward
25800 Carlos Bee Boulevard
Hayward, CA 94542
www.csuhayward.edu/

Loma Linda University
Nicholl Hall
Loma Linda, CA 92350
www.llu.edu/

Biola University
13800 Biola Avenue
La Mirada, CA 90639
www.biola.edu/

California State University, Long Beach
1250 Bellflower Blvd.
Long Beach, CA 90840
www.csulb.edu/

California State University, Los Angeles
5151 State University Drive
Los Angeles, CA 90032
www.calstatela.edu/

California State University, Northridge
18111 Nordhoff Street
Northridge, CA 91330
www.csun.edu/

University of Redlands
1200 East Cotton Avenue
Redlands, CA 92373
http://newton.uor.edu/

California State University, Sacramento
6000 J Street
Sacramento, CA 95819
www.csus.edu/

San Diego State University
5500 Campanile Drive
San Diego, CA 92182
www.sdsu.edu/

San Francisco State University
1600 Holloway Avenue
San Francisco, CA 94132
www.sfsu.edu/

University of the Pacific
3601 Pacific Avenue
Stockton, CA 95211
www.uop.edu/

Colorado

University of Colorado
Boulder, CO 80309
www.colorado.edu/

Metropolitan State College
1006 11th Street, Campus,
Denver, CO 80204
www.mscd.edu/

University of Northern Colorado
501 20th Street
Greeley, CO 80639
www.univnorthco.edu/

Connecticut

Southern Connecticut State University
501 Crescent Street
New Haven, CT 06515
http://scwww.ctstateu.edu/

University of Connecticut
850 Bolton Road
Storrs, CT 06269
www.uconn.edu/

District of Columbia

Gallaudet University
800 Florida Avenue NE
Washington, DC 20052
www.gallaudet.edu/

George Washington University
2201 G Street, NW
Washington, DC 20052
http://gwis.circ.gwu.edu/

Howard University
2400 6th Street, NW
Washington, DC 20059
www.howard.edu/

University of the District of Columbia
4200 Connecticut Ave. NW, Bldg. 48
Washington, DC 20008
www.udc.edu/

Florida

Florida Atlantic University
777 Glades Road
P.O. Box 3091
Boca Raton, FL 33431
www.fau.edu/

Nova Southeastern University
3375 SW 75th Avenue
Fort Lauderdale, FL 33314
www.nova.edu/

University of Florida
335 Dauer Hall
Gainesville, FL 32611
www.ufl.edu/

University of Central Florida
4000 Central Florida Blvd.
Orlando, FL 32816
www.ucf.edu/

Florida State University
107 Regional Rehabilitation Center
Tallahassee, FL 32306
www.fsu.edu/

University of South Florida
4202 East Fowler Ave. BEH 255
Tampa, FL 33620
www.usf.edu/

Georgia

Georgia State University
University Plaza
Atlanta, GA 30303
www.gsu.edu/

University of Georgia
576 Aderhold Hall
Athens, GA 30602
www.uga.edu/

State University of West Georgia
Carrollton, GA 30118
www.westga.edu/

Valdosta State College
Valdosta, GA 31698
www.valdosta.edu/

Hawaii

University of Hawaii at Manoa
John A. Burns School of Medicine
1410 Lower Campus Road
Honolulu, HI 96822
www.uhm.hawaii.edu/

Idaho

Idaho State University
Campus Box 8116
Pocatello, ID 83209
www.isu.edu/

Illinois

Southern Illinois University at Carbondale
Rehn Hall
Carbondale, IL 62901
www.siu.edu/siuc/

University of Illinois
901 South 6th Street
Champaign, IL 61820
www.uiuc.edu/

Eastern Illinois University
600 Lincoln Avenue
Charleston, IL 61920
www.eiu.edu/

Rush University
1653 West Congress Parkway
Chicago, IL 60612
www.univ.rush.edu/univ/

Saint Xavier University
3700 West 103rd Street
Chicago, IL 60655
www.sxu.edu/

Northern Illinois University
Department of Communications
DeKalb, IL 60115
www.niu.edu/

Southern Illinois University at Edwardsville
P.O. Box 1776
Edwardsville, IL 62026
www.siue.edu/

Northwestern University
2299 Sheridan Road
Evanston, IL 60208
www.nwu.edu/

Western Illinois University
121 Memorial Hall
Macomb, IL 61455
www.wiu.edu/

Indiana

Indiana University
Bloomington, IN 47405
www.indiana.edu/

Ball State University
2000 West University Avenue
Muncie, In 47306
www.bsu.edu/

Purdue University
Heavilon Hall, B-13
West Lafayette, IN 47907
www.purdue.edu/

Iowa

Iowa State University
210 Pearson Hall
Ames, IA 50011
www.iastate.edu/

University of Northern Iowa
Cedar Falls, IA 50614
www.uni.edu/

University of Iowa
Iowa City, IA 52242
www.uiowa.edu/

Kansas

Fort Hays State University
600 Park Street
Hays, KS 67601
www.fhsu.edu/

University of Kansas
3031 Dole Center
Lawrence, KS 66045
www.ukans.edu/

Kansas State University
303 Justin Hall
Manhattan, KS 66506
www.ksu.edu/

Wichita State University
1845 Fairmont
Wichita, KS 67260
www.wichita.edu/

Kentucky

Western Kentucky University
Tate Page Hall, Room 111
Bowling Green, KY 42101
www.wku.edu/

University of Kentucky
1028 South Broadway, Suite 3
Lexington, KY 40504
www.uky.edu/

Spalding University
851 South 4th Street
Louisville, KY 40203
www.spalding.edu/

Murray State University
16th and Main Street
Murray, KY 42071
www.mursuky.edu/

Eastern Kentucky University
248 Wallace Bldg.
Richmond, KY 40478
www.eku.edu/

Louisiana

Louisiana State University
Baton Rouge, LA 70803
www.lsu.edu/

Southern University
P.O. Box 9888
Baton Rouge, LA 70813
www.subr.edu/

Grambling State University
P.O. Box 803
Grambling, LA 71245
www.gram.edu/

Southeastern Louisiana University
University Station
P.O. Box 879
Hammond, LA 70402
www.selu.edu/

Northeast Louisiana University
700 University Avenue
Monroe, LA 71209
www.nlu.edu/

Louisiana State University Medical Center
1900 Gravier Street
New Orleans, LA 70112
www.lsumc.edu/

Louisiana Tech University
P.O. Box 3165 T.S.
Ruston, LA 71272
www.latech.edu/

Maryland

Loyola College
4501 North Charles Street
Baltimore, MD 21210
www.loyola.edu/

University of Maryland at College Park
Lefrak Hall
College Park, MD 20742
www.umcp.umd.edu/

Towson State University
Towson, MD 21204
www.towson.edu/

Massachusetts

Boston University
635 Commonwealth Avenue
Boston, MA 02215
http://web.bu.edu/

Northeastern University
360 Huntington Avenue
Boston, MA 02115
www.northeastern.edu/

Bridgewater State College
Bridgewater, MA 02325
www.bridgew.edu/

Elms College
291 Springfield Street
Chicopee, MA 01013
www.elms.edu/

Worcester State College
486 Chandler Street
Worcester, MA 01602
www.worc.mass.edu/

Michigan

Wayne State University
581 Manoogian Hall
Detroit, MI 48202
www.wayne.edu/

Western Michigan University
Kalamazoo, MI 49008
www.wmich.edu/

Eastern Michigan University
115 Rackham Building
Ypsilanti, MI 48197
www.emich.edu/

Minnesota

University of Minnesota-Duluth
10 University Drive, Bohannon Hall
Duluth, MN 55812
www.d.umn.edu/

Minnesota State University, Mankato
MSU 77-Elis & Stadium Road
Mankato, MN 56002
www.mankato.msus.edu/

University of Minnesota
164 Pillsbury Drive SE
Minneapolis, MN 55455
www.umn.edu/

Moorhead State University
1104 7th Avenue, South
Moorhead, MN 56563
www.moorhead.msus.edu/

St. Cloud State University
720 4th Avenue South
St. Cloud, MN 56301
www.stcloud.msus.edu/

Mississippi

Mississippi University for Women
P.O. Box W-1340
Columbus, MS 39701
www.muw.edu/

University of Southern Mississippi
Southern Station
P.O. Box 5092
Hattiesburg, MS 39406
www.usm.edu/

University of Mississippi
University, MS 38677
www.olemiss.edu/

Missouri

Southeast Missouri State University
One University Plaza
Cape Girardeau, MO 63701
www.semo.edu/

University of Missouri, Columbia
303 Lewis Hall
Columbia, MO 65211
www.missouri.edu/

Truman State University
Violette Hall 164
Kirksville, MO 63501
www.truman.edu/

Fontbonne College
6800 Wydown Blvd.
St. Louis, MO 63105
www.fontbonne.edu/

St. Louis University
221 North Grand Street
St. Louis, MO 63103
www.slu.edu/

Southwest Missouri State University
901 South National Avenue
Springfield, MO 65804
www.smsu.edu/

Nebraska

University of Nebraska, Kearney
West Center
Kearney, NE 68849
www.unk.edu/

University of Nebraska, Lincoln
301 Barkley Memorial Center
Lincoln, NE 68583
www.unl.edu/

University of Nebraska, Omaha
60th and Dodge Street
Omaha, NE 68182
www.unomaha.edu/

Nevada

University of Nevada, Reno
108 Redfield Bldg./152
Reno, NV 89557
www.unr.edu/

New Hampshire

University of New Hampshire
4 Library Way, Hewit Hall
Durham, NH 03824
www.unh.edu/

New Jersey

College of New Jersey
Hillwood Lakes, Box 4700
Trenton, NJ 08650
www.trenton.edu/

Kean College of New Jersey
1000 Morris Avenue
Union, NJ 07083
www.kean.edu/

Montclair State College
Normal Avenue
Speech Bldg.K-119
Upper Montclair, NJ 07043
www.montclair.edu/

William Paterson College
300 Pompton Road
Wayne, NJ 07470
www.wilpaterson.edu/

New Mexico

University of New Mexico
901 Vassar, NE
Albuquerque, NM 87131
www.unm.edu/

New Mexico State University
Dept. 3 SPE. Box 30001
Las Cruces, NM 88003
www.nmsu.edu/

Eastern New Mexico University
Station 3, Lee Hall
Portales, NM 88130
www.enmu.edu/

New York

College of St. Rose
432 Western Avenue, Box 100
Albany, NY 12203
www.strose.edu/

State University of New York at Buffalo
109 Park Hall
Amherst, NY 14260
www.buffalo.edu/

Lehman College of CUNY
Bedford Park Boulevard West
Bronx, NY 10468
www.lehman.cuny.edu/

Brooklyn College, CUNY
2900 Bedford Avenue
Brooklyn, NY 11210
www.brooklyn.cuny.edu/

Long Island University
One University Plaza
Brooklyn, NY 11201
www.liunet.edu/

Long Island University
C.W. Post Center
720 Northern Boulevard
Brookville, NY 11548
www.liunet.edu/

Buffalo State College
1300 Elmwood Avenue
Buffalo, NY 14222
www.snybuf.edu/

Queens College of CUNY
65-30 Kissena Boulevard
Flushing, NY 11367
www.qc.edu/

State University of New York
College at Fredonia
Thompson Hall-W121
Fredonia, NY 14063
www.fredonia.edu/

Adelphi University
Cambridge Avenue
Garden City, NY 11530
www.edelphia.edu/

SUNY College of Arts and Sciences
One College Circle, 218 Sturgis Hall
Geneseo, NY 14454
http://mosaic.cc.geneseo.edu/

Ithaca College
301 Smiddy Hall
Ithaca, NY 14850
www.ithaca.edu/

St. Johns University
8000 Utopia Parkway
Jamaica, NY 11439
www.stjohns.edu/

SUNY College at New Paltz
75 South Manheim Bpulevard
New Paltz, NY 12561
www.newpaltz.edu/

CUNY Graduate School
33 West 42nd Street
New York, NY 10028
www.gc.cuny.edu/

Hunter College
425 East 25th Street
New York, NY 10010
www.hunter.cuny.edu/

Teachers College of Columbia University
525 West 120th Street
New York, NY 10027
www.tc.columbia.edu/

Marymount Manhattan College
221 East 71st Street
New York, NY 10021
www.marymount.mmm.edu/

New York University
719 Broadway, 2nd Floor
New York, NY 10003
www.nyu.edu/

Pace University
Pace Plaza
New York, NY 10038
www.pace.edu/newhome.html

St. Joseph's College
155 West Roe Boulevard
Patchogue, NY 11772
www.sjcny.edu/

SUNY at Plattsburgh
226 Sibley Hall
Plattsburgh, NY 12901
www.plattsburgh.edu/

Nazareth College of Rochester
4245 East Avenue
Rochester, NY 14618
www.naz.edu/

Syracuse University
805 South Crouse Avenue
Syracuse, NY 13244
www.syr.edu/

North Carolina

Appalachian State University
124 Edwin Duncan Hall
Boone, NC 28608
www.appstate.edu/

University of North Carolina at Chapel Hill
Wing D, Medical School, CB #7190
Chapel Hill, NC 27599
www.unc.edu/

Western Carolina University
Cullowhee, NC 28723
www.wcu.edu/

North Carolina Central University
P.O. Box 19776
Durham, NC 27707
www.nccu.edu/

Elizabeth City State University
Elizabeth City, NC 27909
www.ecsu.edu/

University of North Carolina at Greensboro
300 Ferguson Building
Greensboro, NC 27412
www.uncg.edu/

East Carolina University
Greenville, NC 27858
www.ecu.edu/

North Dakota

University of North Dakota
University Station, P O Box 8040
Grand Forks, ND 58202
www.und.nodak.edu/

Minot State University
500 University Avenue, West
Minot, ND 58707
http://warp6.cs.misu.nodak.edu/

Ohio

University of Akron
302 E Buchtel Avenue
Akron, OH 44325
www.uakron.edu/

Ohio University
201 Lindley Hall
Athens, OH 45701
www.ohio.edu/

Bowling Green State University
338 South Hall
Bowling Green, OH 43403
www.bgsu.edu/

University of Cincinnati
P.O. Box 379
Cincinnati, OH 45221
www.uc.edu/

Case Western Reserve University
10900 Euclid Avenue
Cleveland, OH 44106
www.cwru.edu/

Cleveland State University
1899 East 22nd Street
Cleveland, OH 44115
www.csuohio.edu/

Ohio State University
1070 Carmarck Road
Columbus, OH 43210
www.acs.ohio-state.edu/

Kent State University
A104 Music & Speech Building
Kent, OH 44242
www.kent.edu/

Miami University
College of Arts & Sciences
2 Bachelor Hall
Oxford, OH 45056
www.muohio.edu/

Oklahoma

University of Central Oklahoma
100 North University Drive
Edmond, OK 73034
www.ucok.edu/

University of Oklahoma
825 NE 14th Street
P.O. Box 26901
Oklahoma City, OK 73190
www.ou.edu/

Oklahoma State University
120 Hanner Building
Stillwater, OK 74078
http://pio.okstate.edu/

Northeastern State University
Special Services Building
Tahlequah, OK 74464
www.nsuok.edu/

University of Tulsa
600 South College Avenue
Tulsa, OK 74104
www.utulsa.edu/

Oregon

University of Oregon
Eugene, OR 97403
www.uoreton.edu/

Portland State University
P.O. Box 751
Portland, OR 97207
www.pdx.edu/

Pennsylvania

Bloomsburg University
400 East 2nd Street
Bloomsburg, PA 17815
www.bloomu.edu/

California University of Pennsylvania
Learning Research Center
California, PA 15419
www.cup.edu/

Clarion University of Pennsylvania
Davis Hall
Clarion, PA 16214
www.clarion.edu/

East Stroudsburg University of Pennsylvania
LaRue Hall
East Stroudsburg, PA 18301
www.esu.edu/

Edinboro University of Pennsylvania
208 Compton Hall
Edinboro, PA 16444
www.edinboro.edu/

Indiana University of Pennsylvania
203 Davis Hall
Indiana, PA 15705
www.iup.edu/

Temple University
109 Weiss Hall
Philadelphia, PA 19122
www.temple.edu/

University of Pittsburgh
3347 Forbes Avenue
Pittsburgh, PA 15260
www.pitt.edu/

Marywood College
2300 Adams Avenue
Scranton, PA 18509
www.marywood.edu/

West Chester University
West Chester, PA 19383
www.wcupa.edu/

Rhode Island

University of Rhode Island
Adams Hall
Kingston, R I 02881
www.uri.edu/

South Carolina

University of South Carolina
Columbia, SC 29208
www.sc.edu/

South Carolina State University
300 College Street NE
Orangeburg, SC 29117
www.scsu.edu/

South Dakota

University of South Dakota
414 East Clark Street
Vermillion, SD 57069
www.usd.edu/

Tennessee

University of Memphis
807 Jefferson Avenue
Memphis, TN 38105
www.memphis.edu/

Vanderbilt University
School of Medicine
1114 19th Avenue South
Nashville, TN 37212
www.vanderbilt.edu/

Texas

University of Texas at Austin
Austin, TX 78712
www.utexas.edu/

University of Texas at Dallas
1966 Inwood Road
Dallas, TX 75235
www.utdallas.edu/

Texas Women's University
TWU Station, Box 23775
Denton, TX 76204
www.twu.edu/

University of North Texas
P.O. Box 5008
Denton, TX 76203
www.unt.edu/

University of Texas, Pan American
1201 West University Dr.
Edinburg, TX 78539
www.panam.edu/

University of Texas at El Paso
P.O. Box 639
El Paso, TX 79968
www.utep.edu/

Texas Christian University
P.O. Box 297450
Fort Worth, TX 76129
www.tcu.edu/

Texas A & M University, Kingsville
Campus Box 178
Kingsville, TX 78363
www.tamuk.edu/

Lamar University
Lamar Station, Box 10076
Beaumont, TX 77710
www.lamar.edu/

University of Houston
4800 Calhoun
Houston, TX 77204
www.uh.edu/

Texas Tech University
P.O. Box 42073
Lubbock, TX 79409
www.ttu.edu/

Stephen F. Austin State University
SFA Station, P.O. Box 13019
Nacogdoches, TX 75962
www.sfasu.edu/

Our Lady of the Lake University
411 Southwest 24th Street
San Antonio, TX 78207
www.ollusa.edu/

Southwest Texas State University
601 University Drive
San Marcos, TX 78666
www.swt.edu/

Baylor University
BU Box 97332
Waco, TX 76798
www.baylor.edu/

Utah

Utah State University
UMC 10
Logan, UT 84332
www.usu.edu/

Brigham Young University
136 John Taylor East
Provo, UT 84602
www.byu.edu/

University of Utah
1201 Social Behavioral Building
Salt Lake, UT84112
www.utah.edu/

Vermont

University of Vermont
461 Main Street, Allen House
Burlington, VT 04505
www.uvm.edu/

Virginia

University of Virginia
2205 Fontaine Avenue
Charlottesville, VA 22903
www.virginia.edu/

Hampton University
Hampton, VA 23668
www.hamptonu.edu/

James Madison University
Harrisonburg, VA 22807
www.jmu.edu/

Old Dominion University
Norfolk, VA 23504
www.odu/edu/

Radford University
P.O. Box 6961
Radford, VA 24142
www.runet.edu/

Washington

Western Washington University
17 Parks Hall
Bellingham, WA 98225
www.wwu.edu/

Eastern Washington University
526 Fifth Street, MS-106
Cheney, WA 99004
www.ewu.edu/

Washington State University
201 Daggy Hall, Box 642420
Pullman, WA 99164
www.tricity.wsu.edu/

University of Washington
1417 NE 42nd Street
Seattle, WA 98105
www.washington.edu/

West Virginia

Marshall University
400 Hal Greer Boulevard
Huntington, WV 25755
www.marshall.edu/

West Virginia University
805 Allen Hall, Box 6122
Morgantown, WV 26506
www.wvu.edu/

Wisconsin

University of Wisconsin, Eau Claire
Eau Claire, WI 54702
www.uwec.edu/

University of Wisconsin, Madison
1975 Willow Drive
Madison, WI 53706
www.wisc.edu/

Marquette University
P.O. Box 1881
Milwaukee, WI 53233
www.mu.edu/

University of Wisconsin, Milwaukee
P.O. Box 413
Milwaukee, WI 53201
www.uwm.edu/

University of Wisconsin, Oshkosh
800 Algoma
Oshkosh, WI 54901
www.uwosh.edu/

University of Wisconsin, River Falls
235 Klienpell Fine Arts Building
River Falls, WI 54022
www.uwrf.edu/

University of Wisconsin, Stevens Point
2100 Main Street
Stevens Point, WI 54481
www.uwsp.edu/

University of Wisconsin, Whitewater
1011 Roseman Building
Whitewater, WI 53190
www.uww.edu/

Wyoming

University of Wyoming
University Station
P.O. Box 3311
Laramie, WY 82071
www.uwyo.edu/

Affiliated Health-Care Careers

MEDICAL SCIENTISTS, EDUCATORS, AND INFORMATION WORKERS

A wide variety of careers are affiliated with the health-care industry. These responsible and challenging positions are of great value to physicians, dentists, and other diagnosing and treating practitioners. The activities of the affiliated health-care professionals have a direct impact on the lives and well-being of patients. In some cases, the professions involve public health and preventive medicine, while in others they may be of direct benefit to sick patients. Some careers involve the continuing education of practitioners and furthering the dissemination of health-related knowledge and information.

The wide-ranging nature of the professions discussed in this section is reflected in the significant differences in their educational requirements. The job prerequisites range from a high school diploma to a master's degree, and each profession demands its own skills. The diversity of occupational opportunities makes this segment especially valuable to those who have not found a suitable occupation in the other four major areas.

BIOMEDICAL ENGINEERS

Principal activity: Designing and testing biomedical products for safety and effectiveness

Work commitment: Usually full-time

Preprofessional education: High school diploma or its equivalent

Program length: 4 to 8 years

Work prerequisites: Bachelor's degree; master's or doctorate preferred

Career opportunities: Very favorable

Income range: $35,000 to $75,000

Scope

Biomedical engineers convert ideas into products and develop solutions to technical problems presented by physicians, dentists, scientists, and other health-care specialists. The problems may be mechanical, electrical, chemical, or a combination of these and thus are wide-ranging. The heart-lung bypass machine, pacemaker, laser, ultrasound, and nuclear imaging equipment are examples of products developed by biomedical engineers in collaboration with physicians. The consequences of their work have been enormous, in both diagnostic and therapeutic aspects of medicine and dentistry. Efforts by bioengineers have not only been life saving but also have improved the quality of people's lives.

Activities

Since the biomedical problems are so variable, the nature of the engineer's work is multifaceted, encompassing divergent specialties. These generally fall into one of four groups:

1. **General bioengineering** involves applying engineering principles to understanding the anatomy and physiology of the normal and diseased body. This area is concerned with enhancing the biological environment by ridding it of pollutants.

2. **Clinical engineering** uses engineering principles and technological advances to enhance health-care delivery systems, including testing and upkeep of medical equipment and training staff in their proper use.

3. **Medical engineering** involves developing biomaterials, diagnostic and therapeutic instruments, and devices needed in both patient care and research.

4. **Rehabilitation engineering** concerns the design of devices for people with disabilities.

Work Settings

Bioengineers work at universities, research centers, industrial laboratories, and governmental facilities.

Advancement

Advancement comes from securing a graduate degree (master's or doctorate) or by demonstrating supervisory or management potential.

Prerequisites

A high school diploma or its equivalent is needed to enroll in a college bioengineering program. For many jobs, a master's or doctorate degree is necessary. Students who are considering this field should take classes in mathematics (including algebra, trigonometry, precalculus, and calculus), biology, chemistry, physics, computers, and a foreign language.

Desirable attributes include inventiveness, the capacity to think in the abstract, analytical skills, and problem solving ability. Personal qualities important for this field include patience, determination, a positive work attitude, and verbal and written communication skills.

Education/Training

Entry-level positions in bioengineering require a bachelor's degree from an accredited program. Undergraduate courses that are commonly offered for majors in this field include biomedical engineering systems and design, biomedical computers, bioinstrumentation, engineering, biophysics, biothermodynamics, biotransport, and artificial organs and limbs.

Graduate-level programs are more numerous than undergraduate ones. A graduate degree is necessary for senior or teaching appointments. Those with traditional undergraduate engineering degrees have the option of securing a graduate degree in bioengineering and entering the field by this means.

Certification/Registration/Licensure

Certification is available for those in clinical engineering through the International Certification Commission for Clinical Engineering and Biomedical Technology. To secure certification one needs an engineering degree, three years of hospital-based experience in the specialty, and successful completion of a five-hour written and oral exam.

For More Information

The professional organization in this field is the Biomedical Engineering Society, P.O.Box 2399, Culver City, CA 90231.

An additional resource is the Alliance for Engineering in Medicine and Biology, 1101 Connecticut Avenue NW, Washington, DC 20036.

Program accreditation is provided by the Accreditation Board for Engineering and Technology.

Biomedical Engineering Programs

Alabama

University of Alabama at Birmingham
UAB Station
Birmingham, AL 53294
www.uab.edu/

Arizona

Arizona State University
Tempe, AZ 85287
www.asu.edu/

California

Southern State University
Costa Mesa, CA 92626
www.ssu.edu/

University of California, Davis
Davis, CA 95616
www.ucd.edu/

University of California, San Diego
Box 0337
La Jolla, CA 92093
www.ucsd.edu/

California State University
6000 J Street
Sacramento, CA 95819
www.csu.edu/

Connecticut

Trinity College
300 Summit Street
Hartford, CT 06106
www.trinity.edu/

University of Connecticut
Storrs, CT 06269
www.uconn.edu/

District of Columbia

Catholic University of America
620 Michigan Avenue, NE
Washington, DC 20064
www.cua.edu/

Florida

University of Miami
P.O. Box 248025
Coral Gables, FL 33124
www.ir.miami.edu/

Georgia

Mercer University
Macon, GA 31207
www.mercer.edu/

Illinois

University of Illinois at Chicago
2318 Alumni Hall
Chicago, IL 60607
www.uic.edu/

Northwestern University
1801 Hinman Avenue
Evanston, IL 60208
www.nwu.edu/

Indiana

Purdue University
Schleman Hall
W Lafayette, IN 47907
www.purdue.edu/

Iowa

University of Iowa
Iowa City, IA 52242
uiowa.edu/

Kentucky

University of Kentucky
Lexington, KY 40506
www.uky.edu/

Louisiana

Tulane University
6823 St. Charles Avenue
New Orleans, LA 70118
www.tulane.edu/

Louisiana Tech University
Ruston, LA 71272
www.latech.edu/

Maryland

Johns Hopkins University
3400 North Charles Street
Baltimore, MD 21218
www.jhu.edu/

Massachusetts

Boston University
121 Bay Street Road
Boston, MA 02215
http://web.bu.edu/

Western New England College
Springfield, MA 01119
www.wned.edu/

Worcester Polytechnic Institute
100 Institute Road
Worcester, MA 01609
www.wpi.edu/

Michigan

University of Michigan
Ann Arbor, MI 48109
www.umich.edu/

Minnesota

University of Minnesota
Duluth, MN 55812
www.d.umn.edu/

Missouri

Washington University
1 Brookings Drive
St. Louis, MO 63130
www.wustl.edu/

New Jersey

Rutgers State University
P.O. Box 2101
New Brunswick, NJ 08903
www.rutgers.edu/

New York

Hofstra University
Hempstead, NY 11550
www.hofstra.edu/

Columbia University
303 Lewisohn Hall
New York, NY 10027
www.columbia.edu/

University of Rochester
Rochester, NY 14627
www.rochester.edu/

Syracuse University
201 Tolley Administration Building
Syracuse, NY 13244
www.syr.edu/

Rensselaer Polytechnic Inst.
Troy, NY 12180
www.rpi.edu/

North Carolina

University of North Carolina at Chapel Hill
Chapel Hill, NC 27599
www.unc.edu/

Duke University
Durham, NC 27708
www.duke.edu/

North Dakota

North Dakota State University
University Station
Fargo, ND 58105
www.ndsu.nodak.edu/

Ohio

University of Cincinnati
100 Edwards Center
Cincinnati, OH 45221
www.uc.edu/

Case Western Reserve University
10900 Euclid Avenue
Cleveland, OH 44106
www.cwru.edu/

Ohio State University
3rd Floor, Lincoln Tower
Columbus, OH 43210
www.acs.ohio-state.edu/

Wright State University
Fairborn, OH 45435
www.wsu.edu/

University of Toledo
Toledo, OH 43606
www.utoledo.edu/

Pennsylvania

University of Pittsburgh
133 Biddle Hall
Johnstown, PA 15904
www.pitt.edu/

Allegheny College
Midville, PA 16336
www.alleg.edu/

Drexel University
Philadelphia, PA 19104
www.drexel.edu/

University of Pennsylvania
1 College Hall Levy Park
Philadelphia, PA 19104
www.upen.edu/

Carnegie Mellon University
Pittsburgh, PA 15213
www.cmu.edu/

Penn State University
University Park Campus
University Park, PA 16802
www.psu.edu/

South Carolina

Clemson University
105 Sikes Hall, P.O. Box 345124
Clemson, SC 29634
www.clemson.edu/

Tennessee

University of Memphis
Memphis, TN 38152
www.memphis.edu/

Vanderbilt University
Nashville, TN 37240
www.vanderbilt.edu/

Texas

University of Texas–Arlington
Arlington, TX 76019
www.uta.edu/

University of Texas–Austin
Austin, TX 78712
www.utexas.edu/

Texas A&M University
College Station, TX 77843
www.tamu.edu/

Utah

University of Utah
250 South Student Services Building
Salt Lake City, UT 84112
www.utah.edu/

Vermont

University of Vermont
Burlington, VT 05401
www.uvm.edu/

Virginia

University of Virginia
Charlottesville, VA 22906
www.virginia.edu/

Virginia Commonwealth University
821 West Franklin Street
Richmond, VA 23284
http://griffin.vcu.edu/

Washington

University of Washington
Seattle, WA 98195
www.washington.edu/

Wisconsin

Marquette University
517 North 14th Street
Milwaukee, WI 53233
www.mu.edu/

Milwaukee School of Engineering
1025 North Broadway
Milwaukee, WI 53202
www.mse.edu/

Wyoming

University of Wyoming
Box 3435
Laramie, WY 82071
www.uwyo.edu/

Biomedical Equipment Technicians

Principal activity: Performing maintainence of biomedical equipment

Work commitment: Full-time

Preprofessional education: High school diploma

Program length: 1 to 4 years; usually 2 years

Work prerequisites: Associate degree

Career opportunities: Quite favorable

Income range: $20,000 to $50,000

Scope

One of the most significant medical events in the past several decades has been the introduction of a continuous stream of innovative instruments and devices that have had a profound impact on improving medical care. Biomedical engineers have used such technologies as lasers, ultrasound, computers, and nuclear science to develop sophisticated diagnostic and treatment equipment. Consequently, a wide range of instruments are in use at medical centers, hospitals, and even small clinics. These include advanced EKG machines, dialysis units, complex incubators for premature infants, and mammoth computerexial topography (CAT) scanners. To be effective, instruments must be safe to use, accurate in their operation and readings, and properly employed to secure reliable and optimal benefits. The people who maintain the equipment at medical facilities are biomedical equipment technicians.

Activities

Biomedical equipment technicians have many different responsibilities at the facilities they serve. They install the equipment, calibrate it so that its readings and operation are reliable, train the personnel who will be working with it, and do preventive maintenance and repairs when necessary. They may also be called upon to evaluate equipment that is being considered for purchase.

Work Settings

These skilled technicians are employed by medical centers, large hospitals, medical schools, research institutions, biomedical equipment manufacturers, service maintenance companies, and government agencies.

Advancement

Being promoted through the four levels of biomedical equipment technician ranks (BMET 1-4) will enhance one's status.

A **BMET-1** is an entry-level worker who does supervised routine maintenance, safety checking, and repairs.

A **BMET-2** has several years of experience and works independently, doing maintenance and repair work.

A **BMET-3** has significant education and training, and can perform challenging assignments requiring highly skilled ability.

A **BMET** supervisor works under a department head or hospital supervisor and oversees the activities of the lower grade technicians.

Prerequisites

A high school diploma or its equivalent is necessary to enter this field. Course work should include algebra, trigonometry, physics, biology, and chemistry. Computer, electronics, and work-shop courses are especially helpful.

Desirable personal attributes include a strong interest in technology, superior eye-hand coordination and vision, aptitude for precise and meticulous work, patience, and the ability to respond quickly to unforeseen problems that arise.

Education/Training

There are two educational routes available to those entering this field:

1. Formal biomedical equipment technician programs are offered by vocational-technical schools, community colleges, collages, and even universities. Most award an associate degree after two years, and some offer a bachelor's degree. These programs provide practical experience at assigned hospitals or labs. A typical program includes courses in biology, chemistry, anatomy, physiology, medical terminology, mathematics, electronics, and computers.

2. One can earn an associate degree from a college offering an A.S. in electronics and then secure on-the-job training. However, one is at a disadvantage in attaining a position with this alternative route.

Certification/Registration/Licensure

Before taking the General Biomedical Equipment Certification Examination, candidates must have four years of experience, or three years of experience and an AS degree in electronic technology, or two years of experience and an AS degree in biomedical technology. Specialty examinations for certification in the areas of clinical laboratory equipment and radiology equipment are also possible.

Career Potential

With the rapid increase in the use of biomedical equipment, the need for technicians is strong and the outlook for employment is favorable for the foreseeable future.

For More Information

The professional organization for this field is the Junior Engineering Technology Society, 1420 King's Street, Alexandria, VA 22314.

For more information, write to the Association for the Advancement of Medical Instrumentation, 1330 Washington Boulevard, Arlington, VA 22201.

Biomedical Equipment Technician Programs

Alabama

Community College of the Air Force
Maxwell Air Force Base
130 West Maxwell Boulevard
Montgomery, AL 36112
www.au.af.mil/au/ccaf/

James H. Faulkner State Community College
1900 Highway 31 South
Bay Minette, AL 36507
www.faulkner.cc.al.us/

Jefferson State Community College
2601 Carson Road
Birmingham, AL 35215
www.jscc.cc.al.us/

University of Alabama
Kirklin Clinic
2000 6th Avenue South
Birmingham, AL 35233
www.uab.edu/

Wallace Community College
P.O. Box 1049
Selma, AL 36707
www.wallace.edu/

Arkansas

Arkansas State University, Beebe
P.O. Box H
Beebe, AR 72012
www.astate.edu/

California

Napa Valley College
2277 Napa Vallejo Highway
Napa, CA 94558
www.nvc.cc.ca.us/

Cerritos College
11110 Alondra Boulevard
Norwalk, CA 90650
www.cerritos.edu/

Santa Barbara City College
721 Cliff Drive
Santa Barbara, CA 93109
www.sbcc.cc.ca.us/

Colorado

Colorado College
4435 N. Chestnut
Colorado Springs, CO 80907
www.cc.coloradol.edu/

Connecticut

Gateway Community Technical College
88 Bassett Road
North Haven, CT 06473
www.commnet.edu/gwctc/

Delaware

Delaware Technical & Community College
400 Christiana-Stanton Road
Newark, DE 19713
www.terry.dtcc.edu/

Florida

Florida Community College
501 West State Street
Jacksonville, FL 32202
www.fccj.cc.fl.us/

Georgia

Dekalb Technical Institute
495 North Indian Creek Drive
Clarkston, GA 30021
www.dekalb.tec.ga.us/

Illinois

Oakton Community College
1600 East Golf Road
Des Plaines, IL 60016
www.oakton.edu/

South Suburban College
15800 South State Street
South Holland, IL 60473
www.ssc.cc.il.us/

Indiana

Ivy Tech State College
4301 South Cowan Road
Muncie, IN 47302
www.ivy.tec.in.us/

Iowa

Des Moines Area Community College
2006 South Ankeny Blvd.
Ankeny, IA 50021
www.dmacc.cc.ia.us/

Kansas

Kansas City Community College
7250 State Avenue
Kansas City, KS 66112
www.kckcc.cc.ks.us/

Johnson County Community College
12345 College Boulevard
Overland Park, KS 66210
www.johnco.cc.ks.us/

Kentucky

Madisonville Community College
2000 College Drive
Madisonville, KY 42431
www.madcc.uky.edu/

Louisiana

Delgado Community College
615 City Park Avenue
New Orleans, LA 70119
www.dcc.edu/

Maryland

Howard Community College
10901 Little Patuxent Parkway
Columbia, MD 21044
www.howardcc.edu/

Massachusetts

Berkshire Community College
1350 West Street
Pittsfield, MA 01201
www.cc.berkshire.org/

Springfield Technical College
1 Armory Square
Springfield, MA 01105
www.stcc.mass.edu/

Michigan

Lansing Community College
P.O. Box 40010
Lansing, MI 48901
www.lansing.cc.mi.us/

Schoolcraft College
18600 Hagerty Road
Livonia, MI 48152
www.schoolcraft.cc.mi.us/

Muskegon Community College
221 S. Qarterline Road
Muskegon, MI 49442
www.musgegon.cc.mi.us/

Minnesota

Anoka-Hennepin Technical College
3300 Century Avenue North
White Bear Lake, MN 55110
www.ank.tec.mn.us/

Missouri

St. Louis Community College
Forest Park
St. Louis, MO 63110
www.stlcc.cc.mo.us/

New Jersey

New Jersey Institute of Technology
323 King Boulevard
Newark, NJ 07102
www.njit.edu/

County College of Morris
214 Center Grove Road
Randolph, NJ 07869
www.ccm.edu/

New York

College of Technology at Farmingdale
Route 110
Farmingdale, NY 11735
www.farmingdale.edu/

Erie Community College
4041 Southwestern Boulevard
Orchard Park, NY 14127
www.sunyerie.edu/

North Carolina

Stanly Community College
141 College Drive
Albermarle, NC 28001
www.stanly.cc.nc.us/

Alamance Community College
Interstate 40 & I-95
Graham, NC 27253
www.alamance.cc.nc.us/

Caldwell Community College
2855 Hickory Boulevard
Hudson, NC 28638
www.caldwell.cc.nc.us/

Ohio

Cincinnati State Technical & Community
College
3520 Central Parkway
Cincinnati, OH 45223
www.cinstate.cc.oh.us/

Cuyahoga Community College
2900 Community College Avenue
Cleveland, OH 44115
www.tri-c.cc.oh.us/

Air Force Institute of Technology
Wright Patterson AFB
Dayton, OH 45433
www.afit.af.mil/

Kettering College of Medical Arts
3737 Southern Boulevard
Kettering, OH 45429
www.ketthealth.com/kcma/

North Central Technical College
2441 Kenwood Circle
Mansfield, OH 44901
www.nctc.tec.oh.us/

Owens Community College
351 First Street
Perrysburg, OH 43551
www.owens.cc.oh.us/

Pennsylvania

Penn State University, Dubois
College Place
Dubois, PA 15801
www.psu.edu/

Delaware Community College
901 South Media Line Road
Media, PA 19063
www.dccc.edu/

Penn State University, Woodbury
P.O. Box PSU
Lehman, PA 18627
www.psu.edu/

Penn State University, McKeesport
University Drive
McKeesport, PA 15132
www.psu.edu/

Penn State University, New Kensington
3550 7th Street Road
New Kensington, PA 15068
www.nk.psu.edu/

Lehigh Carbon Community College
4525 Education Park Drive
Schnecksville, PA 18078
www.lccc.edu/

Johnson Technical Institute
3427 North Main Avenue
Scranton, PA 18508
www.jti.org/

Tennessee

East Tennessee State University
Johnson City, TN 38134
www.etsu-tn.edu/

State Technical Institute at Memphis
5983 Macon Cove
Memphis, TN 38134
www.stim.tec.tn.us/

Texas

Texas State Tech College, Harlingen
2424 Boxwood
Harlingen, TX 78550
www.harlingen.tstc.edu/

St. Phillips College
801 Martin Luther King Drive
San Antonio, TX 78203
www.accd.edu/spc/spcmain/spc.htm

Texas State Tech College
Waco/Marshall Campus
3801 Campus Drive
Waco, TX 76705
www.tstc.edu/waco.html

Virginia

ECPI College of Technology
5555 Greenwich Road
Virginia Beach, VA 23462
www.ecpi.edu/

Washington

North Seattle Community College
9600 College Way North
Seattle, WA 98103
http://nsccux.sccd.ctc.edu/

Spokane Community College
North 1810 Greene Street
Spokane, WA 99207
www.scc.spokane.cc.wa.us/

Wisconsin

Western Wisconsin Tech College
304 North 6th Street
LaCrosse, WI 54602
www.western.tec.wi.us/

Milwaukee Area Tech College
700 West State Street
Milwaukee, WI 53233
www.milwaukee.tec.wi.us/

BIOMEDICAL PHOTOGRAPHERS

Principal activity: Preparing photographs for medical records, education, and research purposes

Work commitment: Full-time

Preprofessional education: High school diploma

Program length: 2 to 4 years

Work prerequisites: Associate or bachelor's degree

Career opportunities: Quite favorable

Income range: $20,000 to $45,000

Scope

Biomedical photographers are skilled professionals who help biologists, researchers, and others establish documentary records of their work. They must be skilled in all aspects of photography.

Activities

Biomedical photographers must be prepared to work with both living and nonliving subjects. They may be called upon to make simple prints of charts, graphs, and transparencies or to carry out more complex tasks, such as producing motion pictures of complex activities, making videotapes or digitized images for teaching, or making presentations at scientific meetings. The work of these specialists may involve photo-recording of a patient's medical condition over an extended period, so as to record changes. They may take motion pictures taken during operations or autopsies. At other times, they might be asked to make images of the tissues seen under a microscope.

With the capacity of computers to enhance the quality of images, biomedical photographers have a host of new tools are at their disposal. Being knowledgeable of advancing technology is essential for anyone in this profession.

Work Settings

Biomedical photographers work in medical centers, medical schools, and research institutes. Some also work for dental and veterinary schools, pharmaceutical companies, museums, and governmental agencies. Some biomedical photographers are self-employed, offering their services on a free-lance basis.

Advancement

In a large department, a photographer can move into a supervisory post. Advancement also comes by specializing in such areas as cinematography, microphotography, pathological photography, or ophthalmic photography.

Prerequisites

A high school diploma or its equivalent is necessary to enter an educational program in this field.

Desirable personal attributes include patience, manual dexterity, a strong interest in photography, good communication skills, and the ability to work under pressure and time constraints.

Education/Training

In the past, on-the-job training at a teaching hospital was the standard route to an entry-level position as a photographic technician. Today, however, candidates should complete at least a two-year associate degree program at a school that offers a biological photography program. Another approach is to combine a two-year college program with two years of commercial photography education or on-the-job training.

The Biological Photographic Association offers several short training programs.

Certification/Registration/Licensure

Biomedical photographers can attain certification by passing written, practical, and oral examinations. Certified professionals are titled *registered biological photographers (RPBs)*, which is accepted as evidence of competency in the field. Certification is useful but not essential for securing employment.

Career Potential

The overall employment prospects in this field are quite favorable. This is the result of the enormous growth of the health-care industry. The demands of educational and research institutions are growing, as are the needs of museums, publishers, and related industries. Technological advances have created for a greater need for specialized personnel.

For More Information

The professional organization in this field is the Biological Photographic Association, 1819 Peachtree Street NW, Atlanta, GA 30309.

 # BIOMEDICAL WRITERS

Principal activity: Preparing written materials on health-related issues

Work commitment: Part- or full-time

Preprofessional education: High school diploma or its equivalent

Program length: 4 years

Work prerequisites: Bachelor's degree

Career opportunities: Favorable

Income range: $25,000 to $85,000

Scope

Biomedical communications is a broad field, covering health materials in print, on the radio, and on television. A biomedical writer may spend the day writing advertising copy, a script to be aired on a radio program, or a documentary to be presented on TV. These writers bring complex information to people in a simple format they can understand.

Activities

Biomedical writers have the challenging job of writing about medical matters so that people outside the medical field can comprehend them. To do this, they must understand, analyze, interpret, and then accurately write about some very complex subjects.

They may prepare sales brochures or instruction manuals for new diagnostic and treatment equipment; write announcements of new medical findings by pharmaceutical companies; draft scripts for radio and television shows on health issues; or write articles for newspapers, magazines, or exhibits. The most successful medical writers have their own regular or syndicated columns.

Work Settings

Biomedical writers are employed by publishers of newspapers, magazines, and textbooks; pharmaceutical and medical equipment companies; medical centers and major hospitals; professional health-care organizations and volunteer health agencies; advertising agencies; and radio and TV stations.

Advancement

Advancement in this field comes by moving to specialty areas, where salaries are higher, or by joining the staff of a larger organization. Earning a master's degree or an advanced certificate from the American Medical Writers' Association also can be helpful.

Prerequisites

A high school diploma or its equivalent is needed to begin studies in this field.

Desirable personal attributes include a genuine interest in writing and in the medical field; good interviewing, research, and interpersonal skills; and the ability to work under deadline pressure.

Education/Training

The basic requirement for entering the field is a bachelor's degree with the appropriate courses and skills. Some positions require a master's degree. Undergraduates should major in English or journalism and minor in the biological sciences. Proficiency with a computer is mandatory.

Certification/Registration/Licensure

The American Medical Writers' Association offers continuing education courses at its annual conference and at regional and chapter workshop meetings. These courses are based on a core curriculum to improve skills in six relevant areas: editing, writing, audiovisual work, public relations and advertising, free lancing, and teaching. A certificate is awarded upon completion of each of these courses. An advanced certificate is offered to eligible candidates who have completed eight in-depth courses.

Career Potential

The overall employment outlook in this field is quite favorable. In recent decades people have become much more health conscious. "Taking charge" of one's own well-being requires good medical information. In addition, radio and TV today devote more time to health-related issues. Pharmaceutical and research companies also actively seek talented research writers. Nevertheless, competition for high-paying positions is quite stiff.

For More Information

The professional organization in this field is the American Medical Writers' Association, 9650 Rockville Pike, Bethesda, MA 20814.

Biomedical Writing Programs

Many colleges and universities offer courses in biomedical or technical communications—far too many to list here. A few also offer master's degree programs. For a list of programs in your area, write to the American Medical Writers' Association at the address listed above.

CERTIFIED ATHLETIC TRAINERS

Principal activity: Supervising the physical well-being of athletes

Work commitment: Part- or full-time

Preprofessional education: High school diploma

Program length: 4 years

Work prerequisites: Bachelor's degree and certification

Career opportunities: Strong

Income range: $20,000 to $40,000

Scope

This is one of the newer health-care occupations. Specialists in this field are educated and trained to identify and evaluate sports injuries, provide prompt treatment to injured athletes, and determine if further medical care is needed. They also develop and implement injury-prevention programs, teach about health care, and supervise athletic training programs.

Activities

Athletic trainers provide initial care for injured atheletes, protect them from further trauma, and ensure that appropriate medical treatment is provided when necessary. They work in collaboration with and under the direction of the supervising institutional physician. Trainers ensure that the atheletes understand and follow the physician's instructions and wear appropriate protective gear during team activities. They also work in liaison with coaches to make sure that athletes are in shape or have adequately recovered from injuries before returning to limited or full sports activities.

Advancement

A trainer can advance by earning a higher degree and by gaining additional professional experience.

Prerequisites

A high school diploma or its equivalent is essential for entering a training program. Students should take biology, chemistry, and physics as well as first-aid. If possible, they should secure some experience as coaches or team captains.

Desirable personal attributes include a genuine interest in both athletics and health care, good hygiene habits, good communication skills, and an understanding and tolerance for human limitations. Trainers also must be able to relate well to people and to inspire them.

Education/Training

Trainers must earn a college degree in an accredited program. This includes courses in human anatomy and physiology, kinesiology, physiology of exercise, psychology, nutrition, personal and community health, first-aid (plus CPR), physical education, coaching, and athletic training. A mandatory part of the program is gaining extensive field experience.

There are a limited number of graduate programs leading to q master's or doctoral degree. These require advanced-level courses in the subjects listed above.

Certification/Registration/Licensure

Certification is a requirement for professional success in this field.

To be certified by the National Athletic Trainers' Association, candidates must earn a college degree with the appropriate course of studies and secure 800 hours of experience. In addition, they must pass a three-part exam that evaluates basic knowledge, clinical skills, and decision making abilities. Continuing education courses are required to maintain accredited status.

Some states also require a license for trainers.

Career Potential

Strong employment opportunities are anticipated in this field. The increased interest in athletics is stimulating opportunities, the majority of them at high schools, where athletic trainers frequently combine teaching with their training activities.

For More Information

The professional organization in this field is the National Athletic Trainers' Association, 2952 Stemmons Freeway, Dallas, TX 75247.

For information on certification, write to the NATA Board of Certification, 3725 National Drive, Raleigh, NC 2612.

Athletic Training Programs

Alabama

Samford University
Box 292448
Birmingham, AL 35229
www.samford.edu/

University of Alabama
Tuscaloosa, AL 35487
www.ua.edu/

California

California State University, Fresno
Fresno, CA 93740
www.fansonly.com/schools/fres/

California State University, Long Beach
Long Beach, CA 90840l
www.acs.csulb.edu/

California State University, Northridge
Northridge, CA 91330
www.csun.edu/

California State University, Sacramento
Sacramento, CA 95819
www.csus.edu/

Colorado

University of Northern Colorado
Greely, CO 80639
ccc.univnorthco.edu/

Connecticut

Southern Connecticut State University
501 Crescent Street
New Haven, CT 06515
http://scwww.ctstate.edu/

Delaware

University of Delaware
Newark, DE 19716
www.udel.edu/

Florida

Barry University
11300 NE 2nd Avenue
Miami Shores, FL 33161
www.barry.edu/

Georgia

Valdosta State University
Valdosta, GA 31698
www.valdosta.edu/

Idaho

Boise State University
Boise, ID 83725
www.idbsu.edu/

Illinois

Southern Illinois University
Carbondale, IL 62901
www.siu.edu/

Eastern Illinois University
Charleston, IL 61920
www.eiu.edu/

Western Illinois University
Macomb, IL 61455
www.wiu.edu/

University of Illinois
Urbana, IL 61801
www.uiuc.edu/

Indiana

Anderson University
Anderson, IN 56012
www.anderson.edu/

Indiana University
Bloomington, IN 47405
www.indiana.edu/

Ball State University
Muncie, IN 47306
www.bsu.edu/

Indiana State University
Terre Haute, IN 47809
www.indstate.edu/

Purdue University
West Lafayette, IN 47907
www.purdue.edu/

Iowa

University of Iowa
Iowa City, IA 52242
www.uiowa.edu/

Kansas

Kansas State University
364 Bluemont Hall
1100 Mid-Campus Dr.
Manhattan, KS 66506
www.ksu.edu/

Kentucky

Eastern Kentucky University
Richmond, KY 40475
www.eku.edu/

Maryland

Towson University
Towson, MD 21252l
www.towson.edu/

Massachusetts

Endicott College
376 Hale Street
Beverly, MA 01915
www.endicott.edu/

Boston University
635 Commonwealth Avenue
Boston, MA 02115
http://web.bu.edu/

Northeastern University
Boston, MA 02115
www.northeastern.edu/

Bridgewater State College
MAHPLS
Bridgewater, MA 02325
www.bridgew.edu/

Salem State College
352 Lafayette Street
Salem, MA 01970
www.salem-ma.edu/

Springfield College
Springfield, MA 01109
www.spfldcol.edu/

Michigan

Grand Valley State University
Allendale, MI 49401
www.gvsu.edu/

Central Michigan University
Mount Pleasant, MI 48859
www.cmich.edu/

Eastern Michigan University
Ypsilanti, MI 48197
www.emich.edu/

Minnesota

Minnesota State University, Mankato
Mankato, MN 56002
www.mankato.msus.edu/

Gustavus Adolphus College
St. Peter, MN 56082
www.gac.edu/

Mississippi

University of Mississippi
Hattiesburg, MS 39406
www.olemiss.edu/

Missouri

Southwest Missouri State University
Springfield, MO 65804
www.smsu.edu/

Montana

University of Montana, Missoula
McGill 126
Missoula, MT 59812
www.umt.edu/

New Hampshire

University of New Hampshire
Durham, NH 03824
www.unh.edu/

Plymouth State College
MSC #1
Plymouth, NH 03264
www.plymouth.edu/

New Jersey

Kean College of New Jersey
Union, NJ 07083
www.kean.edu/

William Paterson University of New Jersey
Wayne, NJ 07470
www.wilpaterson.edu/

New Mexico

University of New Mexico
Albuquerque, NM 87131
www.unm.edu/

New Mexico State University
Las Cruces, NM 88003
www.nmsu.edu/

New York

Canisius College
Buffalo, NY 14208
http://gort.canisius.edu/

State University of New York at Cortland
Cortland, NY 13045
www.cortland.edu/

Ithaca College
Ithaca, NY 14850
www.ithaca.edu/

Hofstra University
Hempstead, NY 11550
www.hofstra.edu/

North Carolina

Appalachian State University
Boone, NC 28608
www.appstate.edu/

University of North Carolina
211 Fetzer Gymnasium
Chapel Hill, NC 27599
www.unc.edu/

East Carolina University
Greenville, NC 27858
www.ecu.edu/

High Point University
University Station
Montlieu Avenue
High Point, NC 27262
http://acme.highpoint.edu/

North Dakota

North Dakota State University
Fargo, ND 58105
www.ndsu.nodak.edu/

University of North Dakota
Grand Forks, ND 58202
www.und.nodak.edu/

Ohio

Mount Union College
Alliance, OH 44601
www.muc.edu/

Ohio University
Grover Bldg. 229-5
Athens, OH 45701
www.ohiou.edu/

Marietta College
Marietta, OH 45750
www.marietta.edu/

University of Toledo
Toledo, OH 43606
www.utoledo.edu/

Oklahoma

University of Oklahoma
Tulsa, OK 74104
www.ou.edu/

Oregon

Oregon State University
Corvallis, OR 97331
www.orst.edu/

Pennsylvania

California University of Pennsylvania
250 University Avenue
California, PA 15419
www.cup.edu/

East Stroudsburg University
East Stroudsburg, pA 18301
www.esu.edu/

Mercyhurst College
Erie, PA 16546
http://eden.mercy.edu/

Messiah College
Grantham, PA 17027
www.messiah.edu/

Lock Haven University
Lock Haven, PA 17745
www.lhup.edu/

Temple University
Pearson Hall
Philadelphia, PA 19122
www.temple.edu/

Duquesne University
123 Health Sciences Bldg.
Pittsburgh, PA 15282
www.duq.edu/

University of Pittsburgh
Pittsburgh, PA 15261
www.pitt.edu/

Slippery Rock University
School of Allied Health
Slippery Rock, PA 16057
www.sru.edu/

Pennsylvania State University
Kinesiology Department
University Park, PA 16802
www.psu.edu/

Waynesburg College
Waynesburg, PA 15370
www.waynesburg.edu/

West Chester University
215 South Campus
West Chester, PA 19383
www.wcupa.edu/

South Carolina

University of South Carolina
Blatt PE Center
Columbia, SC 29208
www.sc.edu/

South Dakota

South Dakota State University
Brookings, SD 57007
www.sdstate.edu/

Tennessee

East Tennessee State University
Johnson City, TN 37614
www.etsu-tn.edu/

Lipscomb University
Nashville, TN 37204
www.dlu.edu/

Texas

Texas Christian University
TCU Box 297600
Fort Worth, TX 76129
www.tcu.edu/

Southwest Texas State University
San Marcos, TX 78666
www.swt.edu/

Utah

Brigham Young University
College of PE & Sports
Provo, UT 84602
www.byu.edu/

Vermont

University of Vermont
College of Education
Burlington, VT 05405
www.uvm.edu/

Virginia

James Madison University
Harrisonburg, VA 22807
www.jmu.edu/

Washington

Washington State University
Department of Kinesiology
Pullman, WA 99164
www.tricity.wsu.edu/

West Virginia

University of Charleston
2300 MacCorkle Avenue, SE
Charleston, WV 25304
www.uchaswv.edu/

Marshall University
Huntington, WV 25755
www.marshall.edu/

West Virginia University
School of Health Promotion
Morgantown, WV 26506
www.wvu.edu/

Wisconsin

University of Wisconsin
LaCrosse, WI 54601
www.uwlax.edu/

CHILD LIFE SPECIALISTS

Principal activity: Addressing the social and psychological needs of hospitalized children

Work commitment: Part- or full-time

Preprofessional education: High school diploma

Program length: 4 years

Work prerequisites: Bachelor's degree

Career opportunities: Limited at this time

Income range: $20,000 to $35,000

Scope

Hospitalization means a complete break in one's life, separation from family and friends, and facing unfamiliar (and sometimes painful) testing and treatment procedures. The potential for intense psychological stress is quite high, especially for children. Child life specialists help children deal with that stress.

Activities

Child life specialists use play therapy to help children deal with the stress of hospitalization. They may have children use dolls to act out their emotions and reveal their fears and distress. These specialists also provide young patients with needed reassurance and emotional support, explain what is happening, and prepare the children for what comes next.

Child life specialists act as story-tellers and sometimes as active listeners. Many times they act as a liason between children and their nurses, physicians, dietitians, and other therapists.

Work Settings

Child life specialists work at medical centers and hospitals, where their involvement may come as early as the time of admission and extend until discharge. Some are also employed by outpatient facilities. While the use of these specialists is not widespread, the profession is growing slowly.

Advancement

Salary increases and tenure are available at hospitals with larger programs. With experience, a child life specialist may become director of the program at a large institution.

Prerequisites

A high school diploma or its equivalent is necessary to train for this profession.

Desirable personal attributes include common sense and judgment, superior communication skills, compassion, an optimistic and outgoing personality, a sense of humor, a caring and giving nature, and the emotional resilience to deal with critically ill children. Above all, these specialists must love children.

Education/Training

There are three routes open to those seeking to enter this field.

1. One can earn a bachelor's degree at one of the few colleges offering a majors in child life.

2. One can secure a bachelor's degree in education, recreational therapy, or child psychology and then complete a practice in child life as part of the program.

3. Those with a degree in a related field can get on-the-job training as a child life assistant.

Undergraduate training usually involves courses in English, speech, biology, education, psychology, medical terminology, and pediatric illnesses. Field work provides practical experience in dealing with issues associated with the field, such as family dynamics, emotional trauma, and professional interaction with health-care providers.

Certification/Registration/Licensure

Certification is voluntary and can be secured through the Child Life Council. Ultimately, states may require licensure in this field.

Career Potential

Employment in this field today is limited because of budgetary cuts to health-care providers. Salaries tend to be low. However, the field is growing slowly.

For More Information

The professional organization is the Child Life Council, 11820 Parklawn Drive, Rockville, MD 20852

Child Life Programs

Most people entering this field major in psychology, education, or recreational therapy. Few schools offer a program in child life. For a list of schools that do, contact the Child Life Council, at the address listed above.

DIETARY MANAGERS

Principal activity: Supervising food service operations

Work commitment: Full-time

Preprofessional education: High school diploma

Program length: 1 year

Work prerequisites: Certification

Career opportunities: Quite favorable

Income range: $30,000 to $60,000

Scope

Dietary managers supervise other workers who are involved in food service operations at hospitals, schools, hotels, prisons, nursing homes, and large companies.

Activities

The job responsibilities of dietary managers vary widely, depending on the size and nature of the institution that employs them. They hire and supervise other staff members, order and purchase supplies, and oversee meal preparation and clean-up. To carry out these duties, they work closely with registered dietitians to ensure that they meet the nutritional needs of their clients.

Work Settings

Dietary managers are employed by hospitals, long-term care facilities, educational institutions, hotels, prisons, and large corporations with in-house food service.

Advancement

Dietary managers can advance by moving to larger facilities. Some go into teaching.

Prerequisites

A high school diploma is necessary to train for this field. Students should take courses in biology, home economics, and business management.

Desirable personal attributes include a strong interests in food preparation, good business skills, and the ability to supervise others.

Education/Training

Dietary management programs ,which typically last one year, are offered by many vocational-technical schools and community colleges. They offer courses in nutrition, food service management, quantity food production, and business practices.

Certification/Registration/Licensure

Graduates of accredited dietary management programs can take an examination to be certified by the Dietary Managers' Association. This qualifies them as a *certified dietary managers*. More than 70 percent of the 15,000 professionals working in this field today are certified.

Career Potential

With the rapidly aging population of the United States today, prospects are quite favorable for long-term employment growth in this field.

For More Information

The professional organization is the Dietary Managers' Association, One Pierce Place, Ithaca, IL 60143.

Dietary Manager Training Programs

Alabama

Auburn University
204 Mell Hall
Auburn, AL 36849
www.auburn.edu/

Florida

University of Florida
2209 NW 13th Street, STED
Gainesville, FL 32609
www.ufl.edu/

Georgia

University of Georgia
Athens, GA 30602
www.uga.edu/

New York

Senior Healthcare Alternatives
103 Head of Neck Road
P.O. Box 927
Bellport, NY 11713
(516) 536-8000

Broome Community College
P.O. Box 1017, T221-A
Binghampton, NY 13902
www.sunybroome.edu/

Dutchess Community College
53 Pendell Road
Poughkeepsie, NY 12601
www.sunydutchess.edu/

SUNY at Farmingdale
Massapequa General Hospital
750 Hicksville Road
Seaford, NY 11783
www.farmingdale.edu/

Suffolk County Community College
533 College Road
Seldon, NY 11784
www.sunysuffolk.edu/

Westchester Community College
75 Grasslands Road
Valhalla, NY 10595
www.wcc.co.westchester.ny.us/

Erie Community College
6205 Main Street
Williamsville, NY 14221
www.sunyerie.edu/

North Dakota

University of North Dakota
Box 9021
Grand Forks, ND 58202
www.und.nodak.edu/

Pennsylvania

Pennsylvania State University
201 Mateer Building
University Park, PA 16802
www.psu.edu/

ENVIRONMENTAL HEALTH SCIENTISTS

Principal activity: Helping reduce the threat to public health due to environmental hazards

Work commitment: Full-time

Preprofessional education: High school diploma

Program length: 4 years

Work prerequisites: Bachelor's degree

Career opportunities: Quite favorable

Income range: $20,000 to $45,000

Scope

Environmental health scientists (or *sanitarians*) work to reduce health hazards due to unsafe food and water or waste and sewage disposal. They also are concerned with atmospheric pollution and radioactive contamination.

A major milestone in the development of this field was an 1850 report of the Sanitary Commission of Massachusetts, which made 50 specific recommendations. It took another 100 years, however, to establish environmental health as a distinct professional discipline. Those working in this field play a vital role in maintaining public health in the United States. The efforts of the government to promote health and prevent disease have enhanced interest in this field.

Activities

Entry-level sanitarians usually act as inspectors, checking restaurants, schools, daycare centers, summer camps, hospitals, bakeries, and grocery stores. In addition, they check water supplies, sewage treatment facilities, and swimming pools.

More experienced sanitarians, in addition to inspection duties, provide education and consultation in this field.

Highly experience sanitarians help organize training programs. Some sanitarians specialize in industrial hygiene, institutional hygiene, or radiation protection.

Work Settings

Most sanitarians are employed by public health agencies at the local level, therefore are civil service employees.

Advancement

After a few years of work experience, a sanitarian may advance to a supervisory position. Such a position might involve planning, organizing, and evaluating activities.

Sanitarians with graduate degrees may conduct research, teach or specialize.

Prerequisites

A high school diploma or its equivalent is the minimum requirement to train for work in this field.

Desirable personal attributes include good health and vision, superior communication skills, a genuine interest in science and health care, and a desire to be in an active and responsible profession.

Education/Training

A bachelor's degree with a basic science background is needed to secure an entry-level position. There are about 25 accredited programs in environmental health in the U.S. These encompass biology, chemistry, physics, microbiology, mathematics, epidemiology, biostatistics, environmental health factors, communication, and behavioral sciences. Field training is also incorporated into the programs.

Many new openings in this field require a master's degree.

Certification/Registration/Licensure

Most states have their own standards for registration or licensure.

Career Potential

Employment prospects for sanitarians will be quite favorable for the foreseeable future. In recent years, the public's concern with health hazards and a clean environment has greatly increased. This forces government agencies to be more cognizant of their responsibilities and more concerned with these issues.

For More Information

The professional association in this field is the National Environmental Health Association, 1200 Lincoln Street, Denver, CO 80203.

For information on certification, write to the National Accreditation Council for Environmental Health Curricula, at the same address.

Environmental Health Science Programs

Arkansas

University of Arkansas at Little Rock
2801 South University Avenue
Little Rock, AR 72204
www.ualr.edu/

California

California State University at Fresno
5241 North Maple Avenue
Fresno, CA 93740
www.fansonly.com/schools/fres/

California State University, Northridge
18111 Nordhoff Street
Northridge, CA 91330
www.csun.edu/

California State University, Sacramento
6000 J Street
Sacramento, CA 95819
www.csus.edu/

San Diego State University
5500 Campanile Drive
San Diego, CA 92182
www.fansonly.com/schools/sdsu/

San Jose State University
1 Washington Square
San Jose, CA 95192
www.sjsu.edu/

Colorado

Colorado State University
Fort Collins, CO 80523
www.colostate.edu/

Connecticut

University of Hartford
West Hartford, CT 06117
www.hartford.edu/

Delaware

Delaware State University
Dover, DE 19901
www.dsc.edu/

Georgia

University of Georgia
Athens, GA 30602
www.uga.edu/

Idaho

Boise State University
1910 University Drive
Boise, ID 83725
www.idbsu.edu/

Illinois

Illinois State University
Normal, IL 61790
www.ilstu.edu/

Indiana

Indiana State University
Terre Haute, IN 47809
www.indstate.edu/

Purdue University
Schleman Hall
West Lafayette, IN 47907
www.purdue.edu/

Kentucky

Eastern Kentucky University
Richmond, KY 40475
www.eku.edu/

Maryland

Salisbury State University
253 Power Building
Salisbury, MD 21801
www.ssu.edu/

Massachusetts

Hampshire College
Amherst, MA 01002
www.hampshire.edu/

Massachusetts Institute of Tech
77 Massachusetts Avenue
Cambridge, MA 02139
www.mit.edu/

Springfield College
Springfield, MA 01109
www.spfldcol.edu/

Michigan

Ferris State University
PRK 211
Big Rapids, MI 49307
www.ferris.edu/

University of Michigan–Flint
Flint, MI 48502
www.flint.umich.edu/

Oakland University
101 North Foundation Hall
Rochester, MI 48309
www.acs.oakland.edu/

Missouri

Missouri Southern State College
Joplin, MO 64801
www.mssc.edu/

New Jersey

Rutgers State University
Cook College
New Brunswick, NJ 08903
www.rutgers.edu/

New Mexico

Eastern New Mexico University
Station #5 ENMU
Portales, NM 88130
www.enmu.edu/

New York

SUNY College at Cortland
Cortland, NY 13045
www.cortland.edu/

North Carolina

Western Carolina University
Cullowhee, NC 25435
www.wcu.edu/

East Carolina University
East 5th Street
Greenville, NC 27858
www.ecu.edu/

Ohio

Ohio University
416 Tower
Athens, OH 45701
www.ohiou.edu/

Bowling Green State University
Bowling Green, OH 48403
www.bgsu.edu/

Wright State University
Dayton, OH 45435
www.wright.edu/

Oklahoma

East Central University
Ada, OK 74820
www.ecok.edu/

Oregon

Oregon State University
Corvallis, OR 97331
www.orst.edu/

Pennsylvania

California University of Pennsylvania
3rd Street
California, PA 15419
www.cup.edu/

Indiana University of Pennsylvania
216 Pratt Hall
Indiana, PA 15705
www.iup.edu/

West Chester University
100 West Rosedale Avenue
W Chester, PA 19383
www.wcupa.edu/

Tennessee

East Tennessee State University
P.O. Box 70731, ETSU
Johnson City, TN 37614
www.etsu-tn.edu/

Texas

Texas Southern University
3100 Cleburn
Houston, TX 77004
www.tsu.edu/

Virginia

Old Dominion University
5215 Hampton Boulevard
Norfolk, VA 23529
www.odu.edu/

Washington

University of Washington
Seattle, WA 98195
www.washington.edu/

Wisconsin

University of Wisconsin–Eau Claire
P.O. Box 4004
Eau Claire, WI 54702
www.uwec.edu/

HEALTH EDUCATORS

Principal activity: Helping to improve people's lifestyles through education

Work commitment: Usually full-time

Preprofessional education: High school diploma

Program length: 4 years; 6 for public health educator

Work prerequisites: Bachelor's degree; master's degree for public health educator

Career opportunities: Favorable

Income range: $25,000 to $45,000

Scope

Health education is performed by people in school, community, and public health agencies. The goal of all three groups is to teach people how to improve their health and prevent disease. By persuading individuals to practice healthy lifestyles, these educators have a profound impact not only on individual lives but on society in general. This is reflected, for example, by the education campaigns against smoking, alcohol and substance abuse, and AIDS.

Activities

School health educators must hold a teaching certificate and have expertise in health education. They teach about the importance of personal hygiene and emphasize the destructive impact of smoking, alcohol, and drugs. Greater emphasis in this area is anticipated, because it is so important to our society's future.

Community health educators reach out to the adult population through places of business, television, and other public media. They use exhibits, public meetings, health runs, and smoking withdrawal clinics to encourage healthier lifestyles.

Public health educators secure information on public health issues and serve as liaisons between government agencies and community groups.

Advancement

Advancement in this field comes with experience and additional education (such as a master's degree).

Prerequisites

A high school diploma or its equivalent is needed to enter a training program. Public health educators must hold at least a batchelor's degree. Some position require a master's degree.

Desirable personal attributes include good communication skills, a desire to teach, the ability to interact in a group setting, and good health and hygiene habits.

Education/Training

Those planning careers as school or community health educators must earn a bachelor's degree in education. Most colleges offer teacher training programs.

Public health educators must earn a degree in public health, which is offered by many universities.

Certification/Registration/Licensure

Most health educators are not licensed. However, those teaching in schools must have a teaching license from their state education department.

Career Potential

Most school health educators work in public schools. Those holding a master's degree, can teach at the college level.

Many health organizations hire health educators as administrative personnel. Educators also work in hospitals, clinics, HMOs, and government agencies.

For More Information

The professional organization in this field is the American Public Health Association, 1015 18th Street NW, Washington, DC 20036.

Health Education Programs

Hundreds of colleges and universities offer teaching programs—far too many to list here. Contact your state university for more information on programs in your area.

HEALTH INFORMATION TECHNICIANS

Principal activity: Maintaining medical records

Work commitment: Usually full-time

Preprofessional education: High school diploma

Program length: 2 to 4 years

Work prerequisites: Associate degree

Career opportunities: Favorable

Income range: $18,000 to $30,000

Scope

A major responsibility of hospitals and other health-care facilities is maintaining complete and accurate records for all of their patients. These records are essential, for example, for insurance or Medicare payments. Moreover, doctors use records to evaluate treatments, and governement agencies use them to determine if facilities are being managed in accordance with legal requirements.

Activities

Health information (medical record) technicians must determine if patient records are complete, including the attending physician's name, admission date, history, symptoms, physical exam records, test results, diagnoses, physician notes, and discharge date. They also must translate diseases and procedures into coding symbols. They are responsible for maintaining all patient records in an organized fashion, so that they can be easily retrieved. The work must be processed accurately and efficiently, so that reimbursement is correct and expedited.

These workers find information for doctors and administrators, and so must interact with health professionals, insurance companies, lawyers, administrators, and patients.

Work Settings

Most medical record technicians work in hospitals. Others work in HMOs, nursing homes, health clinics, and physicians' offices.

Advancement

With experience and education, a medical record technician may advance to a supervisory or managerial position.

Prerequisites

A high school diploma or its equivalent is necessary for admission to college-level programs in this field.

Desirable personal attributes include dependability, a concern for detail, good computer and communication skills, the ability to maintain confidentiality, and organized work habits.

Education/Training

Most people in this field complete a two-year course in medical record technology, leading to an associate degree. An alternate approach is to graduate from an independent study program offered by the American Medical Record Association.

Certification/Registration/Licensure

Meeting the educational requirements and passing a written examination sponsored by the American Medical Record Association assures certification. This status is helpful in finding employment.

Career Potential

Employment prospects for medical record technicians are favorable. The increasing numbers of elderly people in the United States will require more hospitalizations and use of other health-care facilities, with a corresponding rise in the work load for medical record technicians.

For More Information

The professional organization for this field is the American Information Health Management Association, 919 North Michigan Ave., Chicago, IL 60611.

Health Information Technician Programs

Alabama

Samford University
800 Lakeshore Drive
Birmingham, AL 35229
www.samford.edu/

University of Alabama at Birmingham
UAB Station
Birmingham, AL 35294
www.uab.edu/

University of West Alabama
Livingston, AL 35470
www.westal.edu/

California

Charles R. Drew University of Medicine &
Science
Los Angeles, CA 90059
www.cdrewu.edu/

Colorado

Regis University
Denver, CO 80221
www.regis.edu/

Florida

Florida International University
University Park
Miami, FL 33199
www.fiu.edu/

University of Central Florida
Orlando, FL 32816
www.ucf.edu/

Florida A & M University
Tallahassee, FL 32307
www.famu.edu/

Georgia

Clark Atlanta University
James R. Brawley Drive at Fair Street NW
Atlanta, GA 30314
http://galaxy.cau.edu/cau/ctsps.htm.

Medical College of Georgia
1120 15th Street
Augusta, GA 30912
www.mcg.edu/

Columbus State University
209 Arnold Hall
Columbus, GA 31907
www.colstate.edu/

Idaho

Boise State University
1910 University Drive
Boise, ID 83725
www.idbsu.edu/

Illinois

Chicago State University
95th at King Drive
Chicago, IL 60628
www.csu.edu/

University of Illinois at Chicago
P.O. Box 5220
Chicago, IL 60680
www.uic.edu/

Illinois State University
Normal, IL 61790
www.ilstlu.edu

Indiana

Indiana University
300 North Jordan Avenue
Bloomington, IN 47405
www.indiana.edu/

Indiana University Northwest
3400 Broadway
Gary, IN 46408
www.iun.indiana.edu/

Indiana Universty Purdue University
Cavanaugh Hall
Indianapolis, IN 46202
www.iupui.edu/

Kansas

University of Kansas
126 Strong Hall
Lawrence, KS 66045
www.ukans.edu/

Washburn University of Topeka
Topeka, KS 66621
www.wuacc.edu/

Wichita State University
1845 North Fairmont
Wichita, KS 67260
www.wichita.edu/

Kentucky

Eastern Kentucky University
Richmond, KY 40475
www.eku.edu/

Western Kentucky University
Bowling Green, KY 42101
www.wku.edu/

Louisiana

University of Southwestern Louisiana
104 University Circle
Lafayette, LA 70504
www.ce.usl.edu/

Louisiana Tech University
Ruston, LA 71272
www.latech.edu/

Maine

University of Maine
Orono, ME 04469
www.ume.maine.edu/

Massachusetts

Springfield College
Springfield, MA 01109
www.spfldcol.edu/

Michigan

Baker College of Auburn Hills
1500 University Drive
Auburn Hills, MI 48326
www.baker.edu/

Ferris State University
PRK 211
Big Rapids, MI 49307
www.ferris.edu/

Baker College of Mt. Clemens
34950 Little Mack
Clinton Township, MI 48035
www.baker.edu/

Davenport College
4123 West Main Street
Kalamazoo, MI 49006
www.davenport.edu/

Baker College of Muskegan
123 East Apple Avenue
Muskegan, MI 49442
www.baker.edu/

Baker College of Owosso
Owosso, MI 48867
www.baker.edu/

Baker College of Port Huron
3403 Lapeer Road
Port Huron, MI 48060
www/baler/edi

Minnesota

College of St. Scholastica
Duluth, MN 55811
www.css.edu/

Moorhead State University
Owens Hall
Moorhead, MN 56563
www.moorhead.msus.edu/

Mississippi

Jackson State University
P.O. Box 17330
1400 John R Lynch Street
Jackson, MS 39217
www.sjums.edu/

University of Mississippi Medical Center
2500 North State
Jackson, MS 39216
www.olemiss.edu/

Alcorn State University
Lorman, MS 39096
www.alcorn.edu/

Missouri

St. Louis University
221 North Grand Boulevard
St. Louis, MO 63103
www.slu.edu/

Nebraska

College of St. Mary
Omaha, NE 68124
www.csm.edu/

New Jersey

Kean College
1000 Morris Avenue
Union, NJ 07083
www.kean.edu/

New York

St. Francis College
180 Remsen Street
Brooklyn Hts., NY 11201
www.stfranciscollege.edu/

SUNY Health Science Center at Brooklyn
450 Clarkson Avenue
Brooklyn, NY 11203
www.hscbklyn.edu/

Long Island University
CW Post Campus
Brookville, NY 11548
www.liunet.edu/

Ithaca College
Ithaca, NY 14850
www.ithaca.edu/

Pace University
New York City Campus
New York, NY 10038
www.pace.edu/newhome.html

Rochester Institute of Tech
Rochester, NY 14623
www.rit.edu/

Touro College
27-33 W 23rd Street
New York, NY 10010
www.touro.edu/

State University of New York
Institute of Technology at Utica
Utica/Rome, NY 13504
www.cs.sunyit.edu/

North Carolina

Western Carolina University
Cullowhee, NC 28723
www.wcu.edu/

East Carolina University
East 5th Street
Greenville, NC 27858
www.ecu.edu/

Ohio

Ohio State University
3rd Floor, Lincoln Tower
Columbus, OH 43210
www.acs.ohio-state.edu/

University of Toledo
Toledo, OH 43606
www.utoledo.edu/

Oklahoma

East Central University
Ada, OK 74820
www.ecok.edu/

Southwestern Oklahoma State University
Weatherford, OK 73096
www.swosu.edu/

Pennsylvania

Gwynedd- Mercy College
Gwynedd Valley, PA 19437
www.gmc.edu/

Temple University
Broad Street & Montgomery Avenue
Philadelphia, PA 19122
www.temple.edu/

Duquesue University
600 Forbes Avenue
Pittsburgh, PA 15282
www.duq.edu/

University of Pittsburgh
Bruce Hall, 2nd Floor
Pittsburgh, PA 15260
www.pitt.edu/

South Dakota

Dakota State University
Madison, SD 57042
www.dsu.edu/

Tennessee

University of Tennessee at Knoxville
Knoxville, TN 37209
www.utk.edu/

University of Tennessee at Memphis
800 Madison Avenue
Memphis, TN 38163
www.utmem.edu/

Tennessee State University
3500 John A. Merritt Boulevard
Nashville, TN 37209
www.tnstate.edu/

Texas

University of Texas Medical Branch at
Galveston
1212 Ashbel Smith
Galveston, TX 77555
www.utmb.edu/

Texas Southern University
3100 Cleburn
Houston, TX 77004
www.tsu.edu/

Southwest Texas State University
San Marcos, TX 78666
www.swt.edu/

Utah

Weber State University
3750 Harrison Boulevard
Ogden, UT 84408
www.weber.edu/

Virginia

Norfolk State University
2401 Corprew Avenue
Norfolk, VA 23504
www.nsu.edu/

West Virginia

Fairmont State College
Fairmont, WV 26554
www.fscwv.edu/

Marshall University
400 Hal Greer Building
Huntington, WV 25755
www.marshall.edu/

Wisconsin

University of Wisconsin, Milwaukee
P.O. Box 413
Milwaukee, WI 53201
www.uwm.edu/

HEALTH SERVICES ADMINISTRATORS

Principal activity: Overseeing operations at a health-care facility

Work commitment: Full-time

Preprofessional education: Bachelor's degree

Program length: 4 to 6 years

Work prerequisites: Bachelor's degree; master's degree is preferred

Career opportunities: Favorable

Income range: $35,000 to $75,000

Scope

Health services administrators manage medical centers, hospitals, HMOs, and clinics. Their principal responsibility is to ensure that all hospital activities function in a coordinated, efficient way. The chief administrator is the senior nonmedical officer and is responsible for executing policies set by the institution's board of trustees and for the day-to-day activities of the facility. The administrator also acts as liaison between the board and medical staff. Lower-level administrators have more limited and specialized responsibilities over routine institutional operations.

Activities

Senior health administrators usually function by delegating responsibilities to the middle- and lower-level administrators. This includes purchasing, maintenance, admissions, business personnel, security, public relations, and other vital nonmedical jobs. The senior administrator is ultimately responsible for developing the operating budget that is submitted to the trustees or corporate officials for approval each year.

Work Settings

Health services administrators work in medical centers, hospitals, HMOs, public health agencies, clinics, and other facilities that provide outpatient or inpatient health care.

Advancement

Advancement comes with experience and increased education. Lower-level administrators are called *administrative assistants* or *assistant administrators*.

Prerequisites

A high school diploma or its equivalent is necessary to undertake studies for a bachelor's degree in hospital administration. This major is not necessary for graduate work, since a broad liberal arts background can also serve as the basis for graduate work.

Desirable personal attributes include superior oral and written skills, the ability to interact with colleagues and supervisors, a strong interest in following up details, and good business and leadership skills.

Education/Training

Graduate-level work includes course in medicine, public health, and business. The program lasts two years, including a summer internship at a health faculty. An alternative program involves a full year of academic work followed by a second year of residency as a health services administration intern.

Certification/Registration/Licensure

Certification can be secured by meeting the educational and experience requirements of the American College of Hospital Administrators, 840 North Lake Shore Drive, Chicago, IL 60611.

Career Potential

The changing health-care industry, and especially the evolution of HMOs, has increased the demand for administrators. This, together with an increasing population of senior citizens, suggests favorable employment opportunities in this field.

For More Information

The profession organizations are for this field are listed below:

American College of Health Care Administrators
325 South Patrick Street
Alexandria, VA 22314

American College of Health Care Executives
One North Franklin Street
Chicago, IL 60606

HEALTH SCIENCES LIBRARIANS

Principal activity: Collecting and compiling biomedical information

Work commitment: Usually full time

Preprofessional education: Bachelor's degree

Program length: 1 to 2 years

Work prerequisites: Master of library science degree

Career opportunities: Average

Income range: $25,000 to $60,000

Scope

An essential component of any health education institution is its medical library. This is where information is kept—information vital to the teaching and research activities of faculty, staff, and students. With the major technological advances in medicine over the past decades, there has been an explosion of knowledge. Today, in addition to housing books and journals, libraries are linked by computers to a worldwide network that permits unlimited access to information.

Activities

Medical librarians are information specialists trained in the health sciences. They are responsible for securing the most suitable books, journals, and other materials for their institutions, and then cataloging those materials so they can be readily retrieved. Librarians help library users find the information they need for their work or studies. They teach users about the library's organization, acquire materials requested by users from other libraries, and update computer databases with bibliographic information. Thus, librarians at a medical school or hospital have access to MEDLINE, the general medical retrieval system operated by the National Library of Medicine, and to specialized databases focused on major diseases or subjects. Some hospital librarians also bring reading materials to patients.

Work Settings

Medical librarians work in a wide variety of health sciences institutions, including schools of medicine, dentistry, veterinary medicine, nursing, pharmacy, and allied health. Some work in medical centers, hospitals, research institutes, pharmaceutical companies, and professional health-care associations.

Advancement

With experience and certification, a librarian can gain additional responsibilities and become manager of a specialized area of library operations.

Education/Training

A bachelor's degree is the basic prerequisite for undertaking an education in library science. Master's degree programs are accredited by the American Library Association and last one to two years. Courses deal with scientific literature, biomedical communication, use of bibliographic and informational resources, library organization and management, and standard cataloging systems.

Certification/Registration/Licensure

The Medical Library Association offers four levels of accreditation for librarians. Getting a higher-level accreditation can help a librarian advance to a more responsible position or to a management position.

Career Potential

Prospects for employment in this field are stable for the immediate future, because of the enormous quantity of biomedical information being published. Since the number of librarians coming into the profession is significant, however, competition for more attractive positions is intense.

For More Information

The professional organization for this field is Medical Library Association, 6 North Michigan Avenue, Chicago, IL 60602.

Health Sciences Librarian Programs

Alabama

University of Alabama
Tuscaloosa, AL 35487
www.ua.edu/

Arizona

University of Arizona
Tucson, AZ 85721
www.arizona.edu/

California

University of California, Los Angeles
405 Hilgard Avenue
Los Angeles, CA 90024
www.ucla.edu/

San Jose State University
1 Washington Square
San Jose, CA 95192
www.sjsu.edu/

Connecticut

Southern Connecticut State University
501 Crescent Street
New Haven, CT 06515
http://scwww.ctstateu.edu/

District of Columbia

Catholic University of America
620 Michigan Avenue NE
Washington, DC 20064
www.cua.edu/

Florida

University of South Florida
Tampa, FL 33620
www.usf.edu/

Georgia

Clark Atlanta University
J.P. Brawley Drive at Fair Street, SW
Atlanta, GA 30314
http://galaxy.cau.edu/cau/ctsps.html

Hawaii

University of Hawaii
2530 Dole Street, C-200
Honolulu, HI 96822
www.uhwo.hawaii.edu/

Illinois

University of Illinois
2318 Alumni Hall
Chicago, IL 60607
www.uic.edu/

Dominican University
River Forest, IL 60305
www.rosary.edu/

Indiana

Indiana University
300 North Jordan Avenue
Bloomington, IN 47405
www.indiana.edu/

Iowa

University of Iowa
Iowa City, IA 52242
www.uiowa.edu/

Kansas

Emporia State University
Emporia, KS 66801
www.emporia.edu/

Kentucky

University of Kentucky
Lexington, KY 40506
www.uky.edu/

Maryland

University of Maryland
Baltimore, MD 21228
www.umd.edu/

Massachusetts

Simmons College
300 The Fenway
Boston, MA 02115
www.simmons.edu/

Michigan

University of Michigan
Dearborn, MI 48128
www.umich.edu/

Wayne State University
Detroit, MI 48202
www.wayne.edu/

Mississippi

University of Southern Mississippi
Hattiesburg, MS 38677
www.usm.edu/

Missouri

University of Missouri–Columbia
Columbia, MO 65211
www.missouri.edu/

New York

SUNY at Albany
Albany, NY 12222
www.albany.edu/

Long Island University
University Plaza
Brooklyn, NY 11201
www.liunet.edu/

Pratt Institute
Information Science Studies
Brooklyn, NY 11205
www.pratt.edu/

SUNY at Buffalo
Capen Hall
Buffalo, NY 14260
www.buffalo.edu/

Queens College
65-30 Kissena Boulevard
Flushing, NY 11367
www.qc.edu/

St. John's University
8000 Utopia Pkwy
Jamaica, NY 11439
www.stjohns.edu/

Syracuse University
Syracuse, NY 13244
www.syr.edu/

North Carolina

University of North Carolina
University Heights
Asheville, NC 28804
www.unca.edu/

North Carolina Central University
Durham, NC 27707
www.nccu.edu/

University of North Carolina at Greensboro
Greensboro, NC 27412
www.uncg.edu/

Ohio

Kent University
Kent, OH 44242
www.kent.edu/

Oklahoma

University of Oklahoma
407 West Boyd
Norman, OK 73019
www.ou.edu/

Pennsylvania

Clarion University of Pennsylvania
Clarion, PA 16214
www.clarion.edu/

Drexel University
Philadelphia, PA 19104
www.drexel.edu/

University of Pittsburgh
Bruce Hall, 2nd Floor
Pittsburgh, PA 15260
www.pitt.edu/

Rhode Island

University of Rhode Island
Kingston, RI 02881
www.uri.edu/

Texas

University of Texas at Austin
Austin, TX 78712
www.ut.edu/

University of North Texas
Box 13797
Denton, TX 76203
www.unt.edu/

Texas Woman's University
Denton, TX 76204
www.twu.edu/

Washington

University of Washington
Seattle, WA 98195
www.washington.edu/

Wisconsin

University of Wisconsin, Madison
756 University Avenue
Madison, WI 53706
www.wisc.edu/

University of Wisconsin, Milwaukee
P.O. Box 413
Milwaukee, WI 53201
www.uwm.edu/

HEALTH SOCIOLOGISTS

Principal activity: Securing sociological data relevant to health care

Work commitment: Full-time

Preprofessional education: Bachelor's degree

Program length: 2 to 4 years

Work prerequisites: Master's or doctoral degree

Career opportunities: Favorable

Income range: $33,000 to $60,000

Scope

Since the last century, doctors have discovered treatments for many diseases, using antibiotics and other medicines, and such preventive measures as inoculations.

There is another aspect to health care, however: Social factors also influence the incidence and course of disease. Health sociologists track who gets sick and why, and get information on how people respond to different treatment options. Armed with this information, they can advise medical professionals on how to choose the best treatment modes for a widespread disease.

Activities

Health sociologists seek information on a wide variety of issues. They study the underlying social factors that motivate people to seek medical attention, the interactions of health-care providers with patients and with each other, people's reactions to technological advances, and community responses to the danger of infectious diseases. An emerging area of specialization is health issues of the elderly.

Work Settings

Health sociologists are employed by federal agencies, state health departments, research institutes, and universities.

Advancement

With experience a sociologist can be promoted to higher levels of authority and responsibility. Earning a Ph.D. enhances their employment and advancement opportunities.

Prerequisites

A bachelor's degree with a major in sociology or a closely related field is the basis for the advanced degree required to enter this profession.

Desirable personal attributes include sound judgment, superior skills in oral and written communication, computer capabilities, patience, and perseverance.

Education/Training

Candidates should secure a master's degree in sociology, which requires two years of full-time graduate work and completion of a thesis.

Securing a Ph.D. greatly enhances one's marketability. A doctorate degree usually takes about four years and requires completion of a thesis.

Certification/Registration/Licenserure

Certification is offered by the American Sociological Association and the Sociological Practice Association. No license is needed to work in this field.

Career Potential

It is difficult to make a definitive projection for this field, but it appears that employment opportunities will increase. The health-care industry will need much more information on elder-care issues as the population ages.

For More Information

The professional organizations for this field are listed below:

The American Sociological Association
1722 N Street NW
Washington, DC 20036

Sociological Practice Association
Department of Sociology
2247 AB Wayne State University
Detroit, Michigan 48202

INSTRUCTORS FOR THE BLIND

Principal activity: Teaching visually impaired people to be mobile and independent as much as possible

Work commitment: Part- or full-time

Preprofessional education: High school diploma

Program length: 4 to 6 years

Work prerequisites: Bachelor's degree required; master's degree preferred

Career opportunities: Excellent

Income range: $30,000 to $45,000

Scope

The loss of vision, unfortunately, is not a rare occurrence in our society. It can be due to congenital factors, ophthalmologic disease, or injury. While devastating, the impact of blindness can be somewhat diminished by giving the patient the skills that allow for greater mobility. This affords the visually impaired person a greater sense of independence and enhances self-worth. Instructors for the blind provide this training.

Activities

Instructors first evaluate their clients to determine the nature and extent of their visual impairments. Then they form a plan for each individual and outline a schedule to implement them. They teach clients to become physically oriented to their surroundings by using their senses of hearing and touch. The initial goal is mobility within a person's own neighborhood, but then it is broadened as much as possible. Mobility skills usually are taught on an individual basis, but other skills may be presented in a group setting.

Work Settings

These instructors work in private homes, VA hospitals, schools, rehabilitation centers, and community centers for the blind.

Advancement

With experience and a master's degree, an instructor's earning potential increases significantly.

Prerequisites

A high school diploma or its equivalent is required before undertaking studies for a bachelor's degree.

Since a master's degree is the preferred educational level, students should plan on completing a batchelor's degree first, then applying to an accredited master's program.

Desirable personal attributes include patience and perseverance, strong verbal communication skills, compassion, and a desire to help the visually handicapped.

Education/Training

The standard educational requirement is a master's degree. This two-year program involves both classroom and clinical experience, including an internship. More than 15 colleges and universities offer master's degrees in this field.

Because there currently is a serious shortage of instructors, individuals holding a bachelor's degree can readily secure employment.

Certification/Registration/Licenserure

Currently there are no state licensing requirements. Those who meet the educational and experience requirements can be certified by the Association for the Education and Rehabilitation of the Blind and Visually Impaired.

Career Potential

Employment prospects are favorable now because their is an acute shortage of instructors. As the older population increases in this country, many will experience vision problems as well, so the need for instructors should remain strong.

For More Information

The professional organization for this field is the Foundation for the Blind, 15 West 16th Street, New York, NY 10011.

The accrediting agency is the Association for the Education and Rehabilitation of the Blind, 4600 Duke Street, Alexandria, VA 22304.

Instructor for the Blind Programs

For a complete list of schools offering a master's degree in this field, contact the Association for the Education and Rehabilitation of the Blind and Visually Impaired at the address listed above.

MEDICAL ILLUSTRATORS

Principal activity: Providing illustrations for medical materials

Work commitment: Part- or full-time

Preprofessional education: Bachelor's degree

Program length: 2 to 3 years

Work prerequisites: Master's degree

Career opportunities: Favorable

Income range: $35,000 to $65,000

Scope

Medical illustrators provide the visual elements for the textbooks and journals used to train other medical professionals. They also provide illustrations for the journals and magazines that bring medical findings to the attention of the larger community. These illustrations enhance the readability and clarity of sometimes complicated materials. Thus, illustrators are important contributors to health education.

Activities

Medical illustrators are artists who use their creative talents to produce illustrations, charts, and graphs for textbooks, journals, magazines, and exhibit displays. They may graphically represent the steps of an operation or recreate what can be seen under a microscope. Given the wide variety of assignments that may receive, illustrators need to be knowledgeable in a variety of techniques and media, including diagramming, drawing, painting, preparing models, and creating audiovisual aids.

Advancement

Advancement comes with experience and with specialization in different areas of medicine or with different media.

Prerequisites

The standard requirement is a bachelor's degree with a major in art. The courses include drawing, life drawing, painting, design, theory of color, illustration techniques, photography, and layout. Students also should secure a solid background in the sciences, including chemistry, biology, anatomy, developmental biology, physiology, histology, and microbiology. Developing an attractive portfolio of illustrative materials is essential.

Besides an interest in art and science, desirable attributes include creativity, an ability to translate scientific information into a clear and attractive format, patience, and the ability to work with demanding professionals under the pressure of deadlines.

Education/Training

A master's degree in medical illustration is offered by a few institutions, whose programs are accredited by the Association of Medical Illustrators. Most programs include gross anatomy, histology, physiology, human embryology, neuroanatomy, pathology, illustration in print and nonprint media, anatomical and surgical illustration, three-dimensional modeling, graph and chart design, exhibit construction, and cinematography.

Certification/Registration/Licensure

Certification can be secured through the Association of Medical Illustrators.

Career Potential

The employment outlook in this field is favorable, especially for those holding a master's degree from an accredited program.

For More Information

The professional organization is the Association of Medical Illustrators, 1819 Peachtree Road NE, Suite 712, Atlanta, GA 30309.

Medical Illustrator Programs

Georgia

Medical College of Georgia
Augusta, GA 30912
www.mcg.edu/

Illinois

University of Illinois at Chicago
1919 West Taylor Street
Chicago, IL 60612
www.uic.edu/

Maryland

Johns Hopkins University
School of Medicine
1830 East Monument Street, Suite 7000
Baltimore, MD 21205
www.jhu.edu/

Michigan

University of Michigan
2000 Bonisteel Boulevard
Ann Arbor, MI 48109
www.umich.edu/

Texas

University of Texas
Southwestern Medical Center
5323 Hines Boulevard
Dallas, TX 75235
www.swmed.edu/

Canada

University of Toronto
1 King's College Circle
Toronto, Ontario
Canada, M5S 1A8
www.utoronto.ca/

MEDICAL AND PSYCHIATRIC SOCIAL WORKERS

Principal activity: Helping patients adjust to life's circumstances

Work commitment: Full-time

Preprofessional education: High school diploma

Program length: 4 to 6 years

Work prerequisites: Bachelor's degree required; master's degree preferred

Career opportunities: Very favorable

Income range: $25,000 to $45,000

Scope

Medical social workers help patients (and their families) recovering from illness and those who are chronically ill or disabled cope with the varied stresses generated by their conditions. *Psychiatric social workers* focus on the needs of those with emotional problems, helping them adjust to home life and their community with a minimum of anxiety. These social workers are important members of the therapeutic professional community.

Activities

The activities of a medical social worker may involve finding home care for a senior citizen, arranging placement for a patient in a convalescent home, securing help for the parents of a newborn with congenital medical problems, or helping a family cope with a parent who is seriously ill. Medical social workers are often called upon to explain to family members the nature of a patient's illness and its short- and long-term impact on all aspects of their lives. Their duties vary daily, as they play a significant role in the health-care team.

Psychiatric social workers similarly have varied responsibilities. They may serve as a liaison between patient, family, and staff; explain the nature of a patient's illness to the family in understandable terms; write reports on patient progress; help in the relocation of patients to society; maintain contact to monitor their progress; and arrange for them to receive additional services.

Work Settings

These social workers are employed by all kinds of hospitals, nursing homes, long-term care facilities, clinics, home health agencies, crisis centers, public health departments, and residence homes for the mentally disabled.

Advancement

Advancement to a supervisory position may come with increased education, certification, and experience.

Prerequisites

A high school diploma or its equivalent is necessary to undertake college studies for a bachelor's degree in social work.

Desirable personal attributes include a sincere concern for the well-being of others, emotional maturity, sound judgment, the ability to work with people from all social strata, good decision-making skills, patience, and the fortitude for working with people in crisis situations.

Education/Training

The minimum level of education necessary is a bachelor's degree in social work (BSW). Hundreds of colleges and universities offer programs accredited by the Council on Social Work Education. Such programs include courses in human behavior and the social environment, social welfare policy and services, methods of social work, and field experience.

A master's degree (MSW) is advisable for medical social work. It takes two years of study, but it is required for many positions. More than 100 institutions offer such a program, which mandates a bachelor's as a prerequisite.

Those seeking teaching appointments should enroll in doctoral programs that require additional course work and a thesis. About 50 institutions currently offer degrees at this level.

Certification/Registration/Licensure

Voluntary certification can be secured from the Academy of Certified Social Workers. This certification requires an MSW, two years of experience, membership in the National Association of Social Workers, and passing a written examination.

All states require that social workers be certified, registered, or licensed.

Career Potential

The employment outlook for social workers is very favorable for the foreseeable future. This positive outlook is the result of an expanding population, especially of senior citizens. In addition, advances in medical technology and the emphases on community care for the emotionally disturbed and on substance abuse treatment have added to an increased need for social workers in the U.S.

For More Information

The professional organization for this field is the National Association of Social Workers, 700 First Street NE, Washington, DC 20002.

MEDICAL SECRETARIES

Principal activity: Maintaining office duties in a physician's practice

Work commitment: Full-time

Preprofessional education: High school diploma

Program length: 2 to 3 years

Work prerequisites: High school diploma required; college or business courses preferred

Career opportunities: Favorable

Income range: $20,000 to $40,000

Scope

Secretaries are the communication centers of an office. They are largely responsible for the efficient functioning of the facility. Medical secretaries are employed by physicians or by institutions where physicians work.

Activities

Medical secretaries type letters, transcribe dictation, set appointments, arrange for hospitalizations, and order supplies. They operate a variety of different types of equipment that facilitate communication and optimize office efficiency.

Work Settings

Medical secretaries are employed by private practice physicians or by groups of physicians. Some work in hospitals, clinics, HMOs, insurance companies, and other agencies.

Advancement

Opportunities for advancement come with experience and training, and with the demonstration of organizational and managerial talent. It is also facilitated by enhancing one's knowledge of the medical field. Upward mobility may be reflected by being appointed an administrative assistant or office manager.

Prerequisites

A high school diploma or its equivalent is necessary for work in this field.

Desirable personal attributes include a neat appearance, a pleasant personality, attention to detail, and the ability to be discreet and to maintain confidentiality.

Education/Training

Training is offered at many business high schools, but college preparation is preferred. Candidates should take courses in English, typing, computers, and business practices. Courses in medical vocabulary are also desirable.

Secretaries must be able to operate various pieces of office equipment, such as a computer, FAX machine, photocopier, and switchboard. Training in word processing, database management, spread sheets, desktop publishing, and graphics is desirable.

Certification/Registration/Licensure

Highly trained and experienced secretaries who pass a series of examinations offered by the National Secretaries' Association may qualify for the designation *certified professional secretary*. This recognition carries weight with prospective employers.

Career Potential

With the continued growth of the health-care industry, there will be a continuing demand for medical secretaries. Thus, the job outlook in this field is favorable.

For More Information

There is no professional organization for medical secretaries.

Medical Secretary Programs

California

La Sierra University
Riverside, CA 92515
www.lasierra.edu/

Colorado

Denver Technical College
925 South Niagara Street
Denver, CO 80224
www.dtc.edu/

Idaho

Boise State University
1910 University Drive
Boise, ID 83725
www.idbsu.edu/

Indiana

Indiana University
3400 Broadway
Gary, IN 46408
www.indiana.edu/

Kansas

Washburn University of Topeka
Topeka, KS 66621
www.wuacc.edu/

Maryland

Villa Julie College
Stevenson, MD 21153
www.vjc.edu/

Michigan

Baker College of Auburn Hills
1500 University Drive
Auburn Hills, MI 48326
www.baker.edu/

Baker College of Mt. Clemens
34950 Little Mack
Clinton Township, MI 48035
www.baker.edu/

Baker College of Flint
1050 West Bristol Road
Flint, MI 48507
www.baker.edu/

Davenport College
415 East Fulton
Grand Rapids, MI 49503
www.davenport.edu/

Davenport College
4123 West Main Street
Kalamazoo, MI 49006
www.davenport.edu/

Northern Michigan University
Marquette, MI 49855
www.nmu.edu/

Baker College of Muskegon
123 East Apple Avenue
Muskegon, MI 49442
www.baker.edu/

Baker College of Owosso
Owosso, MI 48667
www.baker.edu/

Baker College of Port Huron
3403 Lapeer Road
Port Huron, MI 48060
www.baker.edu/

Cleary College
Ypsilanti, MI 48197
www.cleary.edu/

Nebraska

Midland Lutheran College
Fremont, NE 68025
www.mlc.edu/

New Mexico

Eastern New Mexico University
Station #5, ENMU
Portales, NM 88130
www.enmu.edu/

Western New Mexico University
College Avenue
Silver City, NM 88062
www.wnmu.edu/

North Dakota

Minot State University
Minot, ND 58707
http://warp6.cs.misu.nodak.edu/

Ohio

University of Akron
381 Buchtel Common
Akron, OH 44325
www.uakron.edu/

University of Cincinnati
100 Edwards Center
Cincinnati, OH 45221
www.uc.edu/

Wright State University
Dayton, OH 45435
www.wright.edu/

University of Toledo
Toledo, OH 43606
www.utoledo.edu/

Oregon

Oregon Institute of Technology
Klamath Falls, OR 97601
www.oit.osshe.edu/

Pennsylvania

Waynesburg College
Waynesburg, PA 15370
www.waynesburg.edu/

York College of Pennsylvania
York, PA 17405
www.ycp.edu/

Rhode Island

Johnson & Wales University
8 Abbott Park Place
Providence, RI 02903
www.jwu.edu/

Tennessee

Middle Tennessee State University
Murfreesboro, TN 37132
www.mtsu.edu/

Trevecca Nazarene College
333 Murfreesboro Road
Nashville, TN 37210
www.trevecca.edu/

Martin Methodist College
Pulaski, TN 38478
www.martinmethodist.edu/

Texas

Lamar University–Beaumont
4400 Martin Luther King Highway
Beaumont, TX 77710
www/lamar.edu/

Utah

Weber State University
3750 Harrison Boulevard
Ogden, UT 84408
www.weber.edu/

Washington

Walla Walla College
College Place, WA 99324
www.wwc.edu/

West Virginia

College of West Virginia
Beckley, WV 25802
www.cwv.edu/

Marshall University
400 Hal Greer Boulevard
Huntington, WV 25755
www.marshall.edu/

West Virginia University
Institute of Technology
Montgomery, WV 25136
http://wvit.wvnet.edu/

Wisconsin

Concordia University–Wisconsin
Mequon, WI 53097
www.cuw.edu/

MENTAL HEALTH WORKERS

Principal activity: Helping to care for emotionally or developmentally disabled persons

Work commitment: Full-time

Preprofessional education: High school diploma

Program length: 2 years

Work prerequisites: High school diploma required; associate degree preferred

Career opportunities: Favorable

Income range: $20,000 to $35,000

Scope

For centuries, people with emotional and mental problems were shunned and mistreated by others. Persecution and discrimination still occur in this country. Although there are ongoing debates in scientific circles over how best to treat the mentally ill and developmentally disabled, many workers at various professional levels provide services to these people. Among these are mental health workers. They are responsible for providing a wide variety of therapeutic, supportive, and protective services. They deal with mentally handicapped people of all ages, emotionally ill individuals, and people suffering from substance addictions. These mental workers are important members of the health-care team.

Activities

Mental health workers motivate their clients to use their skills and to acquire new ones, help them carry out therapeutic exercises, administer medications and treatments, take vital signs, provide behavior modifications and counseling, serve as patient advocates, and act as a resource for patients and their families during the transition to an outside home. All of these activities are carried out under the supervision of a registered nurse or social worker.

Work Settings

Mental health workers are employed by mental health facilities such as state and private hospitals, community health centers, mental health clinics, schools for the mentally disabled, crisis centers, nursing homes, child guidance clinics, and private psychiatric offices.

Prerequisites

There are no standard prerequisites for the field at present. While it is not always required, a high school diploma or its equivalent is highly desirable.

The more common route to employment in this field is acquiring some post-high school course work in mental health—perhaps leading to an associate degree, which usually takes two years.

Desirable personal attributes include emotional stability, a strong sense of compassion, good health and stamina, strong verbal communication skills, patience, a good sense of humor, and dependability.

Education/Training

Many community colleges offer programs in mental health and human services, leading to an associate degree. These programs involve courses in basic and psychiatric nursing, general and abnormal psychology, mental health technology, theory of personality and social development, child development and growth, group dynamics, and sociology. As part of the program, students have the opportunity to get experience working with clients in a mental health setting.

Certification/Registration/Licensure

Certification does not as yet exist, but several states have instituted a licensure requirement for mental health workers. Other states are expected to follow suite and institute their own requirements.

Career Potential

We expect that employment opportunities will increase in this field in the coming years. This is due to two major developments in the mental health field: First, more and more patients are being moved from mental health hospitals into community-based facilities. Second, the industry is coming to recognize and accept that mental health workers provide cost-effective service to individuals who are in transition or have been placed in community settings. In either case, patients will need the kind of assistance that mental health workers provide.

For More Information

While there is no professional organization for this field, you can write for more information from one of the agencies listed below:

National Association of Social Workers
750 First Street NE
Washington, DC 20002

Council on Social Work Education
1600 Duke Street
Alexandria, VA 22314.

Mental Health Worker Programs

Arkansas

University of Central Arkansas
Conway, AR 72035
www.uca.edu/

California

California State University
5151 State University Drive
Los Angeles, CA 90032
www.csula.edu/

Illinois

Northern Illinois University
De Kalb, IL 60115
www.niu.edu/

Governors State University
University Park, IL 60466
www.govst.edu/

National-Louis University
1000 Capitol Drive
Evanston, IL 60201
http://nlu.nl.edu/

Indiana

Indiana University Purdue University
2101 Coliseum Boulevard East
Ft. Wayne, IN 46805
www.ipfw.indiana.edu/

Indiana Wesleyan University
Marion, IN 46953
www.indwes.edu/

Kansas

Emporia State University
Emporia, KS 66801
www.emporia.edu/

Pittsburgh State University
Pittsburgh, KS 66762
www.pittsburgh.edu/

Kansas-Newman College
3100 McCormick Avenue
Wichita, KS 67213
www.ksnewman.edu/

Washburn University
Topeka, KS 66621
www.wuacc.edu/

Kentucky

Northern Kentucky University
400 Highland Heights
Highland Heights, KY 41099
www.nku.edu/

Louisiana

Louisiana State University Medical Center
433 Bolivar Street
New Orleans, LA 70112
www.lsumc.edu/

Maine

University of New England
Hill Beach Road
Biddeford, ME 04005
www.une.edu/

University of Maine at Farmington
Farmington, ME 04938
www.umf.maine.edu/

Maryland

Morgan State University
Cold Spring Lane and Hillen Road
Baltimore, MD 21239
www.morgan.edu/

Massachusetts

Boston University
121 Bay Street Road
Boston, MA 02215
http://web.bu.edu/

Emmanuel College
400 The Fenway
Boston, MA 02115
www.emmanuel.edu/

Springfield College
Springfield, MA 01109
www.spfldcol.edu/

Michigan

Lake Superior State University
Sault Sainte Marie, MI 49783
www.lssu.edu/

Minnesota

St. Cloud State University
St. Cloud, MN 56301
www.stcloud.msus.edu/

Missouri

Evangel College
1111 North Glenstone
Springfield, MO 65802
www.evangel.edu/

New Jersey

Thomas Edison State College
101 West State Street
Trenton, NJ 08608
www.tesc.edu/

New York

Elmira College
Elmira, NY 14901
www.elmira.edu/

New York Institute of Technology
Old Westbury, NY 11568
www.nyit.edu/

North Carolina

Western Carolina University
Cullowhee, NC 28723
www.wcu.edu/

Ohio

Wright State University
Fairborn, OH 45435
www.wright.edu/

Franciscan University of Steubenville
1235 University Blvd.
Steubenville, OH 43952
www.franuniv.edu/

University of Toledo
Toledo, OH 43606
www.utoledo.edu/

Pennsylvania

Gannon University
University Square
Erie, PA 16541
www.gannon.edu/

MCP Hahnemann University
201 North 15th Street, Mail Stop 506
Philadelphia, PA 19102
www.auhs.edu/

Texas

West Texas A & M University
P.O. Box 907
Canyon, TX 79016
www.wtamu.edu/

University of North Texas
P.O. Box 13797
Denton, TX 76203
www.unt.edu/

Virginia

Virginia Commonwealth University
821 Franklin Street
Richmond, VA 23284
www.vcu.edu/

West Virginia

Marshall University
400 Hal Greer Boulevard.
Huntington, WV 25755
www.marshall.edu/

APPENDIX A

HEALTH-CARE CAREER OPTIONS: ALTERNATIVE LISTING

Anesthesiology Careers

Anesthesiologist Assistant
Nurse Anesthetist

Cardiovascular Medicine Careers

Cardiovascular Technologist
EKG Technician
Perfusionist
Pulmonary Function Technologist
Respiratory Therapist/Technician

Dental Careers

Dental Assistant
Dental Hygienist
Dental Laboratory Technician

Diagnostic Technology Careers

Diagnostic Medical Sonographer
EEG Technician/Technologist

Dietetic Careers

Dietary Manager
Dietetic Technician

Dietitian

Food Technologist

Eye Care Careers

Ophthalmic Assistant
Ophthalmic Technician
Ophthalmic Technologist
Optician
Optometric Assistant
Optometric Technician
Optometrist
Orthoptist

Engineering Careers

Biomedical Engineer
Biomedical Laboratory Technician

Health Information Careers

Biomedical Photographer
Biomedical Writer
Certified Athletic Trainer
Child Life Specialist
Genetics Counselor
Health Information Technician
Health Sciences Librarian
Health Services Administrator
Instructor for the Blind
Medical Illustrator
Medical Social Worker
Patient Representative

Health Practitioner Careers

Chiropractor
Emergency Medical Technician
Medical Assistant

Pharmacist
Physicians Assistant
Podiatrist
Surgeon Assistant
Veterinarian
Veterinary Assistant

Laboratory Medicine Careers

Blood Bank Technologist and Specialist
Clinical Laboratory Technician/Technologist
Cytotechnologist
Histology Technician

Mental Health Careers

Psychiatric Social Worker
Mental Health Assistant
Mental Health Worker
Psychiatric Aide

Nursing Careers

Licensed Practical Nurse
Nurse Midwife
Nurse Practitioner
Registered Nurse

Nurse's Aide

Public Health Careers

Health Educator
Health Sociologist
Environmental Health Scientist

Radiology Careers

Diagnostic Medical Sonographer
Nuclear Medical Technologist
Radiation Therapy Technologist
Radiological Technologist

Rehabilitation Therapy Careers

Art Therapist
Dance /Movement Therapist
Home Health Aide
Horticultural Therapist
Music Therapist
Occupational Therapist
Occupational Therapy Assistant
Orthotic-Prosthetic-Technician
Physical Therapist
Physical Therapy Assistant

APPENDIX B

ADMISSIONS TESTS

The admission tests listed here are the ones you are likely to face as a health-care student:

Medical College Admission Test (MCAT) for podiatry

Veterinary College Admission Test (VCAT) for veterinary medicine

Pharmacy College Admission Test (PCAT) for pharmacy

Optometry Admission Test (OAT) for optometry

Allied Health Professions Admission Test (AHPAT) applies to a wide variety of professions

Graduate Record Examination (GRE) for admission to some graduate programs

In this appendix, we'll briefly discuss each of these tests, outlining their fees, content, and where to get them.

Medical College Admission Test

The Medical College Admission Test (MCAT) is required for admission to podiatry and medical schools. The extent to which test scores are used in the screening process varies from school to school. Generally, the admissions officer looks at your test scores, your undergraduate records, your references, and your interview performance in making the decision.

The MCAT is administered and scored by the MCAT Program. For an application or more information, contact:

MCAT Program
P.O. Box 4057
Iowa City, IA 52243
(319) 337-1357

Content

The MCAT consists of four separate sections:

1. **Verbal reasoning**: 65 questions (85 minutes)
2. **Physical sciences**: 77 questions (100 minutes)
3. **Writing sample**: 1 question (60 minutes)
4. **Biological sciences**: 77 questions (100) minutes

Test Fees

Fee $155   ***Sunday test fee*** $10 extra

Veterinary College Admission Test (VCAT)

The VCAT measures achievement in the basic sciences. For an application packet containing sample questions, contact:

Psychological Corporation
P.O. Box 96152
Chicago, IL 60693
(800) 228-0752

Contents

The VCAT consists of about 230 multiple-choice questions. Each question has four answer choices, only one of which is correct. The test lasts about 3½ hours, with a short break midway through.

There are five content areas, and you are allowed to work on each area only during the fixed time allotted for it. You cannot go back to earlier sections.

1. **Verbal ability:** 50 questions
2. **Biology:** 50 questions
3. **Chemistry:** 50 questions
4. **Quantitative ability:** 40 questions
5. **Reading comprehension:** 40 questions

Test Fees

Fee $60

Pharmacy College Admission Test

The PCAT measures general academic ability and scientific knowledge. The test is prepared and administered by the Psychological Corporation. For an application packet containing sample questions, contact:

Psychological Corporation
P.O. Box 91518
Chicago, IL 60693
(800) 622-3231

Content

The PCAT consists of about 300 multiple-choice questions. Each question has four answer choices, only one of which is correct. The test lasts 3½ hours, with two short breaks.

There are five content areas, and you are allowed to work on each area only during the fixed time allotted for it. You cannot go back to earlier sections:

1. **Verbal ability:** 50 questions
2. **Quantitative ability:** 65 questions
3. **Biology:** 60 questions
4. **Chemistry:** 60 questions
5. **Reading comprehension:** 45 questions

Test Fees

Fee: $40

Optometry Admission Test

The OAT measures academic ability and comprehension of scientific information.

The test is administered by the Optometry Admission Testing Program. For an application packet containing sample questions, contact:

Optometry Admission Testing Program
211 East Chicago Avenue
Chicago, IL 60611
(312) 440-2678

Contents

The OAT consists of 100 multiple-choice questions. Each question has four answer choices, only one of which is correct. The test lasts 5 hours and 20 minutes, with a 30-minute rest period.

There are three content areas, and you are allowed to work on each area only during the fixed time allotted for it. You cannot go back to earlier sections:

1. **Biology:** 40 questions
2. **General chemistry:** 30 questions
3. **Organic chemistry:** 30 questions

Test Fees

Fee: $80

Allied Health Professions Admission Test

The AHPAT measures general academic ability and scientific knowledge.

The AHPAT is prepared and administered by the Psychological Corporation. For an application packet containing sample questions, contact:

Psychological Corporation
P.O. Box 99596
Chicago, IL 60693
(800) 622-3231

Content

The AHPAT consists of approximately 300 multiple-choice questions. Each question has four answer choices, only one of which is correct.

There are five content areas, and you are allowed to work on each area only during the fixed time allotted for it. You cannot go back to earlier sections:

1. **Verbal ability:** 75 questions
2. **Quantitative ability:** 50 questions
3. **Biology:** 50 questions
4. **Chemistry:** 50 questions
5. **Reading comprehension:** 45 questions

Test Fees

Fee: $40

Graduate Record Examinations

The Graduate Record Examinations (GREs) are taken by persons applying to graduate schools for a post-baccalaureate degree. The test is offered in both computer- or paper-based formats. In addition, the GREs are offered as a general test or as specific subject tests. Most allied health programs that require a GRE score expect the applicant to take the general test.

The test is administered by the Educational Testing Service. For an application packet and a sample general practice test, contact:

Educational Testing Service
Princeton, NJ 08541
(609) 771-7670

Contents

The GRE general test takes 3½ to 4 hours to complete. This test measures verbal, quantitative, and analytical reasoning skills not necessarily related to any particular field of study.

You must work on the different sections sequentially and you cannot return to a section that has been completed. A sample format of a general test follows:

Section 1: 38 questions (30 minutes)
Section 2: 25 questions (30 minutes)
Section 3: 30 questions (30 minutes)
Section 4: 38 questions (30 minutes)
Section 5: 25 questions (30 minutes)
Section 6: 30 questions (30 minutes)
Section 7: 3 questions (15 minutes)

Test Fees

General test fee: $96
Subject test fee: $120

APPENDIX C

ALLIED HEALTH PROFESSIONAL ORGANIZATIONS

American Academy of Anesthesiologist
Assistants
P.O. Box 33876
Decatur, GA 30033

American Academy of Physician Assistants
950 N. Washington Street
Alexandria, VA 22314

American Art Therapy Association, Inc.
1202 Allanson Road
Mundelein, IL 60060

American Association of Blood Banks
8101 Glenbrook Road
Bethesda, MD 20814

American Association of Colleges of Nursing
I DuPont Circle
Washington, DC 20036

American Association of Colleges of Pharmacy
1426 Prince Street
Alexandria, VA 22314

American Association of Colleges of Podiatric
Medicine
1350 Piccard Drive
Rockville, MD 20850

American Association of Medical Assistants
20 N. Wacker Drive
Chicago, IL 60606

American Chiropractic Association
1701 Clarendon Blvd.
Arlington, VA 22209

American College of Nurse-Midwives
818 Connecticut Avenue, NW
Washington, DC 20006

American Dance Therapy Association, Inc.
2000 Century Plaza
Columbia, MD 21044

American Dental Assistants' Association
203 La Salle Street
Chicago, IL 60601

American Dental Hygienists' Association
444 N. Michigan Avenue
Chicago, IL 60611

American Dietetic Assoc.
216 W Jackson Blvd. St800
Chicago, IL 60606

American Health Information Management
Association
919 N. Michigan Avenue
Chicago, IL 60611

American Nurses' Association
600 Maryland Avenue SW
Washington, DC 20024

American Occupational Therapy Association
4270 Mongomery Lane
Bethesda, MD 20824

American Optometric Association
243 North Lindberg Boulevard
St. Louis, MO 63141

American Pharmaceutical Association
2215 Constitution Avenue, NW
Washington, DC 20037

American Physical Therapy Association
1111 N. Fairfax Street
Alexandria, VA 22314

American Podiatric Medical Association
9312 Old Georgetown Road
Bethesda, MD 20814

American Society of Clinical Laboratory
Sciences
7910 Woodmont Avenue
Bethesda, MD 20814

American Society of Cardiovascular
Professionals
10500 Wakeman Drive
Fredericksburg, VA 22407

American Society of Echocardiography
4101 Lake Bone Trail
Raleigh, NC 27607

American Speech-Language Hearing
Association
10801 Rockville Pike
Rockville, MD 20852

American Veterinary Medical Association
1931 North Meacham Road
Schaumburg, IL 60173

Association of American Veterinary Colleges
1101 Vermont Avenue, NW
Washington, DC 20005

Association of Physician Assistant Programs
950 North Washington Street
Alexandria, VA 22314

Association of Surgical Technologists
7108-C South Alton Way
Englewood, CO 80112

Institute of Food Technologist
221 North La Salle Street
Chicago, IL 60601

American Academy of Orthotists and
Prosthetists
717 Pendleton Street
Alexandria, VA 22314

American College of Health Care
Administrators
325 South Patrick Street
Alexandria, VA 22314

American Medical Technologists
710 Higgins Road
Park Ridge, IL 60068

American Society of Electroneuro Diagnostic
Technologists
204 W Seventh Street
Carroll, IA 51401

Foundation of Hospice and Home Care
519 C Street NE
Washington, DC 20002

Society of Nuclear Medicine-Technologists
1830 Samuel Morse Drive
Reston, VA 22090

Society of Diagnostic Medical Sonographers
12770 Cott Road
Dallas, TX 75251

American Society of Radiologic Technologists
15000 Central Avenue, SE
Albuquerque, NM 87123

American Association for Respiratory Care
11030 Ables Lane
Dallas, TX 75229

Opticians' Association of America
10341 Democracy Lane
Fairfax, VA 22030

American Association of Nurse Anesthetists
222 South Prospect Avenue
Park Ridge, IL 60068

National Society for Histotechnology
4201 Northview Drive
Bowie, MD 20716

Joint Commission on Allied Health Personnel
in Opthalmology
2025 Woodlane Drive
St. Paul, MN 55125

National Academy of Opticianry
1011 Martin Luther King Jr. Hwy.
Bowie, MD 20720

American Society of Extra-Corporal
Technology
11480 Sunset Hills Rd.
Reston, VA 22090

National Society for Pulmonary Technology
120 Falcon Drive
Fredericksburg, VA 22408

American Horticultural Therapy Association
362A Christopher Avenue
Gathersburg, MD 20879

National Therapeutic Recriation Society
2775 South Quincy Street
Arlington, VA 22206

Association for the Advancement of Medical
Instrumentation
3330 Washington Blvd.
Arlington, VA 22201

National Athletic Trainers' Association
2952 Stemmons Freeway
Dallas, TX 75247

Child Life Council, Inc.
2910 Woodmont Ave.
Bethesda, MD 20814

Association of Medical Illustrators
1819 Peachtree Road NE
Atlanta, GA 30309

Medical Library Association
6 North Michigan Avenue
Chicago, IL 60602

National Society for Patient Representation
of the Americas
840 North Lake Shore Drive
Chicago,IL 60611

National Association of Dental Laboratories
3801 Mt. Vernon Avenue
Alexandria, VA 22305

National Association of Emergency Medical
Technicians
102 West Leake Street
Clinton, MS 39056

National Association for Music Therapy
8455 Colesville Road
Silver Spring, MD 20910

Society of Vascular Technologists
4601 Presidents Drive
Lanham, MD 20706

APPENDIX D

JOB SEARCH RESOURCES

General Sources

This section lists a variety of general reference sources, such as handbooks and directories, in several fields. They are organized by state, so you can focus on your area.

Arizona

Directory of Nursing Homes
Oryx Press
4041 North Central 700
Phoenix, AZ 85012

California

International Cytogentic Laboratory Directory
Association of Cytogenetic Technologists
616 South Orchard Drive
Burbank, CA 91506

District of Columbia

AMO Directory
Group Health Association of America
1129 20th Street NW
Washington, DC 20036

Federal Job Digest
325 Pennsylvania Avenue SE
Washington, DC 20003

Florida

Blue Book Digest of HMOs
Natl. Assn. of Employers on Health Care Action
420 Clandon Blvd. Ste. 110
P.O. Box 220
Key Biscayne, FL 33149

Medical Laboratory Directory
U.S. Directory Service Publishers
655 128th Street NW
P.O.Box 68-1700
Miami, FL 33168

Georgia

Billan's Hospital Blue Book
2100 Powers Ferry Road
Atlanta, GA 30339

NMTCB Directory
Nuclear Medicine Technology Certification
2970 Clairmont Road
Atlanta, GA 30329

Illinois

ALA Handbook of Organization and Membership Directory
50 East Huron Street
Chicago, IL 60611

Directory of Medical Library Associates
Medical Library Association
6 North Michigan Avenue
Chicago, IL 60602

Freestanding Outpatient Surgery Career Directory
SMG Marketing Group Inc.
1342 North La Salle Drive
Chicago, IL 60610

Organization of Medical Record Departments in Hospitals
American Hospital Publishing Inc.
737 North Michigan Avenue
Chicago, IL 60611

Indiana

Occupational Outlook Handbook
JIST Works, Inc.
8902 Otis Avenue
Indianapolis, IN 46216

Maryland

Directory of Accredited Laboratories
American Association for Laboratory Accreditation
656 Quince Orchard Road
Gathersburg, MD 20878

Michigan

Encyclopedia of Medical Organizations and Agencies
Gale Research Inc.
835 Penobscot Building
Detroit, MI 48226

Nebraska

The City-County Recruiter and the State Recruiter
P.O. Box 2400, Station B
Lincoln, NE 68502

Hospitals Directory
American Business Directories, Inc.
5711 South 86th Circle
Omaha, NE 68127

Laboratories- Medical Directories
American Business Information Inc.
5711 South 86th Circle
Omaha, NE 68127

New Jersey

American Library Directory
R.R. Bowker Co.
121 Chanlon Road
New Providence, NJ 07904

New York

Federal Career Opportunities
Federal Research Services, Inc.
243 Church Street
New York, NY

Virginia

Directory of Community Blood Bank Centers
11117 North 19th Street
Arlington, VA 22209

Journals

Many journals carry help-wanted ads. Listed below are several such journals, arranged alphabetically. You can find journals like these in the libraries of most medical schools and universities.

A

AABB News
Acta Cytology
Aium Newsletter
American Clinical Laboratory
American Clinical Laboratory News
American Heart Journal
American Journal of Health Promotion
American Journal of Public Health
American Journal of Surgery
American Libraries
*American Society of Extra-Corporal
    Technology*
Annals of Surgery
Applied Cyto-Genetics
Applied Radiology
*Archives of Pathology and Laboratory
    Medicine*
Archives of Surgery
ASHA

B ~ C

Biomedical Engineering
Blood Banking
Cardiovascular & Pulmonary Technology
Clinical Imaging
Clinical Medical Laboratories
Clinical Nuclear Medicine
Clynical EEG
Computerized Medical Imaging and Graphics
CP Diggest
Cyto-Technology & Histotechnology
Cytotenetry

E

Emergency Medicine
Emergency Medicine Services

H ~ I

Health and Social Work
Health Education
Information Manager
Information Science–Medical Records
Information Today
Journal of Nuclear Medical Technology
*Journal of Clinical Endocrinology &
    Metabolism*

J

Journal of Computer Assisted Topography
Journal of Histotechnology
Journal of Nuclear Medicine
Journal of the American Record Association
*Journal of the American Society of
    Eco-Cardiography*
Journal of Ultrasound Medicine

L ~ M

Laboratory Medicine
Library
Magnetic Resonance Medicine
Medical Electronic Equipment News
Medical Electronic Products
Medical Imaging & Therapy
MLA News

N ~ O

Nursing
Nursing Economics
Optometry

P

Perfusion Life
Perfusionist
Pharmacy
Pharmacy Times

R

Radiological Technology
Radiology
Radiology And Nuclear Medicine
Review of Optometry

S

Sonography
Speech & Hearing
Surgery
Surgical Rounds
Surgical Technologist

T ~ U

The Information Manager
Transfusion
Vision Monday

APPENDIX E

WEB SITES FOR NATIONAL ALLIED HEALTH ORGANIZATIONS

Art Therapists

American Art Therapy Association
www.arttherapy.org/

Biomedical Engineers

Biomedical Engineering Society
www.bmenet.org/

Biomedical Writers

American Medical Writers Association
www.amwa.org/

Blood Bank Technologists and Spcialists

American Society of Clinical Pathologists
www.ascp.org/

Cardiovascular Technology Personnel

Alliance of Cardiovascular Professionals
www.atlantic.interactive.com/acp/htp

Certified Athletic Trainers

National Athletic Trainers' Association
www.natl.org/

Child Life Specialists

Child Life Council
www.childlife.org/

Chiropractors

American Chiropractor Association
www.amerchiro.org/

Clinical Laboratory Technicians

American Society of Cytopathology
www.cytopathology.org/

Clinical Laboratory Technologists

American Medical Technologists
www.amtl.com/

Cytotechnologists

American Society of Cytology
www.cytopathology.org/

Dance Movement Therapists

American Dance Therapy Association, Inc.
www.adta.org/

Dental Hygienists

American Dental Hygienist Association
www.adta.org/

Dental Laborabory Technicians

National Association of Dental Laboratories
www.nadl.org/

Diagnostic Medical Sonographers

Society of Diagnostic Medical Sonography
www.go-digital.net/SDMS

Dietary Managers

Dietary Manager Association
www.dmaonline.org/

Dietetic Technicians

American Dietetic Association
www.dmaonline.org/

EEG Technicians and Technologists

American Society for Electroneuro-Technology
www.aset.org/

Emergency Medical Technicians

National Association of EMTs
www.naemt.org/

Environmental Health Scientists

National Environmental Health Association
www.neha.org/

Food Technologists

Institution of Food Technology
www.ift.org/

Genetic Counselors

National Society of Genetic Counselors
www.nsgc.org/

Health Educators

American Public Health Association
www.apha.org/

Health Sociologists

American Sociological Association
www.asanet.org/

Histology Technicians

National Society of Histotechnology
www.nsh.org/

Home Health Aides

Home Care Aide Association of America
www.nahc.org/

Horticultural Therapists

American Horticultural Therapy Association
www.ahta.org/

Instructors for the Blind

Foundation for the Blind
www.afb.org/

Licensed Practical Nurses

National Federation of LPNs
www.nflpn.com/

Medical and Psychiatric Social Workers

National Association of Social Workers
www.socialworkers.org/

Medical Assistants

American Association of Medical Assistants
www.aama.ntl.org/

Medical Illustrators

Association of Medical Illustrators
www.medical-illustrators.org

Mental Health Assistants

Center for Mental Health Services
www.mentalhealth.org/

Music Therapists

American Music Therapy Association
www.namt.org/

Nuclear Medicine Technologists

Society of Nuclear Medicine
www.snm.org/

Nurse Anesthetists

American Association of Nurse Anesthetists
www.aana.com/

Nurse–Midwives

American College of Nurse Midwives
www.midwife.org/

Nurse Practitioners

American College of Nurse Practitioners
www.nurse.org/acnp/

Occupational Therapists & Assistants

American Occupational Therapy Association
www.aota.org/

Ophthalmic Assistants, Technicians, & Technologists

Joint Commission of Allied Personnel in Ophthalmology
www.jcahpo.org/

Opticians

Opticians' Association of America
www.opticians.org/

Optometric Assistants & Technicians

American Optometric Association
www.oanet.org/

Optometrists

www.openseason.com/asco/

Orthopists

American Ortheptic Council
www.aoj.org/

Orthotic-Prosthetic Technicians

American Orthotic & Prosthetic Association
www.opoffice.org/

Perfusionists

American Society of Extra-Corporeal
Technology
www.amsect.org/

Pharmacists

American Pharmaceutical Organization
www.apha.org/

Physical Therapists & Assistants

American Physical Therapy Association
www.aptd.org/

Physician Assistants

American Academy of Physician Assistants
www.aapa.org/

Podiatrists

American Podiatric Medical Association
www.apma.org/

Radiation Therapy Technicians & Technologists

American Society of Radiological Technology
www.asrt.org/

Recreation Therapists

National Recreation & Park Association
www.nrpa.org/branches/htrs.htm

Registered Nurses

American Nurses' Association
www.ana.org/

Respiratory Therapists & Technicians

American Association for Respiratory Care
www.aarc.org/

Surgeon Assistants

American Academy of Physician Assistants
www.aapa.org/

Surgical Technologists

Association of Surgical Technologists
www.ast.org/

Veterinarians & Assistants

American Veterinary Medical Association
www.avma.org/

JOB TITLE INDEX